LIVES

OF THE

LORD CHANCELLORS OF ENGLAND.

GREAT SEAL OF CHARLES II.

LIVES

OF

THE LORD CHANCELLORS

AND

KEEPERS OF THE GREAT SEAL

OF

ENGLAND,

FROM THE EARLIEST TIMES TILL THE REIGN OF QUEEN VICTORIA

BY

LORD CAMPBELL.

SEVENTH EDITION.

ILLUSTRATED.

VOL. V.

WILDSIDE PRESS

CONTENTS

OF

THE FIFTH VOLUME.

CHAP.		PAGE
CVIII.—Continuation of the Life of Lord Somers till he was deprived of the Great Seal, ...		1
CIX.—Continuation of the Life of Lord Somers till the death of King William, ...		39
CX.—Continuation of the Life of Lord Somers till his appointment as Lord President of the Council, . . .		57
CXI.—Conclusion of the Life of Lord Somers, ...		82
CXII.—Life of Lord Keeper Wright		119
CXIII.—Life of Lord Cowper from his birth till his appointment as Lord Keeper, ...		135
CXIV.—Continuation of the Life of Lord Cowper till the Accession of George I., ...		166
CXV.—Continuation of the Life of Lord Cowper till the Accession of George I., ...		203
CXVI.—Continuation of the Life of Lord Cowper till his final retirement from office, ...		215
CXVII.—Conclusion of the Life of Lord Cowper, ...		247
CXVIII.—Life of Lord Chancellor Harcourt from his birth till he received the Great Seal, ...		286
CXIX.—Continuation of the Life of Lord Harcourt till the death of Queen Anne, ...		309
CXX.—Conclusion of the Life of Lord Harcourt, . . .		332
CXXI.—Life of Lord Macclesfield from his birth till he received the Great Seal, ...		351
CXXII.—Conclusion of the Life of Lord Macclesfield, . .		377

CHAP. PAGE
CXXIII.—Life of Lord Chancellor King from his birth till his appointment as Lord Chief Justice of the Court of Common Pleas, ... 415
CXXIV.—Continuation of the Life of Lord King till he was made Lord Chancellor, ... 439

LIVES

OF THE

LORD CHANCELLORS OF ENGLAND.

CHAPTER CVIII.

CONTINUATION OF THE LIFE OF LORD SOMERS TILL HE WAS DEPRIVED OF THE GREAT SEAL.

THIS appointment gave satisfaction to every class of the community, except violent ultra-Tories. "All people," says Burnett, "were now grown weary of the Great Seal's being in commission: it made the proceedings in chancery to be both more dilatory and more expensive; and there were such exceptions made to the decrees of the Commissioners, that appeals were brought against most of them, and frequently they were reversed. Sir John Somers had now got great reputation, both in his post of Attorney General and in the House of Commons; so the King gave him the Great Seal. He was very learned in his own profession, with a great deal more learning in other professions, in divinity, philosophy, and history. He had a great capacity for business, with an extraordinary temper; for he was fair and gentle, perhaps to a fault, so that he had all the patience and softness, as well as the justice and equity, becoming a great magistrate. He had always agreed in his notions with the Whigs, and had studied to bring them to better thoughts of the King, and to greater confidence in him."[1]

Thus was the new Lord Keeper hailed in the "DISPENSARY," by Garth, who, after describing the corruption and oppression which prevailed before the Revolution, exclaims:

[1] Burnet iii. 148.

"Haste, and the matchless Atticus address,
From Heav'n and great Nassau he has the mace.
Th' oppressed to his Asylum still repair,
Arts he supports and learning is his care.
He softens the harsh rigor of the laws,
Blunts their keen edge, and cuts their harpy claws;
And graciously he casts a pitying eye
On the sad state of virtuous poverty.
Whene'er he speaks, Heav'ns! how the list'ning throng
Dwells on the melting music of his tongue!
And when the power of eloquence he'd try,
Here, lightning strikes you; there soft breezes sigh.'

On the first day of Easter Term following he was publicly installed in his office, and took the oaths in the Court of Chancery in Westminster Hall.[1] I do not find any account of the procession or of the speeches on this occasion. From the modesty of his nature it is probable that he contrived to avoid the attendance of great nobles and the parade which had given such delight to many of his predecessors, and that, inwardly resolved to do his duty as a Judge, he avoided the ostentatious declaration of his laudable intentions.

He presided in the Court of Chancery for seven years with the unbounded applause of all discerning and candid men, to whatever class or party belonging. The highest testimony to his merit consists in the utterly frivolous charges which were afterwards trumped up by faction against his judicial conduct. All contemporary accounts concur in praising his industry, his patience, his courteousness, and the uniform serenity of his temper under every provocation of petulance, and of dullness, which is still more trying. We must be contented with the general description we have of his judicial excellence; for there is hardly any record of those displays of learning, ratiocination, and eloquence, which might have been handed down to instruct and delight future generations. Vernon professes to report the decisions of the Court of Chancery during the whole of the time that Lord Somers held the Great Seal,[2] and Peere Williams from 1695 downwards;[3] but their statements of his judgments are most scanty and jejune, and we have only a few scattered notices of cases before him in other reporters.

I should say, that the great debt of gratitude we owe him as an Equity Judge arises from his introducing and

[1] Crown Off. Min. fol. 140.   [2] 2 Vern. 287 373.   [3] 1 Peere Wms.

establishing the principles and doctrines of the civil law on the subjects of legacies, trusts, charities, and all others to which they were properly applicable. The early Chancellors were well versed in the civil as well as canon law, but they never thought of laying down general rules; and from the time that Equity began to assume a systematic form, Lord Nottingham was the only Chancellor who had ever opened the Pandects, or read any commentators on that immortal code. The habit of referring to the Civil Law, which he introduced, had been almost forgotten under his successors—the narrow-minded Guilford, whose only solicitude was to please the King, that he might keep his place—and the boisterous Jeffreys, who was early imbued with a good tincture of Common Law, but who, when he rose to eminence, was too much occupied with politics and drinking to do more than try, as occasion required, to recollect what he had formerly learned. But Somers had kept up the familiar and accurate knowledge of the Civil Law which he had acquired while a student at Oxford. Now, frequently referring to it during the arguments at the bar, and in his judgments, he rendered some acquaintance with it indispensable to the practitioners, and he introduced into his Court a fashion for such researches—which lasted a considerable time after he had retired. If, from the training for the Equity bar, more recently introduced, which consists in preparing bills and answers in a draughtsman's office, the pure fountains of Roman jurisprudence are not often approached, the want is not so much felt, after the enlightened system of Equity has been developed and may be found in the Digest of Chancery Reports—and it is not now very material that "the doctrine of the Court" is supposed to be the invention of Lord Somers, Lord Cowper, or Lord Hardwicke, although these great judges drew it from Ulpian, from Vinnius, or from Voet.[1]

I will mention as a specimen, that, following the Civil Law, Lord Somers, contrary to some former English authorities, laid down the rule which has been acknowledged

[1] Let it not be supposed that I mean to throw any peculiar reflection on *Equity counsel*,—who are deserving of all respect ;—for I have heard it repeatedly observed in the Court of King's Bench,—" according to the saying of Lord Hale, *Qui prior est tempore potior est jure*," and " let us never forget the celebrated maxim of Lord Bacon, *Non potest adduci exceptio ejusdem rei, cujus petitur dissolutio*."

ever since, that a bequest of chattels of a durable character, such as pictures, to one for life—remainder to another—is valid, on the ground that the use of the thing only shall be construed to pass to the first taker, and not the thing itself; although a gift for life of chattels *quæ ipso usu consumuntur*, as corn or wine, if specific, is a gift of the property and the old rule shall prevail.[1] So he settled the doctrine, that if there be a legacy to a daughter, on condition that she do not marry without consent of her guardian, the condition shall be construed only *in terrorem*, and, marrying without consent, she shall still have her legacy, unless there be a bequest over to another, in which case, marrying without consent, she loses the legacy.[2]

I do not find that any of Lord Somers's decrees were reversed, except that in *Lawrence* v. *Lawrence*, respecting an implied bar of dower, by acceptance of a bequest of personalty, and a devise of part of the real estate under a will, which devised the residue of the real estate to a stranger. He ruled, according to the *intention*, that dower was barred, but it was held, on a rehearing by Lord Keeper Wright, and afterwards, on appeal by the House of Lords, that dower might still be claimed, as it was not barred *expressly*.[3]

More I can not venture to say of Somers as a dispenser of Equity. But while he held the Great Seal, he had very important judicial duties to perform upon a trial before the Peers for murder, and upon a writ of error from the Court of Exchequer.

The same Lord Mohun whom he had prosecuted for murder when Attorney General, had been concerned, along with the Earl of Warwick, in an affray in a tavern, in which swords were drawn, and a gentleman of the name of Coote was killed. The two noble lords being capitally arraigned, Somers acted as Lord High Steward, and conducted himself on the occasion with true dignity and propriety. Lord Warwick appearing at the bar, with the gentleman-jailor of the Tower standing by his side, holding an axe, the edge as yet turned from the prisoner, his

---

[1] Hyde *v.* Parrat, 1 P. Wms. 1; 2 Vern. 321.
[2] Stratton *v.* Grymes, 2 Vern. 357.
[3] However, Lord Somers's view of making it a question of intention was much favored by Lord Eldon, in Garthshore *v.* Chailie, 10 Ves. 20.

Grace said to him, " It ought to be a support to your mind sufficient to keep you from sinking under the weight of such an accusation, that you are to be tried before so noble, discerning, and equal Judges, that nothing but your own guilt can hurt you. No evidence will be received but what is warranted by law ; no weight will be laid upon the evidence but what is agreeable to justice ; no advantage will be taken of your Lordship's little experience in proceedings of this nature ; nor will it turn to your prejudice that you have not the assistance of counsel in your defense as to the fact (which can not be allowed by law), and their Lordships have already assigned you counsel, if any matters of law should arise."

Lord Warwick was found guilty of manslaughter, and allowed the benefit of his peerage ; but Lord Mohun was entirely acquitted, on evidence that he had himself received a wound in trying to part the combatants, and he volunteered a promise, which he literally kept, " not to give their Lordships any trouble of this sort for the future,"— as in his next duel he and the Duke of Hamilton, his antagonist, were both killed on the spot.[1]

But the grand monument of Somers's stupendous industry, learning, and ability as a Judge, is his celebrated judgment in the " BANKERS' CASE." This arose out of the infamous shutting up of the Exchequer, in the reign of Charles II., whereby the King intercepted, for his own private uses, nearly a million and a half of money, which should have been applied to the repayment of loans to the Government.[2] After this robbery had ruined many individuals, had destroyed public credit, and had paralyzed trade, Charles, as a partial indemnity, granted to the bankers, by way of interest at six per cent. on their debts, certain perpetual annuities which were charged on the hereditary excise. The dividends were paid till the year 1683, but never after. William III., as well as James II., refusing to acknowledge the obligation, the bankers presented a petition or *monstrans de droit*, to the Barons of the Exchequer, praying for payment of the arrears of the annuities, and the Attorney General demurred. Two questions arose—1. " Whether the grant was good ?" 2. " Whether this was the proper remedy ?" The whole Court held that, generally speaking, the King can alienate

[1] 13 St. Tr. 909–1062. [2] Ante, Vol. IV., p. 120.

or charge any part of the public revenue, although Baron Lechmere doubted whether the hereditary excise was not made inalienable by act of parliament; and they all agreed that this petition was the proper remedy. So they gave judgment for the complainants, directing payment to be made to them at the receipt of the Exchequer. Thereupon the Attorney General brought a writ of error before the Court of Exchequer Chamber, created by a statute of Edward II. to review the judgments of the Barons of the Exchequer, consisting of the Lord Chancellor and the Lord Treasurer, assisted by the common-law Judges. At this time there was no Lord Treasurer, the Treasury being in commission. Almost all the Judges adhered to the judgment of the Court below, except Chief Justice Treby, who thought that the Barons had no authority to order the payment, and, therefore, that the remedy by petition to them was inapplicable.

Somers was inclined to this opinion; but before he would give judgment, or say anything to commit himself, or finally make up his mind, he entered into a most laborious examination, not only of all the authorities cited at the bar or by the Judges, but employed many weeks in perusing old books and records which had not before been referred to, and he is said to have spent several hundred pounds in collecting them. He finally satisfied himself that the majority of the Judges were wrong, and he supported his own opinion in a written argument, which is happily preserved to us, and which Mr. Hargrave justly describes as "one of the most elaborate ever delivered in Westminster Hall." Having stated the nature of the case, he thus on very sound principles begins his reasoning :—" The only question is whether this be such a remedy as the law allows for recovering from the King the arrears and growing payments of the annual sums in question? If it be not, I am sure none of us ought to make the parties' case better than the law has made it. We must judge of property according to the rules which the law has fixed, and can make no new ones, nor invent new remedies, however compassionate the case may appear, or however popular it may seem to attempt it." He then gives the history of the royal revenues, and of the Court of Exchequer from the most remote times, with an account of the means afforded for obtaining justice against the Crown, and shows (I think very conclusively) that although the King might alienate or charge any property belonging to the Crown, the Barons of the Exchequer had no authority to order the Lord Treasurer, to whom they are subordinate, to make any payment out of the royal revenue, and that the only remedy was a "Petition of right," addressed directly to the Sovereign, who would indorse upon it *Soit droit fait come il est désiré;* and this being referred to the "Keeper of his conscience," a judgment would be pronounced which, though not enforced by legal process, would effectually procure justice to the petitioner if he was entitled to relief. But a point was then made that in this Court of Exchequer Chamber the Judges were co-ordinate with him, who was only to be considered their president or chief, and therefore that he could not reverse the judgment against the opinion of the majority of them. He therefore put this question to them, "Whether, as this Court is constituted, judgment ought to be given according to the opinion of the greater number of the Judges who are by the Lord Chancellor and Lord Treasurer called to their assistance, notwithstanding they themselves are of a different opinion?" Three declared that the opinion of the majority of the Judges ought to prevail, and seven the contrary. The Lord Keeper said that, on this point, he agreed with the majority, and thereupon he reversed the judgment of the Barons of the Exchequer.—A writ of error on this reversal was brought in the House of Lords, where the reversal was reversed, and the original judgment was restored. But (as we shall see) Lord Somers's political influence was then declining, and in those days, all the Lords voting on appeals and writs of error, the result was often produced by canvass or by political bias. Seven temporal and four spiritual Peers (among them Burnet, Bishop of Salisbury) protested against this reversal. It seems at last to have been made a party question.¹ Indeed, Somers was sus-

¹ The Jacobites rejoiced much in this reversal; and "downright Shippen," in his doggerel, thus insulted Somers:

"An unjust Judge, and blemish of the mace—
Witness the bankers' long-depending case."

Yet by impartial persons the judgment was so much admired, that the compliment to it was eagerly repeated: "The Chancellor's arguments are like geometrical stairs, supporting each other."

pected of a wish to please the King, but his argument is a sufficient refutation of this calumny. On the other side there was much solicitation, the stake being unprecedently great, and many powerful individuals being interested in it.—The matter was finally compromised by a parliamentary grant of half the amount demanded.'

As the granting of divorces in the House of Lords is rather a judicial than a legislative act, I may properly here mention that, while Somers presided on the woolsack, the practice was established of a parliamentary dissolution of marriage by reason of the adultery of the wife. The first case of this sort which came before him was that of the infamous Countess of Macclesfield, the mother of Savage; and, by the Chancellor's advice, the adultery being clearly established, the bill passed, although there had not been a divorce *à mensâ et thoro* in the Ecclesiastical Court.² This was followed by the Duchess of Norfolk's case. She had twice defeated an application to parliament by the Duke for a divorce; but on fresh evidence of her guilt being adduced, together with the verdict of the jury in the Duke's action against her paramour, Lord Somers advised that the relief prayed for should be granted, and the bill passed.³ It is much to be regretted that he did not establish a judicial tribunal, with power to dissolve marriage on proof of the wife's adultery, and that he did not rescue the English nation from the reproach of the action for "criminal conversation," whereby an English husband seeks a pecuniary benefit from his own dishonor.

Lord Somers gave high satisfaction in disposing of the proper judicial business of the House upon appeals and writs of error, and he acquired much credit by vigorously maintaining the jurisdiction of the English House of Lords over appeals from the Irish Courts of Equity.⁴

¹ 12 & 13 W. 3, c. 12, 13. See 14 St. Tr. 1-114.
² 5 Parl. Hist. 1173. Dr Johnson, in his "Life of Savage," incorrectly states that "the Countess confessed that Earl Rivers was the father of her child;"—but she resolutely asserted her innocence.
³ Macqueen, 572 ; Lord's Journ.
⁴ The Irish House of Lords had claimed this jurisdiction, and had committed JOHN CAMPBELL to prison for a breach of privilege, in serving the Bishop of Derry with an order of the English House of Lords.* My clansman was released ; and the attempt was renewed by the Irish House of Lords in 1717; but they did not carry their point till 1782.

* Lords' Journ.

He was likewise of great service in enforcing the attendance of the Judges as assistants to the Peers. While he remained a Commoner, and therefore presided on the woolsack only as Speaker, there was cast upon him the painful duty of reprimanding these venerable sages of the law for negligence. On the 8th of February, 1694, an order was made that "all the Judges do attend this House to-morrow, immediately upon the rising of the respective Courts in Westminster Hall, and do not go away until the rising of the House." The Judges attended accordingly on the following day, and were thus addressed by the Lord Keeper (in pursuance of a previous instruction from the House): "I am commanded to tell you, that you have the honor to be the assistants here; and the House takes notice of your great negligence in your attendance. You have had sometimes warning given you, though not with so much solemnity as I am directed now to do it. If this fault be not amended for the future, the House will proceed with great severity against you." This rebuke seems scarcely to have answered its purpose; for, on the 3rd of December, 1694, it was "ordered that all the Judges do attend this House to-morrow, at twelve of the clock, except such whose attendance is at present necessary in the courts of law or equity; and that the reprimand given to the Judges the 9th of February last be then repeated to them." On the following morning "the Lord Keeper, pursuant to the order of yesterday, repeated to the Judges the reprimand before administered to them." Unluckily, we have no further account of this ceremony; but it proved effectual, as the Judges appear ever after to have given entire satisfaction to the House by their diligence and assiduity.[1]

Having followed Somers as a Judge nearly to the close of his official career, we must now regard him in a character in which he drew much more public attention—as a member of the Government.

[1] Lords Journals. Macqueen's Practice of the House of Lords, 41. At this time, the Judges were expected to attend the House of Lords from day to day, without any special summons, for the purpose of carrying messages to the House of Commons, and giving their advice on any question which might arise. Now they are only employed as messengers on very important occasions, as to carry to the House of Commons bills respecting the royal family; and they are specially summoned when it is wished that they should advise the House on questions of law arising out of judicial proceedings or bills pending.

While he continued in office, the administration of affairs at home was chiefly intrusted to him. The King conducted his diplomatic negotiations nearly as much as his campaigns, without ministerial advice, but he was rather indifferent as to civil appointments and domestic measures, except in as far as they bore upon his foreign policy. Yet it is a curious fact that Somers had a violent *fracas* with his royal master immediately after his appointment, and this led to the cordiality which subsequently prevailed between them. The Great Seal having been in commission since the commencement of this reign, William, without consulting the Lords Commissioners, had personally exercised all the judicial patronage connected with it, and thought he was still to follow the same course. The very day after the transfer of the Great Seal, he set off for Flanders to fight the battle of Landon, and, not a word being said to the Lord Keeper about filling up vacancies then existing in legal offices, sent him orders by the Earl of Nottingham, the Secretary of State—as if he had been a mere clerk in a public office—to make out patents creating Sir William Rawlinson Chief Baron of the Exchequer, Sir William Wogan Chief Justice of Chester, and Mr. Ward Attorney General. Somers resolved not to hold the Great Seal on such terms, believing that the King erred from ignorance of our customs, and, wishing to instruct him in his duties—while William was still at Harwich, waiting for a fair wind—sent to him by a special messenger the following respectful, manly, and dignified remonstrance:—

"March 27, 1693.

"May it please your Majesty,

"It is no small misfortune to me, that before I enter upon the execution of the great trust with which your Majesty has been pleased to honor me, I should find myself under the necessity of giving your Majesty a trouble in relation to it.

"Nothing but the utmost concern for your service could have brought me to do it now, or shall ever hereafter lead me to do the like.

"My Lord Nottingham, since your departure, has told me Sir William Rawlinson is to be Chief Baron, Sir William Wogan Chief Justice of Chester, and Mr. Ward Attorney General.

"Your Majesty having laid no commands on me relating to any of them, I think it my duty, before I act anything in this matter, with all humility, to represent to your Majesty what consequence it may have.

"The lawyers being spread over every part of the kingdom, and having a great influence among the people, the method used to unite them in their service to the Crown had been by obliging them to a dependence upon the Great Seal for their promotion where they merited. This has always given a weight to that office in public affairs, and, if I understand your Majesty aright, the making the Great Seal thus considerable was one of the effects you expected from placing it in a single hand. But I submit to your Majesty how far this is likely to succeed, or any other of your Majesty's ends be answered, if such eminent offices are disposed of in such a manner at my entrance on this charge.

"I do not meddle on any consideration of the persons themselves, though I know not but your Majesty might expect it from me; and it may not be improper to observe to your Majesty how much it has been to the honor of your reign, that your Judges have been of known ability in the law, and that it is the particular concern of the Crown that the Chief Baron should be experienced in the course of the Exchequer, and knowing in the Common Law.

"As to the place of the Attorney, your Majesty having been pleased to express your purpose to advance Sir Thomas Trevor to that office, to several persons, it was not in my power to make it a secret; and your Majesty having divers times commanded me to find out a Solicitor, I was under the necessity of proposing it to Mr. Ward, whom I thought a fit person, before I could name him to your Majesty, and so that could not be concealed.

"This being the case, let me humbly offer it to your Majesty's consideration whether, if the passing these patents must be the first use I am to make of the Seal, it can be supposed I have that credit which ought always to go along with it, and without which it is impossible it should reach any part of what your Majesty aimed at in the change.

"Your Majesty will bear me witness that I had a just prospect of the difficulties of this charge, and that nothing but a perfect resignation to your Majesty, together with a gracious assurance of your support, engaged me to undertake it. Upon this support I do and must depend, and whatever your Majesty might expect from the Seal in my hand must fail if there be any the least want of it.

"Having discharged my duty in this faithful representation to your Majesty, I lay the Seal and myself at your Majesty's feet, with an entire submission to your will and pleasure. "I am,
"May it please your Majesty,
"Your Majesty's most dutiful,
"Most obedient, and most humble
"Subject and servant,
"J. SOMERS."

The result was most creditable to both parties. William declined to accept the tendered resignation of the Great Seal: disclaimed any intention to slight one who had been so useful to his cause, and for whose learning, ability, and integrity he had such respect; and expressing a hope that the persons proposed for the vacant offices in the law, who had been all strongly recommended to him, might be considered not unfit, promised that in future all such appointments should be made by the advice of the Lord Keeper. The patents for Rawlinson, Wogan, and Ward, were accordingly made out,—and William was faithful to his engagement. The office of the Attorney General soon again becoming vacant, Sir Thomas Trevor, the Lord Keeper's protégé, was appointed to it, and the Great Seal was restored to all its ancient consequence. Ever after there was the most perfect good understanding between the King and his minister,—the charge against the latter subsequently being that he had too implicitly complied with the royal will.

Down to 1697 Somers refused to accept a peerage, and the fashion of the Lord Keeper addressing the two Houses at the commencement and close of the session had passed away, the King in person delivering a speech, for which his ministers were considered responsible. For some years, therefore, Somers, sitting on the woolsack in the House of Lords, had only, as Speaker, to put the question, and his name seldom appears in the accounts of parliamentary proceedings, although parliament, which, in the eight years immediately before the Revolution, sat only two months, had now regular sessions lasting a considerable portion of every year.¹ But, taking no part in debate, he regulated, in a great degree, the resolves of the Upper House, and the King was implicitly guided by his opinion in giving the Royal assent to bills, or rejecting them by the exercise of the veto, which had not yet become a dormant prerogative of the Crown.

The first very important deliberation they had together was with respect to the liberty of the press. Notwithstanding Milton's inimitable defense of "Unlicensed Printing,"² even at the Revolution the public mind was not prepared for the abolition of the restrictions which had been imposed upon authors, first by proclamations and decrees of the Star Chamber, and then by statutes. The Licensing Act, which had inadvertently been suffered to expire in 1679, and had been revived by James II.'s parliament in 1685, was in 1692 continued till the end of the then next session of parliament.³ Should the experiment be made, of trusting to the *punishment* of such as publish anything dangerous to the public or injurious to individuals? William, who had seen the harmlessness of a free press in his own country, took the liberal side; but the few Tory members of the Cabinet very plausibly urged that *prevention* was better than *punishment*, and that it was the duty of the state to restrain as far as possible from the publication of libels as from the commission of other crimes. Somers prevailed by pointing out not only the vexatiousness, but the utter inefficiency, of the desired regulations, in spite of which there had been more libels published upon the government and on private character since the Revolution than during any former period of our history. "Unlicensed printing" was thus forever established in England—and now we have only to be watchful that the press be not itself turned into an engine of tyranny.⁴

¹ Under date 2nd May, 1693, when the two Houses met according to the prorogation—that they might be again prorogued, there is this entry in the Journals of the Lords: "This day Sir John Somers, Knight, Lord Keeper of the Great Seal of England, first sat as Speaker in the House of Peers." He was afterwards enumerated at the top of the list of Peers present as "Dom. Cust. Mag. Sig." till he was made Chancellor and a Peer in 1697.

² "Areopagitica; a Speech for the Liberty of unlicensed Printing—to the Parliament of England."

³ Stat. 13 & 14 Car. 2, c. 33. 1 Jac. 2, c. 17. 4 & 5 W. & M. c. 24, s. 14.
⁴ See Hall. Const. Hist. ii. 226.

The next subject of debate in the Cabinet was the "Place Bill." The disappointed Tory party, combining with a few disappointed individual Whigs, and a section of politicians actuated by disinterested but absurd notions of government, had passed a bill by which no one holding any place of profit under the Crown should be permitted to sit in the House of Commons. The great argument for it was, that the misrule in Charles II.'s reign was chiefly to be ascribed to his "Pensioner's Parliament." But wise men clearly saw, that, though the House of Commons might be corrupted by a majority of its members being placemen, it could not possibly exercise the functions vested in it by the constitution, and that it would soon become useless and despised, if all the ministers of the Crown were excluded from it. Somers, therefore, manfully concurred in the opinion that the Bill should be stopped by the royal VETO, and when its title was read in the presence of the two Houses, their Majesties being on their thrones, the answer was, "Le Roy et la Reyne s'aviseront."[1]

In the end of the same year, the "Triennial Bill" a second time passed both Houses. The King had before vetoed it, and Burnet says it was to soften the distaste which this proceeding gave that Somers was appointed to the Great Seal.[2] Most extravagant notions were entertained of the benefits to be derived from the bill, which many thought would produce complete purity of election, would insure the return of independent members, would render all proceedings in parliament patriotic and wise, and would renew and perpetuate the Golden Age in England.[3] We must remember that there were many living who had known one parliament last nearly eighteen years, and who had seen years elapse filled with abuses without any parliament sitting to redress them. The King was still hostile to the measure, remarking that "the Triennial Bill in Charles I.'s time was the signal for the civil war." But Somers pointed out to him that this bill was free from the obnoxious clauses which had been assigned by Lord Clarendon as the reasons for repealing that act; that its provisions were perfectly consistent with the full exercise of the prerogative in a limited monarchy; and that, in the temper in which the nation then was, it could

[1] 5 Parl. Hist. 828.   [2] O. T. iii. 143.   [3] Ibid. 183.

not be again rejected without making many, hitherto well affected to him, turn their longing eyes to St. Germaine's. The royal assent was accordingly given to the bill,¹ and, although much disappointment was experienced (as after the passing of our Reform Bill), it worked well till the accession of George I., when a House of Commons, which had been elected for three years, resolved to sit for seven.

Queen Mary dying soon after the Triennial Bill was passed, the Lord Keeper successfully exerted himself to bring about a reconciliation between the King and the Princess Anne, who had long been estranged from the Court. Entering the royal closet, he found William in such an agony of grief, as not even to be conscious of his presence. When Somers had broken silence, and regretted the feuds in the royal family, the King said, "My Lord, do what you will. I can think of no business." By the agency of Somers an interview was arranged, in which the King received the Princess with cordiality, and informed her that the palace of St. James's should be appropriated for her future residence. The Lord Keeper had still the painful duty to discharge of delivering to the King at Kensington, the address of condolence voted by the Lords on this melancholy occasion, and receiving the King's simple and pathetic answer: "I heartily thank you for your kindness, but much more for the sense you show of our great loss, which is above what I can express."

William now bearing undivided sway, nominally as well as really,—a new Great Seal was immediately ordered, suited to the alteration in the royal style, and was delivered to the Lord Keeper.² But Mary having considered it her duty, as a good wife, not to interfere in the administration of the government, except in matters of form, this melancholy event made no difference in his position.

In 1695 Lord Keeper Somers gave his countenance to the bill for allowing a full defense by counsel, together with a copy of the indictment, and a list of the jurors and the witnesses, in cases of treason; but it is doubtful whether it would have passed if Lord Ashley, afterwards Earl of Shaftesbury, and author of the "Characteristics," had not broken down while delivering, in the House of Commons, a set speech in support of it, and, being called upon to go on, had

¹ 6 W & M. c. 2. ² Books of Privy Council, 1694.

not electrified the House by observing, "If I, Sir, who rise only to give my opinion on a bill now pending in the fate of which I have no personal interest, am so confounded that I am unable to express the least of what I proposed to say, what must the condition of that man be who, without any assistance, is called to plead for his life, for his honor, and for his posterity?"[1] A clause was added in the Lords, (as some very unwarrantably say, on the suggestion of Somers, with a view to defeat the bill,) "that on the trial of a peer or peeress for treason, all peers should be summoned, and be entitled to sit,"—to which it was thought the Commons would not agree. But why should it be supposed that the Commons would object to Peers being fairly tried as well as themselves?—and there is no authority for asserting that Somers disapproved of the bill. The royal assent was given to it without any hesitation.[2]

The Lord Keeper took an active part in what was considered one of the greatest measures of William's reign—the reformation of the monetary system by a recoinage; and he suggested, and strongly urged, a plan by which the clipping of money would have been instantly stopped, and several millions would have been saved to the nation.[3]

There was now a strong desire that he should take part in the debates in the House of Lords, and the King actually made out a warrant for conferring a peerage upon him. This was inclosed to him in a letter from the Duke of Shrewsbury, who was supposed to have great influence over him, and who wrote, "The King is really convinced that it is for his service that you should accept of a title. I beg the answer I may have may be a bill for the King's

---

[1] 5 Parl. Hist. 966.   [2] 7 W. 3, c. 3.
[3] "The Lord Keeper Somers did indeed propose that which would have put an effectual stop to clipping for the future: it was, that a proclamation should be prepared with such secrecy as to be published all over England on the same day, ordering money to pass only by weight: but at the same time, during three or four days after the proclamation, all persons in every county that had money should bring it in to be told and weighed; and the difference was to be registered, and the money to be sealed up, to the end of the time given, and then to be restored to the owners; and an assurance was to be given that this deficiency in weight should be laid before the parliament, to be supplied another way, and to be allowed them in the following taxes." The King liked the proposal; but it was overruled from an apprehension that t might give a shock to commercial credit.—*Burnet*, iii. 203.

signing.[1] As for arguments, I have used all I have already; and by your objections, you may give me leave to tell you, you are as partial and unreasonable with too much modesty as some are with too much ambition."[2] Somers still resolutely refused the offered elevation.

However, he had a temporary dignity thrust upon him. William, after the death of Mary, still going abroad yearly during the campaigning season, he, by virtue of the prerogative, appointed under the Great Seal, "Lords Justices," who might be considered the successors of the "Grand Justiciars" in the times of the Norman Kings and of the early Plantagenets,—administering the government in his absence. The Princess Anne, to her great mortification, was excluded from the regency. The Archbishop of Canterbury was nominally at the head of the Lords Justices who were appointed, but the Lord Keeper, who came next, had the duties of the office cast upon him almost exclusively. If four of them were together, they were entitled to the honors of royalty. But

---

[1] The course of making out a patent of peerage is, that upon warrant under the sign manual, and countersigned by a secretary of state, a bill is prepared on parchment by the Attorney General, which is a draught of the grant. This being superscribed by the Sovereign, passes under the Privy Seal, and then comes the Patent under the Great Seal—before which the Peerage is not completed—although, on kissing hands after the warrant, a member of the House of Commons about to be ennobled vacates his seat. Anciently, a barony was created without patent by a writ of summons to parliament, but was not acquired so as to descend to heirs till the Baron had taken his seat in the House of Peers. Such a peerage descends to heirs female as well as male, and is usually called "a Barony in fee."

[2] Hardw. St. Pap. ii. 429. In the prospect of the accession of the House of Hanover, such a jealousy was there of the Sovereign being absent from the realm, that the Act of Settlement, 12 & 13 W. 3, c. 2, provided "that no person who should thereafter come to the possession of the Crown should go out of the dominions of England, Scotland, or Ireland," without consent of parliament. Queen Anne never was, or wished to be, abroad; but this was repealed by 1 Geo. st. 2, c. 51; and Hallam is of opinion that the first two Georges, by their frequent visits to Hanover, made a bad return for the waiver of the condition on which they were invited to the throne. On going beyond the sea, they invariably, according to ancient usage, appointed a Regent, or Lords Justices, to exercise the royal authority in their absence. George III. was never more than one hundred miles from London, the place of his birth. George IV. was only once abroad, which was in the year 1821, and he then appointed Lords Justices. William IV. never was abroad after he came to the Crown. Queen Victoria going to the Continent in 1843, no provision was thought necessary for the exercise of the royal authority in her absence; and the appointment of Lords Justices may now be considered to have fallen into desuetude. See discussion on this subject in the House of Lords, 7th August, 1845.

Somers ever as much as possible avoided parade, and in the exercise of authority was desirous of acting under the express directions of the King.¹

Upon the discovery of the plot to assassinate William, in the beginning of the year 1696, the Lord Keeper followed a course which was not much complained of at the time, but was afterwards made a ground of heavy charge against him. An association for the protection of the King's person being formed, he announced and acted upon a resolution to remove from the commission of the peace, all magistrates all over England who refused to sign it,—whereby many Jacobites and ultra-Tories were dismissed. Such a punishment for merely not joining in a voluntary ebullition of loyalty, does seem a very arbitrary, though not an illegal, proceeding; but we must recollect that, after the death of the Queen, who, if the pretended Prince of Wales could be considered spurious, was the next heir to the crown, there was a very general disposition to question William's title, notwithstanding all he had done for the nation, and that, to preserve the public tranquillity, measures were absolutely necessary, and therefore defensible, which would be justly condemned in our quiet times.²

The trial and execution of Charnock, King, and Heyes, for high treason, which followed, under the direction of the Lord Keeper, could not be censured. They were regularly brought before a jury; they were fully heard in their defense, and a clear case was made out against them. The only circumstance which excites any sympathy in their favor is their generous anxiety to exempt James II., who was then at Calais planning an invasion to recover his crown, from the suspicion of being engaged in their plot.³

But the proceeding against Sir John Fenwick brings some reproach on the memory of Somers, and shows that after the principles of justice have been for ages violated in any country, they can not suddenly be completely restored to efficiency, the moral perceptions of the most humane and enlightened individuals continuing for a time to be blunted. It appeared by an intercepted letter from Sir John Fenwick to his wife, that he had been engaged

¹ He was a Lord Justice in 1695, 1696, 1697, 1698, and 1699.
² 2 Ralph, 843.   12 St. Tr. 1377—1466.

in the plan for an invasion from France to restore King James, and the Lords Justices directed that he should be brought to trial for high treason, but the witnesses who were expected to prove his guilt left the kingdom, and there was no sufficient legal evidence against him. Thereupon the government resorted to the proceeding which had been invented in the reign of Henry VIII. for perpetuating murder, and which had brought such reproach upon the Stuarts and upon the republican party—A BILL OF ATTAINDER. This was violently opposed in both Houses, and was carried in the Lords only by a majority of sixty-six to sixty.[1] Yet it received the royal assent, and the prisoner refusing to make the disclosures which were required of him, he was executed—throwing luster on the Jacobite cause by his fidelity to his friends, and the calmness and constancy which he displayed.[2]

The Lord Keeper is much to be commended for the liberal zeal he displayed to see the highest talents in every department employed in the public service. He assisted Montagu in the appointment of Newton as Warden of the Mint, to which may be ascribed the successful restoration of the currency by the recoinage; and, on his recommendation Locke was nominated a Lord of Trade, to carry into effect the sound commercial principles which this great philosopher had propounded in his writings. Unfortunately Locke's health was so much impaired, that he was soon obliged to leave the duties of his office and fly to his country retreat at Oates. After he had been there some weeks, he wrote the following letter to the Lord Keeper:—

"My Lord,

"Some of my brethren, I understand, think my stay in the country long, and desire me to bear my part, and to help to dispatch the multitude of business that the present circumstances of trade and the plantations fill

---

[1] The Bishops voted, although this was *causa sanguinis*, and were 12 to 9.
[2] 13 St. Tr. 537–758; 5 Parl. Hist. 998–1156. Although the attainder of Fenwick was supported by Bishop Burnet, and many humane and upright men, Lord Keeper Somers must be held principally responsible for it. Fortunately, he had nothing whatever to do with the warrant for "the massacre of Glencoe," which is the great reproach to the reign of William, and which, I am sorry to say, brought deserved obloquy upon the name of CAMPBELL.

their hands with. I can not but say they are in the right; and I can not but think, at the same time, that I also am in the right to stay in the country, where all my care is little enough to preserve those small remains of health which a settled and incurable disposition would quickly make an end of anywhere else. There remains, therefore, nothing else to be done, but that I should cease to fill up any longer a place that requires a more constant attendance than my strength will allow; and to that purpose I prevail with your Lordship to move his Majesty that he would be pleased to ease me of the employment he has been so graciously pleased to honor me with, since the craziness of my body so ill seconds the inclination I have to serve him in it, and I find myself every way incapable of answering the ends of that commission. I am not insensible of the honor of that employment, nor how much I am obliged to your Lordship's favorable opinion in putting me into a post which I look upon as one of the most considerable in England. I can say that nobody has more warm wishes for the prosperity of his country than I have; but the opportunity of showing those good wishes, in being any way serviceable to it, I find comes too late to a man whose health is inconsistent with the business, and in whom it would be folly to hope a return to that vigor and strength which such an employment I see requires. It is not without due consideration that I represent this to your Lordship, and that I find myself obliged, humbly and earnestly, to request your Lordship to obtain for me a dismission out of it."

The Lord Keeper thus replied:—

"Sir,

"My great fatigue, joined with a very great indisposition, must make my excuse for being so slow in returning an answer to your very obliging letter. I am very sorry for your ill health, which confines you to the country for the present; but now you will have so much regard to yourself, your friends, and your country, as not to think of returning to business till you are recovered to such a competent degree as not to run the hazard of a relapse. As to the other part of your letter which relates to quitting the commission, I must say, you are much in the wrong, in my opinion, to entertain a thought of it; and I flatter myself so far as to believe I could bring you over

to my sentiments if I had the happiness of half an hour's conversation with you. These being my thoughts, you can not wonder if I am not willing to enter upon the task you propose, for me to say something to the King of your wishes. But when the new commission is made, and the establishment fixed, and the parliament up, and you have had the opinion of your friends here, I will submit to act as you shall command me. In the meantime, give me leave to say that no man alive has a greater value for you, or is with more sincerity than myself, Sir,
"Yours," &c.

Locke, however, was firm to his purpose; and, anticipating a personal interview, says gracefully, "Then I, who am so much in your favor, shall not alone, of all the subjects of England, apprehend that, upon a fair hearing, your Lordship will not allow the EQUITY of my case." The resignation was accordingly accepted.

In the following year Locke's health having improved, another effort was made to press him into the public service; and the King, at the request of the Lord Keeper, sent for him in the hope of overcoming his scruples. Of this interview the philosopher gives an account in a letter to his friend:—

"Sunday, in the evening, after I had waited on the King, I went to wait upon your Lordship, it being, I understand, his Majesty's pleasure I should do so before I returned hither. His Majesty was so favorable as to propose the employment your Lordship mentioned; but the true knowledge of my own weak state of health made me beg his Majesty to think of some fitter person, and more able to serve him in that important post—to which I added my want of experience for such business. I must beg your Lordship, for the interest of the public, to prevail with his Majesty to think on somebody else, since I do not only fear, but am sure, my broken health will never permit me to accept the great honor his Majesty meant me. As it would be unpardonable to betray the King's business, by undertaking what I should be unable to go through, so it would be the greatest madness to put myself out of the reach of my friends during the small time I am to linger in this world, only to die a little more rich, or a little more advanced. He must have a heart strongly touched with wealth or honors, who, at my age, and laboring for breath, can find any great relish for either of them."[1]

The wise resolution of the philosopher was not further combated, and he was probably of more use to the public in still being allowed to prosecute his abstract inquiries than if occupied with the details of official business. But we must honor the desire to advance men of literary reputation to employments in the state—which has been so rarely manifested in England.

Somers himself, careless about honors, having, on the 22nd of April, 1697, surrendered the Great Seal, it was returned to him by the King, with the title of Lord Chancellor;[2] and the same day, he was created Baron Somers, of Evesham, in the county of Worcester. To enable him to support his dignity, the King, who still possessed the old prerogative (taken away from his successor) of alienating the royal hereditary revenues, granted to Lord Somers and his heirs the manors of Reigate and Howleigh, in Surrey, and £2,100 a year out of the fee farm rents of the Crown.[3]

The first measure on which he had to express his opinion as a Peer was the Bill sent up by the Commons, requiring property in land as a qualification to be returned representative to parliament for any county, city, or borough,—the object being to weaken the Whig party by excluding men who, like Sir Andrew Freeport, were engaged in commerce, and were of liberal politics. Lord Somers contended that "the nation might reasonably be left to their freedom in choosing their representatives in parliament; that it seemed both unjust and cruel if a poor man had so fair a reputation as to be chosen, notwithstanding his poverty, by those who were willing to pay him wages, that he should be branded with an incapacity because of his small estate; that corruption in elections was to be dreaded from the rich rather than from the

---

[1] Lord King's "Life of Locke," 244-248.
[2] London Gazette 22d April, 1697. "His Majesty, in Council, received the Seals from the hands of the Right Honorable Sir John Somers, Knight, Lord Keeper thereof, and was pleased to return it to him again, with the title of Lord Chancellor of England."
[3] These grants seem to have created a good deal of jealousy and envy, but Somers conducted himself respecting them with great independence.—See Letter from Secretary Vernon to the Duke of Shrewsbury, 1 Vernon's Corr. 223.

poor; and that, at all events, it was absurd that land should be the only property recognized as a qualification." The bill was rejected.[1]

Lord Somers had now reached his highest pitch of worldly prosperity. He was not only the favorite of the King, but he could influence a decided majority in both Houses of Parliament, and his general popularity was such that the high Church party expressed a wish that he were theirs. The Tory fox-hunters could say nothing against him, except that he was "a vile Whig;" the merchants celebrated him as the only Lord Chancellor who had ever known anything of trade or finance; the lawyers were proud of him as shedding new glory on their order; and so much was he praised for his taste in literature, and his patronage of literary men, that all works of any merit in verse or prose were inscribed to him. Thus was he addressed by Addison, in the Dedication of his Poem in praise of King William:—

> "If yet your thoughts are loose from state affairs,
> Nor feel the burden of a nation's cares,
> If yet your time and actions are your own,
> Receive the present of a muse unknown:
> A muse that in adventurous numbers sings
> The rout of armies and the fall of Kings,
> Britain advanc'd, and Europe's peace restor'd,
> *By Somers' counsels* and by Nassau's sword.
> "To you, my Lord, these daring thoughts belong,
> Who help'd to raise the subject of my song;
> To you the hero of my verse reveals
> His great designs, to you in council tells
> His inmost thoughts, determining the doom
> Of towns unstorm'd, and battles yet to come.
> And well could you, *in your immortal strains*
> Describe his conduct and reward his pains;

---

[1] See Tind. Rap. xiv. 373. During the High Tory administration of Queen Anne, the bill was again introduced and passed (9 Anne, c. 5); but on this one point I think the Chartists are right, and, when a member of the House of Commons, I voted in their favor. Let there a proper qualification fixed for the *electors,* and they may be safely left to their free choice. No harm whatever would follow from the introduction of a few operatives into the House of Commons; but in truth, there would be no chance of such an occurrence. There never has been any property qualification for the representative in Scotland; and the English fashion, attempted to be introduced at the time of the Reform Act, was strongly and successfully resisted by us. Yet, whatever objections the Scottish members may be liable to, all that I have ever known could easily have produced qualifications, if the statute of Anne had been extended to them.

> But since the state has all your cares engrost,
> And poetry in higher thoughts is lost,
> Attend to what a lesser muse indites,
> Pardon her faults, and countenance her flights."[1]

At this period of his career the levee of the Lord Chancellor was almost as crowded as that of the King; and he could not have been insensible to the popularity he enjoyed with all ranks of his fellow citizens. But what above all yielded him the most enviable gratification, was the power which he enjoyed from his own great income, and from a just application of a portion of the funds of the state to relieve distress, and to encourage rising merit struggling with poverty. He not only liberally assisted literary men of his own country, but he extended his patronage to foreigners. About this time Bayle's "Historical and Critical Dictionary" being about to appear, and there being much talk of the learning and of the poverty of the author, Lord Somers wrote to a friend in Holland, intimating that "if Mr. Bayle would accept of his patronage for his Dictionary, he had 150 guineas at his service." Bayle, for a supposed plot in favor of France, having been deprived by William of a pension, and turned out of his professorship at Rotterdam, answered, that, although he stood in need of the present offered to him, he could not bring himself to pay that compliment to a Lord who was minister to a Prince of whom he had such reason to complain.[2] The Chancellor found no difficulty in procuring the acceptance of a like sum by a parson of profligate morals, to whom it was offered on condition that he would cease to come to his levee.[3] A more unmixed good action was his procuring a pension for the widow of Archbishop Tillotson, from whose disinterestedness she had been left in great distress.

But his greatest glory was his patronage of Addison, to

---

[1] This versification, if indifferent, was the best then going: for the star of Dryden was disappearing in the west, and that of Pope had not yet begun to illumine the eastern horizon.

As a specimen of the prose dedications, I will copy a few sentences of that by Edmund Gibson of a new edition of Camden's BRITANNIA:

"She (Britannia) still remembers how they all blessed you for your defense of her distressed Prelates, and how upon your Lordship's advancement a general joy ran through the whole family; but that a more particular satisfaction appeared among the learned to see the honor conferred upon a leading member of their own body. She was pleased to hear them say that by such promotions they, as well as their neighbors, might at last have their Richelieus and Colberts." [2] See Biog. Brit. 3749. [3] Ibid.

which we are indebted not only for the "Travels in Italy," and the "Dialogue on Medals," but for the enlarged views and exquisite polish which distinguish the other compositions of this inimitable writer. Influenced much less by the flattering lines which Addison, then unknown, had addressed to him from Oxford, than by the desire to assist in fitting for the public service one so likely to bring credit to the Whig party, and to confer benefits on his country, he eagerly concurred with Montagu, the Chancellor of the Exchequer, in enabling the aspirant diplomatist to improve himself by a residence in France, and by visiting foreign courts. The consequence was, that an annuity of £300 was settled upon him, and paid to him till the King's death. To this kindness in a considerable measure may be ascribed the success of Addison's subsequent career.[1]

One libel appeared upon the Lord Chancellor, which only added to the splendor of his reputation. This was written by a son of the Earl of Abingdon, who had been engaged in a Chancery suit, and who grossly reflected upon a decree pronounced against him. But the House of Lords took up the matter as a breach of privilege, and sent a message by the Lord Chief Baron and Mr. Justice Neville to the Commons, requesting the attendance of one of their members upon the subject. Thereupon, Lord Abingdon, in the name of his son, begged pardon of the Lord Chancellor and the House, for the offense committed. The apology stayed further proceedings, beyond ordering the libel to be burnt in Palace Yard by the hands of the common hangman.[2]

I may here mention the only other question of "privilege" which arose while Lord Somers held the Great Seal, and considering his liberality and good sense, we can not but be astonished at the manner in which it was treated. The House of Lords being the Court of Appeal in the last resort, its decisions settle the law, and are binding on all inferior tribunals. It being deemed material that they should be made known, Sir Bartholomew

[1] He must otherwise have taken orders; and, if we may judge by his very worst production, his "Evidences of Christianity," he would not much have distinguished himself as a divine. Montagu therefore might say, with a free conscience, "I am called an enemy to the Church; but I will never do it any other injury than keeping Mr. Addison out of it."
[2] Lord's Jour. xv. 240, 247.

Shower, an eminent barrister, published a collection of them, still cited under the title of "Shower's Parliamentary Cases," but some of them being freely commented upon, the publication was voted to be a breach of privilege, and a standing order was made, which has never yet been repealed, whereby it was "Resolved, that it is a breach of the privilege of this House for any person whatsoever to print or publish in print anything relating to the proceedings of this House without the leave of this House." The prohibition was thus made to extend not only to the publication of political debates, but to judgments upon appeals pronounced when the House, as a court of justice, sits *foribus apertis*.[1]

The splendid portion of Somers's career, dating from the time when he was made Lord Chancellor and a Peer, soon passed away. Henceforth he was almost constantly involved in political troubles; and although he made a noble struggle against them, and when deprived of office acquired fresh claims to the admiration and gratitude of his country, he had frequent cause to regret that he had not spent his life in comfortable obscurity at Worcester, or in philosophic calm at Oxford.

Immediately after the peace of Ryswick, the English nation being no longer in conflict with the French, became discontented at home, and ceased to consider William their deliverer and their champion. The Tory party grew stronger and more indifferent as to the means they employed to recover power. Louis XIV., although he had reluctantly acknowledged the Revolution settlement in England, was ready to seize any favorable opportunity for reviving the claim of James, and, looking to the Spanish succession, he kept up an immense military force, to be actively employed as soon as fate should put an end to

[1] What seems still more extraordinary,—Lord Hardwicke, so recently as the year 1762, threatened to put it in force against Sir Michael Foster, who, in his admirable work on Crown Law, introduced some cases decided by the House of Lords.—*Life of Sir M. Foster*, p. 45.

It may be compared to the standing order passed in 1721, leveled against Edmund Curl, declaring it to be "a breach of privilege to publish the Life of any deceased Peer or Lord of Parliament, without the permission of his heir or executors." I deemed it necessary to move to have this standing order repealed before I ventured to publish my "Lives of the Chancellors," as I should have found some difficulty in discovering the heir of St. Swithin or Turketel, and I did not like to run the risk of being sent to the Tower for defying the authority of the House.—See *Hansard's Debates*, 28th July, 1845

the inglorious life of Charles II., the last prince of the Austrian line who reigned beyond the Pyrenees.

To preserve internal tranquillity, still threatened by the Jacobites, and as a preparation for foreign war which might at any moment be rekindled, William proposed to keep embodied a few thousand of the veteran troops which had fought with him so gloriously at Namur; but the Commons, under a pretended regard for public liberty, factiously came to a vote " that all the land forces of the kingdom that had been raised since the 29th of September, 1680, should be paid and disbanded."[1] The debates upon the subject in Parliament were most violent, and many publications issued from the press by Tory partisans, inveighing against standing armies, and accusing the King of a design to make himself absolute with the aid of his Dutch guards. In answer to these came out a pamphlet, entitled, " A Letter balancing the Necessity of keeping a Land Force in time of Peace, with the Dangers which may follow therefrom." This was universally ascribed to the Lord Chancellor, and is certainly much after his manner. I believe it to be his; and, proving the author to be far in advance of his age for sound constitutional doctrine and for just views of society and of civil government, it reflects as much credit upon him as any of the popular treatises which he wrote in the reign of Charles II. He professes impartially to state the arguments on both sides, but strongly leans throughout in favor of a small standing army, to be voted annually and paid by Parliament. He shows the absolute necessity for such a force being kept up in the present state of the world, and argues that, being under the control of Parliament, it never can be dangerous to public liberty. He thus concludes:—" From a standing army, now become necessary to defend us from foreign attack, nothing is to be apprehended as long as England is true to herself; and whensoever the nation has lost the noble sense of liberty by which we are now distinguished, we shall soon make fetters for ourselves though we should find none ready made."[2] Considering that even Montesquieu and Blackstone[3] continued to declaim upon the incompatibility of standing armies and national freedom,

---

[1] 5 Parl. His. 1191, 1194.   [2] See Tind. Cont. Rap. vol. xiv. 416.
[3] Sp. L. ii. 6. 1 Bl. Com. 414.

we ought to honor the patriot who, in the 17th century, boldly pointed out that a body of professional soldiers was much better fitted for attaining the ends either of defense or of conquest, than those temporary forces which are raised by occasionally embodying and arming a portion of the citizens; and that though such an institution may be dangerous in a country where the powers of the Prince is ill defined,—after our rights had been declared and guaranteed at the Revolution,—in England it could be attended with no risk, and should excite no alarm. But, although Somers's reasoning has finally prevailed, it produced little effect in his own time, and William was not only obliged to ship off his Dutch guards, but to reduce almost all the English regiments which had returned from Flanders.

As the Tories intended, William took this most grievously to heart, and he became more and more sick of the Whig party, which had not sufficient influence to procure him the gratification of his favorite passion, or even to enable him to provide for the public safety. In those days there was no such thing as a sudden, entire, sweeping change of administration, but henceforth, as a matter of policy, he began to favor the Tories. The Earl of Jersey was made Secretary of State in the room of Somers's friend, the Duke of Shrewsbury; the Earl of Pembroke succeeded the Duke of Leeds as President of the Council; and Lord Lonsdale the Earl of Pembroke, as Lord Privy Seal. Nay, Montagu, with whom Somers had ever so cordially co-operated, and who was considered the second leader of the Whigs, retired from the office of Chancellor of the Exchequer, in which he had gained such reputation,—to make room for Mr. Smith.

Somers was still more obnoxious to the Tories than any of his colleagues who were gone, and they would have been still more delighted to have seen him sacrificed; but the Chancellor did not offer voluntarily to resign, and William could not yet bring himself to dismiss him.

It might have been well for Somers's reputation if he had been deprived of the Great Seal before the misapplication of it which I am now about to relate, and which, though it did not in the event subject him to punishment, certainly casts a shade upon his fame.

In the prospect of the death of Charles II. of Spain without issue all Europe was in a state of anxiety respecting the succession to his vast dominions. "His eldest sister had married Louis XIV.; and in the common course of inheritance the Dauphin would have been his heir. But the Infanta had, at the time of her espousal, solemnly renounced in her own name, and in that of her posterity, all claim to the succession. This renunciation had been confirmed in due form by the Cortes. A younger sister of the King had been the first wife of Leopold, Emperor of Germany. She, too, had at her marriage renounced her claims to the Spanish crown; but the Cortes had not sanctioned the renunciation, and it was therefore considered as invalid by the Spanish jurists. The fruit of this marriage was a daughter, who had married the Elector of Bavaria. The Electoral Prince of Bavaria inherited her claim to the throne of Spain. The Emperor Leopold was son of a daughter of Philip III., and was therefore first cousin to Charles. No renunciation whatever had been exacted from his mother at the time of her marriage. Thus that claim which, according to the ordinary rules of inheritance, was the strongest, had been barred by a contract executed in the most binding form. The claim of the Electoral Prince of Bavaria was weaker; but so also was the contract which bound him not to prosecute his claim. The only party against whom no instrument of renunciation could be produced, was the party who, in respect of blood, had the weakest claim of all."[1] Louis and Leopold each claimed the whole, but, to lessen alarm from excessive empire, proposed that the inheritance should go to a younger branch of the family; the one to the Duke of Anjou, and the other to the Archduke Charles.

William, whose destiny it was to preserve the balance of power in Europe, was placed in a situation of the greatest embarrassment. Although the Spanish King was yet quite a young man, and was married to a young and beautiful wife, from the exhausted state of his health all hope of posterity was gone, and every packet might bring the news of his dissolution.

The diplomacy into which William now entered, and which produced the two Partition Treaties, has been much

[1] Macaulay's Essays, ii. 48.

censured, and does seem to us very inexplicable. The necessity of the case might have justified him in disposing of the sovereignty of great states without the consent of their inhabitants; but the measures he took seem calculated to enhance the danger which he apprehended, and to further the ambitious schemes of his great opponent. Lord Somers, and his more prudent counsellors, were of opinion that the settlement of the Spanish succession should not be attempted without the concurrence of the Spanish government; and that if such a settlement could not be obtained, the wise course would be to wait prepared till the crisis arrived, and then to be governed by circumstances, which the keenest politician could not foresee.

But William, acting without the advice of any English minister, followed a different course, and fell into the snare which was laid for him. Louis XIV., to secure at all events a certain portion of the Spanish dominions to his family, and to disgust Spain with England that he might improve his chance of obtaining all, proposed to William that they two, of their own authority, should settle the question of the succession—by giving Spain, the Indies, and the Netherlands to the Electoral Prince of Bavaria, the two Sicilies to the Dauphin, and the Milanese to the Archduke Charles. Perhaps William thought that the King of Spain, whose great object it was to preserve the integrity of the empire which he ruled, whoever should be the heir, might be offended with France for this interference, and make another disposition of the whole in favor of a German Prince,—or that this was the only mode to prevent the union of France and Spain under the same crown. Whatever might be his reasoning, he was strongly inclined in favor of the arrangement; and he was not swayed by the opinion of Lord Somers, who being consulted, condemned it in as strong language as a minister could venture to employ.

In July, 1698, the King having dissolved the parliament, went over to Holland, and the Partition scheme seemed to be abandoned; but the Chancellor, having retired to Tunbridge Wells to recruit his health from the severe labors he had undergone, was surprised to receive the following letter from his royal master:—

"August, $\frac{14}{25}$, 1698.

"I imparted to you before I left England, that in

France there was expressed, to my Lord Portland, some inclination to come to an agreement with us concerning the succession of the King of Spain; since which Count Tallard has mentioned it to me, and has made such propositions, the particulars of which my Lord Portland will write to Vernon, to whom I have given orders not to communicate them to any other besides yourself, and to leave to your judgment to whom else you would think proper to impart them, to the end that I might know your opinion upon so important an affair, and which requires the greatest secrecy. If it be fit this negotiation should be carried on, there is no time to be lost, and you will send me the full powers under the Great Seal, with the names in BLANK, to treat with Count *Tallard*. I believe this may be done so secretly that none but you and Vernon, and those to whom you shall have communicated it, may have knowledge of it, so that the clerks, who are to write the warrant and the full powers, may not know what it is. According to all intelligence, the King of Spain can not outlive the month of October, and the least accident may carry him off every day. I received yesterday your letter of the 9th. Since my Lord Wharton can not at this time leave England, I must think of some other to send ambassador to Spain : if you can think of any one proper, let me know it, and be always assured of my friendship.

"WILLIAM R."

Lord Somers so far acted properly that he immediately communicated this letter to four of his colleagues, and they all agreeing with him as to the inexpediency of the treaty, he sent their explicit opinion to the King, with the reasons on which it was founded; but it must be admitted that he acted most unconstitutionally in sending at the same time a blank commission under the Great Seal, by which any Commissioners whose names William might please to insert in it should be authorized to conclude the treaty on the terms proposed, or on any other terms which William might dictate. There can be no doubt that if his opinion upon a matter of such magnitude was disregarded, it was his duty to resign; and that at all events he ought not to have enabled the King to conclude an important treaty, by which England was to be bound, without the privity and advice of a responsible English minister. If the government was to be carried on by the Sovereign's personal exercise of the prerogative, what had been gained by the Revolution? Yet in the State Paper Office there is the following letter, with the genuine signature of Lord Somers :—

"Tunbridge Wells, 28th August, 1698, O. S.

"Sir,—Having your Majesty's permission to try if the waters would contribute to the re-establishment of my health, I was just got to this place when I had the honor of your commands; I thought the best way of executing them would be to communicate to my Lord of Orford, Mr. Montagu, and the Duke of Shrewsbury (who before I left London had agreed upon a meeting about that time), the subject of Lord Portland's letter; at the same time letting them know, how strictly your Majesty required that it should remain an absolute secret.

"Since that time, Mr. Montagu and Mr. Secretary are come down hither; and upon the whole discourse three things have principally occurred to be humbly suggested to your Majesty.

"First, that the *entertaining* a proposal of this nature seems to be attended with very many ill consequences if the French did not act a sincere part; but we were soon at ease as to any apprehension of this sort, being fully assured your Majesty would not act but with the utmost surety, in an affair wherein the glory and safety of Europe were so highly concerned.

"The second thing considered was the very ill prospect of what was like to happen upon the death of the King of Spain, in case nothing was done previously towards the providing against that accident which seemed probably to be very near: The King of France having so great a force in such a readiness, that he was in a condition to take possession of Spain, before any other prince could be able to make a stand: Your Majesty is the best judge whether this be the case, who are so perfectly informed of the circumstances of parts abroad.

"But, so far as relates to England, it would be want of duty not to give your Majesty this clear account,—That there is a deadness and want of spirit in the nation universally, so as not at all to be disposed to the thought of entering into a new war, and that they seem to be tired out with taxes to a degree beyond what was discerned till it appeared upon the occasion of the late elections·

This is the truth of the fact, upon which your Majesty will determine what resolutions are proper to be taken.

"That which remained, was the consideration what would be the condition of Europe if the proposal took place: Of this we thought ourselves little capable of judging: But it seemed that if Sicily was in the French hands, they will be entirely masters of the Levant trade; that if they were possessed of Final, and those other seaports on that side, whereby Milan would be entirely shut out from relief by sea or any other commerce, that Duchy would be of little signification in the hands of any prince, and that if the King of France had possession of that part of Guipuscoa, which is mentioned in the proposal, besides the ports he would have in the ocean, it does seem he would have as easy a way of invading Spain on that side as he now has on the side of Catalonia.

"But it is not to be hoped that France will quit its pretenses to so great a succession without considerable advantages; and we are all assured your Majesty will reduce the terms as low as can be done, and make them, as far as possible in the present circumstances of things, such as may be some foundation for the future quiet of Christendom, which all your subjects can not but be convinced is your true aim: If it could be brought to pass that England might be some way a gainer by this transaction, whether it was by the Elector of Bavaria (who is the gainer by your Majesty's interposition in this treaty), his coming to an agreement to let us into some trade to the Spanish plantations, or in any other manner, it would wonderfully endear your Majesty to your English subjects.

"It does not appear, in case this negotiation should proceed, what is to be done on your part in order to make it take place: Whether any more be required than that the English and Dutch should sit still, and France itself to see it executed: If that be so, what security ought we to expect that if, by our being neuter, the French be successful, they will confine themselves to the terms of the treaty, and not attempt to make *further* advantages of their success?

"I humbly beg your Majesty's pardon that these thoughts are so ill put together: These waters are known to discompose and disturb the head so as almost totally to disable one from writing: I should be extremely troubled if my absence from London has delayed the dispatch of the Commission one day: You will be pleased to observe that two persons (as the Commission is drawn) must be named in it, but the powers may be executed by either of them: I suppose your Majesty will not think it proper to name Commissioners that are not English or naturalized in an affair of this nature.

"I pray God give your Majesty honor and success in all your undertakings. I am with the utmost duty and respect,
"Sir,
"Your Majesty's most dutiful
"and most obedient Subject and Servant,
"SOMERS, C.

"P. S.—The Commission is wrote by Mr. Secretary, and I have had it sealed in such a manner that no creature has the least knowledge of the thing besides the persons named."[1]

Under the authority of this Commission, a treaty was signed, and, being sent to England, the Lord Chancellor, by the King's orders, ratified it under the Great Seal, without communicating it to the Privy Council, or any others of his colleagues.—Such is the history of the treaty which, with such exquisite ingenuity and humor, was ridiculed by Arbuthnot, some years afterwards, in his "History of John Bull."[2] Perhaps we ought to give William credit for anticipating "the paroxysm of rage into which poor old Lord Strutt fell, on hearing that his runaway servant, Nick Frog, his clothier, John Bull, and his old enemy, Lewis Baboon, had come with quadrants, poles, and inkhorns, to survey his estate and to draw his will for him." On the arrival of the news of the Partition Treaty at Madrid, Charles did make a will devising the whole of his dominions to the Bavarian Prince, but unhappily this will had scarcely been signed when the Prince died.

William and his Chancellor still both remaining under what seems nothing short of infatuation, a second Partition Treaty was, with equal secrecy and irresponsibility,

---
[1] Ralph 796, 797.
[2] In reality, the King's *proprio vigore* had agreed to all the terms of the treaty four days after writing for powers to a negotiator.

negotiated and ratified;—whereby it was agreed that Spain, the Indies, and the Netherlands should descend to the Archduke Charles,—that France should still have the two Sicilies, and that for her accommodation the Duke of Loraine should surrender his principality to her in exchange for the Milanese. Nothing whatever was stipulated for England, and all sensible standers-by saw that, when the crisis arrived, Louis would utterly disregard the treaty as well as the renunciation, and seek to annihilate the Pyrenees.

Although the manner in which these treaties had been negotiated and concluded was not yet known in England, the terms of them excited there a tumult of disapprobation, and greatly strengthened the Tory party, who not unreasonably threw all the blame upon the Whigs. No direct vote of censure upon either treaty was proposed in parliament, but a series of motions were made on other subjects which were meant to annoy the Government and to irritate the King, with a view of compelling him entirely to banish the Whigs from his councils.

Attacks were made on the Lord Chancellor for his appointment and dismissal of magistrates, and a glowing picture was now drawn of his arbitrary treatment of those who refused to sign the association in defense of the King's safety on the discovery of the "Assassination Plot."

A more factious movement was a charge against the Lord Chancellor of being guilty of piracy on the high seas, and sharing in the booty of which foreigners were robbed, contrary to the law of nations. So far back as the beginning of the year 1696, the Indian seas being much infested with pirates, it was very desirable to send an English ship of war to cruise against them, but there was no fund to bear the expense, for " Parliament had so appropriated the money given for the sea, that no part of it could be applied to this expedition."[1] The King recommended a private subscription, saying that he would lay down £3,000 himself. He afterwards excused himself of his quota, but the Lord Keeper actually contributed £500, and so did the other ministers in proportion. Accordingly a noble vessel, called "The Adventure Galley," was fitted out, and the command of her given

[1] 3 Burnet, 327.

to William Kid, a naval officer, hitherto esteemed for honor as well as gallantry. "The Lord Keeper knew nothing of the matter further than that he thought it became the post he was in to concur in such a public service; but a grant was made to the undertakers of all that should be taken from the pirates by their ship."[1] Captain Kid was regularly commissioned "to sink, burn, and destroy pirates," but, on arriving in the Indian seas, he turned pirate himself, and cruised against the commerce of all nations indiscriminately,—till, after a sharp engagement with an English frigate, in which several fell on both sides, he was captured and brought home in irons. A motion was now unblushingly made in the House of Commons to hold the Lord Chancellor liable for all these enormities, the mover not only inveighing against the illegality of the expedition and of the grant, but broadly insinuating that all the murders and robberies had happened in consequence of his Lordship's orders, for the purpose of swelling his share of the profits, and that he was looked to by Kid for protection and indemnity at home. "Such black constructions are men who are engaged in parties apt to make of the actions of those whom they intend to disgrace, even against their own consciences."[2] However, the charge was so outrageous that none would vote for it who had any regard for character, and it was rejected by a large majority.[3]

The next measure was better imagined, and was attended with brilliant success. A bill was introduced to resume the grants of Irish forfeited estates, which William had very lavishly distributed among his favorites. Being once thrown out by the Lords, it was tacked to a bill of supply,—depriving the Lords (as it was said) of any power to touch it without losing the supply. The Court still made strenuous exertions to stop this multifarious bill. Lord Somers, on the score of ill health was absent from the debates upon it in the Peers, and a charge was brought against him, that, not venturing openly to oppose it, he feigned sickness, and tried to defeat it by intrigue. This was an unlucky time for the Chancellor, as the King most anxious to defeat the bill, was highly dissatisfied with him for not opposing it more actively. It

[1] 3 Burnet, 323. [2] Ibid. 328.
[3] Captain Kid was afterwards tried and executed. 14 St. Tr. 123, 147.

passed both Houses, and such was the strong feeling in favor of it with the public, that Lord Somers would not venture to advise on the present occasion an exercise of the veto by the Crown, so that it received the royal assent.

The Commons not being contented with this victory, a motion was made that an humble address be presented to his Majesty, praying, "that his Majesty will remove John, Lord Somers, Lord Chancellor of England, from his presence and councils for ever." The debate upon this occasion is unfortunately lost; and we only know, generally, that his arbitrary removal of magistrates after the Assassination Plot, and the other charges which were afterwards made the subject of the impeachment, were now hotly urged against him; while he was ably defended by some of his friends, and his merits and services were so powerfully portrayed, that the motion was negatived by a majority of 167 to 106.[2] However, the Commons were determined to carry their object indirectly; and, before separating, they came to a vote which they knew would be most offensive to the King, and would drive him to throw himself into the arms of the party who were strong enough to protect him from such insults—"that an address be presented to his Majesty, praying that no person who is not a native of his Majesty's dominions, except his Royal Highness, Prince George of Denmark, be admitted to his Majesty's councils in England or Ireland."

To avoid receiving and answering this address, William came to the House of Lords next morning, and the Commons being summoned,—by his orders the Earl of Bridgewater, in the absence of the Lord Chancellor,[3] declared that the Parliament was prorogued; and it was not allowed again to assemble.

Lord Somers had been absent from the House above two months. It so happened that the last time he had presided on the woolsack, was the day on which his celebrated judgment in the "Bankers' case" was reversed.[4] Party feeling had mixed itself up a good deal in this

[1] 11 & 12 W. 3, c. 2.
[2] Com. Jour. 5 Parl. Hist. 1221. Burnet iii. 334.
[3] There was a commission from the Crown authorizing John, Earl of Bridgewater, to act as Speaker of the House of Lords in the absence of the Lord Chancellor. [4] Ante, p. 6, *et seq.*

affair, and the story was circulated that he had taken to his bed not only from the slur cast upon his judicial fame, but from the prospect of his approaching fall.

An attempt was now made to induce him to quit his party, and Sunderland pressed him to join with the Tories in a new ministry; but he answered,—"This is neither my custom nor consistent with my honor."[1] Their offer being rejected, the Tories were relentless against him, and Harley, above all, was eager for his dismissal.[2]

William regarded the Chancellor with unshaken confidence, but thought that he could not oppose his own wishes to the national indignation, however unreasonable it might be, and that before calling another parliament his administration must be remodeled. "The first time that the Lord Somers had recovered so much health as to come to Court, the King told him it seemed necessary for his service that he should part with the Seals, and he wished that he would make the delivering them up his own act. He excused himself in this; all his friends had pressed him not to offer them, since that seemed to show fear or guilt, so he begged the King's pardon if in this he followed their advice; but he told the King that whensoever he should send a warrant under his hand commanding him to deliver them up, he would immediately obey it." On the 17th of April the expected warrant was brought to him by the Earl of Jersey, and he delivered to that nobleman the Great Seal, which, although as yet only in the 48th year of his age, for above seven years he had held with so much honor, and which, amidst all the strange vicissitudes which he and his party afterwards experienced, he never recovered.

[1] Cunningham, i. 183.
[2] "The just reputation and high rank which he had justly acquired were intolerable to Harley's envious heart."—*Birch's MSS.* 4223, Brit. Mus.
[3] See Oldm. Hist. 208. Tind. Cont. Rap. xiv. 515. The following extract from Evelyn's Diary shows the feelings of the day, and proves that the worthy author had taken his impressions a good deal from the Tory company which he had been keeping:—"24th April, 1700. The Seale was taken from Lord Chancellor Somers, tho' he had been acquitted by a greate majority of votes for what was charged against him in the House of Commons. This being in Term time put some stop to business, many eminent lawyers refusing to accept the office, considering the uncertainty of things in this fluctuating conjuncture. It is certain that this Chancellor was a most excellent lawyer, very learned in all polite literature, a superior pen, master of a handsome style and of easy conversation; but he is said to make too much haste to be rich as his predecessor, and most in place in this age did, to a more pro-

CHAPTER CIX.

CONTINUATION OF THE LIFE OF LORD SOMERS TILL THE DEATH OF KING WILLIAM.

THE Whigs were highly incensed by the removal of Lord Somers, and loudly complained of the conduct of William. They held the same language during the remainder of his reign, and even invented an anecdote that in his last moments he had expressed deep remorse for his ingratitude to the individual to whom he owed the Crown of England.[1] Lord Somers was too sensible a man to do more than breathe a passing murmur that another effort had not been made to save him. He well knew that after the "Abdication" of James, an English King could only govern through his parliament.[2]

The Chancellor's dismission had produced a deep sensation in Westminster Hall. "The Courts," says Cunningham, "were immediately deserted, the laws silent, and all proceedings at a stand, for no one thought himself worthy to succeed Somers in his high office."[3] William had made no provision for the appointment of a successor, and from the present unsettled state of parties, the Great Seal not only went a-begging, but met with many rebuffs. The first application was made to Sir Thomas Trevor, the Attorney General, but he wisely would not lose his practice at the bar for the prospect of being in a few weeks an ex-Chancellor. Chief Justice Holt next had the bauble held out to him, but he said that both prudence and honesty prompted him to reject it, for he held his present office *quamdiu se bene gesserit*, and he felt himself competent to the discharge of its duties, whereas he had never practiced in a Court of Equity in his life.[4] Even puisne

---

digious excesse than was ever known. But the Commons had now so mortified the Court party, and property and liberty were so much invaded in all the neighbouring kingdoms, that their jealousy made them cautious, and every day strengthened the law which protected the people from tyranny."

[1] Cunningham, vol. i. 252 ; Burnet, iii. 335.

[2] "The removing of the Lord Somers from his high station, though it displeased many people, yet it seemed not to affect his Lordship, who retired with content and temper, and upon all occasions in parliament served the King and the interests of the public with the same zeal as if he had not lost a place."—*Kennet*, iii. 783.   [3] Hist. i. 183.

[4] 2nd May. "Lord Justice Holt," says Prior, "having been at Hampton

judges and barristers without office refused the offer made them, though not yet warned by the lines which have not been able to save others from such folly:—

> "Ambition this shall tempt to rise,
> Then whirl the wretch from high,
> To bitter scorn a sacrifice
> And grinning infamy."

As it was now the middle of Easter Term, and important law business was suspended, the office of Chancellor being in abeyance,—the Great Seal, after remaining ten days in the King's own hands, was delivered into the temporary custody of the two Chief Justices and the Chief Baron as Lords Commissioners.[1] We learn from the letters of Secretary Vernon, lately published,[2] that an intrigue was then entered into by Lord Sunderland with the Duke of Shrewsbury and others, professedly with a view of restoring the ex-Chancellor to his office; but Somers himself was not privy to it, and I suspect that the whole was merely an attempt to mystify the Whigs, by holding out a prospect of returning favor to their chief. On the 21st of May, one NATHAN WRIGHT, Sergeant at Law, was prevailed upon to accept the Great Seal as Lord Keeper.[3]

Lord Somers, on his dismissal from office, having spent some time at Tunbridge Wells for the recovery of his health, retreated to his villa, and there returning to his literary pursuits, which had been long interrupted, forgot his recent mortifications, and felt as if he should be contented never again to mix in political broils. He heard with indifference of the negotiations respecting the appointment of his successor,—although he must have experienced a little glow of satisfaction from the embarrassment produced by the repeated refusals of the Great Seal, —excusable vanity suggesting to him that one reason was the dread of being compared to him who had lately held it with such general applause. He was kept in entire ignorance of the Sunderland intrigue for neutralizing the

Court, and with the King in private, occasioned a report that he had refused the Seals. If it be so or not, I can not say; but as yet the Seals are not disposed of."—*Letters to Earl of Manchester, Cole's Memoirs,* p. 128.

Some say that he exclaimed, "I never had but one cause in Chancery, and as I lost that, I can not think myself qualified for so great a trust."—*Grainger*, i. 164.   [1] Cr. Off. Min. fol. 141.   [2] A.D. 1841.

[3] See Vernon's Letters, written about this time, to the Duke of Shrewsbury, relating to Lord Somers, which are very curious.—Vol. iii. 37-65.

Whigs by the plan for his recall after the conclusion of the next session of parliament, or, as seems to have been pretty well foreseen, he would have indignantly spurned at it.

There was now a lull before the tempest burst forth with fresh violence. The King, having named Lords Justices, went abroad in the beginning of July, and did not return till the end of October. As yet there was perfect tranquillity in Europe, and at home it seemed doubtful which of the two great parties was to prevail, or whether there might not be a cordial coalition, between them. But events were in progress which speedily brought about a party conflict of unexampled violence, and which lighted up the flames of war from the Vistula to the Tagus.

Immediately after the second Partition Treaty into which England had been duped, French intrigue was set to work to convert it into an engine for effecting the object of Louis XIV. to get possession of the whole of the Spanish monarchy; and, through the dexterous management of the Cardinal Parto Carrero, the last male of the Spanish branch of the House of Austria was induced to execute a will, devising all his dominions to Philip, Duke of Anjou, the younger brother of the heir of the French monarchy. Immediately after this solemnity the royal testator expired. With scarcely the show of hesitation, Louis broke through all the obligations of the Partition Treaty, and accepted the splendid inheritance for his grandson. Philip was immediately recognized at Versailles as the successor of Charles II.; the whole court of France accompanied him to Sceaux, on his way to Madrid, and the whole French nation were intoxicated with joy at what they considered an immense accession to their empire.

In England the news excited corresponding consternation and resentment, and there was a violent cry against Lord Somers and the Whigs, to whom the Partition Treaties, and the misfortunes which followed upon them, were not unfairly imputed. A dissolution of parliament took place, and the elections ran strongly in favor of the Tories.

The new parliament met in the beginning of the following year, and the ex-Chancellor had great reason to dread its vengeance. After some time necessarily spent in providing for the Protestant succession, by calling in the House of Hanover,[1] in consequence of the death of the Duke of Gloucester, the promising son of the Princess Anne, the Partition Treaties were hotly debated in both Houses, and a proposal was made in the Commons " to impeach Lord Somers, late Chancellor of England, for the share he had had in these treaties, and for other high crimes and misdemeanors."[2] He thereupon caused it to be intimated to them, " that, having heard that complaint had been made of him in their House, out of his high respect for the Commons of England, he begged that he might have permission to be heard before them in his own defense."

This was granted, although the House, taking umbrage because the proceeding which they intended to keep secret had been divulged, resolved to ask him whence he had the information which induced him to make the application?—"A chair was set by the Sergeant, a little within the bar on the left hand; then the Sergeant had directions to acquaint the Lord Somers that he might come in, and Mr. Speaker acquainted his Lordship that he might repose himself in the chair provided for him; and his Lordship was heard what he had to offer to the House."[3]

Of this memorable speech we have a very imperfect report—from which we can barely trace the line of defense which he assumed. Having given an account of what we know to have passed about the negotiation with Tallard, he makes the King add, " that if he and his other ministers thought that a treaty ought not to be made upon such a project, then the whole matter must be let fall, for he could not bring the French to better terms." Lord Somers said, " he thought it would have been taking too much upon himself if he should have put a stop to a treaty of such consequence: The King's letter requiring the blank Commissions, he construed to be a *warrant* which

[1] See 12 & 13 W. 3, c. 2.
[2] This proceeding had excited great expectation. Thus wrote Prior, still a Whig, to the Duke of Manchester: "I must congratulate your happiness that you are out of this noise and tumult, where we are tearing and destroying every man his neighbor. To-morrow is the great day when we expect my Lord Chancellor will be fallen upon, though God knows what crime he is guilty of but that of being a very great man, and a wise and upright Judge."
—*Pri. Corr.*   [3] 5 Parl. Hist. 1245.

he was bound to obey: But at the same time, he wrote his own opinion very fully to his Majesty, objecting to many particulars, and proposing several things which he thought were for the good and interest of England: That the treaty being concluded, he put the Great Seal to it, by the King's command,—as he thought he was bound to do: That as a Privy Councillor he had offered the King his best advice; and that as Chancellor he had executed the office according to his duty." Having finished, the Speaker asked him " who had informed him that there was a debate in the House about him?" He answered, "that he was strangely surprised at a question which he never knew was put to any man that came to desire the favor of being heard; and that he not only would be content to be under the censure of the House, but would suffer the worst extremity that might befall him, rather than bring prejudice to those who had placed confidence in him." He then withdrew, but came back immediately and desired to leave with the House the King's letter to him, preparatory to the first Partition Treaty, with a copy of his answer, which he said he had permission to lay before them.[1] It is said that his defense was so full and clear, that if, upon his withdrawing, the question had been quickly put, the whole matter had been soon at an end, and the prosecution let fall. But his enemies, assisted by an indiscreet friend, drew out the debate to such a length that the impression which his speech had made was greatly effaced, and, the House sitting till it was past midnight, the resolution was carried by a majority of ten—198 to 188—" That John, Lord Somers, by advising his Majesty in the year 1698 to the treaty for partition of the Spanish monarchy, whereby large territories of the King

[1] This scene calls forth the following observation from Horace Walpole: "The excellent balance of our constitution never appeared in a clearer light than with relation to this Lord, who, though impeached by a misguided House of Commons with all the intemperate folly which at times disgraced the free states of Greece, yet had full liberty to vindicate his innocence and manifest an integrity which could never have shone so bright unless it had been juridically aspersed."—*Royal and Noble Authors.* Yet the Ultra-Tory, Lord Dartmouth, was so far misled by his prejudices as to write, "I never saw that House in so great a flame as they were upon his withdrawing. He left them in a much worse disposition to himself than he found them: and I heard many of his best friends say they heartily wished he had never come thither."

Lord Melville's defense of himself before the House of Commons, in 1806, is the last instance of a Peer claiming this privilege.

of Spain's dominions were to be delivered up to France, was guilty of a high crime and misdemeanor."[1] And the House ordered Simon Harcourt, the great Tory lawyer, who was afterwards Lord Chancellor, to go up to the House of Lords to impeach him in due form.[2]

Having resolved likewise to impeach the Earl of Portland, the Earl of Oxford, and Lord Halifax,—so eager were the Commons in the prosecution, that they immediately after presented an address to the King, praying him to remove all the four from his presence and councils for ever. The Lords, alarmed at this attempt of the Commons to sentence as well as to accuse, voted a counter address, praying his Majesty "not to pass any censure upon the accused Lords until they are tried upon their impeachments, and judgment be given according to the usage of parliament and the laws of the land." The King's answer to the Commons was in general terms, and amounted to a polite reprimand for their irregularity.[3]

Harcourt appearing at the bar of the Lords, "in the name of the House of Commons, and all the Commons of England, impeached John, Lord Somers, of high crimes and misdemeanors," adding that "the House of Commons would, in due time, exhibit particular articles against the said Lord, and make good the same."[4]

Articles, to the number of fourteen, were forthwith regularly exhibited. Had the case come to a hearing, some of them would have been very serious. The first was for *advising* the Partition Treaty, and could not have been supported by evidence. But the second charged, "that for more effectually carrying on that treaty, the said Lord Somers did prepare a commission to which he affixed the Great Seal of England, without any lawful warrant, and

[1] Sir Robert Walpole, then a very young member, took a warm interest for Lord Somers, and voted for him, but, with the tact which he ever displayed, remained silent, that the effect of the Speech might not be weakened by an angry discussion—privately remarking "that the zeal of the warmest friends is oftentimes more hurtful to the person whose cause they espouse than the bitterest accusations of the most inveterate opponents." He was of opinion that if the question had been immediately put, the prosecution would have been withdrawn. Harcourt, to further the impeachment, laid the trap into which Cowper, who was against it, fell. *Coxe's Memoirs of Sir Robert Walpole*, i. 22. Walpole was afterwards Teller on the division respecting the Replication to Lord Somers's Answer to the Articles of Impeachment, when he was in a minority of 90 to 140. *Ib.* 23.
[2] Burnet, iii. 369. 5 Parl. Hist. 1245. [3] 5 Parl. Hist. 1249, 1250.
[4] 14 St. Tr. 233.

without communicating the same to the rest of the Lords Justices, or advising in concurrence with his Majesty's Privy Council thereupon—that no certain persons of known honor, fidelity, and experience, were therein nominated Commissioners, but that a blank, or empty space, was left in the said commission at the time of the sealing thereof, whereon the Commissioners' names were afterwards to be inserted beyond the seas, although an unlimited power was given to such Commissioners to treat with the Commissioners of the French King, and of the States General, touching the succession to the crown of Spain, and his Majesty did thereby engage himself to ratify and confirm whatever should thereupon be concluded by them or either of them." The third was for procuring, *ex post facto*, a warrant to authorize the commission. The fourth was for clandestinely affixing the Great Seal to the ratification of the treaty. The fifth was for doing the like to the second Partition Treaty in 1699. The sixth was for omitting to cause the commissions and ratifications, according to the duty of his office, to be enrolled—the omission being averred to have been for the sake of concealment. The next five articles accused him of passing in his own favor illegal grants of the property of the Crown. The thirteenth was for granting a commission under the Great Seal to Kid, the pirate, who, under pretense thereof, had long preyed upon the ships and property of his Majesty's subjects in the West Indies —and the last article most frivolously charged judicial delinquency—particularly in respect of the celebrated judgment in the "BANKERS' CASE." In his Answers, Lord Somers traversed the first article; as to the second, third, fourth, and fifth, he relied on his Majesty's express command. With respect to the sixth, he denied that the enrollment was a part of his duty. The charges respecting the grants, he repelled, by asserting that they proceeded from the spontaneous bounty of the Crown, and that they all passed in due form.[1] On the thirteenth, he admitted that he had granted a commission to Captain Kid,

[1] Horace Walpole, though friendly to Somers, blames these grants (*Royal and Noble-Authors*); but, says Lord Hardwicke, "One might as well lay a heavy charge on his father's (Sir R. Walpole's) memory for the grants of lucrative offices obtained for his family, and taking a pension when he resigned. Lord Somers raised no more from his offices and grants than a fortune which enabled him to live with decency and elegance."

and had assisted in fitting him out, but denied all privacy with his piracies. In replying to the last article, he excusably dwells upon his great exertions in the Court of Chancery, to the manifest impairing of his health, and upon the anxiety he had ever manifested to do justice between the Crown and the subject, and between man and man.[1]

There evidently was not the slightest color for the impeachment, except with respect to the treaties; and to these very serious charges I must own I think the defense is very inadequate. It does seem astonishing to us that, to humor the King, Somers should have so acted; and still more astonishing, that he should openly rely on the King's command as a justification. This is the language of Attorney General Herbert, in defending himself for impeaching Lord Kimbolton and the five Members for high treason, in the time of Charles I., but could little have been expected from the great contriver of the Revolution, and the author of the " Bill of Rights." The principle would introduce absolutism into the management of all domestic as well as foreign affairs, and is entirely at variance with every notion of responsible government.

Luckily for the ex-Chancellor, the misunderstanding between the two Houses, which originated in the indiscreet attempt of the Commons to prejudge the case while it was pending, gradually increased, and finally rendered the impeachment abortive. The truth is, that at this time (incredible as it may seem to us), the Whigs had a decided majority in the House of Lords, although they were always outvoted in the House of Commons. From the creation of some new Peers—from judicious appointments to the Right Reverend Bench—and from the highest ranks in England being then much better educated than the fox-hunting squires who represented the counties and many of the smaller boroughs, the Upper House in the reign of William was, and for a good many years continued, far in advance of the Lower in liberality and intelligence. The Lords had steadily supported the late ministers now under impeachment, and an acquittal was pretty confidently anticipated, without any nice discriminations of the articles of charge. The Tor-

[1] 14 St. Tr. 263-274.

majority in the Commons, therefore, very injudiciously sought to stop the prosecutions by a quarrel, that the accused might not have the triumph of an acquittal on the merits. Had they abandoned the unfounded and frivolous articles, and proceeded regularly to trial on the charge respecting the Partition Treaties, they must either have obtained a conviction or covered their opponents with disgrace.

Lord Somers's "Answer" being communicated to the Commons, they neglected duly to put in a "Replication" to it, and they had for an unreasonable time omitted to exhibit written articles against other Lords whom they had impeached. Being urged to use dispatch, they returned a saucy message, intimating that they were the best judges of the propriety of their own proceedings. On the petition of Lord Somers "that a day might be appointed for his speedy trial," the Lords resolved to commence it on Friday, the 13th of June. The Commons thereupon demanded a "Conference," in which, after many complaints, they proposed to their Lordships "that a committee of both Houses be nominated to consider of the most proper ways and methods of proceeding on impeachments according to the usage of parliaments in such cases." This proposal was scorned by the Lords, who sent a message intimating "that they thought themselves obliged to assert their undoubted right to appoint a day of trial for any impeachment depending before them without any previous signification from the Commons of their being ready to proceed; that their Lordships, according to the example of their ancestors, would always use that right with a regard to the equal and impartial administration of justice, and with a due care to prevent unreasonable delays; and that the expressions of the Commons were such as never before had been used by one House of Parliament to another, and such as, if returned, would necessarily destroy all good correspondence between the two."

The Commons, however, refused to proceed till the preliminaries of the trial should be adjusted by a joint committee of Lords and Commons, and they should be assured particularly that the Lord to be tried should, during his trial, stand outside the bar, and that the other impeached Lords should not sit or vote;—declaring, "that to depart from these demands would be giving up the rights of the Commons of England known by unquestionable precedents, and making impeachments (the greatest bulwark for the laws and liberties of England) impracticable for the future."

At last the Lords and Commons met in a "Free Conference," in which there was such violence that there seems to have been some danger of their coming to the *via facti*, and rendering it necessary that constables should be called in to preserve the peace. Lord Haversham, in his speech, plainly accused the Commons of "fastidiously instituting these impeachments against Peers *whom they knew to be innocent*." The Commons immediately broke up the conference, and rushed away. As they were withdrawing, the Duke of Devonshire, the Lord Steward, bawled after them, "he hoped they would return back like men of sense to finish the business on which they had been sent, and would not think that that Lord had any authority to use any such language to their Honorable House." On their arrival in their own chamber, they gave an inflammatory account of what had occurred; whereupon it was resolved, *nemine dissentiente*, "that John, Lord Haversham, hath at the Free Conference this day uttered most scandalous reproaches and false expressions, highly reflecting upon the honor and justice of the House of Commons, and tending to the making a breach in the good correspondence between the Lords and Commons, and to the interrupting the public justice of the nation by delaying the proceedings on impeachment." 2. "That John, Lord Haversham, be charged before the Lords for the words spoken by him this day at the Free Conference, and that the Lords be desired to proceed against the said Lord Haversham, and to inflict such punishment upon him as so high an offense against the House of Commons does deserve." The Lords in answer requested that the Commons would forthwith return to the Painted Chamber and resume the Free Conference, "which, they doubted not, would prove the best expedient to prevent the inconvenience of a misunderstanding upon what has passed,"—and the following day they earnestly repeated their request. They likewise required Lord Haversham to answer the charge against him. But the Commons peremptorily refused to proceed till they should have satisfaction for the insult offered to them at the Free Conference, till the joint committee should be appointed, and till they had assurance that each Lord on his trial should stand at the bar, and that the impeached Lords should not sit or vote on the trial of each other. The Lords thereupon peremptorily fixed Tuesday, the 17th of June, for the trial of Lord Somers, and the Commons resolved "that they would not attend."

The day of trial exhibited a series of party struggles rather than a grave judicial proceeding. The Tories in the House of Lords, although a minority, were numerous and determined, and they zealously backed up all the pretensions of the Commons. On the assembling of the Peers in the morning, the first question put was, "Whether the House should go this day into the Court in Westminster Hall, in order to proceed upon the trial of Lord Somers?" After a sharp debate, it was carried in the affirmative; but twenty-six temporal and three spiritual Lords signed a protest in such violent language that it was expunged from the Journals. The impeached Lords having moved "that they have leave to be absent from Lord Somers's trial," this was strenuously opposed by the Tories, on the ground of its indicating that, contrary to the requisition of the other House, they had a right to be present if they chose; but it was carried in the affirmative.

The procession was then formed to Westminster Hall, which had been properly fitted up for the occasion. The Lords being duly seated according to their degrees, Lord Somers was placed *within* the bar, as this was only a case of misdemeanor; and the articles against him, and his answers, were read by the Clerk. The Commons were then solemnly called to appear and make good their impeachment. No one appearing for the prosecution, the Lords returned in procession to their own chamber. But here a tumultuous discussion arose respecting the form of the question now to be put, and this being referred to the Judges, they declared that it ought to be, " Is John, Lord Somers, guilty, or not guilty of the high crimes and misdemeanors whereof he is impeached?" But the Tory party said, "as they could not vote Lord Somers *guilty* upon any notoriety, without legal evidence, so they could not vote him *not guilty*; for, although the Commons were deprived of the opportunity of making good their accusation, he might, nevertheless, have committed all the offenses charged against him, and with every possible aggravation." To give them some content, the question agreed to be put was, "That John, Lord Somers, be acquitted of the articles of impeachment against him exhibited by the House of Commons, and all things therein contained, and that the said impeachment be dismissed." This being settled, the Lords returned to Westminster Hall, and the question being put to all the Lords present, beginning with the junior Baron, fifty-six voted in the affirmative, and thirty-one in the negative. They then returned to their own chamber, and, without another division, judgment was solemnly pronounced by the Lord Keeper, by order of the House, "that the defendant be acquitted, and the impeachment dismissed." Lord Somers's personal demeanor during the whole proceeding was universally admired, and was afterwards celebrated by Addison:—

"This noble Lord, for the great extent of his knowledge and capacity, has been often compared with the Lord Verulam, who had also been Chancellor of England. But the conduct of these extraordinary persons under the same circumstances was vastly different. They were both impeached by a House of Commons. One of them, as he had given just occasion for it, sunk under it, and was reduced to such an abject submission as very much diminished the luster of so exalted a character. But my Lord Somers was too well fortified in his integrity to fear the impotence of an attempt upon his reputation, and though his accusers would gladly have dropped their impeachment, he was instant with them for the prosecution of it, and would not let that matter rest until it was brought to an issue. For the same virtue and greatness of mind which made him disregard fame, made him impatient of an undeserved reproach."[1]

The Commons, at their next meeting after the acquittal, resolved "that the Lords had refused them justice upon the impeachment against the Lord Somers, by denying them a Committee of both Houses, which was desired, as the only proper means of settling the necessary pre-

[1] Freeholder, No. xxxix.

liminaries, and afterwards by proceeding to a pretended trial of the said Lord, which could tend only to protect him from justice by color of an illegal acquittal, and that the Lords had thereby endeavored to overturn the right of impeachment lodged in the House of Commons by the ancient constitution of this kingdom, for the safety and protection of the people against great men, and had made an invasion on public liberty by holding out a prospect of impunity to the greatest offenders; and that if the supplies necessary for preserving the public peace and maintaining the balance of power in Europe shall be withheld, the whole blame must be ascribed to those who have used their utmost endeavors to make a breach between the two Houses to escape from the just punishment of their own enormous crimes."

The Lords, with more dignity, merely intimated, in answer to this message, that " they had appointed a day for the trial of the Earl of Oxford;" and, when the joint committee was again demanded, saying that " this showed that the Commons never intended to bring any of their impeachments to trial." The impeached Lords were accordingly all acquitted, parliament was prorogued, and this ultra-Tory House of Commons never met again—events arising which brought about a reaction on the liberal side, and enabled the King successfully to appeal to the nation in support of the liberties of Europe.[1]

Lord Somers's early friend, Shrewsbury, hearing of these transactions while resident at Rome, thus addressed him: —" I can not help referring to my old opinion, which is now supported by more weight than I ever expected, and wonder that a man can be found in England who has bread, that will be concerned in public business. Had I a son, I would sooner breed him a cobbler than a courtier, and a hangman than a statesman."

Swift, starting as a zealous Whig, published soon after the prorogation his " Discourse on the Contests and Dissensions between the Nobles and the Commons in Athens and Rome, with the consequences they had upon both those States."[2] Having been flattered by the condescen-

[1] 5 Parl. Hist. 1243. 14 St. Tr. 234–350. Burnet, iii. 366–386. 2 Ralph, 955, 968.
[2] It is supposed that he had before *written* " The Tale of a Tub," and " The Battle of the Books," but this was his first prose *publication*. Some years

sion of William, who had shown him, in the garden at Moore Park, "how to cut asparagus in the Dutch way," and hoping for promotion in the Church from the return of the Whig party to power, he strove to damp the warmth of the Commons by showing that their measures had a direct tendency to bring on the tyranny which they professed to oppose, although afterwards, when he had gone over to the Tories, he designated William as "a new King from a Calvinistic republic," and malignantly slandered those whom he now most lavishly commended. In this work he shadowed forth the impeached Lords in the character of Athenians:—Somers as Aristides—Oxford as Themistocles—Halifax as Pericles, and Portland as Phocion, Thus he flatters the same person whom he so grossly libeled in the "Examiner," and in the "History of the Last Four Years of Queen Anne:"—"Their next great man was Aristides. He was a person of the strictest justice, and best acquainted with the laws as well as forms of their government, so that he was in a manner CHANCELLOR of Athens. This man, upon a slight and false accusation of favoring arbitrary power, was banished by ostracism, which, rendered into modern English, would signify that they voted 'he should be removed from their presence and councils for ever.' But, however, they had the wit to recall him, and to that action owed the preservation of their state by his future services. For it must be still confessed in behalf of the Athenian people, that they never conceived themselves perfectly infallible, nor arrived to the heights of modern assemblies, to make obstinacy confirm what sudden heat and temerity began. They thought it not below the dignity of an assembly to endeavor at correcting an ill step, at least to repent, though it often falls out too late." Somers's late colleagues are equally lauded, and proclamation is made that, having been treated most unjustly, England's only chance of struggling against the difficulties which thickened round her was to place them in the offices which they had so ably and virtuously filled.

This "Discourse," however ingenious, made but little impression on the public mind. There seems reason to think that the people madly took part with the House of

before, he had printed some bad Pindaric odes, which called forth the observation from Dryden, "Cousin Swift, you will never be a poet."

Commons, and there was real danger, not only to the tranquillity, but even to the independence of the country. One section of the dominant Tories would have been contented to support the "Act of Settlement," they themselves possessing office; but another section, wealthy and powerful, still adhered to the doctrine of "divine right," and wished to expiate the "sin of the Revolution" by recalling King James. Still further, the grandson of Louis XIV., having quietly mounted the throne of Spain, had been recognized by several European states, and even the liberal party in England seemed indisposed to make any effort with a view to check the career of France towards universal empire.

But the face of affairs all over Europe was suddenly changed on the death of James II., by France recognizing his son as King of Great Britain. Historians have been greatly at a loss to account for this insane step on the part of Louis XIV., to which may be traced all his subsequent misfortunes. Some say that he was influenced by the dying entreaties of the exiled monarch; others, by a promise of Madame de Maintenon to Mary of Modena; and others, by a declaration of the Dauphin, that "it would be disgraceful for the Bourbons to desert the Prince of Wales, who was not only lineally entitled to the throne of England, but was of their own blood." The truth probably is, that Louis was quite intoxicated by the brilliant success of his own crooked policy respecting the Spanish succession, and the rapture with which it had been received in France, where the people, not presaging the calamities by which they were destined to expiate the perfidious violation of the peace of Ryswick, became delirious with pride and delight, as if a great private estate had been suddenly bequeathed to every individual in the kingdom.¹ The "Great Monarch" thought that, substantially, universal empire was already gained, and that England, as a province, he might dispose of at his pleasure. He therefore ordered James III. to be proclaimed King, pretty much as the English Governor General of India announces his intention to elevate the son of an exiled Rajah to the musnud.

[1] Addison, who was in Paris at the time, was obliged to fly to another country, saying, "The French conversation begins to grow insupportable; that which was before the vainest nation in the world is now worse than ever."

The news of this proceeding caused an unexampled sensation in England. Even Jacobites, who would have been charmed to have the true heir spontaneously recalled, were hurt at the thought of his being imposed upon the nation by a foreign power, and all ranks and persuasions enthusiastically rallied round the throne of William. He now formed the GRAND ALLIANCE, which led to the victories of Marlborough. From the change in the public mind at home, he was likewise pleased with the prospect of getting rid of Rochester, who had been forced upon him as minister, and of again putting himself into the hands of the Whigs. Sunderland now sincerely attempted to negotiate Somers's recall, and a coalition between the more enlightened of both parties. In a letter, written to be laid before the King,[1] he said, "The Tories will not be satisfied without ruining my Lord Somers, nor the Whigs without undoing the ministers, in which the latter think they have the whole nation on their side. But, at last, what can the King do? He must certainly do what may determine him to take his measures. For example, let him come into England as soon as he can, and immediately send for my Lord Somers. He is the life, the soul, the spirit of his party, and can answer for it; not like the present ministers, who have no credit with theirs, any further than they can persuade the King to be undone. When his Majesty speaks to my Lord Somers, he ought to do it openly and freely, and ask him plainly what he and his friends can do and will do, and what they expect, and the methods they propose. By this the King will come to a judgment of his affairs, and he may be sure that my Lord Somers will desire nothing for himself, or any of the impeached Lords, but will take as much care not to perplex the King's business as can be desired; and if he can do nothing his Majesty shall like, he will remain still zealous and affectionate to his person and government." The King, in consequence, addressed a short note to Lord Somers, from Loo, accrediting Lord Galway as a confidential agent, and assuring him of the continuance of his friendship.[2] In conseqnence of these

---

[1] September, 1701.
[2] "J'ay chargé Mr. Gallway de vous parler de ma part avec beaucoup de franchise J'espère que vous adjouterez une entière créance à ce qu'il vous dira ; et que vous voudrez bien avec la mesme franchise sans aucune réserve,

negotiations, Somers prepared Heads of Arguments to induce the King to call a new parliament,[1] and on the 10th of November the old parliament was dissolved, that on this unexpected turn of affairs an appeal might be made to the nation.

The result of the elections was very favorable. The King's speech at the opening of the session was prepared by Somers, and is pronounced by Burnet to be "the best this, or perhaps any other, prince ever made to his people."[3] I copy a few of the more striking passages of this composition, which is as remarkable for its simplicity as for its spirit:—

"My Lords and Gentlemen, I promise myself you are met together full of that just sense of the common danger of Europe, and the resentment of the late proceedings of the French King, which has been so fully and universally expressed in the loyal and seasonable addresses of my people. The owning and setting up the pretended Prince of Wales for King of England is not only the highest indignity offered to me and the nation, but does so nearly concern every man who has a regard for the Protestant religion, or the present and future quiet and happiness of his country, that I need not press you to lay it seriously to heart, and to consider what further effectual means may be used for securing the succession of the crown in the Protestant line, and extinguishing hopes of all pretenders, and their open and secret abettors. By the French King placing his grandson on the throne of Spain, he is in a condition to oppress the rest of Europe, unless speedy and effectual methods be taken. Under

---

et estre persuadé de la continuation de mon amitié" Lord Sunderland, at the same time, wrote to Lord Somers: "The King is resolved to discourse fully and plainly with all the good inclinations possible, and knows that the two friends are of a mind in every particular."—*Hard. Stat. Pap.* ii. 446, 452, 453.

[1] This very elaborate paper is extant in Lord Somers's handwriting. I copy the commencement of it:—

"The present ferment and disposition of the nation.
    1st, Art of government in England, in watching and using such opportunities.
    2nd, These opportunities do not last.
    3rd, Neglect of making use of them always must turn to disadvantage.
        1. By disobliging the zealous.
        2. Encouraging the ill-meaning.
        3. Creating jealousies of the King and his measures.'

3 Burnet, 409.

this pretense he is become the real master of the whole Spanish monarchy; he has made it to be entirely depending on France, and disposing of it as of his own dominions; and by that means he has surrounded his neighbors in such a manner, that, though the name of peace may be said to continue, yet they are put to the expense and inconvenience of war. This must affect England in the nearest and most sensible manner in respect to our trade, which will soon become precarious in all the valuable branches of it; in respect to our peace and safety at home, which we can not hope should long continue, and in respect to that part which England ought to take in the preservation of the liberty of Europe. It is fit I should tell you the eyes of all Europe are upon this Parliament; all matters are at a stand till your resolutions are known, and therefore no time ought to be lost. You have yet an opportunity, by God's blessing, to secure to you and your posterity the quiet enjoyment of your religion and liberties, if you are not wanting to yourselves, but will exert the ancient vigor of the English nation; but I will tell you plainly, my opinion is, if you do not lay hold of this occasion, you have no reason to hope for another. I should think it as great a blessing as could befall England if I could observe you as much inclined to lay aside those unhappy, fatal animosities which divide and weaken you, as I am disposed to make all my subjects safe and easy as to any, even the highest, offenses committed against me. Let me conjure you to disappoint the only hopes of our enemies by your unanimity. I have shown, and will always show, how desirous I am to be the common father of all my people: do you, in like manner, lay aside parties and divisions; let there be no other distinction heard of amongst us for the future but of those who are for the Protestant religion and the present establishment, and of those who mean a Popish prince and a French government."[1]

This speech drew forth, not a formal echo, but a manly pledge of support from both Houses: the treaties of alliance were approved of, a liberal supply was voted, and an act passed to attaint the pretended Prince of Wales if he should land in England. William began to get rid of some of his Tory ministers, and it was confidently

[1] 5 Parl. Hist. 1329.

expected that Lord Somers would soon be again his Chancellor, and avowedly his chief adviser. But our illustrious deliverer, having given this impulse to the national feeling, and laid the foundation of national triumph, approached the termination of his earthly career. His health had been long declining, the injury he received by a fall from his horse greatly aggravated his complaints, and on the 8th of March, 1702, he expired, in the 52nd year of his age, and the 14th of his reign.

CHAPTER CX.

CONTINUATION OF THE LIFE OF LORD SOMERS TILL HIS APPOINTMENT AS LORD PRESIDENT OF THE COUNCIL.

THE national misfortune of the King's death fell with particular severity on the Whigs, at the moment when they had confidently reckoned on returning to office in a body. Anne, when young, had been told that they were republicans and atheists, and she had entertained for them a strong distaste, personal, political, and religious. The Whig ex-Chancellor was particularly obnoxious to her. He had been the confidential adviser of her brother-in-law, from whom she had been much estranged; he was suspected by her of crossing her wishes to be put into the council of regency, and to have a separate establishment as next heir to the crown; and his views respecting church affairs had been grossly misrepresented to her. Although he signed the recognition of her title previous to her being proclaimed, and he was ready to have shown her every mark of loyal respect, she at once announced to the confidential friends who gathered round her on her accession, that she would not even admit him into her presence. Accordingly, he was not allowed to be sworn of her Privy Council, when, along with the Privy Councillors of the late King, he attended to take the oaths, as is usual at the commencement of a new reign; and his name was struck out from the commission of the peace in every county in England.[1] What he probably felt more severely as a special

[1] Historians all say that his name was struck out of the list of Privy

slight to him,—orders were given to discontinue the payment of the pension which he had procured for Addison. Thus, instead of being again in possession of the Great Seal, with the patronage of the Crown, and the power of Prime Minister, he found himself proscribed from office, disgraced as far as the spite of the Court could disgrace him, and held up to the world as a man whose good opinion was a bar to all favor.

Now, however, begins what may be considered the most praiseworthy and the most truly glorious portion of the life of Somers. When he found that Godolphin and Marlborough, judging that it would be most for their own advantage to adopt the measures of the Whigs, at the risk of offending the party which had brought them into power, were resolved to fulfill the engagements of the "Grand Alliance," he strenuously supported their foreign policy, and instead of seeking to embarrass them, he did everything in his power, both in and out of parliament, to enable them successfully to carry on the war. Banished from the Court, he was a main prop of the Government. He was diligent in his attendance in the House of Lords, and he lost no opportunity of supporting the honor of the country, or protecting religious liberty against the inroads of the dominant faction.[1]

Apart from politics, his conduct is still more to be admired, as being more rare among English lawyers, who generally, while in practice, or in office, devote themselves

Councillors which is substantially true, as he was not allowed to be sworn of the Council to the new Sovereign. When the commissions of the peace were renewed, his name, which, as Chancellor and Privy Councillor, had been in all, was by the express orders of the Government, omitted from all —even from the commission for his native county. This, although sometimes denied, appears clearly by a letter from Secretary Vernon to the Duke of Shrewsbury, dated March 31st, 1704. Having mentioned an address of the Lords to the Queen, praying "that such as had been put out of commission since the Queen's accession to the throne should be restored," he adds: "When this matter was debated in the House of Lords yesterday, my Lord Keeper (Wright) had many rubs given him about persons put in and left out of the commissions; particularly that my Lord Somers was left out of the commission of the peace for Worcestershire, which they told him was the more scandalous, since that Lord had sat on the woolsack with more reputation than those that came either before or after him."—*Vern. Corresp.* iii. 257.

[1] From a reference to the Journal of the Peers, I find that the House hardly ever met without his being present. The two last almost always are "D⁸. Somers," "D⁸. Halifax," till a few years after there were some new creations.

exclusively to professional avocations, and in their retirement, left without mental resources, waste their declining years in frivolous occupations or in vain regrets.[1] Lord Somers presents the *beau ideal* of an ex-Chancellor,—active in his place in parliament when he could serve the State, and devoting his leisure to philosophy and literature. He had long been a Fellow of the Royal Society ; he now regularly attended the meetings, and assisted in its transactions ; and being elected the President, he did everything in his power to extend its credit and its usefulness. Having held this distinguished post five years, he gracefully resigned it to Sir Isaac Newton. He made a noble use of the wealth he had honorably acquired, by purchasing a fine collection of paintings, engravings,[2] medals, and books—becoming possessed of almost every edition of the Bible that had ever been printed, and of an immense mass of tracts, printed and manuscript, on English history and antiquities. He lived much with literary men, and liberally aided such as were oppressed by poverty. On Addison's return from the Continent, he cordially embraced him ; he introduced him into the Kit-Cat Club,[3] and visited

[1] There has been at least one splendid exception. A right reverend Prelate, whose name, if I were at liberty to mention it, would be considered a grace to my page, thus writes to me: "I remember traveling, many years ago, with Sir S. Romilly one stage in his carriage, which was filled with the best books of the general literature of the day. To a remark from me that I rejoiced to see that he found time for such reading, he answered, 'As soon as I found I was to be a busy lawyer for life, I strenuously resolved to keep up my habit of non-professional reading ; for I had witnessed so much misery in the last years of many great lawyers whom I had known, from their loss of all taste for books, that I regarded their fate as my warning.'"

[2] He first brought into notice Vertue, the celebrated engraver, by employing him to engrave a portrait of Archbishop Tillotson ; and he made the fortune of Simon Dubois by sitting to him. This painter had previously supported himself by selling, as originals, copies he had made of the old masters—saying that "he was justified in being revenged of the public for not sooner discovering his own genius."—*Life of Vertue by Horace Walpole* Works iv. 120.

[3] Somers was an original member of this club, which is said to have been founded by Jacob Tonson, the bookseller. It derived its name from meeting at the House of CHRISTOPHER CAT, in Shire Lane, close by Temple Bar, famous for his mutton-pies. Witness the well-known line :
"Immortal made as Kit-cat by his pies ;"
and the distich :
"Hence did th' assembly's title first arise,
And Kit-Cat wits sprung first from Kit-Cat pies."
Other accounts state that "Cat" was not the surname of the master, but was taken from the sign of his house, the "CAT and FIDDLE."
All the Whigs who pretended to wit belonged to this club. They dined so

him in his garret in the Hay Market, where the poor poet was found out by Godolphin to celebrate the victories of Marlborough. Lord Somers was rewarded by the Dedication of his friend's "Travels in Italy;" and as he seemed now for ever banished from office, he could have no misgivings as to the sincerity of such sentiments as these, from the author of "The Campaign," with the praises of which all England was ringing:—

"I had a very early ambition to recommend myself to your Lordship's patronage, which yet increased in me as I traveled through the countries of which I here give your Lordship some account; for whatever just impressions an Englishman must have of your Lordship, they who have been conversant abroad will find them still improved. It can not but be obvious to them, that though they see your Lordship's admirers everywhere, they meet with very few of your well-wishers at Paris or at Rome. And I could not but observe when I passed through most of the Protestant governments in Europe, that their hopes or fears for the common cause rose or fell with your Lordship's interest and authority in England."[1]

late as three in the afternoon, and often sat till six. In the summer months they met at the "Upper Flask," on Hampstead Heath. To this Sir Richard Blackmore alludes in his poem entitled "The Kit-Cat," which, strange to say, was fashionable in the reign of Queen Anne:

"Or when, great Kit-Cat, thou art pleas'd to lead
Thy sons to feast on Hampstead's airy head—
Hampstead that, towering in superior sky,
Now with Parnassus does in honor vie."

Sir Godfrey Kneller painted the members of this club somewhat larger than a three-quarters, and less than a half-length—a size which painters have ever since denominated a Kit-Cat. Bolingbroke afterwards, in proposals for forming a rival club squeamishly says: "The first regulation, and that which must be inviolably kept, is decency. *None of the extravagance of the Kit-Cat* —none of the drunkenness of the Beef-Steak—is to be endured." "The OCTOBER" must have been very dull, consisting chiefly of Tory fox-hunters; but "The Brothers," enlivened by the sallies of the renegade Swift against his old Whig friends, must have been very delightful society.—See Malone's Life of Dryden, p. 735; History of Clubs, p. 368; Steele's Correspondence, vol. ii. 344; Noble's Continuation of Grainger, iii. 431.

[1] In a "Life of Somers," published when Addison was alive and in the elevated station of Secretary of State, the author says: "I believe the learned, ingenious, and polite Mr. Addison will not take it amiss to have it told that his Lordship took him into his protection and favor when he first came to town; that he obtained a handsome pension for him before he went to travel, and afterwards recommended him so promptly to the Lord Halifax, that he passed through several profitable and honorable employments till he was made as happy in his fortune as in his fame."—*Life*, 1716, p. 110.

Among the other wits of Anne's reign, the ex-Chancellor was likewise on the most familiar footing with Swift—who, as yet having nothing to hope from the Tories, dedicated to him the "Tale of a Tub," stating how "the bright example of his patron's virtue would adorn the history of the late reign," describing him as "the sublimest genius of the age for wit, learning, judgment, eloquence, and wisdom," and celebrating him for "his discernment in discovering, and readiness in favoring, deserving men."

The "Spectator" had not yet criticised PARADISE LOST, and from the personal prejudices entertained against the author the beauties of this divine poem were hitherto little known to the English public. Lord Somers himself superintended a new edition of it, which was published by Tonson, and at his own expense brought it out, with a pure text, with valuable notes, and with every advantage of decoration.

His house in town, and his country residence, Brookmans, in Hertfordshire,[1] were the resort of the most distinguished of all ranks of society, and displayed the intermixture of aristocracy and genius but seldom in any age witnessed in England. He himself, by his courtesy, his affability, his gaiety, and his taste, was the charm of this brilliant circle. Now, indeed, "he had ample amends for the loss of the honors and fatigues of office;"[2] and now he earned the compliment paid to him, which is more valuable than any praise of a judgment pronounced from the bench or a speech made in parliament,—"If he delivered his opinion of a piece of poetry, a statue, or a picture, there was something so just and delicate in his observations, as naturally produced pleasure and assent in those who heard him."[3]

But he was ever ready to sacrifice these calm delights for the *melee* in the House of Lords, when duty called him thither.

---

[1] This place, formerly called Bell-Bar, is in the parish of North Mymms, not far from Hatfield. Lord Somers bought it from Sir Andrew Fountaine. "It has a most delightful prospect from one side into Epping Forest; from the other, towards St. Alban's and the counties of Bedford and Bucks. The house itself is handsome and well situated."—*History of Hertfordshire*, 1728 p. 64.
[2] Life, p. 52.
[3] Freeholder, by Addison, No. xxxix.

The first parliament summoned by Queen Anne assembling in the end of the year 1702. The Tories were found to have an immense majority in the House of Commons; and to perpetuate their power, they introduced a bill "to prevent occasional conformity," whereby all borough electors for members of parliament, as well as all holders of office, were subjected to the Test Act; all persons who had once taken the sacrament according to the rites of the Church of England, were made liable to very high pecuniary penalties, and eventually to transportation, if they afterwards entered a dissenting place of worship; and all offenders were disqualified thereafter for voting or holding office, without reconciliation to the Church, and a long penance. The bill rapidly passed the Commons by great majorities; but it excited a fierce contest in the Lords. It was there supported (I believe reluctantly) by Godolphin and Marlborough, to please the Queen and the clergy. Nay, Prince George of Denmark, who, as Lord High Admiral, had received the sacrament according to the rites of the Church of England, and yet attended a Lutheran chapel of his own,—so that he was himself "an occasional conformist,"—voted in favor of it.[1]

But Lord Somers, indifferent to the obloquy he might incur, gallantly led the opposition against it, being ably seconded by Lord Halifax and Bishop Burnet. Instead of trying directly to throw it out, they considered the more judicious plan of defeating it would be to introduce amendments by way of mitigating its severity—one being to do away with the future disqualification, and another to reduce the penalty for a first offense from £100 to £50. The amendments, being carried in the Lords, were indignantly rejected by the Commons, who were not only chagrined that the stringency of their measure should be at all impaired, but were beginning to set up the most preposterous pretension, that bills imposing penalties by way of punishing offenders were money bills, and could not, without a breach of privilege, be altered by the Lords.

After some conferences, conducted by written statements, "it came to a FREE CONFERENCE in the Painted

[1] The poor Prince, however, was acting under petticoat compulsion; and, when the division took place, he said to Lord Wharton, who was on the the liberal side, "*My heart is vid you.*"--*Tindal.*

Chamber, which was the most crowded that ever had been known, so much weight was laid on this matter on both sides."[1] Lord Somers was the chief manager for the Lords. The managers for the Commons were rather moderate in their language, using such arguments as these:—

"That if a national church be necessary, the only effectual way to preserve it is by keeping the civil power in the hands of those whose practice and principles are conformable to it; that when they enacted that all officers should receive the sacrament according to the rights of the Church of England, it never was imagined that a set of men would rise up whose consciences were too tender to obey, but hardened enough to break through any laws; and that those men may be effectually kept out of offices who have shown they never wanted the will, when they had the power, to destroy the Church;—that the bill does not trench on true toleration, and does not deprive the Dissenters of any rights which they ought to enjoy."

Lord Somers, in the name of his House, had the boldness to say:—

"That the Lords do not consider going to a dissenting meeting to be *malum in se*, for that Dissenters are Protestants, and differ from the Church of England only in some little forms, and therefore the Lords think loss of office a sufficient punishment, without an incapacity, which should be reserved for capital offenses, and that there was no greater reason to visit this act with incapacity than to make it felony: that the Dissenters are well affected to the present constitution, and hearty enemies to the Queen's and kingdom's enemies: that of late, in the great extremity of the church, they joined with her, and as they were when the Bishops were in the Tower, they have since continued to behave themselves: that the Toleration Act ought to be upheld, as it had contributed much to the security and reputation of the Church, and had produced so good a temper among the Dissenters: that the Lords think they have sufficiently shown their dislike of occasional conformity, by allowing that the guilty person shall not only lose his office, but be liable to a reasonable fine: that this bill

[1] Burnet, 459.

disturbs the settlement which took place on the abdication of James, and carries disqualification further than ever was before attempted; that the Lords, allowing that no man can claim a place by birth-right, yet conceive that giving a vote for a representative in parliament is the essential privilege whereby every Englishman preserves his property; and that whatsoever deprives him of such vote, deprives him of his birth-right."

The reasoning employed is very long and very cogent, but it made no impression on the Commons, who still insisted on the bill passing as they had framed it. The most serious apprehensions were now entertained of a fatal collision between the two Houses, and of the supplies for carrying on the war being stopped. Some peers, from terror, went over to the bigots, but Somers remained firm. Such exertions were made on both sides that there were 130 Lords in the House—the greatest attendance that had ever been known. When it came to the final struggle whether the amendments should be adhered to, the numbers were so nearly equal, that, on three divisions, the affirmative was carried but by one voice, and it was by a different person on each division. So the bill was lost.[1]

But in the following year the battle was renewed. As soon as the session began, the Commons again sent up "a Bill to prevent occasional conformity." Somers now took a bolder course, and he procured its rejection on the second reading by a majority of 71 to 59.[2] Still another effort was made in the last session of this ultra-Tory House of Commons, and now an expedient was proposed whereby success was considered certain—which was to "*tack*" the Occasional Conformity Bill to a money bill, so that it must pass, or the supplies be stopped, the war interrupted, and the whole nation thrown into confusion. But Godolphin and Marlborough were now seriously alarmed; the "*tack*" was denounced as a scheme for depriving the Lords and the Queen of their legislative powers, and the whole influence of the Government being exerted against it, it was lost by a ma-

[1] 3 Burnet, 469. 6 Parl. Hist. 59–92.
[2] 5 Parl. Hist. 171. It is curious to observe, that Godolphin and Marlborough, although they were well known now to disapprove of the bill, not only voted for it, but, to please the Tories on this point, signed the protest against its rejection.

jority of 250 to 134. Nevertheless, the bill was easily carried through the Commons, as a separate measure. When it came to be debated in the Lords, the Queen, who in her heart favored it much, was present, and the speakers on both sides exerted themselves to the utmost in the hope of convincing her. Somers was supposed only to have confirmed the bad opinion she had entertained of him; but the bill was thrown out by a majority of 71 to 50,[1] and the persecution of Dissenters subsided for some years.

We next find Lord Somers struggling against an attempt of this same ultra-Tory House of Commons, by an abuse of parliamentary privilege, to encroach on the just rights of the subject. There had been a gross violation of the elective franchise in many boroughs in England, the returning officers making corrupt bargains with the candidates, as they considered themselves sure of impunity if they sent up representatives who would vote with the dominant majority. Petitions to the House of Commons complaining of undue returns, being found wholly unavailing, at last one Ashby, an elector of Aylesbury, brought an action against the bailiffs, who are the returning officers of that borough, for having maliciously rejected his vote at an election of members of parliament. The plaintiff having clearly made out his case before a jury, he recovered a verdict, with damages and costs. But a motion was made in the Court of Queen's Bench in arrest of judgment, on the ground that such an action was not maintainable; and judgment was arrested by the opinions of the three puisne Judges against that of Lord Chief Justice Holt. A writ of error was therefore brought in the House of Lords, and the Judges were called in. They were divided—of those who attended, five being for affirming, and four for reversing. The present Lord Keeper, not being a peer, had no voice, and the House eagerly listened to the opinion of Somers, the only law lord then existing. Reasoning (as I think) unanswerably, he said that "although the action was new, it rested on well established principles of law; that the plaintiff, having been deprived of the exercise of his franchise by the *malicious* act of the defendants (who must

[1] Against the second reading,—peers present, 50; proxies, 21. For,—peers present, 33; proxies, 17.—6 *Parl. Hist.* 368. 4 *Burnet*, 87-93.

now be taken corruptly to have rejected the vote, knowing it to be good), was entitled to legal redress for the wrong he had suffered, and that the objection that such an action infringes the privileges of the House of Commons, could not be supported, for while that House alone could rightfully determine who is duly returned as representative, the elective franchise was a common law right regulated by statute, on which a court of common law was competent to determine." In those days, and long after, all peers voted upon judicial as well as on political questions, and on the motion of Lord Somers, the judgment was reversed by a majority of 50 to 16.

The Commons were thrown into a transport of rage by this decision; and after a long debate, in which Mr. Walpole (afterwards Sir Robert) in vain tried to bring the House to reason, by showing the fatal consequences which would follow from declaring that returning officers are irresponsible, a 'vast majority,' encouraged by Harley, the Speaker, resolved "that the qualification of an elector is not cognizable elsewhere than before the Commons of England in Parliament assembled; that Ashby, having commenced an action against the bailiffs of Aylesbury for rejecting his vote, is guilty of a breach of privilege; and that whosoever should in future commence such an action, such person, and all attorneys, counselors, or sergeants at law, soliciting, prosecuting, or pleading in any such case, are guilty of a high breach of the privileges of this House." [2]

The Lords thereupon appointed a committee to consider what was fit to be done, and, after an admirable report from the pen of Lord Somers, defending their judgment, came to counter-resolutions, "that the assertion that a person wrongfully hindered from giving his vote for the election of members of parliament, by the officer who ought to take it, is without remedy by the ordinary course of law, is destructive of the property of

---

[1] 215 to 97.

[2] It should be borne in mind, that this resolution purported to declare a question of law clearly within common law jurisdiction; and further, that it never was pleaded in any of the subsequent actions; so that these proceedings do not afford (as has been supposed) an instance of a resolution of the House of Commons, on a question of parliamentary privilege, being overruled by the courts of law, although they do afford an instance of privilege being grossly abused.—*See Lord Campbell's Speeches*, 242.

the subject, is against the freedom of elections, and manifestly tends to encourage corruption and partiality; that the vote against Ashby, after he had, in the known and proper methods of law, obtained a judgment for recovery of his damages, is an unprecedented attempt upon the judicature of Parliament, and is in effect to subject the law of England to the vote of the House of Commons; and that terrifying electors, unjustly deprived of the right of voting, from bringing actions in the ordinary course of law, and attorneys, counselors and sergeants from soliciting, prosecuting and pleading in such cases, by voting their doing so to be a breach of privilege, is manifestly assuming a power to control the law and to prevent justice."

Hostilities between the two Houses were suspended by a prorogation; but, encouraged by these resolutions, which were framed by Lord Somers, Ashby levied his damages, and several more actions of the same sort were commenced by Paty, and other electors at Aylesbury.

When Parliament again met, the House of Commons, passing over the offense of Ashby, immediately imprisoned Paty and the other Aylesbury men who had brought the fresh actions. A writ of *habeas corpus* was sued out in the Court of Queen's Bench for their discharge. Holt was carried away, by excusable indignation, to hold that they were entitled to be liberated; but he was properly overruled by the other judges, on the ground that the Court had no power to examine a commitment by either House of Parliament. The prisoners then petitioned the Crown for a writ of error to bring their case before the Lords, and petitioned that House that the writ of error might be ordered to issue.¹

In the subsequent stages of the controversy, I think that Lord Somers was wrong, although the course he recommended was extremely popular with the nation. The constitutional remedy for this abuse of privilege by the members of the House of Commons, would have been found in an enlightened public and the power of the constituencies on the approaching general election. There never had been a writ of error in the House of Lords in a case of *habeas corpus*, and the Lords had no right to interfere with the commitments of the Commons, however tyrannical they might be. Yet Lord Somers moved

2 Lord Raym. 1105.

various resolutions condemning the proceedings of the Commons, upon which there were various conferences between the two Houses, which were very ably managed by him on the part of the Lords, but which led to no practical result The Commons next imprisoned some counsel and attorneys who had been concerned in these actions; and as no redress could be obtained in the ordinary courts of law, the novel device was resorted to of suing out writs of *habeas corpus* returnable in the House of Lords. This was countenanced by Lord Somers; and here again I think he erred, for the independence of that house of parliament was gone whose commitments could be examined by the other; and if the precedent had been established, the Commons ever after could only have enjoyed such functions as were permitted to them by an authority which the constitution considers co-ordinate. After a cross-fire of resolutions, the Commons were so afraid, that they took their prisoners from Newgate into their own immediate custody, and shut them up in "*Little Ease*," directing the Sergeant-at-arms, who acted as their custodian, to disregard all writs of *habeas corpus* that might be served upon him. Lord Somers then drew up a most admirable statement of the whole proceedings,—which the Lords adopted,—in the shape of an address to the Queen; concluding with a prayer "that her Majesty would be pleased to give effectual orders for the immediate issuing of the writs of error."[1]

The wise course was adopted of putting an end to the session by a prorogation, whereby the prisoners were all discharged; and, this being the third session of the Parliament, according to the Triennial Act it could not meet again. In the late controversy, Somers, upon the whole, must be allowed to have done good service to the state. He established the doctrine, which has been acted upon ever since, that an action lies against a returning officer for maliciously rejecting the vote of an elector; and he so forcibly exposed the abuse of privilege by the Commons, that he brought great unpopularity upon them for their proceedings, and they were long more moderate

[1] "This was thought so well drawn, that some preferred it to those of the former sessions; it contained a long and clear deduction of the whole affair, with great decency of style, but with many heavy reflections on the House of Commons."—4 *Burnet*, 100.

and reasonable in their pretensions. His attempt to control the commitments of the Commons by writs of error, or by writs of *habeas corpus* returnable in the House of Lords, has never been revived. There seems no longer any danger of a collision between the two Houses; but to reconcile their power to stop actions brought contrary to their privileges, and the power of the courts of law nevertheless to proceed with such actions,—is a formidable constitutional problem which still remains to be solved.[1]

The violence of the House of Commons in this controversy about *privilege* had its just reward and correction in the reaction which was now visibly proceeding in favor of the Whigs. "The city and the body of the nation were on the Lords' side."[2] and the dissolution which followed was hailed with general satisfaction. The elections for the new parliament went, in many instances, against the Tories. Disappointed by the policy which Godolphin and Marlborough had pursued, they considered themselves betrayed, notwithstanding the pretended zeal of the Government to carry the bill against occasional conformity, and the enthusiasm they displayed at the commencement of the reign had entirely evaporated. The Whigs had been coalescing more and more with the government, and the returns now appeared so much in their favor, that several of them were introduced into the cabinet and into the household.

[1] 14 St. Tr. 695–890; 6 Parl. Hist. 225, 376; 4 Burnet, 96; 2 Lord Raym. 938, 1105; Salk. 503; Holt, 256; 6 Mod. 45; Lord Campbell's Speeches, 242, 327. Some suppose, that nothing would be more easy than by a statute to define all the privileges of Parliament; but (not attaching much weight to the objection that they ought to be undefined) the most serious inconvenience would arise from saying, that the two Houses have no privileges except such as the framers of the statute have specified; and from, as a necessary consequence, submitting the construction of this statute to the courts of common law. Lord Somers saw the evil arising from the vagueness of privilege, but did not venture on a legislative remedy. Swift, in the year 1724, in a letter to Lord Chancellor Middleton, thus wrote:—"Lord Somers, the greatest man I ever knew of your robe, lamented to me that the prerogatives of the Crown, or the privileges of Parliament, should ever be liable to dispute in any single branch of either; by which means, he said, the public often suffered great inconveniences, whereof he gave me several instances. I produce the authority of so eminent a person, to justify my desires that some high points might be cleared." The legislature may usefully interfere on particular points, as to confer a power of at once stopping an action brought to attach the privileges of either House,—but a "Privilege Code" I pronounce to be impossible. [2] Burn. iv. 99.

The fate of the Great Seal I shall hereafter have to detail more particularly. Some think that it might now have been resumed by Lord Somers, if he had been so inclined; but this I much doubt, for he had not yet "gained great esteem with Queen Anne, who had conceived many unreasonable prejudices against him,"[1] and, although "the Lord Godolphin declared himself more openly than he had done formerly in favor of the Whigs,"[2] he was not yet prepared, by making their champion "Keeper of the Queen's Conscience," to shock, alarm, and quarrel forever with his old associates. Lord Somers, on this trying occasion, maintained his character for disinterestedness and magnanimity. Although, upon a favorable turn for the party which he had long led, a younger man than himself, whom he had patronized, was preferred to him, he showed no jealousy or envy, but cordially rejoiced in the appointment, actually attended in the Court of Chancery when Cowper was installed, and continued to do everything in his power to exalt the reputation and the authority of the new Lord Keeper. He himself was now readmitted into the Privy Council; his name was restored to the commission of the peace, from which it had been erased; and, although he was not formally again a member of the cabinet, he was henceforth confidentially consulted on all the measures of the administration.

Soon after the meeting of the new parliament he was of considerable use in quieting the alarm which Lord Rochester attempted to excite from the recent changes by his motion, "that the Church is in danger." Somers, speaking late in the debate, touched very happily upon the topics of his opponents, and thus concluded:—" The nation is now happy under a most wise and just administration, the public money is justly applied, the treasury is kept in a most regular method, the public credit is in the highest esteem, the armies and fleets are supplied, the success of her Majesty's arms gives the nation greater honor and reputation than ever before known, and we have a fair prospect of bringing the war to a happy conclusion, to the immortal renown of the age and the unspeakable benefit of posterity: wherefore for men to rais groundless jealousies at this time of day, it can mea..

[1] Addison.   [2] Burnet.

no less than an intention to embroil us at home, and to defeat all those glorious designs abroad." The question was then put, "Whether the Church is in danger or not?" and, upon a division, it was carried in the negative.[1]

But Lord Somers had soon to counteract a very ingenious manœuvre of the Tories, which had nearly ruined the rising hopes of his party. The Whigs had always supported zealously the succession of the House of Hanover, the next Protestant heirs, and, to embarrass them, a motion was made to call over the Princess Sophia, so that she might be ready to assume the government in case of a demise of the crown. This proposal was known to be most highly distasteful to Queen Anne, who abhorred the idea of a rival court being kept in England by her successor. The Whigs must, therefore, it was thought, offend her past forgiveness by agreeing to it,— or, by opposing it, be guilty of inconsistency, and ruin their interest at Herenhausen. Somers dexterously saved himself and his friends from these perils. He contrived that the Queen should be present to hear herself insulted by those whom she had lately discarded from her service; and the Duke of Buckingham, falling into the snare, urged as an argument for inviting the granddaughter of James I., now in the seventy-sixth year of her age, "that the Queen might live till she did not know what she did, and be like a child in the hands of others."[2] When her Majesty was sufficiently satiated with Tory sarcasms, Somers moved the previous question, which was carried by a considerable majority. He then induced her to consent to the Regency Bill being brought in which made ample provision for the quiet succession of the Hanover family, without wounding the feelings of the Queen by the presence of any of them in England, and completely restored the Whigs to the good graces of Sophia and her son.* This bill was strongly opposed by the Tories, particularly in the House of Commons, but was at last agreed to, with some amendments to limit the

---

[1] Noes, 61 ; yeas, 30. The Queen was present during the whole debate, and no doubt in her heart was with the yeas.—See 6 Parl. Hist. 499.

[2] Conduct of Duchess of Marlborough, p. 159.

4 Anne, c. 8, entitled "An Act for the better security of her Majesty's Person and Government, and of the Succession to the Crown of England in the Protestant Line."

powers of the Lords Justices, who were to exercise the royal authority at the commencement of the new reign, and it received the royal assent.¹ It was so wisely framed, that when the event contemplated happened, although the population of the country numerically would have been for recalling the exiled family, the son of Sophia succeeded as quietly to the throne as if he had been the legitimate heir, and been born and bred a Briton. On the act passing, Lord Somers wrote to the Elector, afterwards George I., the following letter, which gives an interesting view of the state of parties in England at this time :—

"London, April 12, 1706.

" Sir,

" The hopes of having my letter presented to your Electoral Highness by my Lord Halifax, has encouraged me to the presumption of writing. I could not hope for a more favorable opportunity of making this humble tender of my duty, than by the hands of one who has so eminently distinguished himself on all occasions for the settling and establishing of the succession of the Crown of England in your most Serene Family, and who will be a witness, above exception, of my conduct in every part of that affair. I confess I always depended upon it, that my public behavior should be an abundant testimony for me as to my zeal for the Protestant succession, and for promoting the war in order to reduce the power of France, which I take to be the most effectual security to that succession.

"It is with infinite satisfaction we hear that your Electoral Highness has been pleased to approve the measures taken in our Parliament this last winter. My Lord Halifax is able to give so perfect an account of everything that has been done, and of the several means used to bring them all to bear, that I shall not pretend to enter further into that matter than by saying, I hope it will appear that nothing is now wanting to the establishment of the succession that can be done by the provision of laws, and that the administration of the government, when the succession shall take place, will be upon the same foot that it is now in the Queen's reign.

" It might have a strange appearance, that they who by

4 Burnet, 129–134 ; 6 Parl. Hist. 457, 469.

a long and steady series of acting had shown themselves beyond a possibility of dispute the assertors of the succession in the person of her Electoral Highness the Princess Sophia, should in the least hesitate to agree to a proposition, that it was necessary to have the next presumptive heir to the Crown to reside in England. But I beg leave to suggest to your Electoral Highness's consideration, that if this had been allowed for a rule, it might possibly in a little time have pressed very inconveniently upon your Electoral Highness. It was not to be imagined you would leave dominions where you were Sovereign, to reside in England before you were our King; and yet there would have been an inconvenience in rejecting an invitation of that nature, when the kingdom had before declared such a residence to be necessary. But the manner of making this proposal was, above all other things, the strongest objection to it. The speech with which it was introduced is in print, and so can not be misrepresented. The turn of it was to show, first, that we could go on no further with the Dutch (which was, in effect, to say we must make peace); and next to say, the Queen's administration was hardly sufficient to keep us in peace at home, unless the next heir came over. The Queen was present at this discourse, and none can judge so well as your Electoral Highness whether this was a compliment proper to engage her Majesty to enter willingly into the invitation; and if it had been assented to with reluctance, whether it might not have given rise to unkindness that might in the end have proved very fatal.

"They who were afraid of entering into such an invitation (especially coming as it did from those who never till then showed any concern for the Protestant succession), thought it proper to lay hold of that favorable conjunction to push in for those solid provisions which were evidently wanting, and which we hope are brought to effect by the Act that is to be further carried on by the negotiation entered into for engaging the Allies to become guarantees of our succession, and by the treaty between the Commissioners for England and Scotland for a union of the two kingdoms, which seems to be the way now laid open for the obtaining the declaration of the same succession in Scotland which is already effected in England. I believe there is a good disposition in the Commissioners on both sides. I can absolutely promise for one, the meanest of them, that as far as my capacity and application can go, nothing shall be wanting to bring this treaty to a happy issue.

"Having already presumed to take so great a liberty, I humbly beg permission of your Electoral Highness to mention another particular, the Act of Naturalization, which some said was at least unnecessary, if not a diminution, to your most Serene Family. If this be so, not only all our present Judges, but all the lawyers of former ages, have been in the wrong. There are but two ways of making any person born out of the allegiance of the crown of England capable of enjoying inheritances, honors, or offices in this kingdom, the one complete and perfect, which is naturalization by Act of Parliament; the other imperfect, which is by letters patent of denization. That this is so, can not be better proved than by the instance of his Highness, Prince Rupert. For when King Charles I. intended to create him Duke of Cumberland, to make him capable of that title it was found necessary previously to make him a denizen by the King's grant under the Great Seal, the differences then subsisting between the King and his parliament making it impossible to procure a naturalization. But the present Act is attended with all possible marks of honor and respect to the Queen and nation. It extends to all the posterity of her Royal Highness, the Princess Sophia, *born, or hereafter to be born, and wheresoever they are born, which is a privilege that was never yet granted in any case till in this instance.*

"It is only from your Electoral Highness's eminent goodness that I can hope for pardon for this tedious address. I am, with the most profound respect, &c.

"SOMERS."

The following answer was returned by his Electoral Highness—very encouraging to the hopes of the Whigs in a new reign:

"June 20, 1706.

"My Lord,

"The Lord Halifax delivered to me the letter which you was at the trouble of writing to me. I am much obliged to you for the light it gives concerning the affairs of England, but especially for the part which you have had in all that has been done there in favor of my family.

The testimony of my Lord Halifax was not necessary to inform me of this. *He could give you no other in this respect, but that which is due to you by all good Englishmen who love their religion and their country.* I am not ignorant of what influence you may have amongst them, nor of the manner in which you have employed it. Nothing can give me a better opinion of the English nation than the justice they do your merit. My sentiments concerning the invitation of the successor are entirely conformed to yours, and I put all the value I ought upon the acts which the Lord Halifax brought us. He has convinced us of their importance, and hath discharged his commission as a man equally zealous for the prosperity of England, and for the interests of my family. I shall always look for opportunities of showing you how much I am," &c.

Addison, in his *éloge* of Somers, says, "A great share in the plan of the Protestant succession is universally ascribed to him. And if he did not entirely project the Union of the two kingdoms, and the Bill of Regency, which seem to have been the only methods in human policy for securing to us so inestimable a blessing, there is none who will deny him to have been the chief conductor in both these glorious works. For posterity are obliged to allow him that praise after his death, which he industriously declined while he was living."[1]

There is no ground for saying that he *projected* the Scottish Union, for it had been proposed from time to time ever since the accession of James I.; but when great anxiety had been created upon the subject from the refusal of the Scottish parliament to concur with the parliament of England in selecting the Princess Sophia as the root of a new dynasty, the measure was chiefly intrusted to him, and by his prudence and tact it was brought to a happy conclusion. Though at present without office, and though most of the English commissioners were of higher rank, yet, from the station he had once occupied, and his great celebrity, he was the most regarded by the Scottish Commissioners, and he produced a most favorable impression upon them by the courtesy of his manners, as well as by the liberality of his sentiments. On the delicate subject of religion he quieted their fears by at once agreeing to every precaution they could suggest for the

[1] Freeholder, May 4, 1716. No. xxxix.

safeguard of the Kirk and the protection of their beloved Presbytery. These concessions were distasteful to the Tory party, and were highly obnoxious to the University of Oxford,[1] but the necessity for them being apparent, even the Queen was prevailed upon to sanction them. After the sittings of the Commissioners at the Cockpit, Whitehall, had been continued from the 15th of April to the 22nd of July—in the evening of that day the Articles were finally concluded, and next morning Somers attended the Queen at St. James's, when they were delivered to her, to be submitted to the parliaments of the two countries. When the bill for giving effect to them was afterwards introduced into the House of Lords, he warmly defended it,[2] and, by corresponding with the ministers and leaders of parties in Scotland, his advice materially smoothed its progress through the legislature of that country.[3]

The measure being carried, he afterwards conferred a great benefit upon Scotland, and upon the empire, by strenuously insisting upon the abolition of the Scottish Privy Council, the existence of which would for ever have prevented a cordial union of feelings and of interests between the two nations. We have deeply to lament that at the union with Ireland a different course was adopted, and it was thought fit to keep up a Lord Lieutenant and a separate administration for that country.[4]

[1] Wherefore, this University refused to offer an address of congratulation to the Queen when the measure was completed.
[2] Burnet, iv. 150, 166; Defoe's Hist. of the Union; 6 Parl. Hist. 567, 569.
[3] Letters written by Lord Somers on that occasion to the Earl of Leven, then Commander-in-Chief in Scotland.
After all, I am afraid that the measure was successful less by the talents of Somers than by the money remitted to bribe the Scotch nobles and leading commoners, for both the Scotch and the Irish Unions were conducted on the principle then propounded by Prior—
  " The end must justify the means,
    He only sins who ill intends;
  Since, therefore, 'tis to *combat evil*,
    'Tis lawful to employ the DEVIL."
[4] The notes which he made for his speech in the House of Lords on this occasion are still preserved, and some of his observations are most applicable to Ireland at the present moment. " Heartily desirous of the union—no less desirous to make it entire and complete—not at all perfect while his political administrations subsist—the true argument for the union was the danger to both kingdoms from a divided state.—The advantage of Scotland is to have the same easy access to the Prince—to be under the immediate care of the Prince, and not to owe protection and countenance to any subordinate institution—worst state after the union if a distinct administration continue.—Obj.

While engaged in these weighty affairs of state, and attending to the interests of literature and the fine arts, Lord Somers by no means neglected his own profession. He was warmly attached to law reform, but he was aware of the care and caution necessary to enable him to effect his object. Not carried away by a passion for temporary notoriety, he did not toss on the table of the House of Lords, under the name of "Bills," the crudities of himself or others—bringing law reform into disrepute. While at the bar and in office, he had seen the defects in the system administered both in the common law and equity courts, and he had for some years been devoting a considerable part of his leisure to the consideration how they might be remedied. In the spring of 1706 he brought forward his bill "for the Amendment of the Law and the better Advancement of Justice."[1] Unfortunately we have no account of the debates on this occasion, except from the loose recollection of Burnet, who says, "The Lord Somers made a motion in the House of Lords to correct some of the proceedings in the common law and in Chancery that were both dilatory and very chargeable: he began with some instances that were more conspicuous and gross; and he managed the matter so that both the Lord Keeper and the Judges concurred with him. A bill passed the House that began a reformation of proceedings at law, which, as things now stand, were certainly among

'This Council is not a constitution of state and policy, but in effect a sovereign Court of Justice to see the laws effectually executed, and for preservation of the public peace.'—England could never agree with these Courts that are mixed of state and justice.—We had a Privy Council in England with great and mixed powers—we suffered under it long and much." [Having touched upon the "Council of the Marches of Wales" and the "Council of the North," abolished by the Long Parliament, he continues.] "Hope Scotland, though a little further north, will be quiet and happy under the influence of her Majesty and her Council of Great Britain, unless your Lordships shall interpose another council to intercept that influence. For my part I can not agree to it. I wish North Britain as happy as England— I meant it should be so in the Union.— *True way to make the Union well relished is, to let the country see plainly that England means no otherwise than fairly by them, and desires they should be in the very same circumstances they are themselves.*"—HARD. St. Pap. ii. 473.

[1] "It was no inglorious part of this great Chancellor's life, that when removed from the administration, his labors were still dedicated to the service of the government, and of his country. In this situation, above all the little prejudices of a profession, for he had no profession but that of Solon and Lycurgus, he set himself to correct the grievances of the law, and to amend the vocation he had adorned."—*Walpole's Royal and Noble Authors.*

the greatest grievances of the nation; when this went through the House of Commons, it was visible that the interest of under-officers, clerks, and attorneys, whose gains were to be lessened by this bill, was more considered than the interest of the nation itself; several clauses, how beneficial soever to the subject, which touched on their profit, were left out by the Commons. But what fault soever the Lords might have with these alterations, yet, to avoid all disputes with the Commons, they agreed to their amendments."[1] I have not been able to find the original draft of the bill as introduced by its author,[2] but, notwithstanding the mutilations it underwent—as it appears upon the Statute Book, it introduced greater improvements than our "Procedure" ever received from the Revolution till the reign of William IV.—"Whate'er is best administer'd is best," may truly be said of a judicial system, and the due distribution of justice depends much more upon the rules by which suits are to be conducted, than on the perfection of the code by which rights are defined. The scandalous abuse had been established in England of creating sinecure offices in the Courts, payable by fees, some of such offices being grantable by the Crown, and some being salable by the Judges. Nay, the Judges themselves were chiefly remunerated by fees. It was thus utterly impossible that the suitors should not be sacrificed, and that the complaints of delay and expense with which Westminster Hall rang should not be well founded. The abolition of such offices, and the payment of the Judges by fixed salaries, which we have seen accomplished, would not have been endured in that age. But Lord Somers's bill framed most admirable regulations against pettifogging, chicanery, and vexatious litigation. It compelled a party who meant to rely upon any errors of form in the conduct of an action, at once specifically to point them out, that they might be corrected; it provided that no dilatory plea should be received without an affidavit of its truth; it cured the absurd strictness by which a man could not plead payment of money after the day when it

[1] 4 Burnet, 140.
[2] 4 Anne, c. 16. Petitions against it were presented by the Clerks of the Remembrancer's Office, the Exchequer, &c.; and it appears to have been greatly damaged in the Commons.—Com. Jour., 14th Feb.; Lords' Jour., 11th, 19th March.

became due; it permitted persons who had been beyond seas when a cause of action against them accrued, to be sued during a year after their return; it made bail-bonds given to the sheriff available to the creditor; it prohibited the issuing of subpœnas in equity before filing a bill; and it rendered the action of "Account" effectual against executors and administrators. Further, it provided that a defendant might avail himself of several defenses to an action, whereas formerly he could only set up one, and if that by any chance failed, he was undone; it rendered lessees liable to the purchasers of their farms without the ceremony of an attornment; and it enacted that the effect of a fine of lands should not be defeated by an entry, unless an action were brought within a year. It likewise contained useful enactments respecting warrants of attorney, the probate of wills, declarations of uses and trusts, and the payment of costs both in actions of law and suits in equity.[1] When we consider that this "STATUTE OF JEOFAILS"[2] was framed by the author of the "BILL OF RIGHTS," we may truly say that there was nothing too vast or too minute for the grasp of his intellect.[3]

Lord Cowper (holding the Great Seal) and all the other ministers showed the highest deference for the advice of Lord Somers on all subjects. In a life of Freeman, pre-

---

[1] 6 Parl. Hist. 517. From the Report of the Committee of the Lords, appointed on the motion of Lord Somers to consider of amending the law—which was the foundation of the bill—it appears likewise to have contained enactments to allow courts of common law to issue commissions for the examination of witnesses,—and for making debts and all other property available to satisfy judgment creditors,—which have recently been adopted by the legislature. Lords' Jour. xvi i. 68, 17th Jan. 1705.—See a minute statement of the different stages of the bill, Parke's Hist. Ch. 275.

I have found a pamphlet published at this time, entitled "Reasons humbly offered to both Houses of Parliament for passing a Bill for preventing Delays and Expenses in Suits in Law and Equity," showing that the bill contained several very important clauses which had been struck out from a desire to protect profitable abuses, *e. g.* a clause to prevent frivolous writs of error; a clause for shortening decrees and orders in equity, by forbidding recitals; and a clause for taking a bill in equity, *pro confesso* for want of appearance.

[2] Statutes for the amendment of the Law were thus denominated because when the pleadings were carried on in French the pleader who had made a mistake, when he craved leave to amend, was obliged first to say, "Jeo faile." 3 Bl. 407.

[3] Lord Somers the same session attempted most laudably to reform abuses in the passing of private bills through Parliament, but failed, as he touched the fees to be received by the Speakers of the two Houses and by the Clerks. 4 Burnet, 140.

fixed to his "Reports," published in the year 1742, it is said, "His eminent qualities and rare talents introduced him to the friendship and esteem of that truly noble, virtuous, and learned lawyer and statesman, the late John, Lord Somers, who, in the year 1706, had so high an opinion and just judgment of Mr. Freeman's integrity and abilities, as to recommend him to the important office of Lord Chancellor of Ireland, then vacant, in which high post he was deservedly placed by his Sovereign." I have not yet discovered how Freeman conducted himself as Irish Chancellor, but Lord Mansfield and Lord Redesdale repeatedly bore testimony to his learning and his merits as a lawyer and as a reporter.

Lord Somers now drew obloquy upon himself by defending the Government, and, along with several other Whigs, was grossly libeled by a Dr. Brown, who was found guilty of the offense, and set in the pillory, then a very common, and hardly considered a disgraceful, punishment.[1] The patriotic nobleman was defended and eulogized by De Foe, who afterwards, for a season, countenanced the Tories, but now, in the twelfth book of his "Jure Divino," thus sung:—

> "Somers by nature great and born to rise,
> In counsel wary and in conduct wise,
> His judgment steady and his genius strong,
> And all men own the music of his tongue."

Till the end of the year 1708, Lord Somers continued in his present position without office, and without a seat in the Cabinet, but confidentially consulted by the ministers, and lending them all the help he could, both in and out of parliament. He was contented to witness the success of the policy of his party. The GRAND ALLIANCE which he had assisted King William to plan had produced the victories of Blenheim and Ramillies; and Louis XIV., instead of threatening the liberties of Europe, began to tremble for the fortresses by which his capital was protected. Marlborough and Godolphin had now entirely cast off the Tory party, as well as Tory measures. The Whigs were in possession of all the great, and almost all the subordinate offices under the Crown. They not only enjoyed much popularity, but the Queen, still under the dominion of the Duchess of Marlborough, seemed to have

[1] 11 St. Tr. Harg. ed.

laid aside all her prejudices against them, and to have taken them into permanent favor. The union with Scotland being consummated, there had been a prosperous session of the first parliament of Great Britain, and a dissolution then taking place, the elections for the new parliament had gone very generally for the Whigs. A temporary gloom arose from the death of Prince George of Denmark, but this facilitated some ministerial changes which still enhanced the power of the dominant party.

The Earl of Pembroke succeeding as Lord High Admiral, the office of Lord President of the Council became vacant, and Lord Somers was induced to accept it. The present holder of the Great Seal had given such entire satisfaction that he could not be removed; and, from declining health and satisfied ambition, William's illustrious Chancellor had little desire to resume his old office under another sovereign. The announcement that he had consented to become Lord President of the Council gave general satisfaction. "The great capacity and inflexible integrity of this Lord," says Burnet, "would have made his promotion to this post very acceptable to the Whigs at any juncture, but it was more particularly so at this time; for it was expected that the propositions for a general peace would be quickly made; and so they reckoned that the management of that upon which not only the safety of the nation, but of all Europe, depended, was in sure hands when he was set at the head of the councils, upon whom neither ill practices nor false colors were like to make any impression. Thus the minds of all those who were truly zealous for the present constitution were much quieted by this promotion; though their jealousies had a deep root, and were not easily removed."[1]

[1] Burnet, 247-48. If we are to believe Swift when he had abandoned his old friends and was eager to malign them, Somers had been very impatient to be taken into the government, and had thought himself very ill-used by being kept out so long. "Upon the Prince's death, Nov. 1708, the two great Lords so often mentioned (Marlborough and Godolphin) who had been for some years united with the Low Church party, and had long engaged to take them into power, were now in a capacity to make good their promises, which his Highness had ever most strenuously opposed. The Lord Somers was made President of the Council, &c. It should seem to me that the Duke and Earl were not very willingly drawn to impart so much power to those of that party, who expected these removals for some years before, and were always put off upon pretense of the Prince's unwillingness to have them employed.

v.—6

CHAPTER CXI.

CONCLUSION OF THE LIFE OF LORD SOMERS.

SOMERS remained President of the Council till the downfall of the Whigs,—which would probably have been averted if his advice had been followed. He agreed with his colleagues in thinking that the war ought to be carried on till the grandson of Louis XIV. should be driven from the throne of Spain;[1] but he would have saved them from the enormous folly of the impeachment of Sacheverell.

The first session of parliament after the new Lord President was installed passed over very quietly. The Tory party seemed annihilated, and hardly any opposition being offered to the votes for men and money demanded, or to any of the measures of Government, the discussions in the House of Lords were confined to questions on the election of Scotch peers,[2] and the rights of foreign ambassadors.[3] Lord Chancellor Cowper and Lord Somers cor-

---

And I remember some months before his Highness's death, my Lord Somers, who is a person of reserve enough, complained to me with great freedom of the ingratitude of the Duke and Earl, who, after the service he and his friends had done them in making the Union, would hardly treat them with common civility." But the man who would publish to the world such a confidential communication would be quite capable of misrepresenting it, and Swift is here the less entitled to credit, as he states that Somers, in the same conversation, talked disparagingly of the Union, and sneered at the "Act of Security," by which the Presbyterian form of worship was guaranteed to Scotland.—*Memoirs relating to the change in the Queen's Ministry*, written October, 1714. The general opinion was that the new President of the Council was now to direct public affairs, as we may see by the following letter from Lord Shaftesbury, author of the "Characteristics," to a friend, Nov. 20, 1708. "Somers has kissed the Queen's hand, though not directly as minister, pretty near it you may be sure; since at this time of mourning, and so sincere a mourner as the Queen is, she hardly would see a stranger, and what is more, a man so estranged from her, and so wholly off from the Court as he has been, and whom I scarcely believe she has admitted at any time to kiss her hand, he having been for certain the Prince's aversion, as you may judge by those who chiefly influenced the Prince and were the violentest enemies Lord Somers had."

[1] Thus he congratulated Marlborough on the victory of Malplaquet: "I can not but hope this last great success will quite lower the credit of those who may wish for an ill peace, and satisfy the French King at last that he has attempted everything possible for saving his own honor, and that it is time for him in good earnest to think of preserving France from utter ruin."

[2] 6 Parl. Hist. 758.   [3] Ibid. 792.

dially co-operated; and, although there was no Tory law lord to keep them in check, they seem to have conducted themselves with moderation—not imitating the party violence of their supporters in the House of Commons, where, in deciding controverted elections, the partiality of the Tories, so much complained of in the last parliament, was outdone.

The Whigs were at present in their most palmy state. The Queen never liked them in her heart, as she was hostile to religious toleration, and she would have relished highly the doctrine of the divine right of kings, if it could have been made consistent with her own title to the throne; yet even she found it convenient for a time to dissemble, and appear to be reconciled to the new Lord President, for whom, from the beginning of her reign till this time, she had testified the most marked dislike. He now had frequent access to her presence; he took great pains to win her, and, from his polished and deferential manners, he must have made some progress in removing her prejudices against him. All the while, however, she had secret conferences with Harley, the leader of the opposition, who, on account of the principles he professed, after renouncing Whiggery, enjoyed all her confidence—although she complained that he occasionally came to her under the influence of liquor. The correspondence of the Duchess of Marlborough, gives an amusing account of the Court at this juncture:—" I remember to have been at several of Lord Somers's conversations with Queen Anne, to fill out their tea, and wash their cups.[1] 'Tis certain that as soon as he got into his post, to obtain which I so often urged the Queen, he made his court to Abigail,[2] and very seldom came to me; and it is true that Lord Oxford and St. John used to laugh in their cups (which came out by Duke Devonshire), that they had instructed the Queen to behave so as to make Lord Somers think he should be her chief minister. She could act a part very well when

---

[1] Pope says, in the Rape of the Lock—
"Where thou, great Anna, whom three realms obey,
Dost sometimes *counsel* take, and sometimes *tea*."
But at these meetings with Lord Somers she seems to have taken *tea* and *counsel* together.

[2] Mrs. Masham. Lord Somers had incurred the high displeasure of the Marlboroughs by advising Lord Chancellor Cowper to refuse to put the Great Seal to the commission appointing the Duke Commander-in-Chief for life.

her lesson was given her, and in a little time it appeared very plain to the Duke of Marlborough and Lord Godolphin, that Somers thought of nothing so much as to flatter the Queen, and went to her personally in private."

Anne's secret longing after Tory ministers was now strengthened by her quarrel with the Duchess of Marlborough, and she was impatient to be entirely emancipated from the servitude to which she had been reduced. Another danger to the administration arose from a returning wish for peace, the public being almost satiated with military glory, and discerning persons thinking that the legitimate object of the war had been accomplished. But, led by men of the first talents, both for deliberation and action, with a commanding majority in both Houses, and regarded with general favor on account of their brilliant success in humbling the French King, the Whig party seemed secure of the long enjoyment of power.

And they probably would have continued undisturbed in their offices till their tenure had been confirmed by the accession of the House of Hanover, had it not been for their most preposterous prosecution of the contemptible sermon preached before the Lord Mayor of London on the 5th of November, 1709, the anniversary of the Gunpowder Plot, and published a few days after. This composition not only inculcated passive obedience and the divine right of kings, attacked the Revolution, reflected on the memory of King William, and asserted that the Church was in danger from the misconduct of her Majesty's present ministers—but (worse than all) abused several of them individually, and particularly the Lord Treasurer, under his well-known name of "VOLPONE." If they had allowed it to pass unnoticed, it would have fallen into instant oblivion ; but forty thousand copies of it were sold in a few months, and it acquired more celebrity than any production of Milton or Dryden.

Lord Godolphin was so offended by the dull sarcasms which it contained against him, that he indiscreetly called a meeting of the Cabinet to consider what steps should be taken against the author. His colleagues naturally expressing high indignation, he insanely proposed that, from the importance of the topics which the sermon handled, and the dignified station of those whom it assailed, it should be made the subject of a parliamentary impeachment. This proceeding was warmly opposed by Lord Somers, although he likewise was personally struck at by the preacher.[1] But all his arguments were overruled.[2] By a solemn judicial proceeding in the face of the nation, the Revolution was to be defended, the principles of limited monarchy were to be vindicated, the Protestant succession was to be secured, and the character and conduct of her Majesty's ministers were to be cleared from all aspersion. When the mode of prosecution came to be debated, it was perhaps thought that, in the present unpleasant temper of the two Houses, there would be less difficulty in carrying a vote for an impeachment, than in having an indictment found "*a true bill*" by a grand jury, —and in obtaining a verdict of "*guilty*" from a majority of the Lords, than from a petty jury, who must be unanimous.

Lord Somers attended daily during the trial, which lasted three weeks, but does not seem to have taken any part in it till the Lords came to consider of their verdict, when he and Lord Chancellor Cowper were thrown into a great difficulty by an objection which Lord Nottingham started, that the articles of impeachment did not set out those passages of the sermon which were complained of; and the Judges being consulted, gave it as their opinion that, "in an indictment or information for a misdemeanor by speaking or writing criminal words, the particular words supposed to be criminal must be expressly speci-

---

[1] "There is another sort of them who are for neutrality in religion, who really are none, but are a secret sort of reverend Atheists, who always pretend to be of the Church, join in the herd, and will sometimes frequent our public communion. They are equally of all and of no communion; they are the Gallios that 'care for none of these things;' they can see neither sin nor danger in that ecclesiastical bugbear, as they call schism, yet talk very loud about union, comprehension, and moderation; by all which canting expressions they mean nothing but getting money and preferment, by holding in with persons of all parties and characters, halting betwi t the diversity of opinions and reconciling God and Belial for gain."—*Sermon* 15, *St. Tr.* 78.

[2] "The famous trial of Dr. Sacheverell arose from a foolish, passionate pique of the Earl of Godolphin, whom this divine was supposed, in a sermon, to have reflected on under the name of 'VOLPONE,' as my Lord Somers a few months after confessed to me; and at the same time that he had earnestly and in vain endeavored to dissuade the Earl from that attempt."—*Swift's Memoirs relating to Change in Ministry*. Swift, likewise, in his History of the Four last Years of Queen Anne, informs us "that he had heard from Lord Somers himself that he was against engaging in that foolish business, as foreseeing that it was likely to end in the ruin of the Whig party." See also *Examiner*, No. 26.

fied in the indictment or information." But the noble and learned Lords suggested that the Judges had delivered their opinion according to the rules of Westminster Hall, and not according to the usage of parliament. A resolution was passed "that in impeachments the House was to proceed according to the laws of the land, and the law and usage of parliament;" and upon searching the journals for precedents, Dr. Mainwaring's case was found, which occurred in the reign of Charles I., and which was an impeachment for words, without setting out the words specifically. Whereupon, after a long debate, a resolution was carried, "that by the law and usage of parliament in prosecutions by impeachment for high crimes and misdemeanors, by writing or speaking, the particular words supposed to be criminal are not necessary to be expressly specified in the articles of impeachment." Against this resolution many Lords entered a protest,—and with great reason, as it is equally important to a party accused to be fully informed of the charge against him, whatever the tribunal may be before which he is prosecuted. An acquittal on this point of form would not have been such a triumph to Sacheverell as the sentence which followed.

When the discussion arose whether a question should be put separately on each of the four articles of the impeachment, Lord Somers strongly supported the proposal which was adopted, that the only question should be "Is Henry Sacheverell, Doctor in Divinity, guilty of high crimes and misdemeanors charged on him by impeachment of the House of Commons?" By his official rank he was the last but three who voted, and the Lord President, with a firm voice, answered "Guilty." The numbers were pretty much as in any other party division, 69 to 52. However ill-advised the prosecution, I must say that the defendant, in preaching and publishing such a sermon, committed an offense for which he was liable to punishment. For the desecration of the pulpit by making it a platform from which he assailed political opponents, he was to answer to his ecclesiastical superiors, and several parts of his harangue, charged as libelous, did not exceed the just bounds of political discussion; but in others he had publicly denied the lawfulness of the existing government, and incited the people to a violent subversion of the settlement for the succession to the throne established by the legislature.

But, as Somers had foreseen, the Lord Chancellor, in declaring what was the sentence on Dr. Sacheverell, pronounced the doom of the Whigs. The Queen had been present during all the proceedings, and, recollecting that she was the daughter of the last legitimate king, but forgetting that she had a brother who, according to the doctrine of divine right, had a preferable title to the throne, she had been much startled and shocked by the doctrines which Sir Joseph Jekyll and the managers for the Commons had propounded as to the right of resistance; and she had listened with much more complacency to Sir Simon Harcourt and the counsel for the defendant, when they showed that passive obedience was enjoined both by law and religion. The effect upon the public was such, that all moderate friends of the Church and all dissenters seemed annihilated, or become ashamed of their opinions, —and an ultra High-Church enthusiasm raged unresisted throughout the land. Sacheverell himself was considered a greater hero than Marlborough, and, dissenting chapels being burnt as a sacrifice to him, he was received wherever he appeared with more than royal honors. If any of the Whig cabinet had been so silly as to think that the impeachment would amuse the public and allow them without opposition to prosecute their foreign policy, they were miserably deceived, for all the victories they had won abroad were forgotten in the danger that was apprehended to the Church at home; and although the majorities in both Houses remained steady, there was a general desire in the nation that its destinies should be confided to safer and more orthodox counselors. Harley marked with delight the advantage to be gained, and, both during and after the trial, unscrupulously patronized Sacheverell and his doctrines. His secret communications with the Queen became more frequent, and she only waited for a favorable opportunity to change the administration and to dissolve the parliament.

The last act of the Whigs was to reject the overtures made by Louis XIV. at Gertruydenberg, upon which it is now generally thought that peace might have been advantageously concluded. Somers, bent on gaining the specific object of the GRAND ALLIANCE,—to prevent

France and Spain from belonging to the same family, shut his eyes to the reduced condition of the former kingdom, and the devoted attachment of the latter to a Bourbon sovereign; and, although all danger to the balance of power in Europe had passed away, he still cordially supported the Duke of Marlborough in his wish to penetrate the last line of the French defenses on the side of Flanders, and to march upon Paris. He thus wrote to his friend, the Lord Lieutenant of Ireland: "The French ambassadors at Gertruydenberg have sent a very insolent letter, or rather manifesto, to the Pensioner in order to justify their breaking off the negotiation. I hope so unnecessary and so insolent a provocation will give the Dutch courage enough to resent it as they ought; but I have not the resolution taken upon it. It breaks my heart to think what a noble game we are unnecessarily throwing away."

From the odium into which the Whigs had brought themselves by their supposed persecution of the Church, the charge was generally believed that Marlborough's only motive for continuing the war was, that he might retain the command of the army abroad, with the immense emoluments which it brought him; and that all the members of the party were willing to sacrifice religion and the public prosperity for their own individual aggrandizement.

The Tory movement began by getting up petitions to the Queen from the counties and some large cities, complaining of the proceedings of the present House of Commons, accusing ministers of wasting the public resources, and asserting that the Church was in danger. The Whigs attempted counter petitions, but durst not call public meetings for the purpose, and they could obtain comparatively few signatures.[1] The Queen took courage to make some partial changes at Court, and to appoint to situa-

[1] About this time Swift arrived from Ireland on his mission respecting the "First Fruits," and saw the coming change. However, he condescended to take notice of a falling patron: "Paid my first visit to Lord President, with whom I had much discourse, but put him always off when he began of Lord Wharton in relation to me, till he urged it; then I said he knew I never expected anything from Lord Wharton, and that Lord Wharton knew that I understood it so. He said that he had written twice to Lord Wharton about me, who, both times, said nothing at all to that part of his letter. Lord President told me he expected every day to be out, and has done so these two months."—*Journal to Stella*, February 12th, 1710.

tions in her personal gift individuals who had been active in the Sacheverell riots. Rumors were spread of a dissolution of parliament, which called forth the following letter from Lord Somers to Lord Wharton:—"We are not without hopes of a good parliament in case they will put us upon a new election. I can not find a way to preserve credit, or to furnish the necessary sums for the army, unless the present parliament be continued. There is no certainty what the composition of the new parliament will be, nor what will be the turn they will take, since they are not Whigs only who will be affected by the dissolution."

At last, in the end of September,[1] when the Queen was in council, with the Lord Chancellor on her right hand, and Lord Somers on her left, a scene took place which bears no resemblance to the manner in which such changes are announced in our days. Her Majesty being seated in her chair of state at the head of the Board, after some routine business had been gone through, called upon Sir Simon Harcourt, the Attorney General, to produce a proclamation which she had ordered him to prepare for dissolving the parliament. When it had been read, the Lord Chancellor rose up to address her with the intention of dissuading her from such a step, meaning to urge that, as the parliament had only sat two years, and as it had strenuously supported her Majesty in carrying on the war, its sudden dissolution would cause great dismay to her allies and joy to her enemies. But he had proceeded a very little way when the Queen stopped him, saying, "that she had considered the matter well, that she would admit of no debate, and that the writs for a new parliament must immediately issue." She then signed the proclamation. Next she declared her uncle, the Earl of Rochester, President of the Council in the room of the Lord Somers. A similar transfer was made of almost all the great officers of state. "So sudden and so entire a change of the ministry," says Burnet, "is scarce to be found in our history. The Queen was much delighted with all these changes, and seemed to think she was freed from the chains the old ministry had held her in: she

[1] Burnet states this scene to have taken place in October, but the *London Gazette*, and other documents showing the new appointments, prove him to have been mistaken.—O. T. iv. 299.

spoke of it to several persons as a captivity she had been long under."[1] The Bishop's splenetic account of the elections shows that the Queen had the nation completely on her side: "Unheard-of methods were used to secure them in London, and in all parts of England; but more particularly in the great cities there was a vast concourse of rude multitudes brought together, who behaved themselves in so boisterous a manner that it was not safe, and in many places impossible, for those who had a right to vote to come and give their votes for a Whig." The result was a House of Commons still more Toryish than that which passed the bills against occasional conformity.[2]

While the Whigs were in this prostrate condition, an attempt was made by the Tories to ruin all their future prospects, by representing them at the Court of Hanover as republicans and levelers, and openly denouncing the sentiments expressed by them at the late trial as inconsistent with monarchical or hereditary government. Lord Somers thereupon wrote the following letter to the Hanoverian resident :—

"My Lord Halifax and my Lord Sunderland beg of you, Sir, to explain to your Court that the Whigs are by no means for a republic, nor for rendering the Crown elective, as they consider it hereditary in the Protestant line, and belonging to the nearest in that line. But is not possible for the Whigs to abandon the Revolution. They advanced the late King to the throne, and they are obliged to defend his title now. They advanced him then in preference to the Queen who now reigns, although she was nearer and a Protestant. As this could not be done but by the authority of parliament, it is natural for the Whigs to defend that authority, and the parliamentary right to the Crown, for otherwise they would declare

[1] Burnet, O. T. 300.
[2] There is a curious note, by Speaker Onslow, in Burnet's "History of his Own Times," in which he relates some negotiations that were carried on with Harley by Lord Somers, Lord Halifax and Lord Cowper, a short time before this change of ministers, on the basis of an overture made by Harley for keeping them in place if they would consent to the substitution of himself, and some of his friends, for Lord Treasurer Godolphin and his dependents. Onslow says he had his information from Sir Joseph Jekyll, "who," he adds, "had it very likely, and I think he said so, too, from the Lord Somers, to whom he was brother-in-law." The negotiation was broken off in consequence of the opposition of Lord Wharton, who expressed his detestation of having anything to do with Harley.

themselves traitors and rebels; and as the establishment of the Hanoverian succession is a consequence of the Revolution, and a work of the late King, your Court should take it well of the Whigs that they defend the Revolution, and should excuse some expressions in their last writings, which appear to carry too far the authority of the parliament in the affairs of the succession; and the more so that the maxims of the Tories tending directly to prepare the way for the Prince of Wales, and to secure his title from being called in question, it is natural for the friends of the Hanoverian succession to maintain a contrary doctrine." [1]

Lord Somers now went into active, and, I am sorry to say, in some instances, factious opposition. He might well be excused in still standing up for a vigorous prosecution of the war, and in trying to obtain a condemnation of the peace which was concluded; but we can hardly attempt to palliate his combining to undo the great measure of internal policy which illustrates this reign, and which he had himself been so instrumental in accomplishing.

As soon as he was removed from office,—notwithstanding his services and his character, as he was considered the chief counselor of the Whigs, he was relentlessly assailed in parliament, and libeled by the Tory press in a manner to make public men of the present day rejoice that they did not live in the reign of Queen Anne. Complaints are still made, and sometimes with justice, of the licentiousness of our periodical writers; but modern *libelers* are mild, candid, and cautious, compared with the *wits* of the Augustan age of English literature when engaged in political controversy. Private character, which is now almost invariably respected, was then attacked with unfeeling exaggerations of what was true, and with unmixed inventions of malignant falsehood. I shall give one specimen which may be enough to support my charge: Swift was highly indignant that he had not obtained promotion in the Church from the late government. Somers and Montagu had been eager to befriend him, and if he had been a layman, they certainly would have liberally provided for him, as they did for Addison and Congreve; but being in orders, he could not well do the duties of Under Secretary of State, or Commissioner

[1] Macph. State Papers, ii. 202.

of Customs, and Queen Anne had resolved that the author of the "Tale of a Tub" should not hold any high ecclesiastical dignity in England. They proposed to appoint him Secretary of Legation at Vienna, or Bishop of Virginia; but he spurned at such offers, his determination being to enjoy power and preferment at home.¹ When the tide was turning, during the trial of Sacheverell, he formed an alliance with Harley and St. John, and, now the chief prop of their government, and editor of the "Examiner," he vituperated the leaders of the opposition with bitterness, in proportion to the fulsomeness of the flattery he had formerly lavished upon them. In an early number of that journal he compares the late and the present ministers by pairs—and this is his parallel between the patron, to whom he had dedicated the "Tale of a Tub," and his successor: "The person who now presides at the council is descended from a great and honorable father, *not from the dregs of the people;* he was at the head of the Treasury some years, and rather chose to enrich his Prince than himself. In the height of favor and credit, he sacrificed the greatest employment in the kingdom to his conscience and honor. He hath been always firm in his loyalty and religion, zealous for supporting the prerogative of the Crown, and preserving the liberties of the people. But then his best friends must own that he is neither *Deist* nor *Socinian;* he hath never conversed with TOLAND to open and enlarge his thoughts; nor was he ever able to arrive at that perfection of gallantry *to ruin and imprison the husband in order to keep the wife without disturbance.*" ²

¹ It is said, that when the Earl of Wharton was appointed Lord Lieutenant of Ireland, Somers introduced Swift to him as a fit person to be his chaplain, when the profligate peer exclaimed, "We can not afford to countenance such fellows; we ourselves have no character to spare." This may account for the savage ferocity with which he afterwards attacked Wharton. The hatred he bore the Ex-Lord Lieutenant, and his old friends he was at no pains to conceal:—

"In state opinions *à la mode*,
He hated Wharton like a toad,
Had given the faction many a wound,
And libel'd all the Junto round."

² Examiner, No. 26, Feb. 1, 1711. So delighted were the Tories with this lampoon that Lord Oxford, as a reward, offered Swift £50, which he indignantly refused, expecting now that miter which he could not obtain from the Whigs.—(*Journal to Stella*.) It is amusing to find Swift's indiscriminate admirers standing up for his political consistency; whereas, there is not such

In the beginning of this year, an inquiry being instituted in the House of Lords into the manner in which the war had been conducted in Spain, Lord Somers strenuously supported petitions presented by Lord Galway and Lord Tyrawly, that they might be heard upon certain charges brought forward against them; but he had, on this occasion, the mortification to find himself in a minority in that assembly which he had long ruled—a motion for rejecting the petitions being carried by a majority of 57 to 46.¹ In a general debate upon the conduct of the war in Spain, which took place a few days after, he seems to have taken a comprehensive view of the foreign policy of the late Government, and to have strenuously maintained the necessity and practicability of driving Philip beyond the Pyrenees, notwithstanding the unfortunate battle of Almanza.²

a flagrant instance of *ratting* in the annals of English party politics as he exhibits. He easily reconciled his high churchism to whiggery while the Whigs were in power, and he openly professed himself an adherent to that party. Thus he addresses the Honorable Mrs. Finch, afterwards Lady Winchelsea:—

"And last, my vengeance to complete,
May you descend to take renown;
Prevail'd on by the thing you hate,
A Whig, and one that wears a gown."

Again, referring to the time when Somers was Chancellor, he says, "It was then I began to trouble myself with the differences between the principles of Whig and Tory. I talked often on this subject with Lord Somers; I told him that, having been long conversant with the Greek and Latin authors, and therefore a lover of liberty, I found myself much inclined to be what they called a Whig in politics; and that, besides, I thought it impossible upon any other principles to defend or submit to the Revolution." In his Journal to Stella, and in letters to his other correspondents, when he had gone over, and was "giving it to the scoundrel Whigs all round," he repeatedly attempts to justify himself by the personal ill-usage he had experienced in receiving no promotion from them while they were in power. Even when he came to England, in the autumn of 1710, and he pretends that the Whigs were trying to get him back to their party, he betrays the same feeling: "All the Whigs were ravished to see me, and would have laid hold on me as a twig to save them from sinking; and the great men were all making their clumsy apologies. It is good to see what a lamentable confession the Whigs all make of my ill-usage."—*Journ. to Stel.* Yet none of them had ever insulted him by offering him a bank-note for calumniating his private friends. Although he was so much caressed by the Tory ministers, they seemed to have talked very slightingly of their tool. Lord Chesterfield, in commenting on Swift's "History of the Four last Years of Queen Anne," says, "It is a party pamphlet founded on the lie of the day, which, as Lord Bolingbroke, who had read it often, assured me, was coined and delivered out to him to write Examiners and other political papers upon."—*Lord Chesterfield's Works*, ii. 498.

¹ 5 Parl. Hist. 962, 965.   ² Ibid. 980.

When the Tories had been in office a twelvemonth, they were supposed to be going on very indifferently, and a rumor was spread that the Queen was about to recall the Whigs, and to give the Treasurer's staff to Lord Somers. Even Swift gave credit to this, and it alarmed him so much that he earnestly applied to be sent out of the country as secretary to an embassy, that he might be safe from the returning triumph of the party which he had deserted.[1] But the negotiations for peace were opened, and the nation grew more and more sick of the war and the "Grand Alliance."

To our great mortification, there is not to be found any fragment of Lord Somers's subsequent speeches during the negotiations for peace, or upon the treaty of Utrecht, although we see from the Lords' Journals that he continued diligently to attend in his place;[2] and contemporary writers tell us in general terms that he strongly concurred with his party in their censure of the present government for abandoning the great object of the war—the separation of France and Spain—and conceding everything to Louis XIV., when that haughty monarch had been reduced to a situation in which he might have been compelled to accept any terms to be dictated to him by England and her allies.

The health of Lord Somers had long been failing, and from this time he could pay little attention to public business.[3] Periodical visits to Tunbridge Wells had hitherto

---

[1] Journal to Stella, Dec. 9th, 1711.

[2] At this time parties were so equally balanced in the Lords, that the most tremendous exertions were made on both sides to procure proxies and the attendance of members. On Lord Nottingham's motion, "that no peace could be safe unless Spain and the West Indies were taken from the House of Bourbon," the previous question being put, was lost by one vote, and the main question was carried by a majority of three. This led to the making of twelve peers in one day, who gave a majority to the Court —4 *Burnet*, 342, 34c · 6 *Parl. Hist.* 1059.

There were now heavy lamentations over the degeneracy of the Lords, in seldom sitting till near twelve at noon instead of eight in the morning. Burnet complains, likewise, that, "except on a day on which some great points are to be discussed upon which the parties divide, they grew disposed to rise after two or three hours' sitting." He would have had them sit from eight till two.—*O. T.*, iv. 447.

[3] He appears to have had a particularly severe attack of illness, in July, 1712. In a letter then written by an adherent of the abdicated family, there is the following disguised passage : "All friends here are well except Rowley, (Lord Rivers) who is dying ; and poor Sanders (Somers), who can not live long, and is already dead in effect, to the great grief of Harry (Hanover), who

been of service to him; but nothing could henceforth recruit his exhausted constitution. He became paralytic, and his mind was debilitated.

This is the only apology that can be suggested for the part he took in the last parliamentary proceeding during this reign in which he seems to have interfered. On account of the extension of the malt-tax to Scotland, and other supposed grievances, a cry was got up in that country for "a repeal of the Union," and the venerable nobleman who had acquired such credit by bringing about that measure, to insure the Protestant succession, and the tranquillity and prosperity of the island,—now, for the purpose of embarrassing the Government, himself became "a repealer." On account of his indisposition, a meeting was held at his house, which was attended by the discontented Scots; and, after a long deliberation, he strongly urged that a motion should be made on the subject in the House of Lords, where his influence was still so great. Accordingly, by his advice, the Earl of Findlater moved "that leave be given to bring in a bill for dissolving the Union; for restoring each kingdom to its power, rights and privileges; for effectually securing her Majesty in her royal power and authority over both kingdoms; and for asserting and confirming all her royal prerogatives, and effectually securing the succession of the Protestant line in the illustrious House of Hanover, as the same stands limited and secured." The motion was seconded by the Earl of Mar.[1] Although Lord Somers was present, he did not take any part in the debate; but I am concerned to say that the Duke of Argyle spoke warmly in support of the motion, and, allowing that he had a great hand in making the Union, declared his opinion now to be that, for the interest both of England and Scotland, it ought to be dissolved. Lord Sunderland, Lord Halifax and all the Whigs, took the same side. Lord Oxford, Lord Peter-

depends more on him than on any one friend besides."—*Macph. State Papers.* ii. 332.

[1] This appears, then, to have been the course of proceeding in the Lords as it still is in the Commons; but by the usage now established in the Lords, any Peer may, without asking leave, lay a bill on the table, and move that it be read a first time, and no motion requires to be seconded. A bill is invariably read a first time as a matter of courtesy, but a motion is made on the first reading; and if from the title of the bill or the explanation given of its contents, it were thought unfit for discussion, it might be stopped *in limine.*

borough and the Tory Lords, who had opposed the measure, now resisted its repeal, "on the ground that such a contract was like marriage, and, how imprudent soever it might have been, was for ever binding on both parties." "All contracts," said they, "can only be dissolved by the same authority by which they were entered into; but this contract was entered into by the separate legislatures of two independent kingdoms, and can not be dissolved by the single legislature of one kingdom."[1] The Government did not venture to meet the motion with a direct negative, but proposed the previous question, upon which they were beaten. A division then taking place on the main question,—of the peers present there was an equal number on both sides—54 to 54; but proxies being called, there were only 13 for the motion, and there were 17 against it—so the Union stood by a majority of 4.[2]

Lord Somers appears afterwards to have been almost entirely disabled from attending to public affairs till the very conclusion of this reign. Though most remorselessly assailed by his old friend Swift, men of principle were more eager than ever to show respect to him. At Tory dinners his health, if proposed by a stray Whig,

[1] I wish that this reasoning would convince Mr. O'Connell and the Irish repealers. I rejoice that, for better reasons, British Whigs and Tories are of one mind as to maintaining the Union with Ireland.—A.D. 1846.

[2] 6 Parl. Hist. 1214–1220; Lords' Jour.; Speaker Onslow's note on Burnet. Erasmus Lewis, then M.P. for Lostwithiel, gives a curious account of this division in a letter to Swift. He says, that both the Tory peers who voted with the Lord Treasurer against the dissolution of the Union, and those who voted for it, were "under agonies" lest they themselves should be victorious. "In all the time I have been conversant in business I never before observed both sides at the same time acting parts which they thought contrary to their interests." But the most curious document connected with this motion, is Bolingbroke's letter to the Duke of Shrewsbury, when notice had been given of it: "Your grace will wonder when I tell you that they intend to move in our House, on Monday, to dissolve the Union. You may be sure that all those whose spirits are naturally turbulent and restless—all those who have languished under expectation—and all those who have any personal resentment, take this occasion to add to the cry, and to pursue their own views by intermingling them in this cause. We shall, I believe, ground on this motion a bill to make it *high treason*, by any overt act, to attempt the dissolution of the Union. If, after all this, we go on to show them all reasonable indulgence, and at the same time to show to them, and to all mankind, a firmness of resolution and a steadiness of conduct, good will have come out of evil, and we shall reap some benefit from this *contretemps*."—*Bol. Corr.* ii. 409. A serious difficulty in the way of the proposed enactment is, that the agitation would be carried on under the form of petitioning to repeal the act creating this new treason,—unless the act were to contain a clause, that to propose the repeal of any of its provisions should be high treason!

went round.¹ And the "SPECTATOR" now delighting and improving the age, when the papers were republished the first volume was inscribed "TO JOHN, LORD SOMERS, BARON OF EVESHAM:" the dedication being from the pen of Addison. Like the *Eloge* of him in the FREE-HOLDER, it is rather too lengthy and labored, and deals too much in general praise, but some passages of it felicitously hit off the characteristic virtues he was now displaying in retirement:—" It is in vain that you have endeavored to conceal your share of the merit in the many national services which you have effected. Your Lordship appears as great in your private life, as in the most important offices which you have borne. I would rather choose to speak of the pleasure you afford all who are admitted into your conversation, of your elegant taste in all polite arts of learning, of your great humanity and complacency of manners, and of the surprising influence which is peculiar to you, in making every one who converses with your Lordship prefer you to himself, without thinking the more meanly of his own talents."²

Sir Richard Steele likewise now showed a generous attachment to Somers, when no further favor could be expected from him; and, as an excuse for being absent from home in attending on him, thus gallantly wrote to Lady Steele: "Dearest wife, the finest woman in nature should not detain me an hour from you; but you must sometimes suffer the rivalship of the wisest men."³

Lord Somers, though no longer attending the House of Lords, was constantly consulted by the Hanoverian minister respecting the means of securing the quiet succession of the Princess Sophia, and afterwards of her son; and, in conjunction with Lord Sunderland, Lord Cowper, and Lord Chief Justice Parker, gave minute instructions as to all the steps to be taken on the expected demise of the Crown.—But his disease so gained ground, that he was seldom seen except by his private friends.

---

¹ ' Addison and I, and some others, dined with Lord Bolingbroke, and sate with him till twelve. We were very civil, but yet, when we grew warm, we talked in a friendly way of party. Addison raised his objections and Lord Bolingbroke answered them with great complaisance. Addison began Lord Somers health which went about."—*Journal to Stella*, April 3rd, 1713.

² These dedications are rather stiff, except that of the eighth volume, to Will Honeycombe, which is in Addison's happiest manner.

³ Steele's Corr. 246.

In the distractions which preceded the dissolution of Queen Anne, he was again publicly produced upon the scene. The Earl of Oxford having been dismissed, and the intrigues of Bolingbroke being defeated by the Dukes of Somerset and Argyle bursting into the council at Kensington, and procuring the delivery of the Treasurer's staff to the Duke of Shrewsbury from the dying Queen, it was agreed, with the view of securing the succession of the Hanoverian line, that all Privy Councillors, without distinction, should attend. As soon as this resolution was notified to Lord Somers, he repaired to Kensington, and next day, on the report of the Queen's physicians that her recovery was hopeless, concurred in the order by the Council to the Heralds-at-arms, and to a troop of Life Guards, to be in readiness to proclaim the Elector of Brunswick King of Great Britain, and in sending off Mr. Craggs with a letter from them to his Highness, requesting him to repair with speed to Holland, where a British squadron, that was fitting out with all possible expedition, would attend him and bring him over to take possession of the vacant throne. Between seven and eight o'clock, in the morning of Sunday, the 1st of August, 1714, Queen Anne expired.

A meeting of the Lords Justices appointed under the Regency Act was immediately held. On account of Lord Somers's very infirm state of health, he had not been appointed one of them, but he attended as a Privy Councillor, and took the oath of allegiance to the new Sovereign.

On the arrival of George I. in England, the Whigs shared among themselves all the offices of the government, and Lord Somers having contributed so much to this consummation, had his faculties been entire as in the reign of William, he would have been pressed to resume the Great Seal. But he was no longer able even to go through the light duties of President of the Council, During occasional renewals of mental activity, he could enjoy the complete triumph of the policy he had supported, and he was delighted by seeing a parliamentary settlement of the crown substituted for indefeasible right. He declined any office, but, *honoris causa*, he was not only sworn of the Privy Council, but a seat in the Cabinet was assigned to him, along with Marlborough.

Sunderland, Halifax, Townsend, Cowper, and Stanhope. He promised to attend their meetings as often as his strength would permit, and to assist them with his advice when privately consulted by them. At the same time, as a mark of public gratitude, an additional pension of £2,000 a year was settled upon him for life.

Unfortunately his infirmities still increased,[1] and, from

[1] The following statement from the Council Office shows the Councils which Lord Somers attended, and from which he was absent, from the accession of George I. till April 6, 1716.

August 1, 1714. Lord Somers was present at the first Council of George I. Sept. 29th, 1714, Sworn,

Councils.		Lord Somers.
1714.	Oct. 1	Present.
	Oct. 4	Present.
	Oct. 5	Not Present.
	Oct. 12	Ditto.
	Oct. 14	Ditto.
	Oct. 29	Present.
	Nov. 2	Ditto.
	Nov. 16	Not Present.
	Nov. 22	Ditto.
	Dec. 6	Present.
	Dec. 16	Not Present.
	Dec. 30	Present.
1715.	Jan. 5	Ditto.
	Jan. 11	Not Present.
	Jan. 15	Ditto.
	Jan. 26	Present.
	Feb. 7	Ditto.
	Feb. 23	Not Present.
	March 29	Present.
	April 1	Ditto.
	April 30	Not Present.
	June 5	Ditto.
	June 17	Ditto.
	June 30	Present.
	July 20	Not Present.
	July 25	Present.
	July 29	Not Present.
	Aug. 31	Present.
	Sept. 9	Ditto.
	Sept. 15	Ditto.
	Sept. 16	Ditto.
	Sept. 23	Ditto.
	Oct. 18	Not Present.
	Oct. 26	Present.
	Nov. 8	Ditto.
	Nov. 22	Not Present.
	Nov. 29	Present.
	Dec. 13	Ditto.
1716.	Jan. 6	Not Present.
	March 10	Ditto.
	April 6	Ditto.

his paralytic affection he became so torpid and lethargic as to be entirely unfit for public business.

Yet there was a brilliant gleam from this luminary before it set forever. While the Septennial Bill was pending in the House of Peers, Lord Somers had a sharp attack of the gout, which suspended the disease of his nerves. Doctor Friend, the celebrated physician, who attended him, finding his intellect for the time entirely restored, conveyed the news to Lord Townshend, one of the principal authors of the measure. This distinguished statesman immediately ran to consult a colleague whose loss had been so much deplored, and who, bound down by sickness and infirmity, was still mysteriously regarded as the oracle of his party. As soon as he entered the room, Lord Somers embraced him, and said, " I have just heard of the work in which you are engaged, and congratulate you upon it; I never approved the Triennial Bill, and always considered it the reverse of what it was intended to be. You have my hearty approbation in this business, and I think it will be the greatest support possible to the liberty of the country."[1] Such was certainly stated to have been "the response of the Oracle," and it must have made a deep impression upon the public mind. I entertain no doubt that Lord Somers did approve of the bill, but I suspect that, if his faculties were restored, he rather excused it as a necessary *coup d'etat* to keep the new family on the throne, than praised as constitutional the vote of a House of Commons to prolong their power more than double the period for which they had been elected.

When the gout left him, he fell back into his former state of nervousness. A fit of apoplexy happily supervened, for he could only have continued "a driveler and a show." He expired at his villa in Hertfordshire, on the 26th of April, 1716, the very day that the Septennial Act passed.

He was buried in the parish church of North Mymms, where a plain monument was erected to him by his surviving sister, who, knowing and conforming to the mod-

---

1716. April 26. Lord Somers died. The last time of his attendance in the House of Lords was 27th January, 1715. Till then he had attended pretty regularly, but he was often hardly conscious of what was going on; and he must have been a melancholy spectacle to his friends.

[1] Coke's Life of Sir Robert Walpole, i. 130.

esty of his nature. merely inscribed upon it these simple words:—

> "THE RT. HONBLE. JOHN, LORD SOMERS,
> BARON OF EVESHAM,
> LORD HIGH CHANCELLOR OF ENGLAND IN THE REIGN OF KING WILLIAM III.
> To whose Memory this Monument was erected by Dame Elizabeth Jekyll."

She remembered that, at the sight of his name, every one visiting the hallowed shrine would think of the accomplished scholar, the consummate judge, the distinguished orator, the enlightened patriot, the statesman to whom we owe the expulsion of a tyrant, the Bill of Rights, and the settlement of the Protestant succession.

The observations which I have incidentally made in relating the events of the life of Lord Somers obviate the necessity of my attempting any labored analysis of his character. I feel proud of him for having joined a profound and scientific knowledge of jurisprudence with a love of literature and of the fine arts—in England a rare combination. He appears to have been complete master of his own profession—from the technical rules of practice and pleading, to the most important questions of international law—while at the Kit-Cat, at Will's, or at Button's, he could converse on equal terms with Addison, Steele, Swift, Prior, and Congreve.

He likewise carried on a correspondence with the most distinguished men of letters in foreign countries. Of this we have a very striking proof in the "Life of Vincenzio da Filicaja," by Bonaventuri, who says, " Il Conte Lorenzo Magalotti, Cavaliere di quel merito, e di quella virtù, che è ben noto a tutto il mondo, e che era strettissimo amico del Senatore da Filicaja, mi ha cortesemente comunicato una lettera che egli ha avuto di Londra da Mylord Giovanni Sommers, Barone d'Evesham, Presidente del Consiglio Privato della Regina, della Gran Bretagna, Signore arrichito di così maravigliose qualità personali, e adornato di cognizioni e di virtù così distinte, che lasciando ora da parte gli altri grandissimi impieghi, che egli ha sostenuto in quel fioritissimo regno, dal solo avervi esercitato per sette anni la importantissima carica di Gran Cancelliere, in gran copia si spande e che lo rende conosciuto e venerato da tutto il mondo. Questa lettera parla del Senatore da Filicaja in tal guisa, e ne fa un ritratto così vivo e somigliante, che io riputerei di far troppo grave torto alla memoria d'un uomo, che io venero al più alto segno, se io non la trascrivessi in quella forma appunto, che dal Conte Magalotti m' è stata data per autenticare con una così chiara testimonianza quanto fin ora ho narrato. '*Ella è certo proprissima* (parla della lingua Inglese, nella quale è scritta la lettera) *per compiangere in essa la perdita dell' incomparabile Senatore da Filicaja, che ha si altamente lodati diversi della nostra nazione, e più distintamente ha dato a me quell' unico ragionevole fondamento che io poteva avere, per lusingarmi che la mia memoria sia per vivere, in quell' immortale componimento de' suoi versi. Io ho così ben ponderate le sue Poesie, e v' ho letto così a fondo i veri sentimenti del suo cuore, che io mi trovo in istato di pianger la sua perdita come se io l' avessi trattate, e intimamente, ogni giorno: perchè non solamente vi raffiguro un sapere profondo, un ingegno dove si perde la vista una gran sublimità di pensieri e una somma sodezza di giudizzio, ma vi discerno chiaramente la rettitudine, e l' integrità della sua mente, l' uomo dabbene e il perfetto amico.*' Meritò certamente il Senatore da Filicaja tutte le lodi, che gli furono date così avanti, come dopo la sua morte, poichè egli fu un gran letterato, un ottimo cittadino, ed un perfetto Cristiano."[1]

[1] "Count Lorenzo Magalotti, who is a gentleman of such merit and virtue, that he is well known to the public, and who was a very intimate friend of the Senator Filicaja, has politely communicated to me a letter which he received from John, Lord Somers, Baron of Evesham, President of the Privy Council of the Queen of Great Britain, a nobleman enriched with such high personal qualities, and adorned with such accomplishments, that, after passing through other employments in that flourishing kingdom, he filled for seven years the most important office of Lord Chancellor, in which he so much distinguished himself that his name became known and venerated over the whole world. This letter speaks of the Senator Filicaja in such a way, and draws such a lively and striking picture of him, that I should be doing too great an injustice to the memory of a man whom I so much revere if I were not to present it to the reader exactly as it comes to me from Count Magalotti, and so confirm my own observations by a noble testimony, to which all must defer. 'It certainly will be fitly employed (speaking of the English language, in which the letter is written) to lament the loss of the incomparable Senator da Filicaja, who has so highly extolled several of our nation, and, in particular, has given to myself the only reasonable foundation I can have for hoping that my name will be long preserved by introducing it into his immortal verses. I have so treasured up his poetry in my mind, and made myself so familiar with the genuine sentiments of his heart, that I feel myself as qualified to lament his loss as if I had for years been personally intimate with him. His writings not only show profound knowledge, a lively imagination, great sublimity of thought, and an exquisite delicacy of taste, but I clearly discover in them the utmost rectitude of sentiment, the highest principles of

Filicaja never published any Italian verses in praise of the English Chancellor, but in his works there is to be found a Latin ode, " In illustriss. Dominum D. Sommers," from which I extract a few stanzas. After an invocation to the Muses he thus proceeds:—

> " Mathesin illa huic ; hæc Sophiam ingerit ;
> Suadem, Poesinque altera ; et altera
> Legum recludit nunc recentum
>   Scrinia, nunc veterum ; urbium illa
> Artem regendarum, altaque munia
> Et pacis, et belli ; hæc reservare amat
> Arcana regnantum sagax quæ
>   Zelotypæ tegit umbra curæ.
>   *   *   *   *
> Te haud finxit unum (credite posteri)
> Natura, non mens una tibi, neque
> Lingua una ; septeno disertus
>   Ore, aliusque et idem
> Semper, nec unquam, dissitus Anglico
> A sole, septem ferme idiomatum
> Per ostia intras Nili ad instar
>   Immodicæ maria alta famæ." [1]

honor, and the requisites for the most perfect friendship.' The Senator da Filicaja certainly merited all the praises bestowed upon him, as well in his lifetime as after his death, for he was a fine writer, a patriotic citizen, and a sincere Christian."

[1] Opere di Vincenzio da Filicaja, tom. ii. 50. Venice, 1755. Italian being one of the seven languages with which Somers was familiar without ever having been out of England, he was, of course, well acquainted with the writings of his contemporary, Filicaja. It is more difficult to conjecture how Filicaja became aware of the merits of Somers ; but this appears to have been brought about by Henry Newton, our resident at Florence, an exceedingly learned man, and personally acquainted with both of these two distinguished characters. Newton published at Lucca, in 1710, a quarto volume of his own Latin Epistles, Orations, and Poems, in which Filicaja is often celebrated. One of the Epistles, dated Florence, Sept. 1706, is thus addressed :—

" Illustrissimo Domino
 D. JOHANNI
  SOMMERS,
Baroni de Evesham.
Henricus de Nova Villa.—S."

I copy a short passage from it, which is curious as giving a statement of Lord Somers's position at this time, and the services he had recently done in bringing about the Union with Scotland :—

" Dein equidem incidimus in Tempora tristia, Virtutibus infensa et reip. magis quam tibi adversa. Tu verò tandem de malitia hominum, deque ipsa invidia triumphasti ; atque inauditum antea nostris annalibus, neque solum Reipublicæ Atheniensis, Romana ac Batava, optimis et de se optimè meritis civibus ingratæ, ipsos Inquisitores accusationis puduit. Nunc vero sine titulo magnus et potens, nec unius anni Consul, sine fascibus nostrum regis orbem, qui Scotis adjectis, coalitisque in unum gentibus, non situ quidem, sed moribus ac mutuo metu, et solito accolarum odio disjunctis (quantum vestra superant facundiæ sapientique trophæa illa bellica quæ sola majoribus nostris

The friendly pen of Addison represents Lord Somers as himself consummately skilled in composition. "His style in writing was chaste and pure, but at the same time full of spirit and politeness, and fit to convey the most intricate business to the understanding of the reader with the utmost clearness and perspicuity. . . I believe no author of the greatest eminence would deny Lord Somers to have been the best writer of the age in which he lived." Yet it must be acknowledged that there is no piece which we know to be his, either in verse or prose, which can be placed on a level with the classical productions of the reign of Queen Anne. The eulogist, foreseeing that such an observation might be made, laments that "this extraordinary person, out of his natural aversion to vain glory, wrote several pieces, as well as performed several actions, which he did not assume the honor of."

Besides his collection of printed tracts,[1] Lord Somers left behind him an immense mass of MSS., partly composed by himself, partly by others. These came into the possession of the Hardwicke family, who were allied to him by marriage, and being deposited in the chambers of the Honorable Charles Yorke, in Lincoln's Inn, were there nearly all destroyed by an accidental fire. Mr. Yorke collected a few of the papers saved, which he bound in a folio volume. From this a selection was given in the "Miscellaneous State Papers," published in 1778, by the second Earl of Hardwicke, who says, "the world will do that justice to the collection, as not to suppose that these specimens from it, *immitis ignis reliquiæ*, will afford an adequate idea of its merits. It filled upwards of sixty volumes in quarto, and did not contain a paper from Lord Somers's pen which the most intimate friend would have wished to secrete, or the bitterest enemy could have fairly turned to his prejudice." I apprehend, however, that these were all connected with law or politics, and that they contained nothing to show that

nota) amplior sanè, potentior illustriorque et magnitudine, et viribus quodque majus, consiliis redditur. . . . . Te lætus interim sequitur Senatus ; cumque Patribus, optandum magis antea quàm sperandum, immò opus penitùs desperatum, optime convenit populo."

[1] These under the title of "Lord Somers's Tracts," have been twice published ; first in 1748, in sixteen volumes 4to. ; secondly in 1809, in thirteen volumes 4to., under the superintendence of Sir Walter Scott.

Somers could have been the author of the "Tale of a Tub."

The next glory to that of being a classical writer is being the patron of classical writers, and this Somers enjoyed in conjunction with Montagu, to a degree not known in any preceding or succeeding age in England. With us it is a national reproach, that authorship has rather been despised and discountenanced by the great, and it has been deemed somewhat discreditable for a man to earn his bread, or to rise into celebrity, by his pen. A successful lawyer, or a parliamentary debater, may overcome all the disadvantages of obscure origin or of early poverty, but no degree of mere literary eminence leads to political promotion. In subsequent times Addison would not have risen to a post of higher distinction than that of Editor of a Journal. But although he could not open his mouth in parliament, Somers and Montagu justly appreciated his inimitable powers as a writer, and being courted and caressed by them and the other leaders of the Whig party, he became Chief Secretary to the Lord Lieutenant of Ireland, a Privy Councillor, and Secretary of State. The fashion which they set was adopted by Harley and the Tories. Swift was received at the table of the Lord Treasurer with as much distinction as if he had been decorated with the Garter, and Prior was employed as an ambassador to negotiate the peace of Utrecht. Lord Somers was ever eager to do homage to established literary reputation, and to discover rising genius. When Pope, "lisping in numbers," gave his boyish compositions to the world,

"The courtly Talbot, SOMERS, Sheffield read."[1]

We have no adequate means of judging how far Lord Somers deserved his reputation as an orator. Although he sat in parliament from the beginning of the year 1689 till his death, a period not much short of thirty years, and during a considerable part of that time led a great party first in the Lower, then in the Upper House, there is not

[1] At the distance of many years, Swift, notwithstanding the hardness of his nature, retained a tender recollection of the pleasant literary reunions in the early part of Anne's reign, at the houses of Pope, Somers and Montagu. Writing to Pope, in 1721, he says—"I frequently conversed with Mr. Addison during all my Lord Oxford's ministry, and his friendship to me continued inviolable, *with as much kindness as when we used to meet at Lord Somers's* or Halifax's, who were leaders of the opposite party."

as much of any one speech he delivered as would make half a column of a newspaper, and in the very scanty reports of parliamentary proceedings in the reigns of William and Anne his name is rarely mentioned.

But he has a surer claim to our admiration and our gratitude by his deeds. He first gave the model of a *constitutional*, in opposition to an *absolutist* monarchy; and this model, which has been attempted in France and in several other continental states, is now generally allowed to be the form of government which gives the most influence to enlightened public opinion, and best answers the purposes for which civil government is instituted.

The great blot upon his public character was the persecution of Roman Catholics in his time,—which, if he did not prompt, he fully sanctioned. Religious toleration was one great object supposed to be gained by the change of dynasty, and it might have been expected that those who brought in the "Toleration Act," and opposed the "Bill against Occasional Conformity," would have been eager to permit all sects of Christians to worship God according to their consciences. Yet after the Revolution the penal code against the Romanists was made far more severe and revolting than it ever had been under Elizabeth or any of the four Kings of the Stuart line. By acts passed while Lord Somers was in office, Roman Catholic priests were banished the kingdom, and if they returned they were to be hanged;[1] a reward of twenty pounds was given for the discovery of a priest, and a Papist refusing to tell where he last heard mass was to be imprisoned for a twelvemonth;[2] no Papist was allowed to keep a school, and severe penalties were denounced against such as should go themselves or send others abroad to be educated in the Romish religion;[3] no Papist could be guardian to any child, and if the child of a Papist became a Protestant, the Court of Chancery might order any part of the father's estate to be applied to the use of the child;[4] no Papist could be a barrister or solicitor;[5] no Papist was to serve on grand juries, or on any other jury if objected to;[6] and other penalties and disabilities were inflicted equally atrocious. It is a very small miti-

[1] 9 W. 3, c. 1.   [2] 8 Anne, c. 3.   [3] 7 W. 3, c. 4.
[4] 8 Anne, c. 3.   [5] 10 W. 3, c. 12.   [6] 6 Anne, c. 1.

gation of the enormity of this persecuting policy, that it was chiefly directed against the Irish Roman Catholics, and that they were all supposed to be Jacobites. The inexpediency as well as the iniquity of such laws seems palpable to us. One fatal consequence of them was, that they not only permanently alienated the affections of the Irish Roman Catholics from the new dynasty, but made English connection odious to the Irish nation, except to a few Protestants who were encouraged to oppress, rob, and insult their countrymen.

The most curious consideration, in looking back to those times, is, that from a general feeling among English Protestants with respect to Roman Catholics,—resembling that which now prevails in the United States of America among the whites with respect to the negroes,— the authors of such measures had no consciousness themselves of doing anything wrong, and did not at all thereby injure their character for liberality with the great body of their countrymen. We can only lament that Lord Somers was not on this subject in advance of his age. Such contemplations should make us alarmed lest some laws and practices, which seem to us very harmless, may be reprobated by our posterity.

The reproach to which Lord Somers was subject in his own time was, that he was too tolerant; from which some said he was an enemy to the Church, some that he was indifferent about religion, and others that he was an atheist. He likewise incurred much obloquy by having had, at one time, a private intercourse with Toland. But there is every reason to think that he was a sincere believer in the truths both of natural and revealed religion. Although he discouraged the extravagant pretensions of the clergy, —instead of being hostile to the Church of England, himself approving of its doctrines and discipline, and seeing that it possessed the affections of a vast majority of the people, he warmly supported it. Nay, he originally concerted with Bishop Burnet the plan of applying the " First Fruits and Tenths " to the augmentation of small livings, which was afterwards adopted under the name of QUEEN ANNE'S BOUNTY.[1] He did occasionally converse with

[1] Letter from Lord Somers to Bishop Burnet:—
" My Lord, " 22nd November, 1701.
" I acknowledge the honor of your Lordship's letter of the 17th with great

the author of "Christianity not mysterious," but there was a warm and steady friendship between him and the pious Tillotson.[1] "His religion," says Addison, (a moralist not only in his writings, but in his practice—a Christian, who taught us how to live and how to die,) "was sincere, not ostentatious, and such as inspired him with an universal benevolence towards all his fellow-subjects, not with bitterness against any part of them. He showed his firm adherence to it, as modeled by our national constitution, and was constant to its offices of devotion, both in public and in his family."[2]

I hope, likewise, that his morals were unimpeachable. When Solicitor General, he had paid his addresses to a young lady, to whom he seems to have been tenderly attached. This was a Miss Anne Bawdon, daughter of Sir John Bawdon, a wealthy alderman of London. When the lovers had plighted their mutual troth, and thought that a long career of domestic happiness was before them, the flinty-hearted father asked what settlement was to be made upon his daughter, corresponding to the fortune he meant to bestow upon her? A rental (rather a short one) was actually given in. Somers's patrimony was very moderate, and he had added little to it himself, having begun practice late, and having been more solicitous about reputation than money. The sordid City Knight cared little for the fair character or the bright prospects of the poor Solicitor General, and, declaring the house at

---

thankfulness. I wish it may lie in my power to contribute to the excellent design you propose; no man will enter into it more willingly, nor shall labor in it more heartily. The point of the first fruits and tenths is what I have proposed several times with much earnestness, but without success. When I have the happiness of seeing your Lordship, we shall, I hope, discourse at large upon the whole subject. In the mean time, allow me to assure you that I am, with great and sincere respect,
  "My Lord,
  "Your Lordship's most obedient humble Servant,
  "SOMERS."
—*Life*, prefixed to Burnet's *History of his Own Times*, p. lxvii.

[1] Toland obtained access to Somers as a joint admirer of Milton, and was a coadjutor in raising and spreading the reputation of this, his favorite poet, by the superb edition of "Paradise Lost," with cuts, published under his superintendence by Tonson.—*Cooksey*, 27.

[2] This groundless charge of infidelity has caused Somers to be compared, not inaptly, to the pious as well as learned Chancellor de l'Hospital, who, because he was for religious toleration, was looked upon with such horror that it was a common saying among the people, "*Dieu nous garde de la messe du Chancellier.*"

Whiteladies and the farm at Severn Stoke to be no provision for a widow, an eldest son, and younger children, peremptorily broke off the match, and compelled the weeping girl to accept an offer from a rich Turkey merchant,—a step he is said to have heartily repented when, at the end of three years, he whom he had rejected for his son-in-law being made Lord Keeper of the Great Seal, Sir John Bawdon wished, like Sir Giles Overreach, that he could have seen his "Right Honorable Daughter."[1] After this disappointment, which he keenly felt, Somers thought no more of the marriage state, and devoted himself to his public duties and the cultivation of literature and science.

Impartiality, however, forbids me to pass over a specific tale of scandal which was most industriously circulated respecting him.

He had for his housekeeper a Mrs. Blount, the wife of a tradesman at Worcester, and it was alleged that he lived openly with this lady as his mistress, behaving cruelly to the husband, and at last shutting him up in a madhouse.—"*Quibus indiciis, quo teste probavit?*" This story, most improbable in itself, is supported only by the gratuitous assertion of bitter and unscrupulous enemies. The manners of the Court of Charles II. had passed away. William and Mary, and afterwards Anne and the Prince of Denmark, had exhibited to the world a picture of the domestic virtues; licentiousness was discouraged in the highest quarters, and the appearance of it was avoided by the most licentious. It is, therefore, utterly impossible that a grave magistrate like Somers, who, though firm in the discharge of his duty, always showed a solicitude to enjoy the good opinion both of the prince and the people, should have followed a course which was sure to draw down upon him the just censure of all ranks in the state; and the supposition is equally at variance with the prudence and good taste, as with the honor and religious feeling, which we know belonged to him. If the case had been made doubtful by circumstances (which it is not), let me again call a witness to character who is worth a thousand,—Addison, who, if he might have forgiven youthful gallantries when repented of and renounced, would have shrunk with horror from the deliberate, sys-

---
[1] New Way to pay Old Debts, act ii. sc. 1.

tematic wickedness imputed to the Lord Chancellor. Yet Addison, who for many years saw him in his own house at all hours, and continued to be on the most friendly and familiar footing with him, describes him as immaculate.[1]

[1] "The New Atalantis," a more infamous work than the "Memoirs of Harriette Wilson," was published early in the reign of Queen Anne, and passing through many editions, retained its fashion for some years at least,—if not destined to immortality,—as we know from the lines of Pope, in the "Rape of the Lock:"—

> "While fish in streams, or birds delight in air,
> Or in a coach and six the British fair,
> *As long as* ATALANTIS *shall be read*,
> Or the small pillow grace a lady's bed."

I subjoin Mrs. Manley's character of "CICERO," by which she means to describe "Lord Chancellor Somers:"—"Cicero was next called, not he that saved the commonwealth from being made a monarchy, but he that would have made the monarchy a commonwealth; he was advanced by Irene to be Magister Officiorum ; the God of eloquence hung upon his tongue; Minerva herself inspired his brain and fired his heart. His wisdom and sedateness of temper preserved and kept together the cabal. Famous Cethegus and precipitate Catiline could only be restrained by him. He it was that gave them their cue, when to bellow, when to strike, when to comply, but seldom to save ; for, however disagreeing in other points, they used all to come into accord for revenge and persecution.

"And, what is not the least astonishing ingredient of their composition, these zealous reformers! these image-worshippers! these pretended devotees who ran mad after the outside of religion! were as immoral as those that had never heard of any! Cicero himself (an oracle of wisdom) was whirled about by his lusts, at the pleasure of a fantastic worn-out mistress: He prostrated his immutable sense, reason, and good nature, either to revenge or reward, as her caprice directed; and what made this commerce more detestable, this mistress of his was a wife! Impious excess! Abominable adultery! Were there not enough of the frail race unmarried? Had not Sergius's immemorial assiduities corrupted enough of that order, but this patrician, this director of nations and imperial assemblies, must bring his pollutions to defile the marriage bed and corrupt a wife? Nay, which is more execrable, the wife of a friend. Was it not a good comedy, or rather farce, when you behold this sententious man, this decisive orator, who by the enchantments of his persuasion left not even Destiny to herself, for Fate and Fortune were, whenever he spoke, his slaves. To see this great, this stupendous man, that could enchant an empire by the music of his voice, skulking in the obscure habit of a slave, hiding his face in an abject robe, as if that could conceal his vices, waiting at a back-door to get an undiscovered entrance into his own palace, after passing the guilty night in adultery with an infamous prostitute! And this not for once or twice, but for months and years! Till his sin was become as confirmed a habit as his hypocrisy! The poor husband, distracted with his wrongs, grew incapable of following the necessary duties of his calling, by which neglect his maintenance fell, and he drank the bitter draught of poverty. The adulteress rioting in all the luxury of the East! shifting abodes in scandalous by-corners, from place to place, for fear the cuckold's prerogative should seize upon the ornaments and riches of his wife as lawful spoil, which, when he was so lucky to do, the vindictive patrician interposed with a thorough revenge, first casting him into a loathsome prison, where, when he had sufficiently languished, a warrant was produced from the jailor

I do not find any particular account of his habits as to convivial pleasures, in which it was still usual for states-

to deliver his prisoner to some persons, who receiving him into their custody, disposed of him in such sort, that to this day he has never been heard of. Let the idolaters consider how much they ought to pride themselves in the morality, religion, and virtue of this Atlas of their empire."—*New Atalantis*, 6th edition, 1720, vol. iii. p. 200.

In a preceding volume we find rather a flattering character of Lord Somers and his friend Montagu, Lord Halifax.

" May your Ladyships be pleased to stretch your radiant eyes with a more than ordinary regard to those two renowned politicians that stop at the door in deep conference with each other. They have had a successful ministry. Time was when their young ambition durst not cast away an improbable wish of being masters of the tenth part of what they are now in possession of. There all they pursued was to be applauded for men of genius in the airy region of Parnassus; they both wrote, and both with success. Nor can there be better judges of writing; and, as an everlasting monument of their praise, be it recorded, that they have not been afraid to applaud and reward the performances of others; free from that emulation which has stung even some of the great emperors of old who would be thought poets. They have, in their two persons, more conspicuously encouraged and raised the ingenious, than has the whole race of the Atalantic nobility besides. True, they have had a larger power than most, and have more distinguished it. Have they enriched themselves suddenly and surprisingly? 'Tis meritorious in one respect, because they do good with it to others; both have had the lucky circumstance of finding it to be for their interest still to remain of the party they first fixed in. The methods they have took to raise their fortune, give us but little hopes that they would have persevered in any principle that should but once appear to be contrary to their interest: but since no such change has arrived, let us charitably applaud them as men remaining true to their first professions—a virtue rarely found in a statesman."—*New Atalantis*, vol. ii. 309.

Cooksey, in his abortive sketch of the Life of Lord Somers, under pretense of defending him, represents him as one of the most profligate of mankind. After referring to the representation that he was *sprung from the dregs of the people*, he thus proceeds: ' The other charge is founded on a supposed amour and attachment between him and a Mrs. Blount, whose husband had been three several times set up in business by his Worcester friends; who, at length, finding him a man whom it was impossible to serve or save from a jail left him to his destiny, and contented themselves with recommending his wife, a very sensible and deserving woman who had been the mother of a large family, to Lord Somers as a housekeeper; in which capacity she lived at his house at Belbar, and proved an excellent servant and nurse to him as long as he lived. His ideas as to connections with women (having been disappointed in his first attachment, on which he renounced ever after the thought of marrying), were such as he professes in the Tale of a Tub, *Jacere collectum humorem in corpora quæque*. Nor did any man ever suffer more than he did from indulging this favorite maxim, in which he was by no means nice, or in the least degree delicate. To this was owing his frequent illnesses, and calls to Tunbridge: and what was worst of all, that wretched state to which the brightest parts and intellects God ever bestowed on man were reduced before his final dissolution."—*Cooksey*, 27, 28. But there is some reason to think that this gentleman had a spite against the memory of his kinsman; at all events, composing his work at Lausanne, in the very end of the eighteenth century, he could only have spoken from a vague tradition, and

men and wits to indulge too freely; but, considering what he accomplished, he must have been habitually temperate, although he might occasionally have exceeded when he had a *tete-à-tete* with Addison, or when he was in the chair leading the festivities of the Kit-Cat. Swift, in his imitation of Horace, entitled "Toland's Invitation to Dismal [Lord Nottingham] to dine with the Calves' Head Club," written at a time when he was at enmity with the Whigs, does not venture to say more than that the gravity of the ex-Chancellor was relaxed by the bottle:—

> "Who, by disgraces or ill fortune sunk,
> Feels not enliven'd when he's drunk?
> By force of wine even Scarborough is brave,
> Hall[1] grows more pert, *and Somers not so grave.*"[2]

This supposed gravity was frequently mimicked for the amusement of the Tories by Estcourt, the famous player.[3]

we must be slow to give any credit whatever to the testimony of a man who asserts as a fact, that "Lord Somers was the author of THE TALE OF A TUB."

A more startling testimony is that of Mackey, who, in his "Sketch of leading Characters at the English Court," written for the information of the Princess Sophia of Hanover, after exalting the good qualities of Somers, throws in a qualification—as if unwillingly—perhaps deceived by prevailing calumny: "He gives entertainments to foreign ministers more like one always bred up in a Court than at the bar. He is of grave deportment, easy and free of conversation, *something of a libertine,*" &c.

I pay less attention to the repetition of the charge by the vindictive Duchess of Marlborough. "There was one thing that appeared to be a great blemish to a Lord Chancellor, that he lived as publicly with another man's wife as if she had been his own." And I utterly disregard the libelous distich of the "downright Shippen:

> "He is—for satire does the truth declare—
> Deist, republican, adulterer.*

[1] Henry Boyle.
[2] "Quid non ebrietas designat," &c. Ep. lib. i. 5. See Journal to Stella, 7th Aug. 1712.
[3] Halifax, Godolphin, and the other Whig leaders, were likewise *taken off* by Estcourt. "This man was so amazing and extraordinary a mimic, that no man or woman, from the coquette to the privy councillor, ever moved or spoke before him, but he could carry their voice, look, mien, and motion, instantly into another company. I have heard him make long harangues, and form various arguments, even in the manner of thinking of an eminent pleader at the bar, with envy, the least article and singularity of his utterance so perfectly imitated that he was the very *alter ipse*, scarce to be distinguished from the original."—*Life of Cibber*, i. 86. Notwithstanding the liberties he had used with the Whigs, there is a most affectionate tribute to his memory by Steele, in the 468th No. of the Spectator. "He had so exquisite a discerning of what was defective in any object before him, that in an instant he

---

* Dodsley's Miscellanies, iii. 256.

But to the person made the subject of such paltry jocularity might truly have been applied the description of the demeanor of Agricola: "Ubi conventus ac judicia poscerent, gravis, intentus, severus: ubi officio satisfactum, nulla ultra potestatis persona: tristitiam et arrogantiam exuerat: nec illi, quod est rarissimum, aut facilitas auctoritatem, aut severitas amorem deminuit."[1]

Lord Somers is celebrated for having been contented with a very small portion of sleep; and in his advanced life, when he could not conveniently rise and light his own fire, "at waking, a reader attended and entertained him with the most valuable authors."[2]

When associating with nobles and kings he retained all his early attachments, and he kept up a friendly intercourse with all connected with him by blood or affinity, never being ashamed of any of them, however obscure. Thus, having received, when he was Chancellor, the present of a collar of brawn from a Mr. Cooksey, who, as the husband of a distant relation, claimed kindred with him,—at the first instant of leisure he sent him this good-natured acknowledgment:—

"Dear Cousin,

"Though I desired my brother Cocks long since to return you my best thanks for your noble present of as good a collar of brawn as ever was ate, (which I can not doubt he has done in the best manner I could wish,) yet having feasted myself, and made my friends often welcome to it, I can not forbear to return you personally our joint thanks, which I have often promised them to do.

"And so I remain, dear Cousin,
"Your most faithful Servant,
"SOMERS."

His kindness and generosity to all depending upon him could show you the ridiculous side of what would pass for beautiful and just. In the accounts he gave of persons and sentiments, he did not only hit the figure of their faces and manner of their gestures, but he would in his narration fall into their very way of thinking, and this when he recounted passages wherein men of the best wits were concerned, as well as such wherein were represented men of the lowest rank of understanding. I do not know any satisfaction of any indifferent kind I ever tasted so much as having got over an impatience of my seeing myself in the air he could put me when I have displeased him. It is to poor Estcourt I chiefly owe that I am arrived at the happiness of thinking nothing a diminution to me but what argues a depravity of my will."

[1] Tacit. Ag. c. 9.   [2] Madd. 107.

will be easily credited, when it is remembered that his enemies allowed that he was indifferent about money, and that he subscribed liberally to every public undertaking which had the slightest claim to his support.[1]

But let us see how harmless are the bitterest attacks upon his general character. Thus writes Sir John Macpherson:

"Somers, though meanly descended, rendered himself respectable by talents which he knew well to improve to his own advantage. He was a man of abilities in his profession, but his parts were more solid than brilliant, or even clear. He was rather a good Chancellor than a great statesman. His integrity and diligence in office were with reason commended. He was too diffident and compliant with King William to make any splendid figure beyond his own line of the law. His complaisance to the King's humor, his flattering him in his very errors, his feeble manner of recommending what seemed right to his own judgment, bore more the appearance of a convenient than of an able servant. Upon the whole he seemed more calculated to smooth the current of business by amending and softening measures already adopted, than to propose and execute those spirited and manly expedients which times of faction seem to demand at the hands of a great minister."[2]

Swift, in his History of the Four Last Years of Queen Anne, tries to depreciate, but is forced to praise him:—

"The Lord Somers may very deservedly be reputed the head and oracle of that party: he has raised himself, by the concurrence of many circumstances, to the greatest employments of the state, without the least support from birth or fortune: he has constantly, and with great steadiness, cultivated those principles under which he grew. . . I have hardly known any man with talents more proper to acquire and preserve the favor of a prince; never offending in word or gesture; in the highest degree corteous and complaisant: wherein he set an example to his colleagues, which they did not think fit to follow; but

---

[1] We have seen his munificence to his college, and his contribution to fit out Captain Kid—which was wickedly made a ground of impeachment against him; and Evelyn tells us that, in 1696, he subscribed £500 to Greenwich Hospital.—*Evelyn*, ii. 55.

[2] Macph. Hist. G. Brit. ii. 182.

this extreme civility is universal and undistinguished ; and in private conversation, where he observes it as inviolably as if he were in the greatest assembly, it is sometimes censured as formal. Two reasons are assigned for this behavior; first, from the consciousness of his humble original, he keeps all familiarity at the greatest distance, which otherwise might be apt to intrude; the second that being sensible how subject he is to violent passions, he avoids all incitements to them, by watching those he converses with, from his own example to keep a great way within the bounds of decency and respect. And it is indeed true, that no man is more apt to take fire upon the least appearance of provocation ; which temper he strives to subdue with the utmost violence upon himself; so that his breast has been seen to heave, and his eyes to sparkle with rage in those very moments when his words and the cadence of his voice were in the humblest and softest manner; perhaps that force upon his nature may cause that insatiable love of revenge which his detractors lay to his charge, who consequently reckon dissimulation among his chief perfections. Avarice he has none ; and his ambition is gratified by being the uncontested head of his party. With an excellent understanding, adorned by all the polite parts of learning, he has very little taste for conversation, to which he prefers the pleasure of reading and thinking; and in the intervals of his time amuses himself with an illiterate chaplain, an humble companion, or a favorite servant." [1]

The Dean, afterwards, when he had sunk into misanthropy, thus speaks of Somers in a letter to Bolingbroke,[2] where he has been enumerating men of genius who have been unfortunate. " I remember but one exception, and that was Lord Somers, whose timorous nature, joined with the trade of a common lawyer, and the consciousness

---

[1] Swift, in his notes on Davis's "Characters of the Court of Queen Anne," clearly discloses his malignity. "LORD SOMERS: of a creditable family in the city of Worcester," [*very mean : his father was a noted rogue.*] "He is supposed to have been the best Chancellor that ever sat in the chair." [*I allow him to have possessed all excellent qualifications, except virtue ; he had violent passions, and hardly subdued them by his great prudence.*] Yet Swift had courted his society, and had complained of nothing except his *formality*. " I soon grew domestic with Lord Halifax, and was as often with Lord Somers as the formality of his nature (the only unconversable fault he had) made it agreeable to me."—*Memoirs relating to change in Queen Anne's Ministry.*

[2] Dec. 19, 1719.

of a mean extraction, had taught him the regularity of an alderman, or a gentleman-usher."

We must now hear his defenders, beginning with Isaac Bickerstaff, who wished Lord Somers to be prime minister:—" If I were to wish for a proper person to preside over the public councils, it should certainly be one as much admired for his universal knowledge of men and things, as for his eloquence, courage and integrity in the exerting of such extraordinary talents.[1]

Horace Walpole, who must have heard him so often described by Sir Robert, thus among his Royal and Noble Authors describes—" John, Lord Somers. One of those divine men, who, like a chapel in a palace, remain unprofaned, while all the rest is tyranny, corruption, and folly. All the traditional accounts of him, the historians of the last age and its best authors, represent him as the most incorrupt lawyer and the honestest statesman, as a master orator, a genius of the finest taste, and as a patriot of the noblest and most extensive views; as a man who dispensed blessings by his life and planned them for posterity."[2]

The impartial Tindal describes the Chancellor of King William :—" As he was one of the ablest and most incorrupt Judges that ever presided in Chancery, so his great capacity for all affairs made the King consider him beyond all his ministers; and he well deserved the confidence that the King expressed for him on all occasions."[3]

The Tory Smollet can not deny the merits of Somers:—" He was skilled in the law, as in many other branches of polite and useful literature. He possessed a remarkable talent for business, in which he exerted great patience and assiduity; was gentle, candid, and equitable; a Whig in principles, yet moderate, pacific, and conciliating."[4]

Nay, the venomous Ralph, who is disposed to abuse every man of liberal principles, is compelled thus to characterize a Whig leader:—" In his capacity of Chancellor, Lord Somers is undoubtedly irreproachable : and he that did not acknowledge his abilities in state affairs, must either have none of his own, or, through prejudice and

[1] Tatler, No. 130, 7th Feb. 1710. [2] Works, vol. i. 430.
[3] Tind. Cont. Rap. xiv. 445. [4] Smol. i. 166.

perverseness, must have forfeited the use of them. It was to his abilities as a statesman as well as a lawyer he owed his advancement. Whether advising as a minister, or standing in the circle as courtier, presiding in the House of Lords as Speaker, conferring or altercating with foreign ministers, giving dispatch to suitors, or doing the honors of his table, where he 'became all things to all men,' he was the most extraordinary man of his time."[1]

Unlike Lord Thurlow, and others who, having contrived to be celebrated in their own age, have been undervalued by posterity, the fame of the subject of this memoir has gone on increasing from generation to generation, in proportion as his character and his public services have been examined, and as the science of government has been better understood. "Lord Somers," says Mackintosh, "seems to have nearly realized the perfect model of a wise statesman in a free community. His end was public liberty: he employed every talent and resource which were necessary for his end and not prohibited by the rules of morality. His regulating principle was usefulness. His quiet and refined mind rather shrunk from popular applause. He preserved the most intrepid steadiness, with a disposition so mild, that his friends thought it mildness excessive, and his enemies supposed that it could be scarcely natural."[2] Lord John Russell observes that "Somers is a bright example of a statesman who could live in times of revolution without rancor, who could hold the highest posts in a Court without meanness, and who could unite mildness and charity to his opponents, with the firmest attachment to the great principles of liberty, civil and religious, which he had early espoused, long promoted, and never abandoned."[3] And Lord Mahon, in language more impressive than a labored panegyric, referring to Lord Somers, exclaims, "I know not where to find a more upright and unsullied character than his. He had contracted nothing of the venality and baseness of the age."[4]

I may add the sincere though poetical tribute of Warton, in his address to Lord Chatham, upon "Trinity College, Oxford," the place of education of our two most distinguished patriots:—

[1] Ralph, ii. 784.
[2] History of Europe.
[3] Life of Mackintosh.
[4] History of England.

> "In that calm bower which nurs'd thy thoughtful youth
> In the firm precepts of Athenian truth,
> Where first the form of British liberty
> Beam'd in full radiance on thy musing eye—
> That form sublime, whose mien with equal awe
> In the same shade unblemish'd SOMERS saw."

I shall conclude with the crowning testimony of Addison, in the "FREEHOLDER," which, be it remembered, was offered when Somers had been consigned to the tomb, and had left no one to bear his name:—
"He had worn himself out in his application to such studies as made him useful or ornamental to the world, in concerting schemes for the welfare of his country, and in prosecuting such measures as were necessary for making those schemes effectual; but all this was done with a view to the public good that should rise of these generous endeavors, and not to the fame that should accrue to himself. Let the reputation of the action fall where it would, so his country reaped the benefit of it, he was satisfied. As this turn of mind threw off, in a great measure, the oppositions of envy and competition, it enabled him to gain the most vain and impracticable into his designs, and to bring about several great events for the safety and advantage of the public, which must have died in the birth had he been as desirous of appearing beneficial to mankind as of being so. His life was in every part of it set off with that graceful modesty and reserve, which made his virtues more beautiful the more they were cast in such agreeable shades. His great humanity appeared in the minutest circumstances of his conversation. You found it in the benevolence of his aspect, the complacency of his behavior, and the tone of his voice. His great application to the severer studies of the law had not infected his temper with anything positive or litigious; he did not know what it was to wrangle on indifferent points, to triumph in the superiority of his understanding, or to be supercilious on the side of the truth. He joined the greatest delicacy of good breeding to the greatest strength of reason. By improving the sentiments of a person with whom he conversed, in such particulars as were just, he won him over from those points in which he was mistaken; and had so agreeable a way of conveying knowledge, that whoever conferred with him grew the wiser, without perceiving that he had been instructed

His principles were founded in reason and supported by virtue, and therefore did not lie at the mercy of ambition, avarice, or resentment. His notions were no less steady and unshaken, than just and upright. In a word, he concluded his course among the same well-chosen friendships and alliances with which he began it."[1]

This writer, as the climax of his eulogy, seizes upon the great felicity of Lord Somers,—that throughout a long public life he ever steadily adhered to the same principles and to the same party. Respectable politicians have seen reason to adopt a policy which they have long opposed, and, abandoning early associates, to join those whom they have been accustomed boisterously to assail; but although such changes may admit of defense or apology, surely he is most to be envied whose consistent conduct can be liable to no reproach or suspicion,—even should it have prevented his rise, instead of leading him to fame and to power. Lord Somers, like the great Prince whom he served, was most fortunate in this, that duty and ambition always concurred in pointing out the straightforward path for him to tread. His course may therefore be considered more uniformly virtuous, and more truly noble, than that of any man who ever held the Great Seal of England.

Lord Somers not having been married, his title died with him. His heirs were his two sisters, one of whom was married to Charles Cocks, Esquire, of Castleditch, and the other to Sir Joseph Jekyll, the Master of the Rolls. From the former is descended the present Earl Somers, whose grandfather was created Baron Somers in 1784, and whose father, in 1821, was raised to the Earldom.[2]

CHAPTER CXII.

LIFE OF LORD KEEPER WRIGHT.

IT seems strange that I should have to introduce into my list of Lord Chancellors and Lord Keepers of the Great Seal a man so little prominent either for abilities or crimes. To his obscurity he owed his promotion.

[1] Freeholder, No. 39.   [2] Grandeur of the Law, 100.

Burnet, in describing the perplexity which, on the removal of Lord Somers, arose about the appointment of a successor, and the necessity for a temporary commission, says, "They thought that all the great men of the law were aspiring to that high post, so that any one to whom it should be offered would certainly accept it; but they soon found that they were mistaken, for, what by reason of the instability of the Court, what by reason of the just apprehension men might have of succeeding so great a man, all to whom the Seals were offered excused themselves. After a few days they were given to Sir NATHAN WRIGHT, in whom there was nothing equal to the post, much less to him who had lately filled it."[1] The occasional occurrence of such elevations seems wisely contrived by Providence to humble the vanity of those who succeed in public life, and to soften the mortification of those who fail. But this dull man actually held the Great Seal above five years, acting as Lord Keeper to two English monarchs; and it therefore becomes my duty to give some account of his origin and of his career.

Sir Nathan Wright was the son of a clergyman, the Rev. Ezekiel Wright, B.D., Rector of Thurcaston, in the county of Leicester, where he was born on the 11th of February, 1653. In 1668 he was entered of Emanuel College, Cambridge, but I find nothing more of him academically. He studied the law for seven years in the Inner Temple, and is said to have attended diligently at "moots" and "readings." His father died when he was very young, leaving him a moderate fortune. Upon this, in his twenty-third year, he married, and, while it lasted, he rather neglected his profession; but, alarmed by an increasing family and decreasing means, he looked out for clients, and he acquired a considerable share of plodding business. Although he found it convenient to turn out a very stanch Tory, he seems to have started as a Whig, for, having been elected Recorder of Leicester in 1680, he was removed from the office, and replaced by the Earl of Huntingdon, in the year 1685, the town being then deprived of its charter:—and he was reappointed in 1688, when municipal corporations were revived on the approach of the Prince of Orange.

In 1692, he was called to the degree of Sergeant at

[1] Burnet, iii. 335.

Law, with thirteen other utter barristers to whom Lord Commissioner Trevor, when they delivered their rings to him in the Court of Chancery, addressed an eloquent discourse on the duties of their new degree. He now had a controversy (and it then seemed probable that he never would be engaged in one more important), " whether he was entitled to precedence over his brother Bonithon, to whom he was junior as a barrister, but whose writ was tested after his, although the writs were returnable the same day?" The future Lord Keeper succeeded in this noble strife against "brother Bonithon,"—and yet the same question being afterwards raised before himself holding the Great Seal, on another call of Sergeants,—to the horror of Westminster Hall he decided in favor of "ancienty of standing " against " priority of writ."[1]

Professing to support the Government,—in 1696, by the favor of Lord Somers, he was called within the bar as King's Sergeant, and he received the honor of knighthood. He practiced almost exclusively in the Court of Common Pleas, except when "riding the Midland Circuit," but notice is taken of a few extraordinary cases in which he was employed. On the trial of the Earl of Warwick before the Peers, for murder, he was leading counsel for the Crown, but he satisfied himself with reading over the indictment, leaving the statement of the case to the Attorney General;[2]—he made a speech to the jury, in prosecuting a lady at the Old Bailey for forging a bond for £40,000, and obtained a conviction, with a sentence of fine—forgery being then only a misdemeanor at common law,[3] and he gained some little distinction by what really appears to have been rather a spirited harangue, delivered by him at the bar of the House of Commons, in support of the Duke of Norfolk's divorce, which was supposed to have carried the bill through, notwithstanding a strong opposition to it.[4] But he never was himself a member of parliament, and, hardly aspiring to be a puisne Judge, much less Attorney or Solicitor General, his real ambition was to retain his snug business at the bar, and "to die a Nisi Prius leader."[5]

[1] See 1 Lord Raymond, 604. In a note to "Nicholls's Leicester," it is observed that "perhaps, in the language of Plowden, he would say, '*that when he was to determine for another, not for himself, the case was altered.*'"
[2] 13 St. Tr. 939, 954.   [3] Ibid. 1250.   [4] Ibid. 1355.
[5] Memoirs of Mr. Surrebutter's professional career:

What then must have been his astonishment when, in the month of May, 1700, he received an offer of the Great Seal! We must consider how many had already refused it; that he was considered a sound lawyer; that previous equity training was not then much thought of; that he was a man of decent character; that he professed high church principles, which were now gaining the ascendency; and that, seeing the decline of the Whigs, he had for some time renounced all their errors. It is said that even *he* hesitated before he would agree to touch the Great Seal (in such bad odor was it); but he had lately had a severe fit of illness, which rendered it doubtful whether he could much longer undergo the fatigues of bar-practice. He consented, therefore,—and without trying to make any stipulation for peerage, grant, or pension.

The Great Seal was delivered to him by King William at Hampton Court, on the 21st of May, 1700, and he was at the same time sworn a Privy Councillor.[1]

I do not find any record of his inauguration in Westminster Hall, but this, no doubt, took place about a fortnight afterwards, on the first day of Trinity Term. He showed a laudable consciousness of his own deficiency, by having a treatise compiled for him to teach him the rudiments of Equity. This MS. is extant, and is entitled "Rules and Practice in the Court of Chancery, with a Complete Index." At the conclusion is the following memorandum:—"N.B. This Tract was drawn up for the use of Sir Nathan Wright when he was made Lord Keeper."

In the first important case which came before him he got wrong.[2] A testator having bequeathed "£15 a-piece to each of his relations of his father's and mother's side," left several cousins-german, some of whom had children,

"Deaf as a post, and thick as mustard,
He aim'd at wit, and bawl'd and bluster'd,
And died a Nisi Prius leader—
That genius was my Special Pleader."

[1] LONDON GAZETTE.—"Hampton Court, May 21, 1700. His Majesty in Council was this day pleased to commit the custody of the Great Seal to the Right Honorable Sir Nathan Wright, Knight, one of his Majesty's Sergeants-at-Law, with the Title of Lord Keeper of the Great Seal of England; and the usual oaths of Privy Councillor and Lord Keeper being administered to him accordingly, he took his place at the board
[2] *Jones* v. *Beale*, T. T. 1700; 2 Vern. 381.

and the question was " whether these children were relations of the testator within the meaning of the bequest.' The Lord Keeper held that they were; and they had their £15 a-piece as well as their parents. There was no appeal, probably from the small amount of the sums in dispute; but it was before understood, and it has often been decided since, that such a bequest is limited to relations who would take as next of kin under the "Statute of Distributions."[1]

One of the most remarkable decrees pronounced by him while he was in office, was that for dissolving the Savoy (July 13, 1702); and in the same year (Nov. 30) he reversed a decision of his great predecessor, Lord Somers, touching a right of dower. On a bill of review brought upon this reversal, Lord Cowper, C., declared, that as the title of the widow to dower was a point of right so doubtful that the Court had held different opinions, and as the decree last made had been so long unquestioned, his Lordship did not think fit to vary it.[2]

The case before Lord Keeper Wright which excited the greatest interest was one of the same class as *Stradling* v. *Stiles*, respecting the "pye-balled horses."[3] Here the words were, " I give my house, and all the goods and furniture therein, to my son Robert, *except the pictures, which I give to my sons James and Edward*."[4] The testator had been a very great picture fancier, and was constantly changing his pictures. He bought many after making his will, and he had many pictures hung in a gallery, and many packed up in boxes in the house. The Lord Keeper held, with general approbation, that the whole of the pictures of which the testator died possessed went to James and Edward.

He seems to have been very cautious; and, although his insufficiency was often dwelt upon, he was allowed to mean fairly. I find only one of his decrees reversed on

[1] *Gayer* v. *Gayer*, 2 Vern. 558.
[2] 5th Dec. 1715, it was finally affirmed in Dom. Proc. on appeal. Journals, H. of Lords, vol. xx. p. 458; 2 Br. P. C. 597, fol. ed.; *Laurence* v. *Laurence*, 1 Freeman, 234.
[3] Reported by Martinus Scriblerus, where the question was "whether, under a bequest of all the testator's *black and white horses*, PYE-BALLED horses should pass."
[4] *Roach* v. *Hammond*, Pre. Ch. 401; Anon. 1 P. Wms. 327; *Harding* v. *Glyn*, 1 Atk. 469; *Smith* v. *Campbell*, 19 Vesey, 400; Coop. 275.

appeal.¹ On questions of difficulty he prudently called in the assistance of Holt, and other common-law judges.² Although there were always heavy complaints of his slowness, he contrived for some time to get through the business of the Court with decent credit: but arrears grew upon him, and his health declining, "the delays of Chancery" were resounded more loudly than at any former period, and before the end of his five years, there was a general wish that the Great Seal should be taken from such feeble hands.

On the 20th of June, 1700, he first sat Speaker in the Lords, and he constantly occupied the woolsack during the sittings of the House, while he continued to hold the Great Seal—merely putting the question, and having no influence over their proceedings.

On the prosecution of Lord Somers and the late ministers impeached along with him, the Lord Keeper was very unwillingly the organ of the House of Lords in announcing their Lordships' "Resolutions," which refused the requisition of the Commons for the appointment of a joint committee to regulate the trials—which called upon them peremptorily to proceed to make good their charge —and which pronounced a verdict of acquittal.³ Having been brought forward by the Tories, he naturally attached himself zealously to that party, and was very desirous that the Whig leader should be convicted.

As often as the King went abroad, the Lord Keeper was appointed a Lord Justice, coming in the commission of regency after the Archbishop of Canterbury, the Princess Anne being still excluded; but during this reign, even when the Tories were most powerful, he was not at all listened to in the Cabinet, and he seldom ventured to offer any opinion, unless it were for more severe measures against the Dissenters.

When the reaction took place on the recognition by

¹ *Earl of Huntington* v. *Countess of Huntington*, 2 Vern. 437, respecting the redemption of a mortgage. He seems to have exercised an independent judgment in putting the Great Seal to commissions which the Government wished to pass. Vernon, under date June 29, 1700, speaking of the commissions to authorize the ships of the East India Company to capture pirates, says—" My Lord Jersey lately sent one of these commissions to my Lord Keeper, with a warrant to affix the Great Seal to it; but he boggles at it, and takes it to be illegal."

² See *Needham* v. *Smith*, 2 Vern. 463.   ³ Ante, p. 46.

Louis XIV. of the Prince of Wales as King of Great Britain, and a Whiggish House of Commons was about to assemble, Lord Keeper Wright was under constant apprehension of speedy dismission, and his worst fears seemed confirmed by the mortifying fact that, without himself being consulted, the King's speech was prepared by the ex-Chancellor, Lord Somers. But his position was very suddenly altered by the death of William, before the contemplated changes in the government could be carried into effect.

Wright had been represented to Anne as a devoted friend to the Church, and upon her accession she was much pleased with the thought of having him for "Keeper of her Conscience,"—more especially on account of the very strong prejudice which she had been taught to foster against his predecessor.

At her first Council, held on the day of William's death, Sir Nathan Wright surrendering the Great Seal into her hands, she instantly returned it to him, with the title of Lord Keeper, saying, "that she would not have done so, if there had been a worthier man in the kingdom to whom she could have delivered it." He was again publicly installed in the office, on the first day the Courts sat in the following Easter Term.[1]

Marlborough and Godolphin being now completely absorbed in foreign affairs, and resolved to carry on the plans of the GRAND ALLIANCE, which their party had strongly condemned while in opposition, left for a time the administration of the government at home very much in the hands of the Lord Keeper, and the more violent high-church section of the Cabinet. The consequence was that Lord Somers was not allowed to be sworn of the Privy Council to the Queen, and that his name was struck out of the commission of the peace, even in his native county. At the same time, many magistrates were removed who had been appointed while he held the Great

[1] "1702, April 29—(being the first day the Courts sat in Westminster this term by reason of her Maj. writts of adjournment).

"*Sir Nathan Wrighte* having immediately after the decease of the late King delivered the Great Seal to her present Majesty, Queen Anne, and received it from her again as Lord Keeper, came this 29th of April into the Court of Chancery, accompanied with the Master of the Rolls, Judges, King's Sergeants, and Councill, and there standing in his place before he entered upon business, took the oath of the Lord Keeper of the Great Seal of England, the Master of the Rolls holding the book, the oath being read by George Wrighte, Clerk of the Crown." Fol. 144. Roll 1701-1714.

Seal, for being well affected to the Revolution; and they were replaced by others who labored under the suspicion of Jacobitism. This system appears to have been acted upon to a great extent for a long while, but at last (as we shall see) it drew down the strong animadversion of parliament.

Although Wright's influence was now supposed to be much greater than it had been under William, he does not seem to have interfered beyond the exercise of the functions immediately connected with his office. He had nothing to do with the Queen's speech at the opening and close of the session beyond handing it to her Majesty, and he never addressed the two Houses except when announcing the prorogation in her name.

The only opportunity he had for oratorical display was in returning thanks, by order of the House, to the Duke of Marlborough for the great victories obtained over the French. Thus, on the hero's return after the battle of Blenheim, we find the following entry in the journals:—
"The House understanding that his Grace, the Duke of Marlborough was come to town; and being very sensible of the great and singular service done by him to her Majesty and this kingdom, and the honor he has done to the English nation: It is thereupon ordered by the Lords Spiritual and Temporal in Parliament assembled, that the Lord Keeper of the Great Seal of England do (when the Duke of Marlborough is present) give him the thanks of this House for the same."

Accordingly, on the following day, the Duke being present, in his place, Lord Keeper Wright thus addressed him:—

" My Lord Duke of Marlborough,

"The happy success that has attended her Majesty's arms, under your Grace's command, in Germany, the last campaign, is so truly great, so truly glorious in all its circumstances, that few instances in the history of former ages can equal, much less excel, the luster of it.

"Your Grace has not overthrown young, unskillful generals, raw and undisciplined troops; but your Grace has conquered the French and Bavarian armies; armies that were fully instructed in all the arts of war, select veteran troops, flushed with former victories, and commanded by generals of great experience and bravery.

"The glorious victories your Grace has obtained at Schallenburgh and Hochstet are very great, very illustrious, in themselves; but they are greater still in the consequences to her Majesty and to her allies. The Emperor is thereby relieved; the empire itself is freed from a dangerous enemy in the very bowels of it; the exorbitant power of France is checked; and, I hope, a happy step made towards the reducing of that monarch within his due bounds, and securing the liberties of Europe.

"The honor of these glorious victories, great as they are, under the immediate blessing of Almighty God, is chiefly, if not alone, owing to your Grace's conduct and valor.

"This is the unanimous voice of England, and of all her Majesty's allies.

"My Lord, this most honorable House is highly sensible of the great and signal services your Grace has done her Majesty in this campaign, and of the immortal honor you have done the English nation; and have commanded me to give your Grace thanks for the same; and I do accordingly give your Grace the thanks of this House for the great honor your Grace has done the nation, and the great and signal services which you have done her Majesty and this kingdom in the last campaign."

When the dispute arose between the two Houses in the Aylesbury case, the Lord Keeper was strongly inclined to take the part of the Commons, but he had no opportunity of expressing his opinion in the House of Lords, being confined to put the question upon the reversal of the judgment in *Ashby* v. *White*, and upon the several resolutions against the right of the other plaintiffs to bring actions for the corrupt rejection of their votes. It is rather surprising that he was not raised to the peerage, that he might answer the ex-Chancellor in debate. This would have been agreeable to the Queen; but from his deficiency in speaking, and his want of constitutional learning and general information, his colleagues thought it more prudent to keep him silent. Had he possessed much courage he might have gained great distinction, for he might have liberated, by his own single authority in the Court of Chancery, Paty and the others who were committed by the Commons. After they had been remanded by the Court of Queen's Bench, they applied to him for a writ of *habeas corpus,* which was granted by him.¹ But his heart failed him. The Commons immediately resolved "that no commoner of England committed by the House of Commons for breach of privilege, or contempt of that House, ought to be by any writ of *habeas corpus* made to appear in any other place, or before any other judicature, during that session of parliament wherein such person was so committed; that the Sergeant-at-arms do make no return of, or yield any obedience to, any such writ of *habeas corpus*, and for such his refusal that he have the protection of the House of Commons; and that the Lord Keeper be acquainted with the said resolutions, to the end that any such writ of *habeas corpus* may be superseded as contrary to the laws and privileges of this House."

The Lords construed these resolutions into a threat to commit their Speaker; and, in an address to the Crown, drawn by Lord Somers say, "The Lord Keeper is a commoner; and if he disobeys, it is a breach of privilege: that if they should carry it so far as to order him into custody, he may seek, but is not to have, relief from any *habeas corpus*."

Wright seems to have been afraid of being sent to prison, or to have been swayed by a wish to support his Tory partisans in the House of Commons, for he called a meeting of the Judges, and they, with the exception of Holt, having concurred in the opinion that "neither the Keeper of the Great Seal, nor any Judge or Court of Justice, could examine a commitment by either house of parliament for a breach of privilege," he refused to liber-

---

[1] "ANNA Dei gratiâ Ang. Sco. Fran. et Hiber. Regina, Fidei Defensor, &c. Samueli Powel serv. ad arma attend. Honorab. Dom. Com. ejus deputato et deputatis, Salutem. Precipimus vobis et cuilibet vestrum quod corpus Jacobi Montague Ar. nuper capt. et in custod. vestra vel alicujus vel unius vestrum ut dicitur detent. sub salvo et securo conduct. una cum die et causa captionis et detentionis pred. Jac. Montague quocunque nomine idem Jac. Montague censaetur in eadem, habeatis seu aliquis vel unus vestrum neat cor. predilecto et fidel. nostro prehonorab. Nathan Wright Mil. Dom. Cust. Mag Sig. nostri Angl. apud Dom. Mansional. suam in parochia Sancti Egidii in Campis in com. Midd. immediate post acception. hujus brevis ad faciend subjaciend. et recipiend. ea omnia et singula quæ dictus dominus Custos Mag Sig. nostri Angl. de eo adtunc ibidem cons. in hac parte. Et habeatis aliquis vel unus vestrum habeat ibi hoc breve. Teste meipso apud Westm. sexto die Martii anno regni nostri tertio."

Indorsed—"Per statum tricesism. prim. Caroli Secundi Regis.
"N. WRIGHT, C. S."

ate the Aylesbury men, and they remained in custody till the prorogation. When the Crown was petitioned for a writ of error to the House of Lords upon the judgment of the Court of Queen's Bench, " quod cognito captionis et detentionis prædictæ non pertinet ad curiam Dominæ Reginæ," all the Judges except one having given an opinion that the writ was demandable, *ex debito justitiæ*, leaving the question to be decided thereafter whether a writ of error lay,—and the Lords having resolved that it was for them, upon the argument of the writ of error, to determine whether it lay, and not for the Crown by refusing it,—he showed very little spirit by not immediately issuing one under the Great Seal, which was his peculiar function; but he hesitated, and the House of Lords having addressed the Queen to direct the writ of error to issue, he concurred in advising her equivocating answer: " My Lords, I should have granted the writ of error desired by this address, but, finding it absolutely necessary to put an immediate end to this session, I am sensible there could have been no further proceedings upon it." [1] A dissolution of parliament soon followed.

Although the Tories had been so powerful in the House of Commons, Marlborough and Godolphin had been gradually leaving that party, and, adopting not only the foreign policy but the principles of domestic administration of the Whigs, were admitting Whig leaders into the Cabinet as fast as the prejudices of the Queen would permit. The brilliant success of the war against France had given great popularity to those who planned it, and the elections went very much in their favor. " When the elections were all over, the Court took more heart ; for it appeared that they were sure of a great majority, and the Lord Godolphin declared himself more openly than he had done formerly in favor of the Whigs. The first instance given of this was the dismissing of Wright, who had continued so long Lord Keeper that he was fallen under a high degree of contempt with all sides,—even the Tories, though he was wholly theirs, despising him." [2]

Even if the general character of the administration had remained unchanged, he must soon have been removed, notwithstanding the liking that the Queen had conceived for him. In the session of 1704, he had been much

---

[1] 14 St. T. 695-890 ; 6 Parl. Hist. 376-436.   [2] Burnet, iv. 122.

damaged by a motion in the House of Lords respecting his appointment and removal of magistrates. " Many gentlemen of good estates and ancient families had been of late put out of the commission, for no other visible reason but because they had gone in heartily to the Revolution, and had continued zealous for the late King. This seemed done on design to mark them, and to lessen the interest they had in the election of members of parliament; and, at the same time, men of no worth, nor estate, and known to be ill affected to the Queen's title, and to the Protestant succession, were put in, to the great encouragement of ill-designing men. An address was moved to the Queen, complaining of the commissions of the peace, in which the Lords delivered their opinion that such as would not serve or act under the late King were not fit to serve her Majesty."[1] In the course of the debate, it came out that the name of Lord Somers having been removed from all commissions of the peace, had never yet been restored, even for the county in which he was born, or that in which he resided. The vote, which was carried, amounted to an address for the dismissal of the holder of the Great Seal, thus charged with having abused its powers.[2]

If, by such proceedings, he made himself obnoxious to one party, he ingratiated himself with another. But he incurred the contempt of all sides by his vacillation and pusillanimity in the Aylesbury case, and the delays in the Court of Chancery were now such as to amount to a denial of justice.

For all these reasons, before the new parliament assembled, the Great Seal was taken from him, and delivered to that great orator, lawyer and statesman, WILLIAM COWPER. The difficulty was to reconcile the Queen to this transfer, but it was at last accomplished through the influence of the Duchess of Marlborough, which was still irresistible. Sarah represents the whole as her own do-

[1] Burnet, 53.
[2] Sir Nathan, nailed to the woolsack, with his tongue tied, must have felt very uncomfortable during this debate, in which he was so spoken at. Vernon, in a letter dated May 31, 1704, thus describes it: "My Lord Keeper had many rubs given him about persons put in and left out of the commissions; particularly that my Lord Somers was left out of the commission of the peace for Worcestershire, which they told him was the more scandalous, since that Lord had sat on the woolsack with more reputation than those that came either before him or after him."

ing, although on this occasion she was only acting as prompted by her husband and Godolphin. "I prevailed with her Majesty to take the Great Seal from Sir Nathan Wright, a man despised by all parties, of no use to the Crown, and whose weak and wretched conduct in the Court of Chancery had almost brought his very office into contempt."[1]

During his tenure of office he had amassed immense wealth, and he immediately retired to one of the estates he had purchased, Chaldecott, in Warwickshire.[2] There he lived in complete seclusion till he died, almost forgotten, on the 4th of August, 1721.[3]

He was buried in the parish church, where there was erected to his memory an elegant tablet of white marble, bearing his arms finely emblazoned, with his motto "UNICA VIRTUS NOBILITAS," and the following inscription:—

"M. S.
PRÆNOBILIS VIRI D. NATHAN WRIGHT, EQ. AUR.
QUI QUINQUE ANNOS
MAGISTRATU FUNCTUS DNI CUSTODIS M. SIGILLI ANGLIÆ
ÆQUUS ET INTEGER, AC TANTO NIHIL IMPAR MUNERI.
SEDECIM PROPE ANNOS, QUOS EXINDE VIXIT,
FAMÆ SATUR ET QUAM MODICI COMPOS VOTI
EX ANIMO RURA COLUIT VICINA
PIUS ET HUMANUS,
A QUOQUE BONO ET PRUDENTI DESIDERATISSIMUS
OBIT AUGUSTI 4o ANNO DNI. 1721, ÆTAT. SUÆ 68."

We need not dispute that he was amiable in private life, but it is only the piety of a descendant which could prompt the assertion that he was "well qualified for his office." Another panegyrist is John Dunton, who, after

---

[1] She adds, satirically: "His removal, however, was a great loss to the Church, for which he had ever been a warm stickler. And this loss was the more sensibly felt, as his successor, My Lord Cowper, was not only of the Whig party, but of such abilities and integrity as brought a new credit to it in the nation."—*Account of her Conduct*, p. 159.

[2] He likewise bought Brakesly, Hurtshill, and other large estates in Leicestershire.—*Nich. Leicest.* ii. 194; iv. 1036.

[3] It has been supposed that he resumed his practice at the bar, because, in December, 1710, Catherine Hall, Cambridge, having taken the opinion of Sir Edward Northey, the Attorney General, on a question in which they were interested, stated that they were in possession of an opinion given at the same time by Sir Nathan Wright, in which he referred to, and expressed his concurrence in the opinion of Sir E. Northey. But the ex-Lord Keeper must have been consulted only as a friend of the College; and, as *his opinion cost nothing*, according to the well-known maxim, probably *it was worth nothing*. See 2 Russ. & Myl. Ch. Rep. 599.

extolling his talents and virtues, says, "In a word, he excels in every grace; but his great humility is the most shining character of all his actions, and his large charity the most useful:" unfortunately adding this climax,— "and Mr. Luke Dunton, my brother, had an honorable post by his recommendation."[1]

Burnet says, "Wright was a zealot to the party, and was become very exceptionable in all respects: money, as was said, did everything with him; only in his court I never heard him charged for anything but great slowness, by which the Chancery was become one of the heaviest grievances of the nation.[2] He was sordidly covetous, and did not at all live suitably to that high post. He became extremely rich, yet I never heard him charged with bribery in his Court, but there was a foul rumor with relation to the livings of the Crown that were given by the Great Seal, as if they were set to sale by the officers under him."[3]

In Davis's Character's of the Court of Queen Anne there is the following account of him: "SIR NATHAN, WRIGHT is son of a clergyman; a good common lawyer, a slow Chancellor, and no civilian. Chance more than choice brought him the Seals."[4] Granger says, "He was one of those characters that sometimes chance makes great. When Lord Somers resigned, never was such a change. The very men who had erected were ashamed of worshipping the idol they had set up. This weak but incorruptible man presided in Chancery until 1705, when he was fairly hooted out of it, and Cowper, a luminary, succeeded him. What a figure does he make between two such characters as Somers and Cowper!"[5]

To show his wit as well as his honesty, an anecdote of him is related which I must not suppress, lest, in not discovering point in his joke, the dullness should be imputable to the biographer. "A watchmaker who had a cause depending in Chancery, a day or two before it was likely to come on, sent the Lord Keeper a present of a very fine time-piece; but the upright Judge returned it, with this message:—'*I have no doubt of the goodness of the piece, but it has one motion too much for me.*'"[6]

---

[1] Life and Errors, p. 428.   [2] Burnet, iv. 55.   [3] Ibid. 122.
[4] Swift, in his notes on this work, adds "*very covetous.*"
[5] Granger, by Noble, i. 35.   [6] Ibid.

While he was at the head of the law, there was a considerable improvement introduced into the administration of criminal justice, the credit of which may be due to him, although, from his having no voice in parliament, we do not exactly know how he viewed it. In early ages, a person accused of treason or felony was not allowed to produce witnesses in his defense, and down to the beginning of the reign of Queen Anne, although witnesses might be heard for the prisoner, they were examined unsworn, so that little attention was paid to the testimony. But by 1 Anne, stat. 2, c. 9, it was enacted, "that in all cases of treason and felony witnesses for the prisoner shall be examined upon oath, in like manner as the witnesses against him." So slowly does prejudice give way, that near a century and a half still elapsed before he was allowed the benefit of counsel.

Sir Nathan Wright was sufficiently eminent as Lord Keeper to be made the subject of a satire, entitled, " THE COUNTRY PARSON'S HONEST ADVICE TO THAT JUDICIOUS LAWYER AND WORTHY MINISTER OF STATE, MY LORD KEEPER WRIGHT," of which the following may be taken as a fair specimen :—

> " Be wise as Somerset, as Somers brave,
> As Pembroke airy, and as Richmond grave,
> Humble as Orford be, and Wharton's zeal
> For Church and Loyalty would fit thee well,
> Like Sarum I would have thee love the Church,
> He scorns to leave his mother in the lurch;
> For the well governing your family
> Let pious Haversham your pattern be,
> And if it be thy fate again to marry,
> And S—q—r's daughter will thy year out tarry,
> May'st thou use her as Mohun his tender wife,
> And may she lead his virtuous Lady's Life:
> To sum up all, Devonshire's Chastity,
> Bolton's Merit, Godolphin's Probity,
> Halifax his Modesty, Essex's Sense,
> Montague's Management, Culpepper's pence,
> Tenison's Learning, and Southampton's Wit,
> Will make thee for an able statesman fit."

Soon after came out, " THE LOCUSTS, or CHANCERY PAINTED TO THE LIFE: A POEM." The poet, after praising some of the common-law judges, thus proceeds :—

> " Enough of law, my Muse, now Satyr rise
> And show how Chanc'rys stock'd with villanies;
> Let bitter'st gall for ink supply thy pen,
> Spare not their crimes, but lash the worst of men;

> Accursed crew! oh! could I make 'em feel
> My biting words like wounds of perfect steel,
> That on their harden'd consciences I may
> Like the tormenting vultures ever prey;
> Or punish them as Mida's was of old,
> By turning every limb of them to gold."

He then comes, in ironical strains, to the Lord Keeper and the reforms of the Court of Chancey :—

> "Hold, Satyr, stop the venom of thy sting,
> Rise, brighter Muse, and of TREBONIUS sing;
> Tell all the world how justice fills that seat,
> Makes England happy, and TREBONIUS great.
> Does he not guide his conscience by the law,
> And by that conscience keep base rogues in awe?
> Devouring Harpies, that for gold would sell
> Their country, office, or themselves to hell.
> But he their crimes with vengeance will pursue,
> And give to them, as to the just, their due.
> See but how bankrupts are twice bankrupt made
> By double fees, and by the subtle trade
> Of secretaries, sealers, clerks, and knaves,
> That lord it o'er poor suitors as their slaves.
> But let such in eternal flames expire,
> Gorgons and Hydras and Chimeras dire."

I feel every desire to do justice to this successor of à Becket, Wolsey, and Bacon; but I really can find little more to relate of him, except that his arms were, "Azure, two bars, argent, in chief three leopards' heads cabossed, or: Crest, a dragon's head coupé, or, issuing out of a ducal coronet, or." Let me add, "He was a plain man both in person and conversation, of middle stature, inclining to fat, with a broad face, much marked by the small-pox."

His son rose to be Clerk of the Crown in the Court of Chancery; but I can not find that the family ever gained any higher distinction.

I hope I may now, with a safe conscience, dismiss the worthy Sergeant. No blame is imputable to him. The marvel is that the Tory party, having at this time to boast of a Harcourt and other accomplished lawyers as adherents, should so long have submitted to the degradation of such a Lord Keeper.

"PAULO MAJORA CANAMUS!"

[1] Nich. Leicest. iii. 215 *et seq*.

CHAPTER CXIII.

LIFE OF LORD COWPER FROM HIS BIRTH TILL HIS APPOINTMENT AS LORD KEEPER.

WE now come to a holder of the Great Seal whose reputation ever outran his promotion, who was a credit to his party, and who conferred lasting benefits on his country. His life, if written near his own times, might have been most interesting; but the task has been neglected till it must be performed under great disadvantages. Very unaccountably, from the latter end of the seventeenth century till past the middle of the eighteenth, biography was a department of literature almost entirely neglected in England. Little curiosity seems during that period to have existed respecting the private history of men, however distinguished in literature, in statesmanship, or in magistracy. Before the last work of Dr. Johnson, the English public had known no more of many of their eminent poets than, till very recently, they knew of many of their eminent lawyers. What is to be discovered of the Chancellors of Anne and George I. must be searched for in authors who have incidentally mentioned them, or in family papers casually preserved,—and much relating to them, which might have been both amusing and instructive, has irrecoverably perished.[1]

William Cowper is a rare instance of a man born to hereditary rank and competent fortune rising to great distinction in the profession of the law in England. He was the eldest son of a baronet of ancient descent, and possessed of good landed estates in Kent and in Hertfordshire.

---

[1] "The lives of such eminent men," said Lord Henley, in 1833, "as Lord Somers and Lord Hardwicke, have been written in a manner totally unworthy of their high reputation. Of Lord Nottingham, Lord Holt, nay, even of the great Lord Mansfield, we have still but meager and unsatisfactory accounts; whilst of the Chancellors Cowper, Harcourt, Macclesfield, King, and Talbot—all considerable judges and statesmen in their time, and principal actors in the great political events of their day—we have little information beyond the scanty notices of the Peerage."—*Life of Lord Northington*, p. 3.

In the reign of Edward VI., the family was seated at Strood, in Kent. Soon after the accession of James I., William Cowper the head of it, while yet a very young man, was made a Nova Scotia baronet,—I presume, for the pecuniary consideration usually demanded when that order was instituted. Afterwards, being a favorite of Charles I., an English baronetcy, then considered a higher distinction, was conferred upon him. He is chiefly memorable for being the first of the line who rhymed;[1] he erected a monument to the author of the "Ecclesiastical Polity," bearing this epitaph of his own composition:—

> "Tho' nothing can be spoken worthy his fame,
> Or the remembrance of that precious name,
> Judicious Hooker; tho' this cost be spent
> On him that hath a lasting monument
> In his own books; yet ought we to express,
> If not his worth, yet our respectfulness."

When the civil war broke out, he adhered to the royal cause, and, with his son John, he was long imprisoned, by order of the Parliament, in Ely House, Holborn. There John died, leaving an infant son, William, who was the father of the Chancellor. Old Sir William, when liberated, retired to Hertford Castle, which he had purchased and fitted up as a private dwelling. Having seen the great evils which had arisen from carrying to excess high church and high prerogative principles,—although an old cavalier, he instilled a love of civil and religious liberty, as well as of a monarchical form of government, into the mind of his grandson, who became a distinguished "Whig," when this designation was first applied to a party in the state, and from whom sprung a long succession of distinguished Whigs. The first baronet having died at the age of eighty-two, his heir soon after married Sarah, daughter of Sir Samuel Holled, of London, merchant, a lady of great accomplishments, who took unwearied pains with the education of her children. The eldest of these was William, the subject of this memoir, born in the castle of Hertford, in the year 1664. His baptismal register has not been found, and the exact day of his birth can not be ascertained. His parents afterwards resided chiefly in London.

Having been taught to read by his mother, he was sent

[1] Cowper, the poet, was lineally descended from him.

to a private school at St. Alban's. There lies before me the original of a letter written by him when eight years of age, which I can not resist my inclination to copy, as the earliest known composition of him who afterwards refuted Bolingbroke's most powerful paper in the "Examiner," and materially influenced the destinies of the empire:—

"Dear Mother,

"I thanke you for my Bow and Arrows, which I shall never use But when my master Gives us leave to play. I shall hereafter take more care of my spelling and writing even without ruled lines. My mistress was well brought to Bed of a Daughter on Sunday was Seaven-night, who is to be Christened to day. I hope my Brothers John and Spencer are both very well. I present my humble Duty to my Father and Mother, with my love to my Brothers, remaining

"Your ever obedient Sonne,
"WILLIAM COOPER.[1]

"St. Albans, Oct. 27, 1672."

At this school he continued at least till the 5th of August, 1675, as there is a letter by him written from it on that day to his mother, showing that he had been aiming at a more formal style, which she had not approved of and had suspected to be the composition of the usher: "Indeed," says he, "the other letter was my own indicting, and I thought I had pleased you mighty well, but since you like the other stile best, I will wright so hereafter."

From this time till he was entered of the Middle Temple, hardly anything is known of his education or his history. He certainly never was at any university, and it is doubtful whether he was ever at a public school, although from evidence given on his brother's famous

[1] *Sic*, although in his subsequent letters he always signed his name COWPER. They are all directed—

"These
For my ever Honoured
Mother the LADY COWPER,
At her house in the
Charter hous Yard
in
London."

They are written very distinctly in large text—giving earnest of the beautiful hand which Lord Cowper acquired, and always retained.

trial at Hertford for murder, there seems reason to think that they were both for some years at Westminster. Whatever was the nature of his tuition, he became an elegant scholar, and he acquired a taste for polite literature, which adhered to him through life.[1]

In his eighteenth year he became a Templar, more with a view of mixing with the good society and acquiring the fashionable accomplishments for which the Inns of Court were still celebrated, than of professionally studying the law. But he made the acquaintance of some black-letter lawyers of agreeable manners, who gave him a liking for their craft, and he had fits of severe application to legal and constitutional lore. Afterwards he fell into bad company, and was seduced into haunts of dissipation. His morals for a time were much corrupted, and he formed a connection which was the pretense for the charge subsequently so boldly and pertinaciously brought forward against him, that he was guilty of bigamy. He had for his mistress a young lady in rather a respectable situation of life, whose family lived near his father's residence in Hertfordshire;[2] and she is said to have brought him two children, a son and a daughter, the former of whom died in infancy, and the latter grew up to womanhood: but there is no foundation whatever for the assertion that he had married her; and, notwithstanding the calumnies of Swift and Mrs. Manley, and the statement with which Voltaire amused Europe, that the Lord Chancellor of England practiced and defended polygamy, he had dropped all correspondence with this lady before he was introduced to either of the two wives whom he successively led to the altar.

The first of these was Miss Judith Booth, daughter of a London merchant, a young lady of wit and beauty, but no fortune. I will give a specimen of a young lawyer's love-letter in the reign of James II. :—

[1] Mrs. Manley speaking of his father under the name of *Volpone*, in her caluminous manner, says—" Whether it were that he was sordidly covetous, or that he could not spare so much from his own expenses, he did not bestew a liberal education upon his son, but bred him to the practice of the law in that manner that is the least generous and most corrupt; but HERNANDO (Lord Cowper) had natural parts which surmounted all these inconveniences." *New Atalantis*, i. 195. Yet her friend Swift is compelled to admit that " he was what we usually call a piece of a scholar, and a good logical reasoner."
[2] Miss Elizabeth Culling, of Hertingfordbury Park.

> "To Mrs. Judith Booth,
> "Walbrooke,
> "London.
> "This present.'

"Dearest Madam,

"My father hath been with me and employed me some part of this afternoon with himself, and hath ordered me to make some inquiries after a servant; so that I must be worse than my desire in not seeing you this afternoon. I wish my thoughts that are so often with you when I am not, were not invisible; then you might save yourself the trouble of reading such like notes, and see at one view how discontented and vexed they are when I can not waite on you. You would see how forward and impatient they grow under any other business, and I'm sure without further apology would excuse me and forgive my absence for their very looks. But since this can not be, be so good as to think 'em truly and plainly expressed in this paper of

"Your very humble and affectionate Servant,
"WILL. COWPER.

"Temple, June 19–86."

The match was an imprudent one, for he was still only a law student, with the prospect of his profession being to him a source of expense rather than of profit. His father was still a young man and had other sons to provide for Nevertheless, after a year's courtship, and before he was called to the bar, the marriage was celebrated. Though deeply regretted by his family, it proved his salvation, and it may be considered the foundation of all his future prosperity. Mrs. Cowper was soon " as women wish to be who love their lords," and he saw that she and her children must for years depend almost entirely upon his exertions. He therefore forthwith set himself steadily and doggedly to work to fit himself to practice as an advocate in Westminster Hall. No one ever had by nature finer qualities for that profession—a handsome figure, a most intelligent and winning countenance, a silver-toned voice, a quick perception, a lively imagination, and " a head for the

---

* He usually writes this complimentary word in a contracted form, at the right-hand bottom corner of the letter, thus: " pEsent." When he was a member of parliament, on the opposite corner he wrote " Frank, W. Cowper," or "Free, W. Cowper."

law." He gained considerable distinction in the "*moots*," which still went on under the cloisters in the Temple, and great expectations of his future success were formed by those who knew him best.

In Trinity Term, 1688, he was called to the bar, and in a few days he had his first brief, which was to make a motion of some importance in the Court of King's Bench. His wife was then on a visit to his father in the country, and he sent her an account of his performance in a letter thus addressed:—

"To Mrs. Judith Cowper, at
"Hertford Castle.
"Present.

"I have to tell you, my dear Judith, that I have made my maiden motion in the King's Bench, and that by the help of self-persuasion and reasoning with myself, without much of the bashfulness I am naturally inclined to. Upon asking the standers-by their opinion of my Performance, they only found fault that I did not interweave what I said with civil expressions enough to his Lordshipp, as, '*May it please your Lordshipp*,' and '*I am humbly to move your Lordshipp*,' and the like. But that fault will be amended for the future, and to that end you shall find me begin to practis my extraordinary civility on your sweet self. I delivered your letter to your Father with my own hand, who is very well except that his leg begins to trouble him a little again. I was yesterday in the afternoon to see my Lady Parker, who is very well, and sends her service to you all at Hertford. I must keep room to present my Duty to my dear Mother, and to subscribe myself as in duty bound,

"Your very faithful and obedient Husband,
"WILL: COWPER.

"Middle Temple, June 28-88."

He chose the Home Circuit, which began soon after, and at Hertford he had several briefs; but he was made more nervous than he had been in the Court of King's Bench, by his mother, and his wife, and a party of ladies whom he knew, coming from the Castle and placing themselves near the Judge on the Bench to hear him plead. However, his courage rose as he advanced, and he acquitted himself to their satisfaction, taking care to interlard his speech with a sufficient number of "May it please your Lordshipps." He did not make enough to pay his expenses at Chelmsford, Maidstone, Horsham, or Kingston, but he had a little sprinkling of business at each of these places; and upon the whole he felt encouraged by the start he had made.

When Michaelmas Term came round, the laws were silent amidst arms. On the 5th of November, the Prince of Orange landed at Torbay.

Young Cowper, early taught by his father, Sir William, the true principles of the constitution, had indignantly beheld the tyrannical acts which marked the close of the reign of Charles II., and the systematic, incurable despotism which threatened the permanent overthrow of the religion and liberties of the people since the accession of the reigning Sovereign. He saw no possibility of redress from the ordinary means prescribed by the law; he thought that the original contract between the King and the people was broken; and he declared that resistance being necessary, and, on account of the spirit displayed by the people, being likely to be effectual, it had become a right and a duty. So enthusiastic was he, that he induced his brother Spencer, and several other young gentlemen who shared his sentiments, to the number of twenty-eight, to form themselves into a little volunteer corps, and, arming themselves in the best way they could, to march under his command that they might join the Deliverer. James was still at Whitehall, struggling to maintain his authority, when, in the beginning of December, they set forward, and it was thought that a battle might be necessary before he could be expelled. Cowper sent to his wife, in the form of a journal, a minute account of this expedition. Unfortunately the beginning of it is lost, but I am enabled to lay a subsequent part of it before the public. From James's flight the expected campaign had been turned into an ovation:—

"Windsor, Saturday, D^r. 15,—88.

"The continuall hurry wee have been in, & our not coming to post-towns at convenient times, have hitherto hindered me fro writing since my last, fro Ailesbury: Fro whence wee sett out on Tuesday last, & dining at Thame, came about 5 in ye evening safe to Oxford; in this day's journey I came to understand that our delays at London were fortunate, for y ͤ day before a party of 12 of y ͤ King's horse had been as far as Wheatly Bridge, within 5 miles of Oxford, to rob or intercept, w ͨ ͪ Bridge was our way necessarily: att y ͤ gate of Oxford wee were stopt by a guard of y ͤ town militia and disarmed, & it being put to my choice who of severall Lords that were in town wee would wait on, I chose L ͩ Lovelace, who, knowing my name and business, dismist me & company w ͭ ͪ civility and arms returned: I found y ͤ University preparing an entertainment of musick for y ͤ Prince (who they expected the next day fro Abington), at y ͤ Theatre & a Dinner at Christ Church College, but y ͤ news of y ͤ K ͤ departure coming at 12 at night, y ͤ Prince sent word to Oxford of y ͤ alteration of his intentions & y ͭ he would march y ͤ next day to Wallingford (9 miles fro Oxford) for London; so y ͭ on Wednesday morning wee went, & about 2 that day mett y ͤ Prince at Wallingford, where wee saw him dine at a little Inn w ͭ ͪ great variety of meat and sawces, sweetmeats, etc., w ͨ ͪ it seems is part of y ͤ fatigue wee admire in great Generals; he lay at y ͤ Mayor's house. The next day being Thursday, he rode all y ͤ way a foot-pace fro thence to Henley, w ͭ ͪ a small guard of about 12 horse, but a very large attendance of Lords & Gentry, and abundance of acclamations and expressions of joy fro y ͤ country People. Fro thence on fryday wee came with y ͤ Prince to Windsor Castle, where he was received with usuall expressions of joy, w ͨ ͪ is now unfeigned. I have hitherto quartered in y ͤ same town w ͭ ͪ y ͤ Court without difficulty, & intend now to stay till y ͤ Prince comes to London: you cannot conceive y ͤ pleasure there is in seeing y ͤ fountain of this Happy revolution, and y ͤ new face of things at Court, where is nothing of y ͤ usuall affectation of Terror, but extreme civility to all sorts of People; you shall see country women admitted to see him dine, & as many of y ͤ Nobles & Principall men as there is rome for dine w ͭ ͪ y ͤ Prince covered. I omitt private particulars because I hope twill not be long till I see you at London, w ͨ ͪ I guess will be on Tuesday; y ͤ Prince, I am informed, stays here to-day, how much longer I can't certainly tell. The army is much short of y ͤ opin: you conceived of it at London as I'm informed. & y ͤ foot I see are very little men. S^r. H. Ashurst has ventured to come hither. The coach by wch I send is near going. We are all very well."

This must be considered an important historical document, giving a most lively picture of public feeling in the great crisis of our fate as a free nation. The reader will probably be surprised by the language respecting "the usual affectation of terror," contrasted with "the extreme civility to all sorts of people" now supposed to be shown by the future King,—for Charles II. was partly redeemed from his vices by his extreme affability, and even James we regard as rather amiable in private life,—while William's reserve and frigid manners from the commencement of his reign, and, as is generally believed, from the moment of his landing, cast a shade upon his virtues, and greatly impaired his influence and his usefulness. But we must make some allowance for the youthful patriot to whom, in the exultation of victory, the scene on which he looked back had darker horrors breathed over it, and who saw in rosy tints all that was before him.

There is likewise an interesting account of this expedition in a MS. in the handwriting of Lady Sarah Cowper, a daughter of the Chancellor, who says that she had her information in the year 1726, from the mouth of her uncle Spencer. She gives some anecdotes, showing her father's gallantry as a soldier, which he modestly concealed:

" When they came near Oxford, they found the city had a garrison, and heard the King's army, said to be about 20,000 men, was encamped just by, but could not learn whether those at Oxford were of the King's or Prince's party. Coming upon the bridge, they found one of the arches broke down, and an officer, with three files of musketeers, came up to them, presented their muskets, and asked them who they were for. Twenty-seven of the company did not care to return an answer, fearing lead in their guts if these soldiers were of the King's side; and the gentlemen had only pistols, so must have engaged with great disadvantage; but my father seemed unconcerned, and, spurring his horse forward, flung up his hat, and cried ' the Prince of Orange!' which was answered by the soldiers with a shout, and they laid planks for them to enter the town, and they were conducted to Lord Lovelace, who kept it against the King. They stayed there three days, and then went on to meet the Prince of Orange, and came into London with him."

When William and Mary had been placed upon the throne, men soon returned to the ordinary occupations of life, and William Cowper once more diligently plied his profession on the circuit and in Westminster Hall. A few extracts of letters to his first wife, when they were occasionally separated, while he was getting on at the bar, will be interesting to those engaged in the same struggle, and may amuse the general reader :—

"I envy you who are in the country, 'tis so close in town; and heartily could wish myself with you, if being in the country in Term time would not look like giving over the profession."[1] . . . "As for my boy, I would have you venture and hope this cast of the die may prove fortunate, for in all applications we run some hazard, and nothing is certainly beneficial to a child but the care of so good a mother as I am sensible you are."[2] . . . "Tuesday, six in the afternoon. Word is now brought me, that the great cause of the Farmers of the City Markets is set down before the Lord Chancellor for to-morrow. If it comes on in the morning, I will be with you (if alone) in the afternoon, though I have two Excise causes for Friday in the afternoon. The trial of the Pirates, which I must attend, is on Monday next. So that all I can do is to go backwards and forwards to show my willingness to be with you as much as I can. I know all this does not satisfy you, but this and more I could allege, for my story is true. If I am so unfortunate as not to be credited, I know no way to help that but your coming up to see if it be so or no. I am sure I had so much rather be with you, that the present profit would not tempt me from the country, if it were not for the consequence of throwing myself altogether out of the little good business I have."[3] . . . [From Kingston, on the Spring Circuit, after excusing his not writing to her from Horsham, from which they were obliged to send the letters "six miles to meet the horse post."] "I write to you from this place, as soon as I arrive, to tell you I have come off without hurt, both in my going and return through the Sussex ways, which are bad and ruinous beyond imagina-

[1] 21st June, 1690.   [2] 29th July, 1690.   [3] 6th July, 1694.

tion. I vow 'tis a melancholy consideration that mankind will inhabit such a heap of dirt[1] for a poor livelihood. The country is a sink of about fourteen miles broad, which receives all the water that falls from two long ranges of hills on both sides of it, and not being furnished with convenient drains, is kept moist and soft by the water till the middle of a dry summer, which is only able to make it tolerable to ride for a short time. The same day I entered Surrey, a fine champaign country, dry and dusty, as if the season of the year had shifted in a few hours from winter to midsummer."[1] . . [From Chelmsford on the Circuit.] " We had very little to do at Hertford; we hanged more than we tried causes." . . . [Addressed to his wife living at Twickenham from a house in the country.] " My mother was to visit Mr. Justice W——'s study to choose some books to read. On his desk, just against him, so that his eyes must frequently direct themselves to it, there is writ this following distich, or couple of verses of his own composing (as he assured my mother over and over),

'IN WISDOM'S SCHOOL THIS MAXIM I HAVE GOT,
THAT 'TIS MUCH BETTER TO BE PLEAS'D THAN NOT.'

I tell you the author that I may not arrogate to myself this metrical maxim, which is likely to prove so beneficial to you and all that hear it. Mr. Crawford is another cause of some mirth here: he was asked why he quitted his friends and party; his answer was, that he had read Machiavel, and learned from him he was to own no cause or party longer than they could protect him, and, in the present condition of the Whigs, as he no longer had their protection, they must no longer expect his allegiance."[2]

Although Cowper, in his correspondence, speaks so modestly of his own progress, there is no doubt that in a few years after he was called to the bar he was not only the decided leader of the Home Circuit, but that he had extensive practice in Westminster Hall, particularly in the Court of Chancery. There he attracted the notice of Lord Somers, who, appreciating his high qualities for public life, and anticipating the service he might render

---

[1] I am now copying this on the boundary between Sussex and Surrey, which at this day it is a common expression that those who live on the south side of Leith Hill are "in the dirt."—Abinger Hall, 3rd October, 1845.
[2] 24th March, 1696.   18th Sept. 1701.

to the Whig party, strongly advised him to get into the House of Commons. We are now to view him on the political stage.

In the year 1695, the Whigs were rather popular, and William III., on his return from the capture of Namur, having dissolved the parliament, the new elections ran in their favor. Sir William Cowper felt his interest so strong at Hertford, that he started his eldest son as a candidate along with himself, and, after a sharp contest, they were both returned. On this occasion they were warmly supported by the Quakers, and particular by an eminent maltster of that persuasion of the name of Stout, the melancholy fate of whose daughter afterwards caused such a public sensation, and was so perilous to the family of Cowper.

The younger Cowper, like the younger Pitt, is a rare instance of a member of the House of Commons being considered from his maiden speech a consummate debater, and ever afterwards maintaining his reputation. Yet, while we are told that "the very day he took his seat he had occasion to speak three times, which he did each time with great applause," we are not even informed of the subject that was discussed; and although, when appointed Lord Keeper, in 1705, it was said that "he had for many years been considered as the man that spoke the best of any in the House of Commons,"[1] there is scarcely a fragment remaining of any speech delivered by him in that assembly. It might have been expected that, after popular government had been established in this country by the Revolution of 1688, great publicity would have been given to the proceedings of the two Houses; but, in truth, the prohibition against printing the speeches of members was much more rigorously enforced than it had ever before been;[2] and the practice being discontinued, which prevailed at an early time, of entering on the Jour-

[1] Burnet, O. T. iv. 122.
[2] We consider the lists of the divisions so essential to inform the constituent bodies how their representatives are conducting themselves, that they are printed and circulated authoritatively by order of the House of Commons; but in the year 1696 the printing and circulating the names of a minority in the House of Commons was unanimously voted "a breach of privilege, and destructive of the freedom and liberties of parliament."—*Com. Jour.* xi. 572. So in 1699 the Lords made a new standing order, which has not been repealed, against "publishing anything relating to the proceedings of this House."—*Die Lunæ, 27th Februarii, 1698.*

nals the substance of what was said on both sides of a question, we are less acquainted with parliamentary eloquence under William III. and Queen Anne than in the reigns of some of the Plantagenets; and we learn only from personal anecdotes and tradition that St. John was the greatest orator who had appeared in England.[1]

Cowper, like other lawyers who have followed him, seems to have rendered himself particularly obnoxious in the House of Commons to the "Squirearchy." "Mr. Cowper," says Vernon, "has provoked the country gentlemen by saying that 'an active, industrious man who employed £5,000 in trade was every whit as fit to be a member there as a country gentleman of £200 a year, who spent all his time in hawking and hunting, and was over head and ears in debt.' My Lord Norreys answered, that 'he was one of those country gentlemen, and thought himself as fit to sit there as those who were used to take money for their opinion.'" At this time the Court was strongly opposed by the landed aristocracy, and relied chiefly on the moneyed interest.[2]

The honorable and learned member for Hertford, as a reward for his services, was raised to the rank of King's Counsel, then considered a high professional distinction. In consequence he assisted in the state trials which arose out of the discovery of the Assassination Plot.[3] In Sir William Parkyn's case, he replied after Sir John Hawles, the Solicitor General, had made "a sad hash of the evidence," and given the prisoner great hopes of an acquittal, and he put forward the strong points for the prosecution with the utmost clearness, precision, and seeming candor. He admitted that the overt act, in planning the attack upon the King on the road from Kensington

[1] While we have some shreds of Cowper's parliamentary eloquence, and some of his forensic efforts are well preserved, St. John, though a finer speaker, has been more unfortunate, as we can judge of his powers of persuasion from his writings alone. Mr. Pitt thought that one of his speeches would be a more valuable discovery than any of the lost works of the ancients.

[2] Vernon's Letters. The "Members' Qualification Bill" passed the Commons, but was thrown out by the Lords, and did not become law till the next reign.

[3] The assassination was to have taken place on a Saturday when the King was to go a-hunting; and the hunting party being deferred, on account of some discoveries which had been made in the design, was renewed for the following Saturday

to Richmond, could not be relied upon, being proved by only one witness; but he dwelt with much force upon the proofs that the prisoner had invited a French invasion, and he enumerated, with great skill, all the corroborating and aggravating circumstances. Thus he concluded:— " The prisoner at last makes an appeal to your compassion, and speaks of his education in the profession of the gown, of his infirmities, his age, and his family. I am very unfit to observe on such topics, and I should be very unwilling to extinguish in your minds the feelings which they are calculated to excite; but I must remind you, gentlemen, that he should have had some pity on the country when he planned the confusion and desolation which would have followed from the landing of a French army on our shores, and that he should have felt some pity for the Prince now on the throne, who has saved our religion and our liberties,—whom the prisoner and his associates, after they had once been disappointed in an attempt upon his life, a second time remorselessly doomed to destruction.' Though these considerations may not quite remove all compassion, yet they may serve to confirm you in a resolution of doing justice to the King, the kingdom, and yourselves; and that is all we ask of you."[2] The prisoner was found guilty and executed.[3]

Cowper's next public appearance was not quite unexceptionable. The principal conspirator was Sir John Fenwick, and it had been intended to arraign him at the Old Bailey, along with the others; but he contrived, under various pretenses, to have his trial postponed, and in the meanwhile to send out of the country one of the two witnesses who were to prove the overt acts of his guilt. If ever a bill of attainder could be justified, it would be under such circumstances; but to legislate capitally and retrospectively against an individual, must ever be an abuse of the supreme power of the state; and if crimes can not be punished judicially by the established tribunals of the

---

[1] 12 St. Tr. 1446; 13 Ibid. 1.   [2] 14 Ibid. 125.
[3] There was abundant evidence to support the conviction for high treason; and there can be no doubt that the prisoner was concerned in the assassination plot. Although he, and Sir John Friend, who suffered along with him, would express no repentance, they were solemnly absolved from all their sins by three nonjuring clergymen. Cowper was afterwards counsel in a prosecution against the clergymen for this outrage; but the report does not show what part he took in it.—14 St. Tr. 406.

country, it is better that they should go unpunished than that a precedent should be set which may be applied to the shedding of innocent blood. We are, indeed, amazed to see that a mode of proceeding, invented in the arbitrary reign of Henry VIII., and then thought violent and unconstitutional, should have been adopted after the " Bill of Rights " had passed under the auspices of Somers, and that, to please William III., it should have been eagerly supported by Cowper and by Bishop Burnet. The bill for the attainder of Sir John Fenwick being introduced into the House of Commons, the Tory lawyers made a noble stand against it.[1] The Attorney and Solicitor General being very indifferent spokesmen, the defense of the measure fell chiefly upon Cowper, and we have some account of what he urged on the occasion. He began by alluding to the delicacy of his situation in mixing the functions of counsel for the Crown and member of Parliament:

"Sir, being concerned in prosecutions without-doors arising out of this transaction, although I had not been professionally consulted respecting the case of Sir John Fenwick, I have hitherto abstained from taking any part in the debates upon the bill for attainting him; but before giving my voice upon it as a Judge, I feel bound to state the grounds on which I have come to the conclusion that it ought to pass. Consider his crime and his subsequent conduct. His crime, as proved against him at your bar, is the reason why I think, before God and man, I ought to give my affirmation to this bill by which you sentence him to die. What he hath done in protracting his trial, and spiriting away the witness, convinces me that we are in a proper method of proceeding against him. Let no man say that you have condemned him because he hath protracted his trial. No: you have condemned him for having been guilty of high treason, manifestly proved against him. Then they ask, ' *Will you condemn any man that is at any time guilty of high treason?*' No; only when a man having been guilty of the worst of treasons, which would have been clearly proved against him in the ordinary course of law, undertaking to atone for his crime by

[1] See in particular the admirable speech of Mr. Harcourt, afterwards Lord Chancellor, *post.*

making discoveries important to the public safety, protracts his trial till the chief witness against him is gone, and then sets the justice of the country at defiance. Gentlemen are afraid that this will be made use of by posterity to the disadvantage of honest men. Must not the guilty be punished because the same methods may be perverted to the ruin of the innocent? By this very precedent the innocent may be protected. If in future times an attempt should be made to condemn a man in parliament without hearing him and without proof, he may say, 'Sir John Fenwick was heard personally and by his counsel; evidence was produced before him and confronted with him; his case was a most extraordinary one and required an extraordinary remedy; he would have introduced a foreign army into the heart of the kingdom, and lifted his hand against the sacred life of the King.'"
—He then very sophistically attempts to answer the argument that the evidence was insufficient to support the bill, there not being two witnesses to the overt act, by contending that the statutes 1 Edward VI. and 5 Edward VI., requiring two witnesses, are only binding on the inferior courts, and do not apply to a bill of attainder. Having next struggled for the doctrine that in legislating they were to be governed, not by technical rules, but by the dictates of conscience,—contrary to his usual tact he seems rather to have shocked the House by trying to induce them to pass the bill under the pretense that it might be hung over Sir John Fenwick *in terrorem*, to induce him to make the discoveries which he had often promised but always withheld: "I am satisfied he hath not made that atonement to his injured country which we have a right to expect from him. I am persuaded that unless this bill proceed steadily against him, you will have none of that discovery——" [Here, says the report, he was interrupted by the noise of some gentlemen showing dissatisfaction at the way of arguing]—" Do not let gentlemen pervert this argument and say, '*Will you hang a man if he do not confess?*' No! but when I have heard proof that he is guilty of the worst of treasons, and hath aggravated his crime by subterfuges to elude justice, he deserves to die,—unless he will merit his life by a discovery of what he knows. I think it of the highest importance that you should be able to trace the other

branch of this conspiracy—the meeting of the French King's forces in England. I think you a e in the proper method, and this bill may have a better issue than his death; but if not, he will only pay the debt which he owes to the justice of his country."[1]

The bill passed the Commons by a majority of only 33, —169 to 136; and the Lords by a majority of 6,—66 to 60. Nevertheless it received the royal assent, and Sir John Fenwick was beheaded on Tower Hill.[2] This proceeding, however irregular it may appear to us, was not much condemned at the time, except by the violent Jacobites, who considered him a martyr; and Cowper, by the share he had in it, rather increased his reputation.

During the trial of Lord Mohun before the Lord High Steward, for the murder of Richard Coote, which took place soon after, we have a remarkable proof of the opinion entertained of Mr. Cowper's elocution:—"Mr. Solicitor General (Sir John Hawles) began to sum up the evidence for the King, but his voice was so low and the noise in the hall was so great that he could not be heard. *Lord High Steward*,—' Mr. Solicitor, pray raise your voice that all my noble Lords may hear you.' Several Lords then moved that one who had a better voice might sum up—*and particularly* Mr. COWPER; but it being usually the part of the Solicitor General to reply, and he only having prepared himself, he was ordered to go on."[3] The Peers, condemned to have their ears tortured, as by the sharpening of a saw, took compassion on the noble prisoner whose head was in jeopardy, and unanimously acquitted him.

Cowper, now an universal favorite, was on the highway to preferment, when an occurrence arose which threw him and his family into the greatest alarm, and threatened to cover with disgrace a name hitherto held in respect. He had a younger brother, Spencer Cowper, to whom he was fondly attached, who had been at school with him, who, being called to the bar, went the Home Circuit with him, occupying the same lodgings at every assize town,

[1] 5 Parl. Hist. 1057, 1141.
[2] See Burnet, iv. 204-266. It is very amusing to see how the good Bishop persuaded himself that it was his duty to interfere in this affair of blood.
[3] 13 St. Tr. 1055

and who spent his vacations in the neighborhood of Hertford, showing, for the sake of the family interest in that borough, very marked attention to the electors, and their wives and daughters. A charge was brought against his brother that he was guilty of a foul murder, and there ran such a strong popular prejudice against him that he was in great danger of an ignominious end.

Mr. Stout, the Quaker, had died since the last election, leaving his widow and an only child, an unmarried daughter, named Sarah, in affluent circumstances. The Cowpers still kindly took great notice of them, visited them at Hertford, and invited them to the house of Sir William, in Hatton Garden. Spencer Cowper had been particularly serviceable to Mrs. Sarah (as she was called) in managing her pecuniary affairs; and although she was a very handsome young Quakeress, and rather of a romantic turn, it seems now quite certain that he had never made her any improper overtures, or at all encouraged a fatal passion which she cherished for him.

It so happened that early in the morning of Tuesday, the 14th of March, 1699, the day after the commencement of the Spring Assizes at Hertford, the dead body of this unfortunate girl was found in the Priory River, which flows through that town, and Mr. Spencer Cowper was certainly the last person who had been seen in her company the night before. Suspicion immediately fell upon him; but he appeared as a witness before the coroner's jury, and so far cleared himself that they brought in a verdict that "she had drowned herself being *non compos mentis*." William Cowper (as we shall see) had been luckily detained in London by business in the House of Commons, or he might have been afterwards charged as an accomplice. Spencer proceeded with the Judges and the other counsel to Chelmsford, and finished the circuit, lamenting the fate of Sarah Stout, but without any dread of being further questioned respecting her death.

In the mean time, two parties were at work, from very opposite motives, planning measures which nearly brought him to the gibbet. An unfounded rumor was spread that she was pregnant, and that she had made away with herself to conceal her shame. The Quakers, with Mead at their head, thought that such an imputation brought disgrace upon the whole of their society, and had the body disinterred to be examined by surgeons after it had been some weeks in the grave. It was proved that she had died a virgin. Her friends would no longer allow that she had drowned herself, but insisted that she had been murdered by Mr. Spencer Cowper, and that he had thrown the dead body into the mill stream. The charge was now most eagerly seized by the political opponents of the Cowpers who easily persuaded themselves of its truth, and who considered it the certain means of extinguishing the Whig interest in the borough. The excitement was greatly increased by a statement that, on the night of the supposed murder, two attorneys and a scrivener from London, shutting themselves up together in a room at Hertford, had exhibited appearances in their dress, and had used expressions, which clearly proved that they were accomplices. An information was laid against all the four before Lord Chief Justice Holt,[1] and they were committed to prison. Upon an application to the Court of King's Bench, the supposed accomplices were admitted to bail; but the Judges being equally divided on Spencer Cowper's case, he was remanded, and he remained in close custody till the Summer Assizes.

The trial took place at Hertford, on the 16th of July, 1699, before Mr. Baron Hatsel, a very well-meaning, but very weak Judge, who seems to have been strongly imbued with the vulgar prejudices which existed against all the prisoners. The case against Spencer Cowper was thus shaped,—that Sarah Stout must have been murdered by some one before her body was thrown into the water,—because it was discovered floating on the surface, which was impossible if she had drowned herself,—and that under the circumstances he alone could have done the deed. The first proposition was negatived even by the witnesses for the prosecution. Beyond the objection to the theory propounded respecting the floating and sinking of dead bodies, the corpse of Sarah Stout was found under the water supported by stakes in a mill race, there being nothing visible on the surface except a part of her petticoat. But a servant maid of Mrs. Stout created a very

[1] Down to this time the Chief Justice of England, on great occasions, still acted as a magistrate in committing criminals for trial, and even in quelling riots.

strong impression against the young barrister, by swearing "that on Monday, the 13th of March, the first day of the Spring Assizes, he alighted from his horse at the house, and dined there; that a bed-room was prepared for him; that having gone out, he returned to supper; that in his hearing she was ordered to go up stairs to warm his bed; that when she went to do this she left him and Mrs. Sarah in the parlor together, Mrs. Stout having before retired to rest; that while she was warming the bed, about a quarter before eleven at night, she heard the slamming of the outer door; that when she came down Mr. Cowper and Mrs. Sarah were gone; that she and Mrs. Stout remained up for them all night, believing that they had walked out together, but did not alarm the neighborhood for the sake of the young lady's reputation; and that their suspense was at last terminated in the morning, by the news of the body being found in the river, about half a mile from the house." By other witnesses it was proved that the three accomplices had been together in a room at Hertford soon after eleven, one of them being wet, and in a great perspiration; that they had talked much of Mrs. Sarah Stout, saying, "that she had behaved ill to a lover, but that her courting days were now over," and that a piece of rope and a bundle were found in a closet belonging to the room they had occupied.

Spencer Cowper not being allowed the assistance of counsel defended himself with firmness and presence of mind, and, by his cross-examination of the witnesses, showed the fallacy of a great part of the case for the Crown. When he came to address the jury, he pointed out how the prosecution had arisen from the zeal of the Quakers to maintain the reputation of their sect, and from the feuds occasioned by the election of his father and brother for the borough of Hertford. He then proceeded to explain the circumstances employed to raise a suspicion against him—which he protested that, out of tenderness to the memory of the deceased, he would not have done had it not been to rescue from danger the three innocent men who were on their trial along with him. He detailed the following facts, which were satisfactorily proved by the evidence of his brother William, afterwards Lord Chancellor, Mrs. Cowper, the Chancellor's first wife, and other witnesses of undoubted credit :—that the fair Quakeress, although Spencer Cowper was a married man, had conceived an uncontrollable passion for him, which he in vain had attempted to repress ; that when in London she wrote to him "she was coming to visit him at his chambers in the Temple ;" that he communicated this assignation in confidence to his brother, and they agreed that as she was to dine that day with their father, in Hatton Garden, William should say, as if casually, in her hearing, "Spencer was gone into the country on business:" that this scheme of inducing her not to go to the Temple was carried into effect; that she had solicited him to lodge at her mother's house during the assizes in the spring of this year which he declined, as he was to occupy lodgings at a Mr. Barefoot's, in the Market Place, which were usually kept for his brother, who was detained in London by parliamentary business; that on the 5th of March she wrote to him, saying, "I am glad you have not quite forgot there is such a person as I in being ; but I am willing to shut my eyes and not see anything that looks like unkindness in you, and rather content myself with what excuses you are pleased to make, than be inquisitive into what I must not know: I am sure the winter has been too unpleasant for me to desire the continuance of it ; and I wish you were to endure the sharpness of it but for one hour, as I have done for many long nights and days; and then I believe it would move that rocky heart of yours that can be so thoughtless of me as you are: When you come to H—d, pray let your steed guide you, and do not do as you did the last time ; and be sure order your affairs to be here as soon as you can, which can not be sooner than you will be heartily welcome:" that on the 9th of March she wrote him another letter, in which she plainly proposed that they should live together, adding this expression, "for come life, come death, I am resolved never to desert you; therefore, according to your appointment, I will expect you ;" that from the rebuffs she met with she had fallen into a melancholy, and had several times threatened to destroy herself: that on the Monday in question he took possession of his lodgings at Barefoot's, and was to sleep there, but that to soothe her he went to her mother's house, and was prevailed upon to stop to dinner, and to promise to call again at night; that he did call, but refused supper, and that the maid, in his hearing, being ordered to warm his bed (as she had truly sworn), did leave the room for that purpose, he then making no objection to the proposal. He abstained from stating the conversation which then passed between him and the young lady, there being no third person present, but he gave the Judge and jury to understand that, for the sake of her character, having remained silent in the presence of the maid,—as soon as they were alone together he positively refused to sleep there, and he immediately left the house. He proved, in the clearest manner, that before the clock struck eleven he had returned to his lodgings at Barefoot's, and that he never went out again till next morning—after news of the catastrophe which had happened had been spread over the town. Mr. and Mrs. Wm. Cowper, when examined, particularly spoke to Mrs. Sarah's frequent fits of despondency, her repeated expressions of her wish to be rid of life and of prognostications she had uttered of her approaching death.

With respect to the two attorneys, it was proved that, coming to attend the assizes, they had taken a room jointly, meaning, after the fashion of the age, to sleep together; and that the scrivener, a particular friend of theirs, arriving late at night, after galloping the greater part of the way from London in a heavy rain, and not being able to find a lodging, they had invited him to take a part of their bed. Before going to rest, for the refreshment of the scrivener they sent out to a tavern for some wine, which they called upon their landlord to partake of; and, as the glass went round, they talked merrily of the Quaker beauty, well known in those parts, who was supposed to have jilted a friend of theirs, of the name of Marshal, and whose coquetries they predicted would soon come to an end, as she had reached her twenty-fifth year, and "her courting days were nearly over."

In modern times, at the close of such a case, the Judge would interpose and direct an acquittal, and the counsel for the prosecution would readily concur in this course; but Mr. Jones, the counsel who conducted this prosecution, having made several speeches very irregularly during the trial, still pressed for a conviction of all the four, and Mr. Baron Hatsel put their lives in jeopardy. After a most imperfect sketch of the evidence about finding the body, he says,—

"You have heard also what the doctors and surgeons said on the one side and the other concerning the swimming and sinking of dead bodies in the water, but I can find no certainty in it, and I leave it in your consideration.[1] Gentlemen, I was very much puzzled in my thoughts, and was at a loss to find out what inducement there could be to draw in Mr. Cowper, or those three other gentlemen, to commit such a horrid, barbarous murder. And, on the other hand, I could not imagine what there should be to induce this gentlewoman, a person of a plentiful fortune, and a very sober, good reputation, to destroy herself. Now, gentlemen, I must confess, the evidence the defendants have given by these letters, if you believe them to be this gentlewoman's handwriting, do seem to fortify all that Mr. Cowper's witnesses have said concerning her being melancholy: It might be a love distraction, and she might have been a virtuous woman for all that; for it might be a distemper which came upon her and turned her brains, and discomposed her mind; and then no wonder at her writing thus, in a manner different from the rest of the actions of her life. Gentlemen, you are to consider and weigh the evidence, and I will not trouble you any more about that matter. As to these three other gentlemen, that came to this town at the time of the last assizes, what there is against them you have heard: They talked at their lodgings at a strange rate concerning this Mrs. Sarah Stout. What you can make of it, that I must leave to you; but they were very strange expressions, and you are to judge whether they were spoken in jest or in earnest. There was a cord found in the room, and a bundle seen there, but I know not what to make of it. As to Mrs. Sarah, there was no sign of any circle about her neck, which *as they say*, must have been if she had been strangled. Truly, gentlemen, these three men by their talking, have given great cause of suspicion; but whether they and

---

[1] Medical jurisprudence, still imperfectly cultivated in this country, seems then to have been at a very low ebb. A doctor, on this trial, being checked by Baron Hatsel, when about to quote the opinions of Galen and Hippocrates upon death by drowning, said,—" I see not, my Lord, why I should not quote the fathers of my profession, as well as you gentlemen of the long robe quote Coke upon Littleton in yours."

Mr. Cowper are guilty or no, that you are to determine. I am sensible I have omitted many things, but I am a little faint, and can not repeat any more of the evidence."
—*Foreman of the Jury:* "We have taken notes, my Lord."—*Baron Hatsel:* "Well, then, gentlemen, go together and consider the evidence, and I pray God direct you in giving your verdict."

The jury deliberated as much as half an hour, and then delivered a verdict of *Not Guilty* as to all the prisoners. William Cowper and the rest of the family were in an agony of suspense; but when the jury came back into court, and Spencer was desired to hold up his hand, he did so with the utmost composure while uncertain as to his doom.[1]

The verdict was unquestionably just, but fanaticism and faction are blind, and an attempt was made to bring all the four again to trial, by the process called "an Appeal of Murder"[2] sued out in the name of the heir at law of Sarah Stout.[3] There were various hearings on the subject, before Lord Keeper Wright, who called to his assistance the Master of the Rolls, Lord Chief Justice Treby, Lord Chief Baron Ward, and Mr. Justice Powell. William Cowper attended as counsel for his brother, and argued the case for him with great talent; his energy being stimulated, not subdued by the anxiety which he felt.[4] No misgiving was ever felt by him for a moment respecting Spencer's innocence, but, considering the perverted and infuriated state of the public mind, it was of the highest importance that the

---

[1] He resumed his practice at the bar—afterwards sat in the House of Commons as member for Berealstone, was made a Judge of the Court of Common Pleas, and presided on many trials for murder; ever cautious and mercifully inclined—remembering the great peril which he himself had undergone. He was buried in the church of Hertingfordbury, where a splendid monument is erected to his memory, while there is no stone to commemorate the Chancellor, although he lies close by.

[2] This mode of proceeding was not abolished till the reign of George IV. It was generally considered odious as a species of private revenge, depriving the Crown of the power to pardon; but Lord Holt declared it to be "a noble badge of the liberties of an Englishman."

[3] 13 St. Tr. 1190–1250; Lord Raymond, 560; 12 Mod. 372.

[4] I have now lying before me two long "playdoyers," which he used on those occasions—one entitled "Notes and Authority's preparatory to my argument against a new writ in my brother's case, and as the counsel's instructions." The other, "Argument for my brother Spencer, at Lord Keeper Wright's chamber in the Inner Temple, May 27, 1700."—They display vast research and acuteness.

risk of a mistaken verdict should not be again run. Upon a capital conviction in this form of proceeding, the Crown had no power to pardon. On account of an informality, the first appeal was quashed, and the Lord Keeper, with the unanimous concurrence of his assessors, refused to issue a writ for another.

All unprejudiced persons, and even many violent political opponents, allowed the acquittal to have been honorable.[1]

[1] The malevolent turn given to the affair by Mrs. Manley, in the *New Atalantis*, in her story of "Mosco and Zara," was that Spencer Cowper had yielded to Sarah Stout's solicitations: that, having grown tired of her, he wished to shake her off; that on the night in question, when she wished that they should retire together to the chamber prepared for him in her mother's house, he prevailed upon her to take a walk with him by the river side; that he then refused to agree to her scheme of abandoning his wife for her; and that having actually run off from her, she, in despair, threw herself into the water. This last scene will show what faith is to be given to the narrations of Mrs. Manley:—" *Zara speaks :* 'I have told my mother of my design to take you for a husband; my despair and melancholy has drawn her at length to consent. Do but utterly forego that woman you call your wife, and we require no more for making mine (in our opinion) a lawful marriage. We are above the little censure of others; the law nor magistrates do not frighten us. I make you absolute master of my fortune, only upon these conditions— My Dear! why do you not speak? Thou art not come here to disappoint me.'—'Alas! beautiful *Zara*, what can I answer? You don't know the world; you are ignorant of mankind. 'Tis in our power to marry ourselves but once as long as that wife shall live. I said the contrary, only to leave your virtue that pretense for yielding; but we must both be utterly void of common sense to pass such a marriage upon the world. No wise woman reckons on the performance of those extravagant things that are said to gain her. Be content with my love; there's nothing I shall omit to please you; I will lose no opportunity to entertain you with my passion, provided you are discreet, and do not expose us both.' He was going on, when *Zara*, not able to hear any more, sunk upon her knees, and catching hold of his coat with both her hands, interrupted him thus: 'Kill me upon the instant! I have something more than the pains of death upon me. Words can not express them! O, if you ever intend to meet mercy (as certainly you'll one day stand in need of it), have mercy upon me, a creature undone by love, agonized by passion, tortured by despair! Kill me, or comply with my request. I shall never live, I can not live to see another day. Pity me; pity the lost, expiring *Zara ; Zara*, who adores you; *Zara*, enchanted by your powerful magic; *Zara*, that even now dies, and can live no more without some returning kindness.' Here her sobs choked her words. He striving to get loose from her, she grasping to retain him; he saw he could not bring her to reason, and, therefore, since they must quarrel, the breach had best be made in the open fields, where nobody could hear them. He would take the pretense, and break from her, never to be plagued with her importunity again. 'You would do well, madam,' says he, aiming to unlock her hands, 'to leave me in peace, and go home to compose your brain by sleep. You happen to be amorous, and fantastically mad, and I must be the sufferer. Are you the first woman who has gone upon a wrong principle? Thy family and reputation are not to be staked for trifles. Be more moderate, or assure yourself, I'll never, from this

The prosecution, however, had the desired effect of subverting the Cowper interest in Hertford. At the next general election, it was manifest that no one bearing that name had the slightest chance of being returned for that borough. Sir William forever retired from parliament.

Fortunately Lord Somers took compassion on young William, and recommended him to the Duke of Bolton, a great Whig borough proprietor. In consequence, his Grace, in a manner rather more open than was practiced when the system of Peers interfering at elections was better established, wrote a letter to the Mayor of Totness, to be communicated to the burgesses, recommending "Counselor Cowper" as a fit and proper person to represent them; but the Mayor, from mistake or treachery, held back the recommendation, and allowed Mr. Gwynne, the candidate favored by the Seymour family, to get an advantage which could not be retrieved. At last, the Mayor having published the recommendation of Cowper, the Bolton party in the borough wrote this dispatch to the Duke:—

"Totness, Dec. 24, 1700.

"May it please your Grace,—We humbly beg pardon instant, see you more.' Here he threw abroad her hands, and broke from her. She fell her length upon the ground; then getting up as fast as she could, strove to follow him, but he was at too great a distance. Revenge and despair worked her up to the height of lunacy: she tore off her hood, her coif, her gown that hung loosely about her, trampling it under foot, and calling after him, 'Turn, turn but a moment; turn,' she cried, 'and see what love and rage can do; return, and see what *Zara* can perform. Ruin—despair—destruction—death—eternal misery overtake me! Heaven, earth, and hell revenge my wrongs. I devote myself to eternal misery, in view of returning in the most affrighting form to haunt this barbarian. Let me mingle among all the traitor's pleasures; let him attain to no honors but what may be blasted by the remembrance of *Zara*. Receive me, O hospitable flood, into thy cold bosom; receive a devoted wretch, whose flame thy waters only can quench.' Here she flounced with all her strength into the river; to the last moment persisting in a desire of speedy death."—*New Atalantis*, i. 221. Refutation and comment would be ridiculous; but it is curious to see what gave such delight in the reign of Queen Anne, and what, though disbelieved, was read by all.

In an early number of the European there is the following statement on the authority of the Rev. J. Hinton, Rector of Alderton, in Northamptonshire:—"Mrs. Sarah Stout, whose death was charged upon Spencer Cowper, was strangled accidentally by drawing the Steenkirk too tight upon her neck, as she, with four or five young persons, were at a game of romps upon the staircase; but it was not done by Mr. Cowper, though one of the company. Mrs. Clavering, Lord Chancellor Cowper's second wife, whom he married during the life of his first, was there, too; they were so confounded with the accident, that they foolishly resolved to throw her into the water thinking it would pass that she had drowned herself."

for not giving an answer sooner to your obliging letter, which was indeed communicated to some of us by our Mayor the day he received it, but he deferred calling a Hall to impart its contents to our burgesses and freemen till this day, when we perceived by them that they were most of them engaged by the interest of Sir E. Seymour for Mr. Gwynne. But what did most surprise us was his showing us a copy, which he had written, he said to your Grace in his own name, without our knowledge wherein he intimated that we were not now in a capacity to serve you as you desired. Indeed, the difficulties by his delays are now very great, but not, as we hope, insurmountable; and you recommending to us such a person as is well qualified for such a trust, and consistent with your honor and our reputation, we hope we shall be able to give you a good account of our proceedings at our next election, and that we are really,

"May it please your Grace,
"Your most humble and obedient Servants,"
&c., &c.

The Duke forwarded this document to Mr. Cowper in the following letter:—

"Sir,

"I inclose you a letter I received yesterday from Totness, by which you will see that the Mayor not communicating the contents of my letter in due time to the burgesses and freemen has occasioned a greater difficulty than I could have imagined; but you will see they are in hopes to give me a good account of their proceedings at the next election, and therefore I think it absolutely necessary that you, immediately upon receipt of this, go down post, for your presence there would be of great service. I sent my secretary post thither on Tuesday last, upon some letters I received from thence; he is upon the place, and will be assistant to you. I am in so great a hurry that you will, I hope, excuse my making use of another hand than that of

"Sir,
"Your very humble Servant,
"BOLTON."

Cowper immediately returned the following answer:—
"I received, last night, your Grace's letter with that from Totness inclosed. The first time I knew of your

favorable intentions towards me, which, however ineffectual they may prove by the practice of the Mayor (who, 'tis plain, hath endeavored, by better advice than his own, to avoid as civilly as he could the authority your Grace's letter would otherwise have had in his Corporation), will always be valued by me as an evidence of your good opinion, and acknowledged to the best of my power, —I had immediately obeyed your Grace in going post to Totness, if want of exercise¹ had not made it impossible for me to perform such a journey in that manner, though I fear my presence there would add nothing to what your power and interest has done for me in that place, especially hindered by the Act of Parliament from using the only means a stranger can on a sudden recommend himself by. What I can think of to contribute on my part, is to empower your Grace's secretary, if he sees it useful, and can do it so as not to let the other side prove it upon him, to insinuate to some one that he can trust that he may disperse it to the rest, that 'I will be a benefactor to the town as soon as I safely may,' and if we succeed, your Grace may rely on me for making good your servant's promise to your satisfaction, who, by your Grace's unmerited goodness to me, will in that, and in everything else, have a right to command, your Grace's most faithful and most obedient Servant,

"W. COWPER."

Had the prospect been more encouraging, "want of exercise" would not have prevented the young lawyer, accustomed to ride the circuit, from speedily setting off "post" for Totness.² His subsequent observations clearly show, that the act lately passed against treating and bribery³ had only introduced a little more care to preserve secrecy, and that, detection being avoided, to corrupt a borough was not then considered disreputable.

It would appear from the following letter, that the Duke of Bolton, hurt that Cowper, who was to be his candidate, declined to present himself immediately to the electors of Totness, had applied to Lord Somers to

¹ This copy I have taken from the draught of the letter, in which, for "want of exercise," the words were originally, "my way of life."
² Of course the reader is aware, that traveling post at that time meant *riding on horseback*, all persons attempting to travel in carriages going slowly with their own horses, and post horses to draw carriages not being kept till half a century after. ³ 7 & 8 W. 3, c. 4.

engage him in the contest, but that the attempt was vain :—

"My Lord Duke,

"My Lord Somers having favored me with an account of what your Grace has done for me since I had the honor of your last letter, and that 'tis thought my being at Totness might be of some use there; I could not but lay hold of this opportunity of writing by your Grace's servant, as well to assure you that although I must for ever acknowledge by what hand your favor is derived to me, I mean that of my Lord Somers, yet I shall never suffer any consideration whatsoever to lessen that sense I have of your great goodness to me in taking care of my concerns to a degree I am not capable of doing it for myself; as likewise to confess how much I am ashamed, that when I understand so much hardship is undergone by others for me, I should not be able to set a helping hand in that part which is at present expected from me. I have but one short and true apology, that I am sorry how my state of health renders it at this season absolutely impossible for me, which I beg your Grace's belief of; since nothing else could in the least excuse me, and that only is the real excuse why I did not set out on the first intimation I had of your Grace's opinion in that particular.

"I am, &c.,
"W. COWPER."

He took refuge in Berealstone, which was entirely close, and was one of a class of boroughs so convenient and useful that we can not help sometimes regretting the scandal which rendered their abolition necessary; for I fear we can not deny that they sent to parliament members more eloquent and better qualified to serve the state than the new boroughs with larger constituencies which have been substituted for them. Cowper continued to sit for the same place, while he was the leader of the Whig party in the House of Commons, till he accepted the Great Seal.[1]

Though for a time deeply grieved by the loss of Hertford, he was now in high spirits on account of the reaction in favor of the Whigs, caused by Louis XIV.'s foolish recognition of the pretended Prince of Wales as King of Great Britain,—confidently expecting to see his

[1] Gwynne was returned for Totness on the Seymour interest.

patron, Lord Somers, forthwith holding the Great Seal, and his own speedy advancement to the office of Attorney or Solicitor General. But his prospects seemed forever blighted on the accession of Queen Anne, when there was such a proscription of the Whigs that Lord Somers's name was struck out of the list of the Privy Council, and out of the commissions of the peace all over England. Cowper was even apprehensive that his silk gown would be taken away from him:—and of six Whig King's counsel, four who had give particular offense to the high-church party were actually cashiered. However, his patent was renewed—perhaps upon the consideration that with a stuff gown, and standing without the bar, he would have maintained his professional ascendency.

In the new reign, as a politician he followed the magnanimous example set him by his chief,—supporting ministers when they adopted the measures of their predecessors, and mitigating as far as he could the bad consequences of the illiberal domestic policy to which they for some time adhered. On the assembling of Anne's first parliament, the ghost of Sarah Stout was still supposed to haunt the streets of Hertford at midnight on its way to the mill race,—and he was again obliged to fly to Berealstone.[1]

Although we know that he continued a frequent debater, and that as a leader of the small Whig minority in the House of Commons he strenuously supported the war with France, and opposed the bills against "occasional conformity," there is no shred preserved of any other speech he ever made while he remained a member of the House of Commons, except in the great privilege case of *Ashby* v. *White*. He had tried to resist the infamous party decisions on election petitions out of which the controversy arose; and when the obnoxious judgment of the Lords came to be discussed, while he allowed that the Commons must themselves decide upon the returns of members, he insisted that it would be no violation of their rights to allow an elector whose vote was maliciously refused to maintain an action against the returning officer, and that the House of Lords was fully justified in deciding that such an action might be maintained. He

[1] 6 Parl. Hist. 42.

contended that the elective franchise vested in an individual was a privilege; that the willful violation of it was a private wrong, working a loss to the party injured; and that there being "*injuria cum damno*," it would be contrary to all principle, and a reproach to the jurisprudence of the country, if a remedy by action was not afforded. The House of Commons might rectify the return, and punish the returning officer for his offense against the public, but could give no compensation to the injured elector. He illustrated his position happily by the case of a battery, for which not only the wrong-doer may be punished by indictment, but for which a reparation in damages is given by civil action. He ridiculed the quibble, that by the ancient theory of the constitution the obligation to return members to parliament was considered a burden, when in reality the legitimate possession of power to interpose in the making of laws and in the government of the country was a noble distinction,—and as a vote for members of parliament was a right on which a high value was placed, he who was wrongfully deprived of it ought to have legal redress, in the same manner as for an injury to his person or his property. As for the argument that the Lords were deciding on the privileges of the Commons, he said, "The Lords have not judged the fact; they are bound as to the fact by the verdict, and they are unquestionably the judges of the law on a writ of error. And, therefore, as to what has been said that any fact of an election might come to be determined before the Lords, it is a great mistake, for they judge purely of the law on writs of error, as every one knows who knows anything of our constitution. I fear we are taking from the subject in effect what the law hath adjudged his right, and we are seeking to reverse a legal judgment given in the subject's favor. Upon the whole, I am for so much of your resolutions as serves only to declare that you have the sole power of determining the rights of all elections, and even the elector's right to vote, to the end to try who is your member, or to punish the officer as an offender against the constitution: so far, is agreeable to the constant law and practice of parliament. But for that part of the resolution which relates to the restraining of the electors from bringing their actions for the personal or private damage done to them, I think it is not agreeable to the constitution of parliament or the law of the land."[1] He was beaten by a majority of 215 to 97, and a dangerous wound was given to parliamentary privilege by this outrageous abuse of it.[2] However, he greatly raised his reputation by this effort, and he was soon to be placed in the highest civil station which a subject could enjoy.

CHAPTER CXIV.

CONTINUATION OF THE LIFE OF LORD COWPER TILL THE ACCESSION OF GEORGE I.

THE general election which took place in the summer of 1705 having turned out very favorably for the Whigs, the Earl of Godolphin and the Duchess of Marlborough having softened Anne's prejudices against that party, and all the world having grown sick of Lord Keeper Wright, it became clear that the Great Seal must soon be transferred to other hands. Lord Somers was still so obnoxious to the Queen and to the clergy, that the leaders of the Cabinet had not the courage to propose to make him again Chancellor. Northey, the Attorney General, was considered quite unequal to the post, even if there had been no objection to his politics; and there was a dread of another incompetent appointment, after the loud and long-continued complaints against poor Sir Nathan, who was about to be cashiered. Harcourt, the Solicitor General, was a man of great talents, and of high honor; but he was a very strong and consistent Tory, and as it was thought that he would always be true to his

[1] 6 Parl. Hist. 279.
[2] When arguing for the privileges of the House of Commons in the famous case of *Stockdale* v. *Hansard*, I had more difficulty in dealing with *Ashby* v. *White* than with any authority cited against me. The mere decision of the House of Lords holding the action maintainable amounted to very little, as the resolution of the House of Commons did not in any shape appear upon the record; but it was not easy to contend, that a resolution of the House of Commons respecting their privileges is binding on all other tribunals, when it may be, and has been, carried to such an extravagant pitch.—See *Lord Campbell's Speeches*, p. 136. The court of law must at least be allowed to judge whether the resolution is on the subject of privilege, so as to be within the peculiar jurisdiction of the House.

party and his principles, his promotion would not have been endured by the rising Whigs. All eyes were turned to Mr. William Cowper, although he had never been a law officer of the Crown. He was by far the most distinguished Whig barrister; he had for some years been regarded as the leader of his party in the House of Commons; and, by his agreeable manners and gentlemanlike bearing, while a zealous politician, he had gained the general good will of his profession, and of public men. There was only one obstacle to his promotion—arising from the rumor to which I have alluded, and which I shall afterwards be under the necessity of considering more minutely—that he had been guilty of bigamy. This charge had been most industriously circulated in society from the time that he became formidable to the Tories, and had been repeatedly stated in the libelous publications of the day, with many particulars and much declamation—but although now brought forward against him, the Queen was persuaded by the Duchess of Marlborough (who, without scandal, was supposed to be much touched by the beauty of his person) that it was groundless—and Godolphin, the Treasurer, was authorized to negotiate with him for his promotion to the woolsack.[1]

They met by appointment on the morning of Thursday, the 11th of October, at Lord Halifax's.[2] The Great Seal being now distinctly offered to Cowper, who had been before sounded on the subject, he stipulated that he should have, like his predecessor, £2,000 for his equipage or out-

---

[1] "Some former passages of his life were thought to disqualify him for that office by which he was to be the guardian of the Queen's conscience: but these difficulties were easily overcome by the authors of his promotion, who wanted a person that would be subservient to all their designs, wherein they were not disappointed."—SWIFT, *History of Four last Years of Queen Anne.*

[2] I have now the invaluable assistance of Lord Cowper's own DIARY. It begins this very day, and continues pretty regularly till the end of January following. There are a few entries in the beginning of February, 1706, but on the 11th of that month there is this notice between brackets, ["Here I broke off, wanting time, and eyes being sore,"] and there is a hiatus till 23rd January, 1709. There is a single entry on that day, and no other is found till 27th August, 1710, about the time when the Whig government was breaking up: we have this notice, "My great business and want of health, forced me to interrupt this course in a great measure; but I hope, on quitting my office, to be at leisure to resume it, though in matters of less moment." Then follow some very interesting details respecting the change of government, and the attempts to retain him in the office of Chancellor. But the entries are very rare during the remainder of the reign of Queen Anne. On the

fit, and a salary of £4,000 a year.¹ He next demanded what his predecessor had not aspired to—a peerage There never hitherto had been an instance of making a man, taken from the bar, a peer on his first receiving the Great Seal, and he said he should be contented to receive this distinction at the "next promotion." To this Godolphin immediately assented, observing, that "he should have been created a peer immediately, if there had been any precedent for it." Some accounts say that Cowper likewise wisely bargained for a retiring pension of £2,000 a year as a compensation for the loss of his practice at the bar; but he does not himself mention this in his diary.² At the same meeting the Treasurer showed him a private letter from Queen Anne, in which she intimated that "Rochester and Nottingham had so behaved themselves that it was impossible for her ever to employ them again, and she looked for support from the Whigs."

All preliminaries being settled, they proceeded together in a coach to Kensington. Having arrived there, the Treasurer was admitted into the Queen's closet, while Cowper remained in her chamber. Her Majesty soon came in and said to him, "Mr. Cowper, I am very well satisfied of your fitness for the office of Keeper of the Great Seal, and I am pleased to give it to you."—*Cowper.* "The honor your Majesty is pleased so graciously to bestow upon me, can not make me more zealous and faithful to your interest than I have always been out of principle, the surest ground to rely on. I am very distrustful that I may not prove equal to so great a post; and all I can promise your Majesty with certainty is, that I will behave myself in it with industry and honesty." He then kissed her hand, and asked and obtained permission from her to go out of town the following day, and to remain in the country till Sunday. He had been advised to do so, that

cession of George I., we have an account of his receiving the Great Seal from that Sovereign; and there, unfortunately, the Diary closes.

¹ At this time, these allowances were paid out of the Civil List, and were still matter of bargain with the sovereign, on whom they fell.

² "October, 1705. Mr. Cowper made Lord Keeper. Observing how uncertain greate officers are of continuing long in their places, he would not accept it unless £2,000 a yeare were given him in reversion when he was put out, in consideration of his losse of practice. His predecessors, how little time soever they had the Seal, usually got £100,000 and made themselves Barons."—*Evelyn.*

he might avoid as much as possible solicitation for places now in his gift.

When he got home he found a summons from Secretary Hedges to attend a Council at Kensington, at six in the evening. Then and there the Great Seal, which had been in the Queen's own custody since the Saturday preceding, was formally delivered to him, with the title of Lord Keeper.[1] He took the oath of office, and he was sworn a Privy Councillor.[2] Having disposed of all his places, " reserving nothing to himself, nor taking the value of one farthing reward " (which he seems to have considered a rare merit), he went to his house in Hertfordshire, and remained there till Sunday morning. He then repaired to St. James's Palace, in compliance with the custom still kept up as in the reign of Charles II., that the Keeper of the Great Seal attended the Sovereign to chapel, and fortunately, there being now the most perfect purity of manners at Court, there was nothing in this ceremony inconsistent with the character of a grave Judge. Lord Keeper Cowper, having conducted the Queen to her closet, carrying the Great Seal, " took his place in the chapel below : and after sermon, a little before anthem finished, went up to her closet, and so returned before her to her lodgings again."[3] The three

---

[1] London Gazette.—" Kensington, Oct. 11, 1705. This day her Majesty in Council was pleased to commit the custody of the Great Seal to the Right Honorable William Cowper, Esq., one of her Majesty's learned Counsel in the Law, with the title of *Lord Keeper of the Great Seal of England;* and the usual oaths being administered to him, his Lordship took his place at the board accordingly."

[2] Each oath cost him £26.

[3] Diary, p. 3. This custom evidently originated from the Chancellor having been an ecclesiastic, Confessor to the King, and Warden of the Chapel Royal. It was still preserved with lay Chancellors, and after the Reformation. We have a very graphic description of it from Paul Hentzer, a German, who published Travels in England in the time of Queen Elizabeth. Giving an account of her going to chapel at her palace at Greenwich, he says, " It was Sunday, when there is usually the greatest attendance of nobility. In the same Hall were the Archbishop of Canterbury, the Bishop of London, a great number of councillors of state, officers of the Crown, and gentlemen who waited the Queen's coming out; which she did from her own apartment, when it was time to go to prayers, attended in the following manner: first went Gentlemen, Barons, Earls, Knights of the Garter, all richly dressed, and bareheaded; NEXT CAME THE CHANCELLOR, BEARING THE SEALS IN A RED SILK PURSE, between two ; one of which carried the royal scepter, the other the sword of state, in a red scabbard studded with golden *fleurs de lis* the point upwards ; next came the Queen, very majestic," &c. I presume the procession on Sundays was laid aside at the accession of the House of

following days were occupied in receiving visits. Among those who called to offer their congratulations was Sir Nathan Wright;—"both, at first meeting, were a little out of countenance." On Thursday, the 18th, he kept his first public Seal in the Middle Temple Hall, and in the evening paid his respects to the Duchess of Marlborough, whom he seems truly to have considered the chief author of his advancement; but she declined all acknowledgment, and, "waiving that talk, expressed herself very averse from the High Church party."¹ Next night by appointment he visited the Prince of Denmark at Kensington, whose compliment was "that he was glad the Queen had made so good a choice."—*Lord Keeper.* "I beg leave to assure your Royal Highness that no one can be more devoted to your service; both because you, Sir, have always been in the true interest of England, and also for that I know there is no surer way to render my poor services acceptable to her Majesty than by my being first accepted by your Royal Highness."²

He continued to attend the Queen every Sunday morning to chapel; and every Sunday evening at six there was a Cabinet Council, in which the Queen presided, and all public business, foreign and domestic, was debated and determined upon.³ When the Queen withdrew, she

Hanover, but it is still preserved when the Queen comes to the House of Lords.

¹ At this time, and for some years after, the names of "Whigs and Tories," were generally laid aside, and the opposing factions were known by the "High and Low Church parties."

² There is a memorandum in the handwriting of his daughter, Lady Sarah, still preserved, which gives a very interesting account of his appearance at this time:—"1705. The Queen after this was persuaded to trust a Whigg ministry; and in the year 1705, Ocbʳ., she made my father Lᵈ Keeper of the Great Seal, in the 41ˢᵗ year of his age—'tis said the youngest Lord Keeper that had ever been. He looked very young, and wearing his own hair made him appear yet more so; which the Queen observing, obliged him to cut it off, telling him the world would say she had given the Seals to a boy."

³ E. G.—"Sunday, 21st Octʳ. 1705. Letters were read from Whitworth, who was with the Russian army, respecting its strength and operations. The next naval campaign was discussed, and the force was fixed which should be required from the Dutch. Reinforcements were ordered for Gibraltar. The propriety of sending a mandate to choose Sheriffs for the city of York after the charter day for that purpose was debated, ' to which the new Lord Keeper spoke the first time in Council.' The Queen desired her speech might be prepared by the Secretary of State for the opening of parliament (the topics, I presume, being then agreed upon), and to be reported at a Cabinet on Friday morning."

generally gave him an audience, that he might take her pleasure on filling up vacancies in the Church, and on legal promotions.¹ There were occasionally "Committees of Council," attended by the ministers, without the Queen; but till the accession of the Georges, who did not understand the English language, all important measures of the government were supposed to be deliberated upon by the Cabinet in the presence of the Sovereign.

On Tuesday, the 23rd of October, the first day of Michaelmas Term, the Lord Keeper took his seat in the Court of Chancery, in Westminster Hall. He held a levee in the Parliament Chamber of the Middle Temple, which was attended not only by the Judges and Queen's Counsel, but likewise by the Lord Treasurer, the Lord Privy Seal, the Lord Chamberlain, the Duke of Somerset, the Duke of Montague, Lord Halifax, Lord Somers, Lord Cornwallis, and many other Peers and Privy Councillors; who made a grander procession than had for a long time been seen on such an occasion. They all escorted him to Westminster Hall, and remained in the Court of Chancery till he was sworn in and began business.² He piously says, in his Diary: "During these great honors done me, I often reflected on the uncertainty of them,

---

¹ E. G.—" The same evening after the Q. withdrew, I was admitted into her bed-chamber, and there laid before her two livings, for which presentations desired; which she received very kindly, and said she would discourse me further next opportunity. Then I begged of her Majesty that Sir James Montague, brother to Lord Halifax, might be her counsel in my place, which she readily granted."—*Diary*, p. 5, 6.

² "Anno Quarto Anne Reginæ, 11th October, 1705.

Wᵐ. Cowper, Esq. } Wᵐ. Cowper, Esq., one of her Majesty's Councill
Lord Keeper. } learned in the law, received the Great Seal of England as Lord Keeper from her Maʸ at Kensington on Thursday in the evening, being the 11ᵗʰ day of October in the year aforesaid, the Queen having sent for it the Saturday before from Sir Nathan Wright, Knt., Lord Keeper, by Mr. Secretary Hedges. And on Tuesday, the 23ʳᵈ of the said October, being the first day of Michaelmas term, the Lord Keeper went to Westminster Hall, accompanied by the Ld. Godolphin Ld. Treasurer, the Duke of Newcastle Ld. Privy Seal, the Dᵉ of Somerset, Mʳ of the Horse, the Earl of Kent Ld Chamberlain, the Earl of Stamford & Essex, the Lds. Mohun, Colepepper, Cornwallis and Somers, and several other persons of honor, and most of the Judges. The Lords accompanied him into the Court of Chancery, where he took the oaths of Allegiance and Supremacy, and of Ld. Keeper of the Grt. Seal of England, the Mʳ of the Rolls holding the book, and the Clerk of the Crown reading the oaths. After a motion made, the Lords departed, and left the Lord Keeper in the Court."—*Crown Off. Minute Roll*, 1701–1714.

and even of life itself: I searched my heart and found no pride or self-conceit in it: and I begged of God that he would preserve my mind from relying on the transient vanity of the world, and teach me to depend only on his providence; that I might not be lifted up with the present success, nor dejected when the reverse should happen; that I might not be confounded or dismayed by the unusualness of my circumstances (and the like): and I verily believe I was helped by his Holy Spirit, from my sincere dependence on his good providence, in this great undertaking." Then follows an addition, which must have been made after his fall: [" Glory be to God, who hath sustained me in adversity, and carried me through the malice of my enemies;—so as that all designed for my hurt turned to my advantage."][1]

The Whigs were much delighted by Cowper's elevation; but it caused great alarm to the High Church party, and as Godolphin still wished for their support, he pretended that he had no hand in it, and even that it had taken place against his wishes. Lord Dartmouth, in his notes on Burnet, says: " The day after Cowper had the Great Seal, I met Lord Godolphin at St. James's where in discourse I told him that the world was in high expectations from the new Keeper: he said he had the advantage to succeed a man that nobody esteemed; but the world would soon have other sentiments, for his chief perfection lay in being a good party man; and seemed desirous I should understand that it had not been done with his approbation, which I did not doubt, knowing it was part of his penance for having passed the Scotch Act of Security, and that there were things of a harder digestion to follow."[2]

The new Lord Keeper devoted himself most earnestly to the discharge of his judicial duties. He not only gave rapid dispatch to the business which came before him, but he earnestly consulted with Lord Somers about re-

---

[1] Diary, 6, 7.
[2] Burnet, v. 220. The last sentence, I presume, means to express the writer's high disapprobation of the Act for securing the Presbyterian Religion in Scotland preparatory to the Union. This was condemned by many of the High Church party as irreligious, and leading to a dangerous toleration of heresy. The truth is, that Godolphin and Marlborough from this time were obliged heartily to coalesce with the Whigs, for the genuine Tory or High Church party were desirous to turn them out for Rochester and Nottingham.

forms in the Court of Chancery. Some abuses were corrected by Orders; and others, requiring the interference of the Legislature for their removal, were reserved for Lord Somers's great bill to amend the law, now about to be introduced.[1]

One most beneficial change he effected by his own authority, and from his own sense of what was right. Hitherto, according to ancient custom, large "New Year's Gifts" were annually made by all the officers of the Court of Chancery to the Lord Chancellor or Lord Keeper. The consequence was, that, for their reimbursement, they were allowed to extort large fees from the suitors; constant reluctance was felt to visit their delinquencies with suitable punishment, and the Judge was crippled in the discharge of his most important duties. This usage was common to all the Courts in Westminster Hall. But there was another of a more monstrous nature —and still more pernicious—which was peculiar to Chancery—that all the Counsel who practiced in the Court came to breakfast with the Chancellor on the 1st of January[2] in every year, and, in the hope of being raised to the bench, or of obtaining silk gowns, or of winning "the Judge's ear," made him a pecuniary present, according to their generosity or their means, or their opinion of his venality or of his stability.[3] Lord Keeper Cowper resolved entirely to abolish all these "New Year's Gifts."

He first, out of delicacy, mentioned the subject to Godolphin, the Prime Minister, knowing that he was likely to be privately censured, although no one could openly oppose him. In his Diary, under date "*30th Dec.*," he says, " I acquainted the Lord Treasurer with my design to refuse New Year's Gifts, if he had no objection against it, as spoiling, in some measure, a place of which he had the conferring. He answered it *was not expected of me, but that I might do as my predecessors had done; but if I refused, he thought nobody could blame me for it.*'

Accordingly, the Lord Keeper gave notice that no New

[1] Ante, p. 77.
[2] For certain purposes this day was considered the commencement of the year, although the dating of the year was not altered till 24th March.
[3] Burnet, iv. 141. I suppose the Counsels' presents varied a good deal, according to the prevailing opinion of the Chancellor's tenure of his office. If it was suspected that he might go out before the first day of Hilary Term (23d January), they must have dreadfully dwindled away.

Year's Gifts would be received by him. Nevertheless, on the morning of the 1st of January, several came to his house with the usual offerings, but they were all denied admittance; and with self gratulation, though not without apprehension of consequences, he immediately wrote in his Diary, "New Year's Gifts turned back: and pray God it doth me more credit and good than hurt, by making secret enemies *in fæce Romuli.*" The storm that he dreaded arose. No sooner was the fact known that the holder of the Great Seal had refused all New Year's Gifts, than the Chiefs of the King's Bench, Common Pleas, and Exchequer, were thrown into a state of consternation; and alarm was felt by the Heads of the Treasury, and other departments of the government, who derived considerable advantage from the present-giving custom.[1] To mitigate the ill-will which he had incurred with those who might have done him a mischief while he was not yet warm in his seat, he resorted to what he considered the justifiable artifice of pretending that it was only by mistake that he had refused the presents of the officers of his Court, and that he had intended to confine the refusal to the presents of the Counsel practicing before him. In execution of this device, he wrote the following letter to his father, Sir William, which the old gentleman was to show about to the offended chiefs and all others whom it might concern:—

"Jan. 2, 1705 (6).

" Honored Sir,

"Your saying yesterday I was y. talk of coffee-houses, and on recollection apprehending you to be in a mistake as to some particulars, and therefore fearing you should be necessitated by others to speak of that subject, I send you this to prevent mistakes: y. rather, because what you say will reasonably be thought of authority as to my concerns. The true fact is this. I had alwaies resolved to refuse the Counc. N. Y. gifts, as that which no Court or Judge in England or elsewhere received; and therefore y. day before sent word to all y. Counc. I could think likely to come to forbid it: but I sent to none of y. Officers, intending to make the same distinction y. other

[1] This, as we have seen, (Vol. II. p. 433), in Elizabeth's time, extended to the Sovereign.

Chiefs do: I had accordingly prepared a cold breakfast for the reception of the Officers as usual, but finding several Counc. came who I had not thought of, and that they would come thick on one another, I could not be at home to some and not to others, and therefore to prevent disputing wth ye Counc. I was denyed to all: But I never forbid ye other Officers, otherwise I would have this distinction made, ye rather because I find, by being abroad, y^t to carry it so far, doth not please others besides ye Chiefs, who probably submit to the same practise. Be pleased to let my Mo. see this, fro

"Y^r most dutifull
"and affectionat Sonne,
"WM. COWPER."[1]

He adhered, however, to his resolution to reject all New Year's Gifts whatsoever, saying that "he could not accept them even from the officers, after having once refused them, though unintentionally."

Notwithstanding the opposition which the reform at first encountered, Lord Cowper's disinterestedness was afterwards gratefully acknowledged by his colleagues,[2] and was rewarded by the well-known lines of Ambrose Philips:—

"He the robe of justice wore,
Sullied not as heretofore,
When the magistrate was sought
With 'YEARLY GIFTS.' Of what avail
Are guilty hoards? for life is frail,
And we are judg'd where favor is not bough'."

When Lord Cowper was a second time Chancellor in the reign of George I., he was still resolute, and we have the following amusing entry in Lady Cowper's Diary, in reference to the abolished custom:—"*Jany.* 17. This month used to be ushered in with New Year's Gifts from the Lawyers, which used to come to near £3,000 to the Chancellor. The original of this custom was from presents of wine and provisions, which used to be sent to the Chancellor by the people who practiced in his Court, but in process of time a covetous Chancellor insinuated to

---

[1] This letter is addressed:—
"To my much honourd
Fa. Sr W. Cowper,
psent"

[2] Letter from Harley, 3rd Nov. 1706.

them that gold would be more acceptable; so it was changed into gold, and continued so till the first time my Lord had the Seals, everybody having blamed it that ever had the Seals, but none forbidding it. The Earl of Nottingham, when Chancellor, used to receive them standing by a table, and at the same time he took the money to lay it upon the table, he used to cry out, 'OH, TYRANT CUTHTOM!' (for he lisped).—My Lord forbid the bringing them."[1]

The arrears left by the late Lord Keeper were very formidable, and from his low reputation there were many applications for rehearings; but by diligence, method and capacity, the business of the Court in a few terms was brought nearly into as good order as in the time of Lord Somers. The new Lord Keeper heard causes in the morning (from eight till one), and motions in the afternoon (from three till eight).[2]

His judgments are to be found in "Vernon,"[3] "Peere Williams,"[4] "Precedents in Chancery,"[5] and "Reports in Chancery." He is little indebted to his reporters, who give us but an imperfect notion of his powers of reasoning, and often substitute their own ungrammatical and quaint phraseology for the correct and simple flow of diction for which we know that he was remarkable. I do not think that he can be considered a profound jurist. He was not very familiar with black-letter books; he does not seem to have devoted much time to the civil law; and I do not perceive him drawing illustrations from the codes of the Continental nations. But, possessing great natural quickness and a retentive memory, he had diligently studied the more practical parts of the common

---

[1] So disinterested was Lord Cowper in money matters, that he not unfrequently refused his regular fees on patents. Thus Colley Cibber tells us, that when Steele's patent, as governor of the Theater Royal, passed the Seal, the Lord Chancellor, in compliment to Sir Richard, would receive no fee.—*Life*, ii. 47. His example, with respect to New Year's Gifts, was not speedily followed; and it is said that, till very recently, the Chief Justice of the Common Pleas invited the officers of his Court to a dinner, at the beginning of the year, when each of them deposited under his plate a present in the shape of a Bank of England note—instead of a gift of oxen, roaring at his levee, as in ruder times.

[2] Nisi Prius sittings after dinner had been abolished just before I entered the profession; but evening sittings at the Rolls continued during the early part of the 19th century.

[3] Vol. II.   [4] Vol. I.   [5] Vol. III.

law of England, with the little to be found in print respecting proceedings in Equity; and, almost from the time of his being called to the bar, he had had great experience on the circuit, and in all the courts in Westminster Hall. Without becoming, when called upon to distribute justice, such an indefatigable student as Lord Nottingham, he took some pains to keep up and to enlarge his stock of legal lore. Above all, he looked so young and so handsome, and so good natured, and his demeanor on the bench was so courteous while it was so dignified, that there was at once a strong prepossession in his favor; he was hailed as "a lawyer and a gentleman,"[1] and the public formed even an exaggerated estimate of the good qualities which belonged to him. His excellent sense and knowledge of the world prevented him from displaying ignorance, and kept him out of the embarrassments into which indiscreet judges are betrayed. He was said even to send away the defeated party contented with him:—" Hujus sors ea fuit, juris dicendi, in quâ gloriam conciliat magnitudo negotii, gratiam, æquitatis largitio; quâ in sorte sapiens Prætor offensionem vitat æquabilitate decernendi, benevolentiam adjungit *lenitate audiendi*."[2]

In reviewing his decisions, one is struck by observing how, in the construction of wills, he repeatedly admitted evidence of parol declarations by the testator relative to intention; but this does not seem then to have been much objected to.[3]—There being a devise of a trust of lands to A. for life, with a power of leasing, remainder to the heirs male of the body of A., he erroneously decreed the trustee to convey to A. an estate for life only, with remainder to A.'s first and other sons in tail male; but Lord Macclesfield reversed this decree, directing the trustees to convey an estate tail to A., although it was admitted that upon articles of marriage so framed the husband would have been made only tenant for life.[4]

He likewise fell into an error in holding that an executor to whom a specific legacy is given is not entitled to the surplus of the personal estate, and his decree was

---
[1] I remember its being said of the four Judges of one of the Courts in Westminster Hall, "A. is a lawyer, but not a gentleman; B. is a gentleman, but not a lawyer; C. is neither a lawyer or a gentleman; but I. is both a lawyer and a gentleman."
[2] Cic. pro Muræna.
[3] See 2 Vernon, 252, 517, 601, 736
[4] *Baile* v. *Coleman*, 2 Vern. 670.

reversed on appeal to the House of Lords, on the motion of Lord Guernsey, who had then great weight as a law lord.[1] All Lord Cowper's other decrees stood, and, as far as I am aware, would now be considered of authority. One of the most important settled the question in favor of the law-making sex, whether a husband should have courtesy out of a trust estate of the wife, although the wife was not dowable of the trust estate of the husband,[2] He laid down the rule, which has been since followed, that if there be a devise of lands to trustees to convey in a manner forbidden by the law against perpetuities, the devise is not void, and the conveyance shall be made as near the intent of the testator as the rules of law will admit.[3]—He decided the famous case of *Onions* v. *Tyrer,* upon the revocation of wills, more frequently cited than almost any other in our books; laying down, that if there be duplicates of a will, a cancellation of one duplicate operates as a revocation of both, and that a will well executed is not revoked by a will intended to revoke it if there be any defect in the execution of the revoking will.[4]—He laid the foundation of a valuable title in the law of "Principal and Surety," by holding that the master who obtains a bond for the good conduct of a servant has no remedy upon it for a loss which might have been prevented by ordinary diligence on his own part.[5] He had a very nice point to determine upon the law of "*donatio mortis causâ.*" A testator, after making his will appointing an executor and residuary legatee, when dangerously ill gave £100 to a person not named in the will, to be retained as a gift if he should not recover, and died of that illness. The question was, whether this was not a parol alteration of the will?—*Lord Cowper.* "The objection is not so strong as if there had been a specific bequest of a chattel, and then a gift, *mortis causâ,* of the same chattel. Devising the *residuum* is only the rest of his estate that he should die possessed of: but this is a gift in the testator's lifetime, although *mortis causâ,* and the

[1] *Lady Granville* v. *Duchess Dowager of Beaufort,* 1 Peere Williams, 114; and See *Ball* v. *Smith,* 2 Vern. 675. Lord Guernsey was one of the Finches; our greatest *famille de robe.*
[2] *Watts* v. *Ball,* 1 P. W. 108.
[3] *Humberston* v. *Humberston,* 1 P. W. 332; 2 Vern. 737.
[4] *Scott* v. *Houghton,* 2 Vern. 760; *Onions* v. *Tyrer,* 2 Vern. 741; Pri. Ch 459; P. W. 343.   [5] *Montague* v. *Tidcombe,* 2 Vern. 518.

possession was transmuted. Notwithstanding the will, the testator had the power to give away any part of his estate in his lifetime, either absolutely or conditionally. The will, therefore, shall have its full operation, although the donee of the £100 *mortis causâ* retains his gift."[1] Lord Cowper, backed by Lord Chief Justice Trevor, had the courage to decide a case, upon the execution of a leasing power under a settlement, against the opinion of Lord Chief Justice Holt—with the general approbation of the profession. Tenant for life, with a power " to grant leases of all lands anciently demised, reserving the ancient rents, and of the other lands, reserving the best improved rents," granted one lease of the whole, " rendering for the lands anciently demised the ancient rents, and for the other lands the best improved rents." Holt thought the lease valid, being in the words of the power; but it was decreed to be void, as contrary to the intention of the settler.[2]

I will finish with a case more amusing to the general reader:—" One Mr. Cornwallis having set up a lottery called ' *The Wheel of Fortune, or a Thousand Pounds for a Penny,*' Mrs. Fuller, the wife of Dr. Fuller, sent for twenty-four of those tickets, and gave them among the servants, upon condition, if twenty shillings or more should come up, her daughter should have a moiety of the prize; and one of them, thus given to her foot-boy, came up a prize of £1,000. The daughter brought this bill for the moiety of the money, and it was undeniably proved by the rest of the servants and others that the ticket, which cost but one penny, was given the foot-boy on that condition. *Lord Cowper.*—' " Cujus est dare ejus est disponere." The foot-boy is an infant, but he is bound by the condition as well as one of full age; he may be a trustee, and is a trustee as to £500 for the young lady.'—*Decree accordingly.*"[3]

Although the Lord Keeper remained a Commoner above a year after he received the Great Seal, his political avocations, from the first, demanded a great deal of his time and attention. On the 25th of October, at the meeting of the new parliament, he took his place on the woolsack as Speaker of the House of Lords;[1] and, with-

---

[1] *Drury* v. *Smith*, 1 Peere Williams, 404.
[2] *Orby* v. *Lord Mohun*, 2 Vernon, 531, 542; Eq. Cas. Ab. 343; Prec Chan. 257. [3] Burnet, iv. 141.

out a right to debate or vote, he was of great service by his advice in appeals and writs of error, and in the general business of the assembly.[2]

Early in the session, the important measure of the Scottish Union being brought forward, he was named one of the Commissioners for England. The Archbishop of Canterbury, nominally at the head of the Commission, did not attend, but the Lord Keeper, who was next in point of rank, was at the conferences which were held with the Scotch Commissioners almost daily. He wisely deferred much to the experience and authority of Lord Somers; but by his insight into character, and his conciliatory manners, he had wonderful success in soothing Caledonian pride, and in quieting Presbyterian jealousy. On the 23rd of July he delivered to the Queen, at St. James's, the articles agreed upon, which were afterwards, with some small alterations, confirmed by the parliaments of the two countries.

In the meanwhile, he notices several occurrences in his Diary, which, though of much less importance, still retain some interest. On "Gunpowder Plot Day," he attended divine service in Westminster Abbey as Speaker of the House of Lords; and, much as he may be supposed to be superior to such a gratification of vanity, he seems to have been much tickled with the precedence yielded to him on this occasion even by the Archbishop of Canterbury himself.[2]

He was still more pleased, soon afterwards, by a vote of the House of Commons—the result of a good deal of canvassing and management—which restored to his family the borough of Hertford, lost to them ever since the trial of his brother Spencer for the murder of Sarah Stout. This victory is commemorated in the DIARY:—"The Hertford election carried for the petitioner. The question passed as I had worded it,—a fair step to deliver a pure town from manifest oppression and wrong."[4]

[1] He says, in his Diary, recording this fact, "All the Lords who were against my advancement all wished me joy,"—a statement which somewhat keeps in countenance the courtly insincerity of our own times.
[2] Burnet, iv. 141.
[3] Diary, p. 11.—Our Chancellors now-a-days (no doubt much to their *mortification*) are cheated out of this distinction by the House of Lords being always adjourned over Gunpowder Plot Day, Charles the Martyr's Day, and Ascension Day, that there may not be a procession to the Abbey.
[4] Diary, 18.—He suspected that Harley was already intriguing against him,

Not being permitted to share in the debates in the House of Lords, he amused himself by taking notes of the speeches on the opposite sides, and marshaling on paper the conflicting arguments.[1]

He furnishes us with an amusing account of a dinner given about this time by Harley, who still remained in office, though discontented, and plotting against his colleagues:—" I believed, when I saw the company, this to be a meeting to reconcile Somers and Halifax with Harley, which was confirmed to me when, after Lord Treasurer was gone (who first went), the Secretary took a glass and drank to LOVE, AND FRIENDSHIP, AND EVERLASTING UNION, and wished we had more Tokay to drink it in (we had drank two bottles good but *thick*). I replied,—' His white Lisbon was best to drink it in, being very *clear*.' I suppose he apprehended it (as I observed most of the company did) to relate to that humor of his, which was never to deal clearly or openly, but always with reserve if not dissimulation, or rather simulation, and to love tricks even where not necessary, but from an inward satisfaction he took in applauding his own cunning. If any man was ever born under a necessity of being a knave, he was."[2]

The Tories out of office were now going into open opposition, but a good many were retained in place ; and Cowper pressed that these, called the "Court Tories," should be made to act as one party with the Whigs— when Halifax observed to him, "We are mixing oil and vinegar."[3]

The Lord Keeper was allowed to name the English puisne Judges, and all the Irish Judges, although, in exercising this patronage, he was influenced by the opinion of Godolphin.[4]

and trying to get a decision in the House of Commons on the Hertford Election Petition, contrary to his interest. Diary, 25.—"After the Q. gone, I asked Secretary Harley what he thought would be the success of Hertford business next day. He said it would certainly do well if yesterday's business did not spoil it. This I then understood as a menace from him, that he would do all he could underhand to spoil the Hertford business.

[1] Diary, 15.
[2] "Sunday, January 6, 1706."—*Diary*, 33. It is curious to see how he wrote of his then colleague—the future Lord Treasurer of the famous Tory ministry. [3] Diary, 12.
[4] Extracts from *Diary*.—27th, Sunday: "A Cabinet. Spoke to Lord Treasurer about Judges ; he said he inclined to Mr. Dormer." 30th, " Was

He thus very naturally expresses his delight with the attentions he received from the great hero of the age: "Lord Marlborough sworn in Chancery. He took occasion to speak much and very kindly to me in public. He is a great master of a very winning address."[1] About the same time he makes an entry respecting the leader of the High Church party, showing liberality on both sides: —"Lord Rochester, a good-natured man, though hot. He had during the debate, signified to me (civilly enough) that I should sit when I happened to be standing; and he afterwards came and asked my pardon in a very kind and obliging manner. He formerly did the same when I was counsel at the bar, and he had stopped my going on (as he ought) in a matter which was not open for me to speak to by the strict rules of the House. What related to one so inconsiderable as myself, especially when at the bar, could only proceed from good nature; for which, if it ever should be in my power, I should be glad to do him kindness, though a violent man of a contrary party to that I think most in the interest of England."[2]

The custom now prevailed, which was continued till the accession of Queen Victoria, that a report was made to the Sovereign in council of all persons capitally convicted at the Old Bailey Sessions. Thus he notices his own humane conduct on the first report after he was in office: —"Sunday, 9. A Cabinet. The Recorder reported the convictions. I spoke to save one, the evidence being doubtful; and the other for first offense. One respited till further order; the other transported."[3]

Before we proceed further with his political career, we must pause for a short time to view him in his domestic circle, where, as far as I can trace, after he recovered from the errors of his early youth, he always appears most amiable. He had some years before been thrown into deep affliction by the loss of his first wife, and the only

---

alone with the Queen in her closet. She asked me to propose a Judge for England, and Chief Baron for Ireland. . . . As to the Irish Baron, I stated the difficulty in procuring a fit man; but told her it was certainly the interest of England to send over as many magistrates thither as as possible from hence, that being the best means to preserve the dependency of the kingdom on England. The Queen said she understood they had a mind to be independent if they could; but they should not." Friday, Jan. 8.—"At night I waited on the Queen, and introduced Mr. Dormer to kiss her hand for Judge's place." —*Diary*, 37.   [1] Diary, 39.   [2] Ibid. 15, 16.   [3] January 26.

child which she brought him. When he received the Great Seal he had recovered his spirits, and being so young and handsome, and holding so high an office, he was looked to as a great *parti* by all the maids of honor and aspiring beauties who adorned the drawing-room of Queen Anne. At last he fixed his affections on a young lady of extraordinary vivacity and accomplishments, though she was of a Tory family,—Mary, daughter of John Clavering, Esquire, of Chopwell, in the Bishopric of Durham; and in the long vacation of 1706 he was happily united to her in marriage. A few of his letters to her may interest the reader, as showing the manners of those times, and the human heart—the same at all times :—

"Sept. 19, 1706.[1]

"The first thing I doe this morning is to sit down to write this to acquaint my life what I am very sure your concern for me will not think impertinent, y^t I got safe at last to my house yesterday, after a very troublesome journey. Wee met the cold northern wind and rain all the way, and being perfectly in ye dark ye three last miles, ye coach was forced to goe very slow, and ye poor servants, through ye violence of ye storm, could not use their eyes, wch they could have done if it had been calm. The coach was two or three times in danger, but got no hurt. The only consolation I had was to think your journey was shorter, and by daylight, so that I was not in fear for what I was most concerned for. You declare against speeches, and I believe care as little to read as hear them, and certainly never man stood less in need of them if the truest love and highest esteem are able to give undeniable evidence of themselves. I believe they are, and therefore shall depend for ever on making love to you that way. Though ye part I act is very painfull, yet 'tis heaven to what I should have felt if I had left you for any time with distrust of the sincerity of my intentions towards you, and I am farther satisfyed in having given you proof that what I have done is not to please an ungovernable appetite, wch perishes as soon as gratifyed, but that I have been led by motives of love and value of you, wch are of such a nature that they can never end but by God's or

[1] This letter is indorsed in the handwriting of Lady Cowper: "My L^{ds} first letter to me after we wer marry'd."

your own act. I beg you to take the best care of your health, and to preserve and improve that degree of affection wch I flatter myself you have for me, or ye little temptation I laid in your way (much less than I design) would not have prevailed. Take care of the points wherein my interest is so much concerned, wch is now become yours, and I hope so to order things as in a little time, without any disadvantage that may incurr ye censure of ye pretended wise, to spend ye remainder of my life in ye enjoyment of that happiness my imagination hath laid up for it. I am, with the greatest truth,

"Your most affectionat Husband and humble Servant
"WM. COWPER.

"Next Saturday's, Tuesday's, or Thursday's post will bring yours to me directed to me at my house in Hertingfordbury, near Hertford, Hertfordshire."

"Septr 24, 1706.

"Mad^m,

"I had a messenger to wait at ye Posthouse for the pleasure of yr lre, by wch means it came to my hands on Sunday as soon as I came fro church in ye morning. I do not fear any one suspecting by it my corresponding wth a lady; ye hand is like the writing of one used to much business of that kind. I dare not tell you, even at this distance, how much it pleased me, and how great an opinion it has given me of your abilitys in that way, for fear I should provoke y^r modesty to bear malice against me for complimenting you (as you will call it) till I am so happy as to see you. You say had you known the danger before, you would have put out of my power to have run into it. I thought I had before acquainted you with my design of carrying ye Lady you mention down wth me,[1] and therefore inferred y^t fro my writing she was here, you would inferr I did so: We were run upon a bank in ye dark, and ye coach was in some danger, as wee could just see, of falling into much lower ground. At that instant I could not but think of ye fable, wher ye man that's going to be cast away is pleased that ye end of ye boat wher his enemy sat was going to sink first. I would have taken care, I assure you, to have fallen as soft as I could,

[1] I presume an old, fat housekeeper—not the simultaneous wife, who, according to Voltaire, formed with them such an amicable trio.—*Phil. Dict.*

for my side would have been uppermost. Having supplyed y⁴ defect you put me in mind of in my Ire, let me do so wth yours: you do not mention the occasion of your taking so unlikely a resolution to be preferred, and what could put so improper a purpose into your heart. I took the first opportunity of giving you my handwriting to what I had before done, but you have far outdone me, when you let me see that those severe words concerning obedience w_{ch} the church and custom exacted fro you, were not merely submitted to as necessary, and of course, but y^{t} you will voluntarily run into a lasting assurance of ye same matter. I know not how to be even with you but by begging to beleiv this great truth, y^{t} if you design to deal so by me, you shall be the best dissembler in the world of y^{r} inclinations, if ever you catch me at willing anything you do not like, or denying anything that you doe. I hope the picture goes on successfully; if done by the time my next banishment begins, it will serve to support me under it, for do not imagine from anything that may look a little trifling or chearfull in this letter y^{t} my mind is here constantly in that tune; 'tis only while I enjoy this half conversation wth you, who I assure you are ye only satisfaction I propose to my hopes in this life. I am most faithfully,

"Your affectionate Husband and humble Servant,
"W. C."

"Fryday, Dec. 20, 1706.

"Mad^{m},
"I cannot pass this day without g^{t} uneasiness unless I inquire of y^{r} health, and hear from you; but I beg it may be very little, if at all troublesome to you to write. I am going to visit my Mother, and perhaps shall begin to prepare her for what she must, I hope, know in a little time. Let me now beg of you, when I cannot see you frown, to give me leave to know, either fro yourself or some other, your pleasure in ye maters I would have talked of wth you. I verily think one reason of my writing to you this night, was my seeing Camilla up for to-morrow. I have so often interfer'd with her, y^{t} I am ashamed of it, and beg y^{t} if you would have been there, if I had not spoke of waiting on you, you will not let that hinder you, and I will make myself amends by seeing you ye first minute I

can afterwards. I beleiv I shall take courage to goe once incognito (I don't mean in disguise) ye approaching time of liberty for those that work hard: That you may be alwaies most happy, shall be the constant prayrs and endeavors of him who is only yours, C."

"Dec. 21,—1706,—11, night.

"D. M.

"I cannot go to rest without expressing, so as you may have it early to-morrow, my concern and amazement to consider by w^{ht} steps you could collect so much disquiet fro so harmless a passage. I cannot recollect I said any one thing, that should give my life ye least occasion for such a charge as I find in y^r letter: heaven is my witness I never did, nor meant to reproach you for anything, nor did I ever beleiv or think I had ye least reason so to do: much less for the quality you mention, fro wch I ever did and do think you the furthest removd of any one under heaven. The only expression on my part y^t could be s^d to sound like reproof, was, y^t I would wait on you o' Saturd. *notwithstanding* wch I intended only for, and I really think was no other than a kind reproof for your unreasonable modesty; and 'tis my want of Skill, if it be not ye language of a Lover. I am sure it proceeded from a heart entirely, at the moment it spoke, possessed wth that passion for you, fully convinc'd of your great merit, for wch I really revere you, and perfectly satisfyed of your lovⁱng me to the extent of my eag'rest wishes. If I have any fault to find, 'tis rather y^t you love too much; nothing else could fro so small a spark blow up such a flame of apprehensions that, beleiv me, are unwarrantable. The expression in my letter, wherein I mention y^r frown, is utterly perverted by my d. Love's melancholy fancy; if you look again, you'll find it nothing but raillery, and I meant it only to make you merry; so y^t I was extremely concerned to find you undertake it as gravely as you do. I never thought of being at Camilla to-morrow, but some time in Xmas, as you'll find by my letter on a review; and yet that you apprehend as if I meant to goe though you did not. I am very desirous to set all your mistakes right, and in order to do it, will wait on you the first minute I can to-morrow, (Saturday). There is nothing I have so much at heart, as to please you in all my words and actions; and therefore I am very unfortunate whenever, contrary to my endeavors, it proves otherwise. I can never mean better, but since I see how dangerous it is to jest upon so nice a subject, I shall learn hereafter to tread wth more care, and not leave ye most innocent expression, if I can, to a possibility of misconstruction. I'll conclude wth owning I am highly guilty of ye vanity of beleiving wh{t} you desire me to beleiv in ye conclusion of yr letter; and in gratitude, I hope, you'll give me credit, when I assure you I have no prospect in life I set ye least value upon, but the continuance of yo favor, and ye unspeakable pleasure and satisfaction I shall ever find in doing you all the good that is in my power. God bless us. Good night!"

These epistles I think, place the Lord Keeper in a very amiable point of view, showing how he could forget the anxieties of business and the struggles of ambition. At the very time when he wrote them, Marlborough was conducting one of his most critical campaigns, on which the fate of Europe and of the Whig party mainly depended; and a great rivalry was raging between opposite factions in the English cabinet.

Harley, intriguing to give a superiority to the Tories, preserved a very civil exterior to the Whig Lord Keeper, and pretended even to be impatient to see his merits rewarded by his elevation to the peerage—as we learn from the following letter,—which may be said to show that the art of writing, as well as speech, is given us to *conceal* our thoughts:—

"Nov. 3, 1706.

"My Lord,

"I received the honor of your Lordship's letter at this place, and I did intend to have been in town as soon as I could have sent an answer, but the excessive floods have confined me; and therefore I will not longer delay the making the most hearty acknowledgments to your Lordship for your favor; I heartily wish it were in my power, by any effectual service, to express the just esteem I have for your Lordship: I do take it to be the best service to the Government, as well as justice to your Lordship in all places, and upon all fitting occasions, to show the world with how great integrity and dispatch that great office is discharged; and as your Lordship's unparalled generosity, the refusing the New Year's Gift, hath brought honor to the Queen's service, so I never omit saying to proper persons that it is a justice due to your Lordship's merit to let the world see the esteem the Queen has for you by a public mark of honor.

"If your Lordship had been in town when I came away, I would have asked your Lordship's opinion upon what heads I should discourse the gentlemen of the county against the next session of parliament: I have seen a great many in several counties, and of both parties, and I find both sorts are very desirous to quit their (pretended) leader, and unite in the Queen's service, if they may be permitted. I see plainly that a few good words, and a little impartiality, will make everything easy; and it is as plain that the other scheme will not subsist more than one session, if it does that; but I will not trouble your Lordship farther upon this head, 'till I have the honor to wait upon you in Lincoln's Inn Fields. I beseech your lordship to be so just as to believe me to be with the utmost esteem,

"My Lord,
"Your Lordship's most humble, and
"Most obedient servant,
"Ro. Harley."

With the assistance, or in spite, of Harley's efforts, "the justice due to his lordship's merit" was soon after done. On the approach of another session of parliament, there being a large promotion in the peerage, he was created Baron Cowper, of Wingham, in the county of Kent. It might be expected that I should now be able to gratify the reader by proofs of the Lord Keeper's great powers as an orator. The Scottish Union, with many other important measures, came on to be debated, and he fully sustained the reputation for eloquence which he had acquired as a commoner. Yet from the time when he took his seat in 1706 till he resigned the Great Seal in 1710, his name is not to be found in the "Parliamentary History," unless on the occasion of his returning thanks to the Duke of Marlborough by order of the House of Peers. I may present, as a specimen of the style of parliamentary reporting in the reign of Anne, the fullest account of the principal debate in the Lords on the Union with Scotland. The names of some of the opposers of the measure are first given, with a slight touch of the objections which they urged, and then the leaders on the other side are thus grouped and complimented:—"The Lords Somers, Halifax, and others, made very pertinent answers to these objections, after which the House divided, and the contents were 71, the non-contents 22."[1]

Lord Cowper's address to the Duke of Marlborough, in returning him the thanks of the House for the victory at Ramillies, was ordered to be entered in the Journals, and is thus preserved to us:—

" My Lord Duke of Marlborough,

" I am commanded by this House to give your Grace their acknowledgment and thanks for the eminent services you have done, since the last session of parliament, to her Majesty and your country, together with their confederates, in this just and necessary war.

" Though your former successes against the power of France, while it remained unbroken, gave most reasonable expectations that you would not fail to improve them; yet what your Grace has performed this last campaign, has far exceeded all hopes, even of such as were the most affectionate and partial to their country's interest and your glory.

" The advantages (I use the lowest expression for everything) which you have gained against the enemy, are of such a nature, so conspicuous in themselves, and so undoubtedly owing to your courage and conduct, so sensibly and universally beneficial in their consequences to the whole Confederacy, that to attempt to adorn them with the coloring of words would be vain and inexcusable; and therefore I decline it, the rather because I should certainly offend that great modesty, which alone can, and does, add a luster to your actions, and which, in your Grace's example, has successfully withstood as great trials as that virtue has met with in any instance whatsoever.

" Only I beg leave to say, that if anything could move your Grace to reflect with much satisfaction on your own merit, it would be this, that so august an Assembly does with one voice praise and thank you; an honor, which a judgment so sure as that of your Grace's to think rightly of everything, can not but prefer to the ostentation of a public triumph."[2]

[1] 6 Parl. Hist. 568. The Lord Chancellor was among the "others."
[2] 18 Lords' Journ. p. 177. 6 Parl. Hist. 546.

The Act of Union provided that there should be one Great Seal for the United Kingdom; although a Seal should still be used in Scotland in things relating to private right;[1] and Lord Cowper was the first Lord Chancellor of Great Britain, being so declared by the Queen in Council, on the 4th of May, 1707, four days after the Act came into operation.[2] On the assembling of the United Parliament, the Queen, in a speech which he prepared, said piously and pointedly, "It is with all humble thankfulness to Almighty God, and with entire satisfaction to myself, that I meet you here in this first parliament of Great Britain; not doubting but you come with hearts prepared, as mine is, to make this Union so prosperous as may answer the well-grounded hopes of all my good subjects, and the reasonable apprehensions of our enemies."

At this period of Anne's reign, the Whig star was in the ascendant. The Duchess of Marlborough still kept Anne under much subjection. Prince George, who was supposed to have had an antipathy to them, and to have exerted against them any little influence he enjoyed, was no more,—and they gained considerable popularity from the brilliant success of the war, which was considered their measure. On the dissolution of parliament in the following year, they gained a decided majority in the House of Commons; Harley and St. John were obliged to retire from office, and Lord Somers being made President of the Council, they considered the government free from Tory taint.

The session of 1708-9, began with placing the Lord Chancellor rather in a delicate position. The two Houses having voted a condolence to the Queen on the death of her husband, which was privately presented to her, she proceeded to give a very necessary order—(she now being a widow)—that the prayer should be discontinued, which, from her accession, had been put up in all churches and chapels during divine service, "to make her an happy mother of children," and the Commons, after the fashion of Queen Elizabeth's parliaments, unanimously resolved

[1] Art. xxiv.
[2] London Gazette.—"Whitehall, May 4, 1707. This day her Majesty in Council was pleased to declare the Right Honorable William, Lord Cowper, Lord High Chancellor of Great Britain."

that an address should be presented to her, praying "that she would not suffer her just grief so far to prevail, but would have such indulgence to the hearty desires of her subjects as to entertain thoughts of a second marriage." This resolution was sent up to the House of Lords, who were bound unanimously to concur in it, and the joint address of the two Houses was ordered to be delivered to her Majesty by the Lord Chancellor. He was a member of a joint committee for drawing it up; and, on his suggestion, the following address was adopted, which, considering that her Majesty was not only in her first weeds, but in the forty-fourth year of her age, with a constitution much impaired by good living and by the gout, shows some tact on the part of the framer of it :—

"MOST GRACIOUS SOVEREIGN: We, your Majesty's most loyal and dutiful subjects, the Lords spiritual and temporal, and Commons, in Parliament assembled, being truly and deeply sensible of the many and great blessings we have enjoyed during the whole course of your Majesty's most glorious reign, do most humbly conceive we should be inexcusably wanting to ourselves and the whole kingdom, if we should neglect to use our most zealous endeavors that those blessings may be derived down to future ages: and, therefore, with hearts full of the most profound respect and duty to your royal person, we most humbly beseech your Majesty graciously to consider the universal desires and most humble supplications of your faithful subjects, that your Majesty would not so far indulge your just grief as to decline the thoughts of a second marriage. This would be an unspeakable joy to your people, who would join their most fervent prayers to Almighty God to bless your Majesty with royal issue; all of them concurring in this opinion, that no greater happiness can be desired for your kingdom than that they and their children may long continue under the gentle and gracious government of your Majesty and your posterity."

The poor Queen, much embarrassed, after expressing her gratitude for the marks of affection she received from the two Houses of Parliament, and her anxiety for the Protestant succession, concluded by saying, "The subject of this address is of such a nature, that I am persuaded you do not expect a particular answer."[1]

[1] 6 Parl. Hist. 777.

The remainder of the session exhibited a series of easy victories gained by the Whigs; but we have no account of any speech of Lord Chancellor Cowper in the course of it, except another address of thanks, by order of the House, to the Duke of Marlborough, for his eminent services. On this occasion the Chancellor, with good taste, was very brief, and touched all ministerial hearts by pronouncing these words with solemn and tremulous voice, to indicate that they proceeded from patriotic piety: " I can not conclude without acknowledging with all gratitude the providence of God in raising you up to be an instrument of so much good, in so critical a juncture, *when it was so much wanted,"*—although profane scoffers pretended that the Lord Chancellor was thinking less of the fate of the nation, than of the fate of the Whigs.

Whether this party had offended Heaven by any profanity, or for what cause they were to be subjected to divine vengeance, we know not; but certainly soon after this time they seem to have been deprived of their understanding, and they were given as a prey into the hands of their enemies.

Now was preached the famous sermon of Dr. SACHEVERELL against VOLPONE and his colleagues, and now was commenced the preposterously foolish impeachment which I have inadequately censured in the life of Lord Somers.[1] It is understood that Lord Cowper joined with the more Whiggish section of the Cabinet in recommending that the sermon should (according to a very prevalent fashion) be, like the Non-resistance Decree of the University of Oxford, merely burnt by the hands of the common hangman, or that it should be left to the cognizance of the ordinary courts of justice, or that it should be passed over with silent contempt—but that Godolphin being furiously bent upon an impeachment, by which he hoped successfully to vindicate his private character and the public principles on which he had acted, they were afraid of a fatal split in the Cabinet by further resistance. They all honestly exerted themselves to bring it creditably to a termination ; and Mr. Burke thought that in the speeches which they delivered are to be found the true principles of genuine Whiggism and of the English constitution.[2]

[1] Ante, p. 84.   [2] "Appeal from the New to the Old Whigs."

Lord Cowper presided as Chancellor when the hearing began in Westminster Hall, and he comported himself during the long trial which ensued with great dignity and propriety. Thus he addressed the defendant, who appeared when proclamation was made for him, and he knelt at the bar:—" Dr. Sacheverell, it is needless to give you any directions concerning your behavior during the time of your trial or the ordering your defense, because the Lords have not only allowed but assigned you the counsel you desired, some both of the civil and common law, who will be able to direct and advise you not only in the substance, but form of your defense. The Lords have also made an order for summoning all such witnesses as you have propounded to appear for you; and, that you might be the better able to provide for your defense, you have had your liberty on the first application for it, and giving security for your appearance. You have also had all the time you thought fit to desire, in order to prepare for your defense, so that you ought ever to remember that their Lordships have used towards you all the indulgence you could reasonably expect." While the Peers were sitting in Westminster Hall, the Chancellor did not interfere further than by saying, " Gentlemen of the House of Commons," or, " Gentlemen, you that are counsel for the prisoner, may proceed," When the great difficulty arose from the objection that the articles of impeachment did not set out the passages of the sermon complained of as libelous, he very fairly put the question to the Judges, " Whether, by the law of England and constant practice in all prosecutions by indictment or information, for misdemeanors by writing or speaking, the particular words supposed to be criminal must not be expressly specified in such indictment or information?" I should have thought there was great weight in the objection, and should have yielded to it; but I make no doubt that it was conscientiously overruled by Lord Cowper and Lord Somers, notwithstanding the habit of imputing party motives to Peers in all judicial cases connected with politics.[1]

When sentence was about to be pronounced, an altercation arose below the bar of the House of Lords, which, but for the discretion of the Lord Chancellor, might have

[1] See Layer's case, 10 St. Tr. 93

led to very serious consequences. Sir Richard Onslow, the Speaker, coming up to demand judgment, " the Gentleman Usher of the Black Rod " insisted that the mace of the Commons was not to be admitted, but should be left outside the door—which he said was according to ancient precedent. The Speaker threatened to return to the House of Commons and complain of this indignity, but Lord Cowper ordered that the mace should be admitted. " Black Rod " being then ordered to produce his prisoner, was going to put him on the right hand of Mr. Speaker, who was thereupon very wroth, and exclaimed, " My Lords, if you do not order the Black Rod to go with the prisoner on the left hand of me at some distance, I will return to the House of Commons,"—upon which the Lord Chancellor directed Black Rod so to do, and then Mr. Speaker demanded judgment.[1] .

The Lord Chancellor, addressing the prisoner, recapitulated the proceedings against him, and, coming to the objection to the framing of the Articles, said :—" Their Lordships have resolved that by the law of parliament, which is part of the law of the land, in prosecutions by impeachment for high crimes and misdemeanors, by writing or speaking, the particular words supposed to be criminal are not necessary to be expressly specified in the articles of impeachment. So that, in their Lordships' opinion, the answer of the Judges, which related only to the course used in indictments and informations, does not in the least affect your case. The Lords, therefore, find themselves obliged by law to proceed to judgment against you, which I am ordered to pronounce, and in which you can not but observe an extreme tenderness towards your character as a minister of the Church of England. This High Court doth adjudge that you, Henry Sacheverell, Doctor in Divinity, shall be and you are hereby enjoined not to preach during the term of three years next coming."[2]—O! most lame and impotent conclusion!!! The driveling parson was considered a greater

---

[1] The Lord's Journals are silent respecting this controversy, but all the particulars are carefully recorded in the Journals of the Commons, who have ever since enjoyed the privilege of taking their mace, with the Speaker, into the House of Lords, and of having the prisoner placed at some distance on the Speaker's left hand,—which were considered great constitutional triumphs. —15 St. Tr. 472; 4 Hats. Prec. 293.   [2] 15 St. Tr. i. 522.

hero than Marlborough, and his prosecutors were scattered to the winds.¹

The Whigs showed the infatuation or *dementation* under which they were laboring, and considerably increased their unpopularity by very improper prosecutions for high treason which they now instituted, and for which the Lord Chancellor, as head of the law, deserves severe blame. During the impeachment, the High Church mob, who accompanied their idol daily to Westminster, pulled down a dissenting meeting-house in Drury Lane, and another in Lincoln's Inn Fields—burning the pulpit and the seats, and huzzaing for " High Church and Sacheverell!"² They might very properly have been prosecuted for a riot, and sentenced to a short imprisonment, but that they should be hanged, beheaded, and quartered as traitors, for " compassing the death of the Queen," or " levying war against her," was contrary to the plain dictates of humanity and justice. Nevertheless, upon the doctrine that an insurrection to destroy all inclosures, or all brothels, is high treason, the rioters were indicted for that offense, and two of the leaders, Damaree and Purchase, a waterman and a joiner, being found guilty, had the fright-

¹ Although he was silenced in the pulpit, he was not incapacitated from receiving ecclesiastical preferment; and a fine living in Wales was immediately bestowed upon him. His journey to take possession of it resembled a royal progress. The nobility and gentry were eager to have the honor of entertaining him, afterwards looking with reverence on the bed in which he had slept; and in all the towns through which he passed he was received with processions, ringing of bells, bonfires, and every demonstration of joy. Upon the dissolution of parliament, which soon followed, the members who had voted for his impeachment were almost universally cashiered, and many with great property and hereditary influence, and heretofore enjoying much individual popularity, did not venture to show themselves at the hustings, not only from the despair of success, but from the dread of personal danger. In the " Memoirs of P. P. Clerk of this Parish," is to be found the most striking testimony to the celebrity conferred upon this *charlatan*. "We are now (says he) arrived at that celebrated year in which the Church of England was tried in the person of Dr. Sacheverell." And in drawing the characters of the members of the association which he formed to defend the Church, he mentions " Thomas White, a man of good repute, for that his uncle, by the mother's side, had formerly been servitor at Maudlin College, where the glorious Sacheverell was educated."

² The Latin special verdict in one of the cases is curious. " Progressi fuer' exultantes et clamantes, '*Huzza High Church and Sacheverell!*' et declarantes qd ipsi omnes domos protestan' dissentien ab Ecclesia anglican' pro divino cultu allocat' diruerent et præd' domu' in vico præd vocat *Drury Lane* adtunc freger' et spoliaver' et subsellia rostrum (angl. *pulpit*) et al' ad inde spectan' in publico vico ibm adtunc protuler' ad comburend' et cum igne postea in eodem publico vico consumpser'." &c.—*15 St. Tr. 693.*

ful sentence, which till lately disgraced our law of treason, pronounced upon them.[1] Although they were afterwards pardoned, the Whig ministers were very justly blamed for vindictively bringing into jeopardy the lives of men attached to the Queen and the constitution, who had merely been betrayed into a breach of the peace from an excess of religious or party zeal.[2]

When the crisis came, the whole conduct of Lord Cowper is highly to his credit for discernment, integrity, and public spirit. Taking (I think) a juster view than his colleagues of the question of peace and war, he in vain tried to save them from the odious charge of continuing the struggle for their own advantage, by representing to them that the object of the Grand Alliance had been gained by the humiliation of Louis XIV., and that this haughty sovereign, amidst all his reverses, never would submit to the disgraceful mandate to assist in driving his own grandson from the throne of Spain. "For my own part," says he, in his Diary, "nothing but seeing such great men believe it, could ever incline me to think France reduced so low as to accept such conditions."[3]

The Queen, prompted by Harley and Mrs. Masham, giving signs of the coming change, it was apprehended that the Duke of Marlborough, then in Flanders, would immediately throw up all his offices; and Lord Cowper, with the Dukes of Newcastle and Devonshire, jointly wrote him a letter, earnestly recommending, both for the sake of the country and of the party, that he would retain

[1] 15 St. Tr. 522–703.
[2] It may be too late to controvert the law laid down in this case, but no government would now direct such a prosecution to be instituted. In Frost's case, which occurred when I was Attorney General, I had no difficulty in advising a prosecution for high treason, as with an organized military band of 10,000 men he attacked the Queen's troops, and tried to storm the town of Newport, intending, by force, to change the constitution of the country, and to establish "the PEOPLE'S CHARTER;" but, in cases which afterwards occurred in the north of England, bearing much more the aspect of "levying war," than the Sacheverell riot, I prosecuted only for a misdemeanor.—The Tories may be excused for rewarding the zeal, and compensating the sufferings of the honest Damaree, by making him chief waterman to the Queen and appointing him to steer her barge.
[3] "Lord Treasurer, Lord President Somers, and all others, Lords, did ever seem confident of a peace (on the terms they wished to prescribe). My own distrust was so remarkable, that I was once perfectly chid by the Treasurer, (never so much in any other case) for saying, 'such orders would be proper if the French King signed the preliminary treaty.' He resented my making a question of it, and said there could be no doubt," &c.—*Diary*, 41.

the command, so that there might still be a Whig gaining victories in the field, or that the odium of dismissing him should be thrown upon the Tories. Marlborough, who, although converted into a very good Whig and for ever alienated from the party now eager to put an end to the war, having still a steady regard for his own interest, thought of a much better expedient than resignation, and proposed that, to increase the confidence of the Allies, he should receive a patent as " COMMANDER-IN-CHIEF FOR LIFE," so that an office which ought not to be connected with party politics might not depend upon the casualties of party struggles. He accordingly, without the previous sanction of his colleagues, caused this scheme to be submitted to the Queen, by Sarah, his Duchess, now in the last agonies of expiring influence. Anne said "she would consider of it," and, under the advice of those who now possessed her confidence, asked the Lord Chancellor whether such a patent would be legal and constitutional? Cowper was aware that grants somewhat similar and not more objectionable, proposed to be made by Queen Elizabeth to the Earl of Leicester, and by Charles I. to the Duke of Buckingham, had been opposed by Lord Chancellor Hatton, and by Lord Keeper Coventry, and he unhesitatingly declared, that whether the proposed patent would be legal or not, it certainly would be unconstitutional, as, under a monarchy, military command could only be properly held during the pleasure of the monarch. Anne was thus enabled to say, that, however willing to gratify the Duke of Marlborough, she found, by the opinion of him in whom she and all her ministers confided so much, his request could not be complied with. The attempt was turned to great advantage by Harley and the Tories, who, during the rest of this reign, represented that the Duke of Marlborough had wished to make himself " Perpetual Dictator." Swift, in his " History of the Four last Years of Queen Anne," pretending to be very mild and candid, says: "We are not to take the *height of his ambition*[1] from his soliciting to be *General for Life;* I am persuaded the chief motive

[1] An expression probably taken from the epigram upon the high bridge, over the little stream in Blenheim Park :—

" The arch, the height of his ambition shows,
The stream, an emblem of his bounty flows."

was the pay and perquisites by continuing the war; and that he had *then* no intentions of settling the Crown in his family, his only son having been dead some years before."[1] In allusion to this attempt it was, that when Addison's CATO came out in the year 1713, and the two rival factions strove which should applaud it most, Bolingbroke called Booth into his box at the theater, and gave him a purse with fifty guineas "for defending the cause of liberty so well against a PERPETUAL DICTATOR."

Although the Whig party had so much fallen in reputation, partly from their rejection of the overtures for a peace made by the French king at Gertruydenberg, but infinitely more from the charge to which they had foolishly exposed themselves of being the enemies of the Church, the Chancellor individually stood high in public estimation; and, for the credit of his name, the Tories were very desirous of retaining him in office. They had one great lawyer, of whom they were justly proud;[2] but he, seeing the precarious tenure of office in such a juncture, would have been better pleased to have been Attorney General,—with his practice at the bar to retreat upon in case of a reverse.

Accordingly, Harley, who at this time did not wish to give a complete triumph to the ultra-Tory party, which might endanger not only the Protestant succession, but his own stability, employed one Moncton to treat with Lord Cowper for his remaining Chancellor. An offer by letter having been declined, the negotiator, who was a common friend of the parties, made a journey from Yorkshire to London, and, in a personal conference, offered Lord Cowper his good offices to preserve him in his place. Lord Cowper made suitable explanations to acknowledge so great a favor, but said "things were too far

---

[1] This character of Marlborough, by Swift, ought to make us look with some indulgence on the licentiousness of the press in our own times, which, being "pretty considerable," some suppose "unexampled." *Our* Marlborough is treated by political opponents with uniform deference and respect: but thus writes Swift, in what he calls "History"—of the hero of Blenheim, Ramillies, and Malplaquet, who never once retreated before an enemy—deliberately representing him even as a coward, "Those maligners who deny him personal valor, seem not to consider that this accusation is charged at a venture, since the person of a wise general is too seldom exposed to form any judgment in the matter; and that fear, which is said sometimes to have disconcerted him before an action, might probably be more for his army than for himself."   [2] Sir Simon Harcourt.

gone towards the Tories for him to think it prudent to keep his place if he might; and that, in case of a Tory parliament, Mr. Harley would find himself borne along into measures he might not like." The following day Harley himself came privately to Lord Cowper, who gives in his DIARY this amusing account of their interview:[1]—

"Munday, 18, 5 o'Clock. Mr H. came to me & made great Expressions of his Esteem &c.; owned he came by the Q. leave & D. of Shrewsbury's consent, & undertook for L. Harc^{tt} Approbation, to offer me to continue in my station, to act with me with Confidence and better friendship than the Junto had for me. He could say much of that, but would accuse none.—Gave me the History of the 3 months past, short & broken so that hard to be remembered. [Then follows a confused statement of intrigues between Godolphin, Marlborough, Harley, St. John, Harcourt, and Shrewsbury.] Used all Arguments possible to perswade me to stay in place:—All should be easy:—The Danger of going out:[2]—a Whig game intended at bottom; enumerated w^t Whigs in; declined (shuffling) to tell all the removes intended, tho asked; endeavoured to possess me with opinion of Injustice of L^d T^r and D. of Malb. towards him, & much broken unintelligible Matter *prout Mos* &c. To which I express'd great Hon^r done by his kind Advances; but as to my staying in, shew^d him a design I had open'd to L^d T^r before I knew his interest decay'd of getting a succ^r, being weary of my place; that being so indifferent towards it, I was not prepared to bear much for it; that I had already tasted Mortifications from Ld Dart^m, encouraged as I had reason to believe from . . . . ; that things were plainly put into Torys hands; a Whig Game, either in whole or in part, impossible; that to keep in, when all my friends were out, wo^d be infamous; that in a little time when any Tory of interest would press for my place, he must needs have it; that it was necessary a man in that place who had so much to do & judge of should sit easy in his mind as to the circumstances he was in; that 'twas impossible I sho^d be so during Measures I could

---

[1] Copied with the original spelling and abbreviations.
[2] This reminds me of a saying I have heard of the late Lord Melville: "Never resign; for when you are once out, the Lord Almighty only knows when you may get in again."

not but think hurtful to the publick, & contrary to the true Interest of my Countrey; and on the whole desired him not to think of continuing me, but only to prepare the Q: to believe my true professions,—that I wo^d always endeavour to serve her, to assist her against any hard Attempts on either side, & to live well with the Ministry when I was out of place, if they pleased to allow me that favour.—He seem'd not much to beleive my declineing to stay in, & after much discourse, desireing me not to resolve, went away."[1]

In this belief, that the Great Seal could not be sincerely repudiated, Moncton returned to the attack, and in a visit of two hours, went over all the arguments again, saying, " he had undertaken to succeed, and that, if he failed, he must throw himself into the Thames." But Cowper was firm, and intimated that, his official functions being substantially finished, he was going to Colegreen, in Hertfordshire, to visit his wife, who had lately lain in there. Moncton actually followed him, and still pressed him to continue to hold the Great Seal, suggesting that he might thereby save the Whigs. Certain news arrived that there was to be a complete sweep, with the exception of the Lord Chancellor, and they returned to town together.

The same day a council was held, and the scene took place which Burnet so circumstantially describes, when the Queen ordered the Attorney General to produce the proclamation for the dissolution of parliament, and the Chancellor was interrupted in his speech to oppose this measure.[2]

---

[1] Diary, 44.
[2] 4 Burnet, 290, 291.—The Diary notices a council, but is silent as to its proceedings. It appears, however, that Lord Cowper had received previous notice from some quarter, that the proposal of dissolution was to be made at the Council, and had prepared himself to resist it. I have, on a narrow slip of paper subsequently indorsed by him, " Heads prepared to speak from— nst Dissol. Parl. 1710. Denyd to be heard"—what he had jotted down just before going to St. James's:

" Hazardous—Dangerous
  To home &
      abroad
  Honour of M.
  & Peace of ye K.
      Worth hearing both sides.
1. Cond. of last Sess.
  Done nothing since to demerit
  —must be something extra w^{ch}

An ineffectual attempt was still made next morning by Moncton to shake his resolution; but Lord Somers and all his friends being actually dismissed, he would no longer allow the matter to be discussed, and putting the Great Seal into the purse, he proceeded with it to St.

    since happened
     O. Vox populi
     P. not so &c.
     If so — an arg^t
       ag^t it
    —wounds prerog.
    —crown approves
    Proph: disapp. Ergo
    (This if in eq. Balance)
    But hurtfull &c.
  2. A certainty
    for an uncertainty
    —put it all ways
     1. Wh. displeased
     2. To (word illegible) **Taxes**
     3. Mixt
      Contention.
  3. Too late for
    Timly Supplys
     Arrest the proceedings
     in Spain, &c.
  4. Encouragm^t to
    enemy
    —to retard peace.
    They build upon
    it, &c.
  5. If invasion
    Who can answer
    ye objection.
    Why such a step un-
    necessary.
  6. The present ani-
    mositys, heats, &c.
    encreased by it.
     Concl.
    Can't suggest any
    reasons on publ. acc^t
    And if this advice be
    only to prep. revol.
    in ministry
    I think it is to sacr.
    too much of ye publ. in-
    terest to such a cause."

We have here an instance of the continuance of the practice of debating subjects in council before her Majesty, and making set speeches upon them. It would be thought strange now, if, at a council held at Windsor for a proclamation to prorogue parliament, a councillor should rise and harangue her Majesty against the measure.

James's Palace. Being admitted to the Queen, he laid before her the reasons of his resolution to surrender it. "This," he says, "she strongly opposed, giving it me again at least five times after I laid it down, and at last would not take it, but commanded me to hold it, adding, 'I beg it as a favor of you, if I may use that expression,' on which I took it again; but after some pause told her, 'I could not carry it out of the palace unless she would promise me to accept it to-morrow if I brought it,' which I think she did, saying, 'she hoped I would alter my mind.' The arguments on my side, and professions, and the repeated importunities of her Majesty, drew this into the length of half an hour." He adds: "The reason of all this importunity, I guess, proceeded from the new minister not being prepared with a successor to me who would be able to execute the office well; Sir S. Harcourt having chose to be Attorney General, and her not knowing if he would take it; her having been informed I executed the office well; the disreputation it might bring on their late proceedings with as many as had any opinion of my probity or understanding; Mr. Harley and the Duke of Shrewsbury being afraid of the old Tories overrunning them, and willing, for a while at least, to have a little counterbalance if they should disagree: so, much to my dissatisfaction, I returned home with the Seal." On the morrow he repaired to the palace as the day before, and being introduced into the Queen's closet, said to her, "Madam, I come now with an easier heart before your Majesty than yesterday, since your Majesty was then pleased graciously to accept my surrender if I should continue of the same mind, which, with a deep sense of your Majesty's condescension and kindness, I do."—*Queen.* "I was in hopes, my Lord, that you would have changed your mind; but I can use no more arguments to persuade you than I did yesterday." Thereupon he fell on his knee, and delivered the purse with the Great Seal into her Majesty's hand, and she accepted it from him. Having offered her some advice about his successor (which she had the day before given him leave to do), he withdrew, and he carried with him what was far more precious than the bauble he had rejected—the consciousness of having acted honorably.[1]

[1] The Duke of Somerset was the only Whig in high office who *ratted.*

CHAPTER CXV.

CONTINUATION OF THE LIFE OF LORD COWPER TILL THE ACCESSION OF GEORGE I.

LORD COWPER immediately retired to his house at Colegreen, leaving the new ministers in undisturbed possession of the field, to complete their arrangements and to prepare for the general election now approaching. Here he heard that the Great Seal was put into commission, the Commissioners being Lord Chief Justice Trevor, Mr. Justice Tracy, and Baron Scrope,[1] Sir Simon Harcourt declining to accept it till the returns to the House of Commons should show what chance there was of stability to the Tory government. But all doubt upon this subject was soon terminated, the elections running in their favor more than in their most sanguine moments they had ventured to anticipate. The cry of "Sacheverell forever, and down with the Whigs!" resounded throughout the length and breadth of the land; there had not been such a burst of High Church feeling since the election of Charles II.'s first parliament at the Restoration, and there was now a House of Commons which could be thoroughly depended upon to pass any laws against Dissenters, or to weaken the influence of the moneyed interest, supposed to be still inclined to Whiggism. The Ex-Chancellor had little consolation from a visit he received from the Duchess of Marlborough, who relieved her bile by giving this character of the Queen:—"She has no original thoughts on any subject; she is neither good nor bad, but as she is made so by others; while pleased, she has much love and passion for those who please; she can write pretty, affectionate letters, but she can do nothing else well."[2]

In his retirement he was violently assailed by the man who at this very time was treacherously carrying on a double courtship with STELLA and VANESSA, pre-

---

When he came to excuse himself to Cowper for being "over persuaded by the Queen to keep his place," we have this conclusion to the entry in the Diary, giving an account of the interview: "On the whole, he appeared to me a false, mean-spirited knave; at the same time he was a pretender to the greatest courage and steadiness."—p. 50.

[1] Patent Roll, 9 Anne, Part 2, No. 8. [2] Diary, 49.

pared to break the hearts of both.¹ Alluding to the ex-Chancellor, Cowper, Swift wrote in the 22nd No. of the EXAMINER, published soon after the change of ministry: "This gentleman, knowing that marriage fees were a considerable perquisite to the clergy, found out a way of improving them cent. per cent. for the benefit of the church! His invention was to marry a second wife while the first was alive, convincing her of the lawfulness by such arguments as he did not doubt would make others follow the same example. These he had drawn up in writing with intention to publish for the general good, and it is hoped he may now have leisure to finish them." This was followed up in a few days with the celebrated comparison between the new and the old officials—containing in the character of Lord Keeper Harcourt the following calumnious sarcasms on his predecessor: "It must be granted that he is wholly ignorant of the speculative as well as practical part of polygamy; he knows not how to metamorphose a sober man into a lunatic; he is no freethinker in religion, nor has courage to be patron of an atheistical work while he is guardian of the king's conscience."² The first charge, to which I have before referred, was supported by the appellation of "Will Bigamy," now applied to the object of it; the second, by an assertion that Lord Wenman, against whom a commission of lunacy had lately very properly issued, was in full possession of his senses; and the third, by the fact that Tindal had dedicated to the late Chancellor a pious work, which was not altogether orthodox. But while Lord Cowper, through the medium of the press, ably defended the policy of his party, he passed over these personalities with contempt.

About this time appeared St. John's celebrated "Letter to the Examiner," which established his fame as a political writer, and had as great an effect as any of the effusions of Swift in bringing about a change in the public mind unfavorable to the Whigs. The unscrupulous author, after ably pointing out the evils arising from the unnecessary continuance of the war by the late ministers, for their own advantage, indulged in a most furious per-

---

¹ In perusing the Journal to Stella, it is curious to observe that, in the minute and circumstantial accounts he gives of all his other visits, he studiously and systematically suppresses his visits to Mrs. Vanhomrigh, and his acquaintance with her daughter.   ² Examiner, No. 26.

sonal assault on the Duchess of Marlborough. He describes the Queen indiscreetly raising one of her servants to be mistress over herself, and, in this single instance, as grieving her subjects. "Instead of the mild influence," says he, " of a gracious Queen, governing by law, we soon felt the miserable consequences of subjection to the will of an arbitrary junto, and to the caprice of an insolent woman. Unhappy nation! which, expecting to be governed by the best, fell under the tyranny of the worst of her sex. But now, thanks be to God! that Fury who broke loose to execute the vengeance of Heaven on a sinful people is restrained, and the royal hand is reached out to chain up the plague." Lord Cowper, although he had resisted the "Dictatorship," thought that he was bound to come forward in defense of his patroness, and, while Addison and Steele attempted to answer the arguments respecting the policy of the war, he, in the form of a letter to ISAAC BICKERSTAFF, took up the cause of the insulted Sarah. The recent change having been brought about through the waiting maid, Mrs. Masham, he turns with justice upon St. John the accusation of governing the Queen by female intrigue:—" Nothing is more probable than that some female attendant of the Queen might be instigated to undermine and supplant a lady on whom the long favor of her royal mistress and the merits of her Lord's services, with her own undisguised zeal for the British liberty, had drawn the envy and hatred of the adverse party; and that this lady, having the judgment to discern the persons and principles that prompted such inferior attendant, and the spirit and honesty to do her duty, by remonstrating (with all modesty, yet with all plainness) against such slavish insinuations of the power of princes as tend, in their natural consequence, to the impairing her Majesty's true title and interest, might easily acquire from the party, so opposed in their agent, the civil appellations of '*insolent woman*,' '*the worst of her sex*,' '*a fury*,' and '*a plague*.' Nothing is more common in courts than calumny; and 'tis no wonder those persons should pursue that lady with the utmost malice, who could have the disingenuity to suggest to her Majesty that the wits of the Kit-Cat have taken pains to lessen her character in the world. In a word, what is it indeed that party can be supposed incapable of attempting privately by their principals and agents, who in their public addresses to her Majesty offer her the powers and authority of an eastern sultan rather than of a British queen, and brand with the names of *atheists* and *republicans* all those who assert the principles which put the Crown upon her Majesty's head; and which if they had not been asserted by the Revolution, her Majesty must at this day have been a private subject, notwithstanding that hereditary title which they make the ground and reason of their proffered unlimited obedience?"[1]

Lord Cowper likewise bestirred himself very actively to defeat the ungrateful and factious efforts soon after made in parliament to ruin the reputation of the "Dictator" himself. Thus he wrote to a leading member of the House of Commons respecting the intrigues then going forward for that purpose:—

"Wensd. 19 Dec. 1711.

"S^r,

"I write this at ye request of the D. of Marlborough, who is apprehensiv (I beleiv with reason) y^t ye Report expected to-morrow may mention such facts as may amount to a reflection, without stating other equally true & appearing to ye Com^n wch would explain & clear ye former; for this reason he is desirous y^t you would meet some of y^r friends of the h. of Com: at Sr R. Onsloes this night, in order to be apprised of such things as may justly be taken notice of in his behalf, if a fit occasion should be given for it: I am very desirous to express myself more fully to you by waiting on you at any time before that meeting if I should not be troublesome to you, & you would mention time and place: but least that should not be convenient to you, I beg leave to add only this; that what assistance can be given him in this case con-

---

[1] Somers's Tracts, by Scott, xiii. 71, 75. Supplement to Swift's Works, i. 13. Sir Walter Scott, in his edition of Somers's Tracts containing these two letters, says in reference to them:—"This and the preceding tract exhibit the singular picture of two statesmen, each at the head of their respective parties, condescending to become correspondents of the conductors of the periodical writings on politics,—a sure proof of the extensive influence which these writings must have acquired over the mind of the public." Vol. xiii. p. 75. Lord Cowper's gallantry on this occasion called forth from Steele, in the dedication to him of the third volume of the Tatler, the following compliment: "Forgive me, my Lord, when I can not conceal from you that I shall never hereafter behold you, but I shall behold you as lately defending the brave and the unfortunate."

sistent with Truth and Justice, is not only extremely due to him in respect of his great Merit and Services; but will be of great use to the publick in supporting his Character so necessary to his success & weight abroad, if the war should continue, and for my own part, if it was in my power, I would espouse his case with all the zeall I justly could, as contributing in so doing not only to the publick gratitude but security for the future. I beg pardon for this liberty, assuring you I will alwaies be willing at your comand to serve in anything I can doe the least good in; & shall be pleased to be so employed. I am with perfect respect,

"Sir,
"Your most faithful
"humble Servant,
"COWPER." [1]

The new Government was all powerful in the Commons, but the Whig Peers, with very few exceptions, resisted the strongest solicitations to gain them over, and were rather more numerous than their opponents, although parties were for some time so equally balanced in the Upper House, that it was often doubtful on a division which would have the majority. They were animated by the hope, which comes in the place of power and salary, that the "administration could not last." [2] The infirmities of Lord Somers increasing upon him, Lord Cowper was regarded as the actual leader of the Opposition. Waiting on the Queen soon after the meeting of Parliament, she said "she hoped he would still serve her in the House of Lords." He answered "that he would be sure to do just as he would have done if he had continued in the great place she had honored him with." As the policy of her new ministers, both foreign and internal, was directly at variance with that of their predecessors, he can not be accused of a breach of good faith for the active opposition he offered to them during the remainder of her reign.

The first time we have any notice of his efforts in his new capacity of an Opposition orator, is in the debates on the conduct of the war in Spain. He appears repeatedly to have addressed the House respecting the disputes be-

[1] From the MSS. of the Earl of Lovelace.   [2] Diary, 51.

tween Lords Galway and Tyrawley, and the Earl of Peterborough, who had commanded with such various success in that country, and to have entered at considerable length into military details, as well as questions of general expediency connected with the peninsular campaigns; but the fragments of his speeches which we find scattered about can not be put together so as to give us any notion of his reasoning or of his eloquence.[1]

When the negotiations for peace were going forward, Lord Cowper waited upon the Queen as a Peer and Privy Councillor, ostensibly to warn her against improper concessions to France, but (as would seem) really to try to deter her from the scheme, known to be in contemplation, of turning the balance in the Upper House in favor of the Tories by a large creation of Peers. We are not informed how he tried to impress her with the unconstitutional nature of such a proceeding, but we find the following entry in the Diary, showing that even the Good Queen Anne considered that speech was given to enable us to conceal our intentions:—"In speaking on this subject, she was pleased to say to me that the House of Lords was already full enough. I'll warrant you I shall take care not to make them more in haste."[2] A few days afterwards twelve new Lords were introduced, and they were asked, "Whether they would vote by their foreman?"[3]

The terms of the peace agreed to at Utrecht coming afterwards to be discussed, the Duke of Marlborough represented "that the measures pursued in England for a year past were directly contrary to her Majesty's engagements with the allies, sullied the triumphs and glories of her reign, and would render the English name odious to all other nations." The Earl of Strafford said, "that some of the allies would not show such backwardness to a peace as they had hitherto done but for a member of that illustrious assembly [looking at the Duke of Marlborough], who maintains a correspondence with them, and endeavors to persuade them to carry on the war,—feeding them with hopes that they will be supported by a strong party here."
—*Lord Cowper.* "My Lords, the noble Earl who last addressed you did not express himself with all the purity of

[1] 6 Parl. Hist. 955, 963, 966, 971, 972, 975, 977.
[2] Diary, 53.   [3] 6 Parl. Hist. 1059.

the English tongue, but he has been so long abroad that he has forgot as well the constitution as the language of his country. According to our laws it can never be suggested as a crime in the meanest subject, much less in any member of this august assembly, to hold correspondence with our allies, such allies, especially as her Majesty in her speech at the opening of this very session declared to be inseparable from her. But, my Lords, it would be a hard matter to justify—to reconcile with our laws, or with the laws of honor or justice, the conduct of some persons in clandestinely treating with the common enemy of our allies, our Queen, and our country."[1]

There was no part of the Treaty of Utrecht which gave such dissatisfaction, or which was probably so liable to censure, as that which delivered up the Catalans, who bravely stood by us, to the vengeance of Philip. Lord Cowper dexterously hit this blot, and moved an address to her Majesty "that she would be graciously pleased to continue her interposition in the most pressing manner that the Catalans may have the full enjoyment of their just and ancient privileges." The feeling of the House, as well as of the public, on this subject was so strong, that Ministers were obliged to agree to the motion without a division.[2]

When the grand debate arose on the ministerial motion for an address to her Majesty, "to acknowledge her goodness to her people, in delivering them, by a safe, honorable, and advantageous peace with France and Spain, from the burden of a consuming land-war unequally carried on, and become at last impracticable, and to entreat her Majesty to pursue such measures as she should judge necessary for completing the settlement of Europe," Lord Cowper is said to have spoken as follows,—alluding particularly to an attempt of Lord Clarendon, the mover, to induce the Opposition to propose a vote of censure:—" My Lords, this is the most barefaced attempt that ever was made by

---

[1] 6 Parl. Hist. 1146. This is a very lively sally, and might screen Marlborough from censure for caballing with the Dutch to defeat the negotiation which the English government had been carrying on for a general peace. But the Ex-Chancellor's reasoning is certainly fallacious: a private subject can not treat with a friendly foreign power, as was universally admitted when Mr. Fox was supposed to have sent Sir Robert Adair to the Empress Catherine; and the government may treat with a public enemy in any way that may be deemed most advisable.   [2] 6 Parl. Hist. 1332.

the present or any other Ministry to secure themselves by endeavoring to get the sanction of this House for their blunders. Are the Ministers themselves conscious that they must be condemned by the public, or why this endeavor at an address to identify us with their imbecility? The Lord that spoke first, acting like a soldier, would, by skirmishing, have drawn on a general engagement; but the troops are too well disciplined to fall into an ambuscade of his laying. I can not remove my finger from the original of our misfortunes, 'the cessation of arms.' We were then told, that if a blow had been struck it would have ruined the peace. Would to God it had done so!"—This was the language of faction, and was so considered, for the address was carried by a majority of 82 to 69. The Ex-Chancellor had forgotten his own pacific policy when he was in office, but he tried to defend his consistency by saying, that the terms were worse and the situation of the allies better than at Gertruydenberg; and he treated with just contempt the importance attached to the renunciation by Philip of the throne of France, when—if there had been any virtue in renunciations—the War of the Succession would never have commenced. In a private conversation he had upon the subject about this time with Harley, now become Earl of Oxford, he said, "I believe, if we had made one campaign more in conjunction with our allies, we must have had a much better peace."—*Oxford*. "If we were at the gates of Paris we could not have had a better peace than what we are now to have." *Cowper:* "We might then have had Strasburg for the Empire, and a better barrier for the Dutch, and in all other respects a better peace."—*Oxford:* "The Emperor would not accept a present of Strasburg; and as for a barrier, it signifies nothing, and is all a mere jest." The Diary says,— "the Lord Treasurer's discourse was either obscure and broken hints, or imposing and absurd to the highest degree,"—but I must own I think he has the best of the argument.¹ The peace of Utrecht might have been more skillfully negotiated, but it was, upon the whole, a good conclusion of a war, the legitimate object of which had been gained, and its justification is the profound tranquillity which Europe long subsequently enjoyed.

¹ Diary, 56.

Lord Cowper, some time afterwards, stood forth to much greater advantage as the defender of religious liberty. The profligate Bolingbroke, not only a confirmed infidel, but zealously resolved by his writings actually to subvert the Christian religion, was now ostensibly the champion of the High Church party; and having fraudulently repealed the act against lay patronage in Scotland, he introduced into the House of Lords the celebrated "Schism Act" for England—the object of which was utterly to crush the Dissenters. Among other things of a similar character, it enacted, "that no person in Great Britain shall keep any public or private school, or act as a tutor, who has not first subscribed the declaration of conformity to the Church of England, and obtained a license from the diocesan, on pain of being committed to prison without bail; and that no such license shall be granted before the party produces a certificate of his having received the sacrament according to the communion of the Church of England within a year last past." We have no further account of his speech than that he said, "It was a bill of the last importance, since it concerned the security of the Church of England, the best and firmest support of the monarchy; both which all good men, and in particular that august assembly, who derive their luster from and are nearest to the throne, ought to have most at heart."

Lord Cowper answered him, but we are only told that, after professing a sincere regard for the church, he declared that, in his opinion, this bill would be equally pernicious to Church and State, and that upon those two heads he spoke near half an hour—saying, "Instead of preventing schism, and enlarging the pale of the Church, this bill tends to introduce ignorance, and its inseparable attendants, superstition and irreligion; that in many country towns, schools for reading, writing, and grammar, were chiefly supported by the Dissenters, not only for the instruction of their own children, but likewise for the children of poor churchmen; so that the suppression of those schools would, in some places, suppress the reading of the Holy Scriptures." He likewise strongly objected to the summary and final jurisdiction given by the bill on matters of such importance and delicacy to "Justices of the Peace—men sometimes illiterate, and frequently bigoted and prejudiced." The other Whig Lords made a resolute stand, but they were all surpassed by the Earl of Nottingham, who had some revenge upon Swift by savagely saying, "My Lords, I own I tremble when I think that a certain divine, who is hardly suspected of being a Christian, is in a fair way of being a Bishop, and may one day, under this act, give licenses to those who shall be intrusted with the education of youth."[1] Nevertheless, with the assistance of the newly created Peers, the bill was carried, having received the preposterous amendment, "that it should not apply to any tutor employed in the family of a nobleman." Lord Cowper signed a strong protest against it, containing this among other unanswerable arguments, " Because the Scots, whose national church is Presbyterian, will not so heartily and zealously join with us in our defense when they see those of the same nation, same blood, and same religion, so hardly treated by us." The bill passed the House of Commons by an immense majority,[2] and disgraced the statute book till the following reign. It was the last attempt in our parliamentary history to abridge the rights of Protestant Dissenters, although disgraceful additions were yet made to the penal code against the Roman Catholics.

While Lord Cowper eagerly stood up for the rights of all white Protestants, he not only joined with Lord Somers in inflicting new penalties on the Roman Catholics, but he was not in advance of his age with respect to men with a black skin. These, without regard to their religion, were, he imagined, not to be distinguished from cattle or inanimate merchandise. I find him taking part in the discussions which went forward at this time about the "ASSIENTO Contract," by which England eagerly bargained for the monopoly of carrying on the African slave trade in her own ships to supply the Spanish colonies with negroes—not hinting a suspicion that the traffic could be at all discreditable—but deliberately considering in what proportion the profits of it should be divided, between the Queen, the South Sea Company, and

[1] He had been the object of some of Swift's fiercest attacks. See especially "Orator Dismal, of Nottinghamshire." Swift's Works, x. 375.
[2] 237 to 126. See 6 Parl. Hist. 1351-1358. Stat. 12 Anne, sec. 2, c. 7, repealed 1718.

private adventurers.[1] The last speech made by Lord Cowper, in the reign of Queen Anne, was in support of an address " to thank her Majesty for giving to the South Sea Company the quarter part of the ASSIENTO Contract, which she was pleased at first to reserve to herself; and that she would be pleased that such other advantages as were vested in her by the said contract might be disposed of for the use of the public." The address was carried, and was considered rather a triumph to the Whigs. The Queen, in her answer, said, "she would dispose of these advantages as she should judge best for the service;"— which is said to have been " very ill relished by the Whig Lords."[2] On the morrow parliament was prorogued to the 10th of August, and before that day arrived the Queen was gathered to her fathers.

I find very little of Lord Cowper, unconnected with politics, during the four years he was in opposition—between his first and second Chancellorships. Except when Parliament was sitting, he resided at his house in Hertfordshire, and avoided all public meetings as much as possible. The following letter he wrote to the Lord Chief Justice Parker, to excuse himself for not waiting upon him at the Hertford Assizes:—

"Aug. 11, 1712.

"My Lord,

"Although during my being in place and since, I have looked on myself as escaped fro the ceremony and business of ye publick meetings of ye county: yet I had y greatest inclination to have waited on your Lordshp, as well for the pleasure of seeing so good a friend, as to congratulate you on ye impartiality, courage, and great wisdom wth wch your Lordshp is allowed by persons of all kinds to have conducted yourself in a late party business that came before you, in w^{ca} ye world will have me a little concerned. As this consideration, among many others, was on one hand a strong motive for me to have waited on y^r Lordship, so on ye other, considering I had never done it to any other Judge at an assize, I doubted whether the boundless malice of those who watch our actions might not raise some reflections on it, how groundless soever they may be; and therefore, though I

---

[1] 6 Parl. Hist. 1362.   [2] Ibid.

observe y̅e̅ scandal office of yᵉ party is plainly afraid of your Lordsp̅, yet I chose this way of paying my duty, as impossible to be perverted: and if I have ever thought upon this subject, I hope you will ascribe it to my retirement and solitude, wᶜʰ are apt to produce that excess. I am, with perfect truth and sincerity

"My Lord,
"Your much obliged,
And most faithfull humble
"Servant,
"COWPER."

Having received from Newton the present of a copy of one of his immortal scientific works, he returned thanks in the following letter, in which he gracefully refers to his patron and predecessor, Lord Somers, who had made Sir Isaac Master of the Mint :—

"Colegreen, 29 Au. 1713.

"Sʳ,

"I chose not to acknowledge & thank you for yᵉ receipt of a very valuable present, your book, till I had read it. It became me, I am sensible, to have made you my compliments upon it in yᵉ same language, but my disuse of writing in Latin, considered wᵗʰ the perfection in wᶜʰ you do it, (I will venture to say preferably to yᵉ learned Italian, your correspondent,) quite discouraged me. I find you have taken occasion to do justice abroad to the character of that truly great man, my Lord Somers; but give me leave to say, yᵉ other parts of yᵉ book (in which he seems at first sight not to be concerned) are a lasting instance, among inumerable others, of his clear judgment in recomending yᵉ fittest person in yᵉ whole kingdo̅ to that employment, which gave a rise to so learned a correspondence. I am, with all sincerity,

"Yʳ most oblidged & humble Servᵗ,
"COWPER."

During the violent struggle which took place, in the last days of Queen Anne, between Oxford and Bolingbroke, the former threw out overtures for a coalition with Lord Cowper. They had sat for two or three years in the same cabinet, and when politically opposed a private intimacy had to a certain degree been kept up between them, insomuch that the Ex-Chancellor had acted as arbitrator in a dispute between the Harley family and the Pelhams;[1] and the Whigs might now have been inclined to give him some support, being convinced that he was a friend to the Protestant succession, while Bolingbroke was plotting to bring in the Pretender. But this negotiation was suddenly broken off by Oxford being deprived of the Treasurer's staff, and Bolingbroke being empowered to form a new administration—at the head of which he meant that he himself should be placed, while he continued Foreign Secretary.

Instantly followed the news of the Queen's dangerous illness,—of the abrupt intrusion into the Cabinet of the Dukes of Argyle and Shrewsbury,—and of the delivery to the latter of the Treasurer's staff by the dying hand of the Queen. On the summons for all Privy Councillors to attend, Lord Cowper repaired to Kensington along with Lord Somers, and joined in directing preparations to be made for the accession of the new Sovereign.

CHAPTER CXVI.

CONTINUATION OF THE LIFE OF LORD COWPER TILL HIS FINAL RETIREMENT FROM OFFICE.[2]

AS soon as the Queen had expired, on the morning of Sunday, the 1st of August, the Council assembled, attended by Baron Kreyenberg, the Hanoverian resident. According to the Regency Act, seven great

[1] The following is the commencement of his letter to Lord Pelham on that occasion:—

"My L^d,

"I am very sensible of the great honour done me in your Lordsps naming, and my Ld Treasurers readily approving me as a fit person to make a scheme for an amicable acomodation of the matters in difference between y^r Lordsp and his family. I am very zealously inclined to endeavour to doe you both this service—your Lordsp for reasons I need not mention to you, and my Ld. T^r for the favours He alwais shewed me when wee were in ye service together, and especially at ye time of the late changes, w^{ch}, however wee differ in Politicks, I ought to remember whenever I have an opportunity of doing him any service without detriment to the publick."

[2] Lord Cowper's Diary ceases at the accession of George I., the last entry being dated 21st Sept., 1714; but fortunately a charming Diary of the second

public functionaries[1] were authorized, on the demise of the Crown, to act as Lords Justices for the administration of the government, along with such others as the Princess Sophia, or her son after her, should name in a sealed paper, of which one copy should be deposited with the Archbishop of Canterbury, another with the Lord Chancellor, and a third with the Hanoverian resident at the English Court. The three copies of the nomination by the Elector of Hanover, executed on the death of his mother, were now produced, opened, read, and found to agree,—and thereby Lord Cowper was one of eighteen added Lords Justices. There were not, and from the nature of the case there could not be, any instructions for their conduct, and, subject to the statutable limitation of their authority, that they should not assent to a repeal of the Act of Uniformity, they were left for some time in the uncontrolled exercise of the prerogatives of the Crown.

The added Lords Justices of the Whig party greatly outnumbered the Tories and those entitled to act by virtue of office. In their proceedings they were chiefly guided by Lord Cowper, although he was lowest in rank of the whole number. Their first measure was to appoint Addison their Secretary, and to order all dispatches directed to the Secretary of State to be delivered to him. This, I am afraid, was meant as an insult to Bolingbroke, who was now obliged to stand at the door of the Council Chamber with his bag and papers under his arm, waiting to be called in and to receive orders from those whom a few days ago he had expected to command.[2]

No change took place in the offices of the government

Lady Cowper, beginning at this time, is preserved. It remains in MSS. but it well deserves to be printed, for it gives a more lively picture of the Court of England at the commencement of the Brunswick dynasty than I have ever met with.

[1] The Archbishop of Canterbury, the Lord Chancellor, the Lord President of the Council, the Lord Treasurer, the Lord Privy Seal, the Lord High Admiral and the Lord Chief Justice of the King's Bench.

[2] There was unfortunately a striking contrast between the two functionaries in point of aptness as well as honesty. Mr. Secretary Addison being desired to write an official notice of the Queen's death, he was so distracted by the choice of words, and so overwhelmed by the importance of the crisis, that at length the Lords Justices, losing all patience at his bungling, summoned a common clerk, who, superseding the author of "Cato," readily did what was required in the usual form of business.

till George's arrival from Hanover, except the removal of Bolingbroke, on the ground that he had notoriously attempted to defeat the Protestant succession. In obedience to a royal mandate received from Herenhausen in the end of August, Shrewsbury, Somerset, and Cowper, three of the Lords of the Regency, abruptly took the Seal of Secretary of State from him, and locked the doors of his office. He had been professing his readiness devotedly to serve the new dynasty, and he was not without hopes of being taken into favor on account of his influence with his party. The fallen minister felt the blow severely, but attempted to conceal his personal mortification. He pretended to be much hurt at the manner of his removal, which, notwithstanding the usual good nature and gentlemanly demeanor of Lord Cowper, seems to have been marked by studied rudeness; but thus he wrote to Atterbury, who had been willing to head a procession in his lawn sleeves to proclaim King James III.,—"To be removed was neither matter of surprise nor of concern to me. But the manner of my removal shocked me for—at least two minutes. I am not in the least intimidated from any consideration of the Whig malice and power; but the grief of my soul is this —I see plainly that the Tory party is gone."

The King did not reach England till the 18th of September. In the mean time, notwithstanding the dismissal of one leader who had made himself so obnoxious, it was matter of conjecture "which political party he would favor," and many supposed that he would try to form a balanced cabinet from both. But as soon as he had landed at Greenwich, his demeanor showed that, either from gratitude for past services, or from the conviction that he could only have a strong government by exclusively employing those who had always appeared well affected to his family, it was evident that a complete ascendency was to be given to the Whigs. The King would take no notice of the Tory Lord Chancellor, who was strongly suspected of being a Jacobite, while he was exceedingly civil to Lord Cowper and Lord Somers.

Two days after, Lord Townshend, who had been appointed Secretary of State, fortified by a royal warrant, demanded, somewhat abruptly, the Great Seal from Lord Harcourt, and Lord Cowper was immediately summoned to receive it.' He gives in his *Diary* the following interesting account of his interview on this occasion with the new Sovereign and the Prince (afterwards George II.): —" I waited on K. accordingly at St. James's in the closet, where the Q. used to receive me. The purse was lying in the window, which the K. gave me, speaking to me in French very shortly,—'That he was desirous I should be restored to the charge of the custody of the Great Seal, he having been well satisfied with the character he had heard of me,' and I answered in English,— 'That it was now just four years since I surrendered the same into the hands of her late Majesty; that she was so good as to press me to keep it, but that I refused, believing that she was going into measures which would raise France again and ruin the common cause, and such I could not bear any part in; that I now received it again from his Majesty with the utmost gratitude, and would serve him faithfully, and, as far as my health would allow, industriously.' The Prince was in the outward room, and made me a very handsome and hearty compliment, both in French and English, and entered very kindly into talk with me. Among other things, speaking of the Princess's[2] coming,—'I wished she was here while the weather was good, lest she should be in danger in her passage.' He said, 'Providence had hitherto so wonderfully prospered his family's succeeding to the Crown in every respect, that he hoped it would perfect it, and believed they should prosper in every circumstance that remained.'"[3]

Next day a council was held, and Lord Cowper was in due form sworn in as Lord Chancellor.[4] On the 20th of October he assisted at the Coronation, and was treated with marked distinction by his new master.[5] Three days after began Michaelmas Term, when, after a most splendid

---

[1] Sept. 21, 1714.—His Matie sent for the G^t Seal of G^t Britain from Simon, Ld Harcourt, and the same evening delivered it to Wm Ld Cowper, with the title of Ld Chancellor of G^t Britain.—*Cr. Off. Min.*

[2] Afterwards Queen Caroline. [3] Diary, 57, 58.

[4] London Gazette.—" St. James's, Sept. 22, 1714. His Majesty having been graciously pleased to deliver the Great Seal of Great Britain to the Right Hon. William, Lord Cowper, his Lordship this day took the oath of Chancellor of Great Britain."

[5] Lady Cowper gives a very amusing account of the feelings and deportment of the different parties at this ceremony: *e. g.*, "One may easily conclude that this was not a day of real joy to the Jacobites: however, they

procession from the Middle Temple, he was installed in the Court of Chancery in Westminster Hall.¹ During the last four years he had been out of office and in active opposition, he had occasionally sat at the Council table when judicial cases were to be decided there; he had regularly attended the hearing of appeals and writs of error in the House of Lords; he had seen MS. notes of the judgments of his successor, and he had found time to revive his knowledge of our institutional writers. He, therefore, now presided in the Court of Chancery with fresh luster; and, aspiring after something more than the glory of avoiding difficulties, of not getting into scrapes, and of jogging on without any very loud complaints being made against him in parliament, he secured to himself the respect of his own generation, and a lasting reputation with posterity.

For a considerable time he enjoyed the entire confidence of the Sovereign. He had drawn up for his Majesty's perusal, to influence him in favor of the Whigs, a very clever statement, entitled "An impartial History of Parties." In spite of his professed impartiality, the writer undoubtedly betrays a leaning to his own party, but he communicates a great deal of valuable historical and constitutional information with captivating clearness.

---

were all then looking as cheerful as they could, but very peevish with every body that spoke to them. My Lady Dorchester stood underneath me, and when the Archbishop went round the throne demanding the consent of the people, she turned about to me and said, 'Does the old Fool think that any body here will say NO! to his question, when there are so many drawn swords?' There was no remedy but patience; and so everybody either was pleased or pretended to be so."

¹ 23 Oct^r., 1714.—"His Majesty having received the G^t Seal of Great Britain from the Rt. Honble Simon, Ld Harcourt upon the 21st Sep^t. A.D. 1714, and having been pleased to deliver it the same day at his palace of St. James to the Rt. Honble Wm Ld Cowper, with the title of Lord Chancellor of Great Britain, which his Lordship formerly enjoyed, his Lordship, the 23rd of Octr. following, came from the Middle Temple Hall to the Chancery Court in Westminster Hall, accompanied by the Earl of Nottingham, Ld President, the Earl of Wharton, Ld Privy Seal, the Dukes of Bolton, Argyll, and Roxburgh, the Earl of Halifax, 1st Ld Commissioner of the Treasury, the Ld Viscount Townshend, Secretary of State, M^r. Walpole, the Judges, and several other officers and persons, and in their presence did then and there take the oaths appointed to be taken by the 1st of Will. and Mary, and the oath of Ld Chancellor, the Ma^r of the Rolls holding the book, and the Clerk of the Crown reading the said oaths."—*Roll*, 1714-1727.

He was soon after gazetted as Lord Lieutenant and Custos Rotulorum of the County of Hertford.

Having given an account of the principles and proceedings of the Whigs and the Tories, from the origin of the two parties, he sums up with an air of great candor:—" I shall only add, that 'tis not to be doubted but your Majesty's known goodness and experienced wisdom will necessarily incline you to such moderate counsels as will render you King of all your divided people. But I humbly conceive it not possible so to distribute your royal favor but that one or other of the parties will appear to have a superior degree of trust reposed in them; and if such a perfect equality was possible to be observed, perhaps it would follow that an equal degree of power, tending at the same time different ways, would render the operations of the government slow and heavy, if not altogether impracticable. It remains, therefore, in my humble opinion, for your Majesty to determine which of these shall have the chief share in your Majesty's confidence, as most likely to support your title to the crown with the greatest zeal and most untainted affection to it. For as to their power to do it, give me leave to assure your Majesty, on repeated experience, that the parties are so near an equality, and the generality of the world so much in love with the advantages a King of Great Britain has to bestow, without the least exceeding the bounds of law, that it is wholly in your Majesty's power, by showing your favor in due time (before the elections) to one or other of them, to give which of them you please a clear majority in all succeeding parliaments." [1]

This, in its original language, would have been a sealed book to George I.; but a translation of it into French by Lady Cowper, was put into the hands of Baron Bernstorff, the Hanoverian Minister, to be submitted to his Majesty at an auspicious moment, and was supposed to have strongly confirmed the royal prepossessions in favor of the Whigs, and of their leader, Lord Cowper.[2]

[1] See Appendix to ch. cxvi. in former editions.

[2] Lady Cowper in her Diary, under 24th Oct., 1714, says she presented it to Baron Bernstorff, when he announced to her that she was to be *une Dame du Palais*: "I gave him, at the same time, a treatise (which I had transcribed and translated for my Lord) in French and English to give the King." Although of a Tory family, Lady Cowper, after her marriage, became a very zealous Whig, and corresponded with the Hanoverian Princess, afterwards Queen Caroline. We may judge of her activity while the Whigs were in opposition during the four last years of the reign of Queen Anne, by an anecdote she mentions in her account of the coronation of George I. She had been shoved

Till the unhappy differences arose in the royal family, which gradually undermined his influence, he was the King's chief counselor in the internal government of the country. His first service in the new reign was to advise his Majesty respecting Judges to be retained and to be dismissed. According to the understood state of the law, which was not without its advantages, although George III.'s alteration of it, at the expense of his successor, must be considered on the whole an improvement, they were all removable on a demise of the crown.[1] Lord Cowper presented a scheme for all the changes and promotions in the profession of the law, framed with great discernment, moderation, and fairness, which was carried into effect very much to the advantage of the community.[2]

out of her place in the Abbey by the Tory Lady Nottingam, and forced to mount the pulpit stairs: "However, her ill-breeding got me the best place in the Abbey; for I saw all the ceremony, which few besides did. The Lords that were over against me, seeing me thus mounted, said to my Lord [Chancellor], that 'they hoped I would preach;' to which my Lord, laughing, answered, that he believed I had zeal enough for it, but that he did not know that I could preach; to which my Lord Nottingham answered, 'No, my Lord? indeed you must pardon me; she can, and has preached for these last four years such doctrines as, had she been prosecuted in any court for them, your Lordship yourself could not defend.'"

[1] "A Judge," says Dr. Johnson, "may become froward from age. A Judge may grow unfit for his office in many ways. It was desirable that there there should be a possibility of being delivered from them by a new King."—*Bos.* ii. 365.

[2] This is a curious document, and to lawyers will be found very amusing:

"JUDGES.
King's Bench.
Lord Chief Justice Parker.
Sr Littleton Powis.
Mr Justice Eyre.
Sr Thomas Powis.

"This Court has ye great influence on Corporations. The 2 brothers generally act, in those maters, in opposition to ye Ch. Justice and M^r. J. Eyres: therefore it would be of great use if one of their places was supplyd by another fit man.

"Sr Littleton, ye elder Bro., is a man of less abilitys and consequence, but blameless. Sr Tho. of better abilitys, but more culpable; having been Attorny General to ye late K. James to his abdication, and zealously instrumental in most of ye steps wch ruind that Prince, and brought those great dangers on the kingdom. Besides having fro that time practised the Law wth great profit, he lately, when ye Hopes of ye Pretender's party were raisd, laid down his practise of near £4,000 an: to be a Judge not worth £1,500 an: for no visible Reason, but if ye Pretender had succeded, he would have made, and that very justly, a merit of this step.

"If either of these be remov'd, I humbly recomend Serjeant Prat, who the

The Chancellor's political functions occupied a considerable portion of his attention; for on him lay the chief burden of domestic administration, Lord Somers being Ch. Justice, Mr J. Eyres, and I beleive every one that knows him, will approve.

"Comon Pleas
L^d Ch. J. Trevor
Mr Just. Blencoe.
Mr Just. Tracey.
Mr Just. Darmer.

Ther seems to be no objection to the three last. The first is an able man, but made one of the twelve Lords wch the late Ministry procur'd to be created at once (in such haste, y^t few, if any, of their patents had any Preamble, or reasons of their creation), only to support *their Peace*, wch the House of Lords, they found, would not without that addition. From that time, at least, he went violently into all the measures of that ministry, and was much trusted by them; and when they divided, a little before the Queen's death, He sided with Ld Bolingbr., and for so doing, 'tis crediby said, was to have been made Ld President. Many of y^e Lords thinks His being a Peer an Obj^n to his being a Judge; because, by y^e constitution, y^e Judges ought to be *assistants* to the House of Lords, wch they can't be, if a *Part* of that body. Ther is but one example known of the like; wch is that of L$_d$ Jeffreys, Ch. Just. of the King's Bench, and after Chancellor to K. Ja. y$_e$ 2nd.

"'Tis natural to think, y^e other Judges stomach y^e distinction, while He is among them: and 'tis said y^t y^e suitors dislike y^e difference they find in his behaviour to them since he had this distinction. He is grown very wealthy If it be thought fit to remove him, Sr Peter King, Record^r of the City of London, I should humbly propose as fit to succeed him.

"Exchequer.
L^d Ch. Baron.———Vacant.
Baron Berry.
Baron Price.
Baron Smith, Ch. Baron of ye Exchequer in Scotland also.
Baron Banister.

"The general opinion of Westminster Hall is, y^t Mr. Dodd, an antient Practiser of this Court, is the fittest person to supply the place of Ch. Baron now voyd, and I must confess experience is requisite for this post above all others.

"Ld Halifax recomends his Bro: Sr James Montague, who has been Attorney General to ye late Queen; and my partiality to gratify my Lord's desires, would incline me to wish he may succeed.

"But if Mr. Dod should be thought more proper, Perhaps Sr James M. would be pretty well content to be a Baron at least for the present.

"W^{ch} might be effected by removing Baron Banister, a man not at all qualify'd for his place (wch he owes to ye friendship of ye late Chancellor), as any Lord will inform yr M.

"If S^r Ja: Montague be made Ch. Baron, and your M. should be pleased to let Sr T. Powis be remov'd gently out of the King's Bench, He would supply y^s place of B. Banister with more abilitys, and not be capable of doing much hurt in that station, as he may in his present.

"As I desire all possible inquiry may be made into any of the particulars above-mentioned: so I humbly request that this Paper may not goe out of y^r Majesty's hand, nor be shewed to more than of necessity.

almost entirely disqualified by growing infirmities for interposing in public business. A dissolution of parliament taking place, the elections ran strongly in favor of the Government, and the returns showed a decided majority in the House of Commons for the Whigs. I must own, that I think they greatly abused this change of fortune by seeking indiscriminately to bring their political rivals to the block.

At the meeting of the new parliament a considerable embarrassment arose from the King's entire ignorance of our language. William, though he might be detected by his accent to be a foreigner (which had added much to the unpopularity caused by his reserved manners), spoke and wrote English with fluency and correctness; and Anne's graceful delivery of her speeches (scarcely excelled by what we ourselves so warmly admire) had charmed all ears and hearts; but George—having been in the direct succession to the throne of England ever since the death of the Duke of Gloucester and the Act of Settlement, a period of fourteen years—had such a dislike to all sorts of learning, that he had not acquired the first rudiments of the language of the country he was to govern,—while it was well known that the Pretender, the son of James II.,

"Of your M.^{s} Council learned in the law.
"I beg leave to mention at this time only ye Attorney General, and Sollicitor General.
"They who are at present in your Majesty's service generally incline to remove both, and put in their places
Sr Peter King, above mentioned, and
Mr Lechmere.
But they are so near rivals they will never agree, ye one to act under the other in those stations. W^{ch} is another reason why Sr Peter may be more fitly disposd of as above said, in ye Comon Pleas.

"The Attorney General, Sr Edward Northy, is an excellent lawyer, and a man of Great abilitys in ye Law, a moderate Tory, and much respected by that Party, and no further blameable, than by obeying those, who could comand him, if he kept his place.
"If he should not be removd, 'tis reasonable to think Mr. Lechemere would accept of being Sollicitor under him: He being old and infirm, and ther being no competition between them, as to Seniority or Preheminence in their Profession.
"Ther may be other expedients thought of to salve any difficultys that may arise on this scheme, but it is needless at present to trouble y^r M: therewith."

The removal, for political reasons of Trevor, admitted to be a good Judge, was a strong measure. The other changes certainly appear for the public service.

who had been driven from his native country in early infancy, although he obstinately refused to adopt the national religion, spoke the English language as if he had never seen a foreign shore, and could converse with all his countrymen inclined to take up his cause in the thrilling accents of genuine Anglicism. George is reported, when seated on the throne, to have uttered the words following; but, notwithstanding all the drilling to which he submitted, it must have been a very awkward, if not a ludicrous exhibition:—"My Lords and Gentlemen, I have ordered my Lord Chancellor to declare to you, in my name, the causes of calling this parliament." Then Lord Cowper, going through the form of conferring with his Majesty, although they had no language in common in which they could converse, thus addressed the two Houses: "My Lords and Gentlemen, his Majesty hath commanded me to declare to you the causes of his calling this parliament, as they are contained in this his Majesty's most gracious speech, now delivered into my hands by his Majesty from the throne. '*My Lords and Gentlemen, this being the first opportunity that I have had of meeting my people in parliament since it pleased Almighty God, of his good Providence, to call me to* THE THRONE OF MY ANCESTORS,'" &c.

No personal blame could be imputed to George for this discourse; but I think Lord Cowper is chargeable with some bad taste and some bad feeling displayed by it. Not only the Jacobites, but Constitutionalists must have been a little inclined to sneer at the *ancestral rights* of the new dynasty, considering that preferable claims, according to the rules of descent, might be set up not only by the son of James II., but by the descendents of Charles I., through the Princess Henrietta, and by all the many children of the children of the Queen of Bohemia, born before the Princess Sophia. It would have been more graceful, therefore, to have rested on his Majesty's undoubted title by act of parliament and the will of the people. The reflection which followed on the Peace of Utrecht, and the measures of the last years of the late reign, were undignified if not unfounded, and showed George as head of the Whig faction rather than the monarch of a mighty nation.

Bolingbroke, addressing a house of parliament for the

last time, made a noble stand for his party, and delivered a speech which excited universal admiration, being superior to all past or contemporary oratory in the English senate; but, like all his other speeches, it has irrecoverably perished. We only know that he vindicated the memory of the late Queen, which he maintained was now wantonly assailed, and that he moved an amendment to the address, in the clause about "*recovering* the reputation of the kingdom in foreign parts;" to substitute the word "maintain" for the word "recover;" saying that, "having been one of the late Queen's servants, if he had done anything amiss, he would be contented to be punished for it; but that he thought it an unjust fate to be censured and condemned without being heard."

Lord Cowper answered him, contending that "they did not condemn any particular person, but only the peace in general, because they felt the ill consequences of it; that they who advised and made such a peace deserved indeed to be censured, but that the words in the address being general, no private person was affected by them; and that the alteration of the word 'recover' into that of 'maintain' would signify no more towards the justification of the guilty, than the word 'recover' towards the condemnation of the innocent."[1] The amendment was negatived by a majority of 66 to 33.

A similar address being carried in the Commons by a majority of 244 to 138, the victory was followed up by moving impeachments for high treason against the three chief leaders of the late Government, the Earl of Oxford, Viscount Bolingbroke, and the Duke of Ormond. The last two fled (I think) injudiciously and unnecessarily. Evidence might have been given that they had corresponded with the Court of St. Germaine's; but if this was treason in the eye of the law, it was not an offense for which the public could have endured to have seen noblemen's heads chopped off,—and, at any rate, the Duke of Marlborough and some of his Whig associates were *in pari delicto*.[2]—The Chancellor

[1] 7 Parl. Hist. 42–46.
[2] Bolingbroke gave as a reason for flying, "that his contempt for Oxford was so great he could not endure concerting with him measures for their common defense." The manner of his flight was characteristic. Having used a tone of calmness and firmness, saying that "he found by experience he could be unfortunate without being unhappy," and having announced his

had no difficulty in passing bills of attainder against the fugitives.[1]

But the prosecution of Oxford caused much embarrassment to his enemies, and drew down no little disgrace upon them. Twenty-two articles of impeachment were exhibited against him. These contained no charge of aiding the exiled royal family; and on his behalf it was contended, that, if well founded in point of fact, none of them amounted to high treason,—so that the accused party was entitled to be liberated on bail, and to sit within the bar on his trial. Having carefully perused the articles, I can find in them nothing of treason. If the Peace of Utrecht were to be again discussed after a vote of approbation by two parliaments, it could not, however blameable, be said to have been a "compassing of the Queen's death," or "levying war against her within her realm." The effort to obtain Tournay for the French was, indeed, gravely contended to be "an adhering to the Queen's enemies," within the meaning of the statute of Edward III.; but this was only by confounding all legal distinctions, and violating the plainest dictates of common sense. Indeed, we now know that the very Cabinet who directed the impeachment against the Earl of Oxford, soon came to the resolution "that the charge of high treason should be dropped, it being very certain that there is not sufficient evidence to convict him of that crime, but that he should be pushed with all possible vigor upon the point of misdemeanor." Yet when a motion was made in the House of Lords, by Lord Trevor, that the opinion of the Judges should be taken whether the charge contained in the articles amounted to treason, Lord Chancellor Cowper showing how a mixture of judi-

---

resolution to meet his accusers, he appeared at Drury Lane Theater, and having, according to the custom of the time, ordered another play for the next night, he disguised himself as a servant of La Vigne, a messenger of the King of France, set off to Dover, and reached Paris undiscovered,—where he soon became Secretary of State to the Pretender.—His real motives for flight were despair of ingratiating himself with the new dynasty, and the hope of a Restoration. Lady Cowper says in her Diary, "At the coronation my Lord Bolingbroke for the first time saw the King. He had attempted it before without success. The King seeing a face he did not know, asked his name when he did him homage, and he hearing it as he went down the steps from the throne, turned round and *bowed three times down to the very ground.*"

[1] Dispatch from Lord Townshend and Secretary Stanhope, 2nd Nov., 1716. 2 Coxe, Sir R. Walp. 70.

cial and political functions may cloud the clearest understanding, strenuously contended that some of the articles, if proved, amounted to high treason, "and challenged all the lawyers in England to disprove his arguments." The only plausible objection to the motion was started by Lord Nottingham, who urged that it might turn out to the hurt of the accused; for if the Judges on this preliminary consultation should say the charge amounted to treason, he would stand prejudged before he was brought to his trial. The motion was negatived by a majority of 84 to 52. Oxford was then allowed to address the House, urging "that he was taking leave of their Lordships perhaps for ever." He seized upon the only real ground of criminality alleged against him, which, as "a high misdemeanor," we should say he could not satisfactorily answer—the secret order sent to Ormond for a cessation of hostilities—which he justified by the Queen's immediate command; and (so unsettled was even now, in the third reign after the Revolution, the doctrine of ministerial responsibility) he said, with sincere confidence:—"If ministers of state, my Lords, acting by the immediate commands of their sovereign, are afterwards to be made accountable for their proceedings, mine may one day be the case of any member of this august assembly."

In spite of a touching appeal to their justice and their mercy, he was committed to the Tower, where he lay two years without being brought to trial; and it is smartly observed by a noble historian, that "the proceedings against him seemed to partake of his character, and could scarcely have been more slow and dilatory had they been directed by himself." [1]

In the meantime the Rebellion broke out in Scotland, and Lord Cowper, alarmed by the supineness of his colleagues, addressed the following letter to the King:—

"Sire,

"I would not trouble your Majesty in this manner, but on some very great crisis, as I take the present to be, when I should desire not to be in the least mistaken by a sudden interpretation. On your Majesty's receiving certain advice from Scotland of an open rebellion not only begun but declared there, and even hostilities commenced, I own my concern to find nothing moved to be

[1] Lord Mahon's History of England, vol. i. p. 414.

considered, but whether circular letters should not go to the Lord Lieutenants, &c., to seize Papists and non-jurors in the North of England.

"Your Majesty's Attorney and Solicitor General were both of opinion with me, that the law doth not warrant the import of such letters; the Chief Justice did not give an opinion either way. Two or three precedents were found in the Council Books of such letters, which were, indeed, strains of the law, in hopes of some good effect, which always failed. However, the most of your Majesty's Council were for making an experiment once more, and to that I refer myself, to have it seen what fruits it will produce when the returns come to be made, if any.

"It was agreed that the method I preferred, of learning the names of all the great Papists and non-jurors in the North, and taking them up, and securing them by warrant of six Privy Councillors or a Secretary of State, in virtue of a plain law made on purpose this session, should be likewise practiced. And lest the using of the first insufficient remedy should, as is usual, slacken the making up of the true, I humbly beg your Majesty to remind your servants that this be forthwith and effectually done, since the former method will take up the inconsiderable people, if any, and be longer in doing also.

"But what seems to me to be the more important and natural consideration on this news from Scotland, is—whether the forces now in Scotland, or going thither, are probably sufficient to stop the march of the rebels; and if not, whether the consequences of that are not bad enough to require some augmentation, wherever it can be had without exposing too much of this part of the kingdom.

"As to the first: I think your General or Secretary at War should state plainly before your Majesty in the Cabinet, what number of effective men are now, or will be in a short time, of your forces in the field, and then by comparing that number with what the rebels will probably march, or your Majesty by the next advices may hear they have got together, a judgment may be formed on that point. If your Majesty's forces are found insufficient to stop the rebels, I humbly think your troops there should be immediately augmented by all means consistent with the not leaving this part of the kingdom so unguarded as to invite an insurrection or invasion to be made here. For it seems certain that if any disgrace befall your Majesty's troops in Scotland, insurrections will immediately follow in England in many places. On the other hand, if the rebels get no advantage in Scotland, my conjecture is, there will be no considerable rising in England. And I take it to be much safer to prevent commotions in England by securing that the rebels shall make no progress in Scotland, than it will be, when any success of the rebels in Scotland shall have made many insurrections to break out in England, to find means to suppress them.

"The Scotch magnify their danger something, and perhaps press for more assistance than can be reasonably spared from home; but I beg leave to assure you, I cannot but observe the prevailing inclination here is to supply the forces there too sparingly, and as, on the one hand, it would be extremely wrong to draw the bulk of your Majesty's forces to that end of your kingdom, so, on the other, the not making the Duke of Argyle strong enough to secure himself against a defeat, or a necessity of retreating, or of letting them go by him towards the South, will thoroughly engage England in a civil war, of which none can answer for the consequence.

"And therefore I humbly advise that this great point should be thoroughly stated and considered by all such as have the honor at any time to advise your Majesty."

Afterwards, when a foreign invasion was seriously threatened, to put the Pretender on the throne, Lord Cowper thus again appealed to him who seemed about to be driven from it:—

"Sire,

"I humbly beg leave to lay a few observations before your Majesty in this great conjuncture of the intended invasion,—not with the least view of traducing any one's conduct, but purely that, if any errors be committed, as short an end may be put to 'em as possible, and the like avoided for the future.

"The fidelity of all who are principally intrusted by your Majesty is unquestionable. But if your Majesty's affairs and those of the public are in the opinion of any of us like to be hazarded in so dangerous a crisis as the present, by any sort of failing or mistake among us, I think it his duty to lay the matter clearly before your Majesty, whose supreme station and power in the state set your judgment above being influenced by considerations which ought not to have any share in the public councils, and which yet the best of your subjects may be more or less liable to.

"Not to delay your Majesty with a longer preface, I can not but think on this important occasion we have already fallen into two very great, I may truly say fundamental errors, either of which may prove, though I trust they will not, destructive to your Majesty's interest in this kingdom, and consequently to that common cause of which your Majesty is, and will every day appear more conspicuously, the head.

"The fault is, the not quelling immediately on their first appearance those rebellious tumults which have been raised on purpose to encourage, indeed invite over, the invasion,—and without which being continued and repeated in the manner they have been, the invasion had never been undertaken. It is a clear and natural inference for the Pretender to make, that if your Majesty's administration has not vigor enough to extinguish these commotions, but only to keep 'em down in one place while they break out in another, much less will you be able to deal with the discontented party when their King shall appear among 'em with officers, money, and arms from abroad, and persons of quality shall also publicly join with them.

"This obvious inference from the experiments they have made of the strength and zeal of their party, is in my humble opinion the main cause why they now undertake to set up this Pretender, rather than on your Majesty's first accession to the Crown, when your Government was not so well settled as it is.

"On the other hand, I take it to be evident that if the first commotions had been instantly extinguished, and others discouraged and prevented, such an instance of the weakness of the Pretender's party and vigor of your Majesty's Government had effectually hindered any designs abroad from taking place to disturb the peace of your Majesty's reign. Your Majesty by this time will naturally inquire by what means might this have been effected, and if by any lawfully, why were they not made use of? The affair was too big for your civil magistrates.

"The militia of the counties was quite out of order, so that no remedy remained but for your Majesty's troops to countenance and assist such of your subjects as voluntarily took arms in defense of your Majesty's Government and of the public peace. These together have been able to disperse the rebels, and make some degree of quiet whereever they have appeared; but in so gentle a manner, that the disaffected rabble have rather been encouraged thereby to try their fortune in another place, finding by experience that where the troops come, 'tis but dispersing for the present, and they are safe as if nothing had been done. The public peace can never be maintained in this method, while the disaffected endeavor to disturb it. But your Majesty has not, nor, when the army is completed, never will have troops sufficient for every place where disturbances may happen, if they are merely to look on; and I beg leave to say, with some assurance, that such is the rage and zeal of the adverse party, that no way is left to preserve the public quiet, but the making some one or more of their essays to a general rebellion so very exemplary, as to deter and to prevent many others which would otherwise be undertaken. I can only say, that no man has naturally a stronger aversion to anything severe than myself; but where a seasonable use of some severity may probably prevent the extensive cruelties and miseries of a civil war, the inclination of the best natured ought to be made to give way to what reason and the public safety so strongly demand."

The Lord Chancellor was still thought too much to advocate military government; and the Riot Act was passed, making it a capital offense for any twelve persons to continue together an hour after they had been ordered by a magistrate to disperse: this was perhaps a harsher law than ever was proposed in the time of the Stuarts,[1]— and though not abused in practice, it brought great obloquy upon the new dynasty.

Some reliance was placed upon the loyal charges to be delivered by the Judges on their circuits. The ancient custom of the Chancellor haranguing them on their duties in the Star Chamber had been laid aside since the

[1] Bl. Com. vol. iv. p. 142.

breaking out of the civil war in the preceding century; but Lord Cowper now sent to each Judge a copy of the following "ORDERS:"—

"His Majesty, understanding that you are about to go your several circuits, and being well assured that your known learning and integrity, together with the authority you are vested with, must necessarily give you the greatest weight in the counties to which you are sent,—

"Has commanded me to mention to you a few particulars relating to that very important service you are so near entering upon.

"His Majesty expects that as well in your charges as otherwise, you will lay hold on this occasion to cultivate in the minds of those you shall have occasion to speak to, a good affection and reverence towards his Majesty and his government: (your own prudence and impartial administration of justice, will not contribute a little to this good end).

"More especially it is his Majesty's pleasure, that to the utmost of your power you excite in his subjects a just abhorrence of the intended invasion, and of that implacable and ungrateful faction by whose instigation and encouragement it was undertaken; by showing that any degree of success in that design must prove very calamitous, and, if complete, destructive to the religion and liberties, as well as to the property, of the people of this kingdom; and by such other arguments as shall occur to you.

"But at the same time you thus prepare the King's people to detest the design, and resist the danger that is threatened, you are to endeavor to create in them a firm confidence that his Majesty's wisdom and vigilance, with the affectionate zeal of his good subjects, aided by the Providence of God, (which has already in this instance so visibly espoused his Majesty's cause, by a timely detection of the conspiracy), will make it end in the ruin of those only who shall join in it. The inconveniences which must follow such undertakings, though not successful, you will take care to lay at the right door, that is, of those whose restless discontents are the true and principal, if not the only, cause of them.

"His Majesty thinks it unnecessary to mention to you any further particulars, and entirely leaves you to your own prudence and perfect knowledge of your duty. But he expects that at your return you inform him of all such things as you shall observe, and may be for his service to know."[1]

By these exertions of Lord Cowper energy was infused into the public councils, the spirit of the people was roused, and the new dynasty kept possession of the throne. He has very undeservedly been censured for the judicial trials and executions which soon followed. The "Rebellion of 1715" being suppressed in Scotland, the rebel Lords were lodged in the Tower of London, and the House of Commons proceeded against them by impeachment for high treason. Having been taken with arms in their hands in flagrant war against the reigning Sovereign, they all pleaded guilty except the Earl of Winton; and a day was named for passing sentence upon those who had thus confessed their legal guilt. Lord Cowper was constituted Lord High Steward, and Westminster Hall was fitted up for the occasion.[2]

At the time appointed, the Earl of Derwentwater, the

---

[1] The Judges now-a-days would be surprised to receive such a circular. They are left to their own discretion as to the topics they shall enlarge upon. It being contrary to etiquette for barristers to be present, so that the "sages of the law" may have greater license, and may, without scruple, repeat the same fine sentences in every county on the circuit, I never myself heard any of these discourses, but I have been obliged in the House of Commons to censure some of them. Addresses to the Grand Jury are certainly best employed in commenting upon the cases in the Calendar which are coming on for trial. Observations may be permitted on the general state of the country, but I hope the Judges will henceforth ever eschew party politics and vexed questions of political economy. A noble friend of mine who was foreman of the Grand Jury some years ago in a northern county, told me that having heard from a Judge of assize a panegyric on the corn laws, he had a great inclination to answer him, and—he would have been fully justified in doing so.

[2] *Extract from Lady Cowper's Diary.*—" Feb. 9th, the day of the trials: My Lord was named Lord High Steward by the King—to his vexation and mine, but it could not be helped, and so we must submit, though we both wished heartily it had been the Earl of Nottingham. The form of the attendance was this from hence:—The servants had all new liveries—ten footmen,—four coaches with two horses, and one with six,—eighteen gentlemen out of livery, and Garter at Arms and Usher of the Black Rod in the same coach,—Garter carrying the wand. I was told it was customary to make fine liveries on this occasion, but had them all plain. I think it very wrong to make a parade upon so dismal an occasion as that of putting to death one's fellow creatures, nor could I go to the trial to see them receive their sentences, having a relation among them, my Lord Widdrington. The Prince was there, and came home much touched with compassion for them. What pity it is that such cruelties should be necessary!"

Earl of Nithisdale, the Earl of Carnwath, Viscount Kenmure, Lord Widdrington, and Lord Nairn, were brought to the bar by the Deputy Governor of the Tower, the gentleman jailer standing on their left hand, holding the axe, with the edge turned towards them. The necessary forms being gone through, the Lord High Steward addressed them, saying:—

"You stand impeached by the Commons of Great Britain, in parliament assembled, of high treason, in imagining and compassing the death of his most sacred Majesty, in levying war against him, and proclaiming a Pretender to his crown to be King of these realms. There is nothing unusual or disadvantageous to you in this mode of proceeding. The whole body of the Commons of Great Britain, by their representatives, are your accusers, and the resolution thus to put you on your trial passed the Lower House, no one contradicting. You would have been sure of a patient and impartial trial by your Peers forming this august assembly; but you have severally admitted the truth of the charges alleged against you, accompanying your pleas with some variety of matter to mitigate your offenses, and to obtain mercy. The circumstances said to have attended your surrender I do not now notice, and all due weight will be given to them; but it is fit that I should make some observations to your Lordships on your attempt to extenuate your guilt,—to the end that the judgment to be given against you may clearly appear to be just and righteous as well as legal. It is alleged by some of your Lordships, that you engaged in this rebellion without previous concert or deliberation, and without suitable preparation of men, horses, and arms. If this exempts you from the charge of being the planners of the treason, it aggravates your criminality in the execution of it, and shows that you were so eagerly bent on insurrection, that at the first invitation you flew into the field without any reasonable hope of success, and reckless of the ruin in which you were to involve yourselves, your friends, and your kindred. Another extenuation you rely upon is, that no cruel or harsh action (I suppose is meant no rapine, or plunder, or worse) has been committed by you. But your Lordships will consider that the laying waste a tract of land bears a little proportion, in point of mischief, compared with the crime of which you stand convicted, —an open attempt to destroy the best of Kings, and to raze the foundation of a government the most suited of any in the world to perfect the happiness and to support the dignity of human nature. Besides, much of this was owing to accident; your march was so hasty, partly to avoid the King's troops, and partly from the vain hope to stir up risings in all the counties you passed through, that you had not time to spread devastation without deviating from your main and (as I have observed) much worse design. No, my Lords, these and such like are artful colorings, proceeding from minds filled with expectation of continuing in this world, and not from such as are preparing for their defense before a tribunal where the thoughts of the heart and the true springs and causes of action, must be laid open." He then proceeds to state the circumstances which aggravated their Lordship's guilt, the first being the high personal character of George: " It is a trite, but very true remark, that there are but few hours between kings being reduced under the power of pretenders to their crown and their graves. Had you succeeded, his Majesty's case would, I fear, have hardly been an exception to that general rule, since it is highly improbable that flight would have saved any of that illustrious and valiant family.¹ It is a further aggravation, that his Majesty, whom your Lordships would have dethroned, affected not the crown by force or by the arts of ambition, but succeeded peaceably and legally to it. On the decease of the late Queen without issue, he became undoubtedly the next in the course of descent capable of succeeding to the crown by the law and constitution of this kingdom. The right of the House of Hanover was limited and confirmed by the Legislature in two successive reigns. How could it then enter into the hearts of men to think that private persons might, with a good conscience, endeavor to subvert such a settlement by running to tumultuary arms, and by intoxicating the dregs of the people with contradictory opinions and groundless slanders?" After excusably dwelling on the prosperity the nation was enjoying, the additional fiscal burdens brought on the country by the rebellion, and the

* This is an ungenerous sarcasm on the old Pretender's recent escape from Scotland, and other similar adventures of the Stuarts.

horrors of civil war, he comes to the subject of religion, and here, if he does not incur personal blame, he shows strikingly the lingering illiberality of the age: "I must be just to such of your Lordships as profess the religion of the Church of Rome, that you had one temptation, and that a great one, to engage you in this treason, which the others had not,—in that it was evident success on your part must for ever have established Popery in this kingdom, and that probably you could never have again so fair an opportunity. But then, good God! how must those Protestants be covered with confusion who entered into the same measures, without so much as capitulating for their religion (that ever I could find, from any examination I have seen or heard), or so much as requiring, much less obtaining, a frail promise that it should be preserved, or even tolerated! It is my duty to exhort your Lordships thus to think of the aggravations as well as the mitigations (if there be any) of your offenses; *and if I could have the least hopes that the prejudices of habit and education would not be too strong for the most earnest and charitable entreaties, I would beg you not to rely any longer on those directors of your consciences by whose advice you have very probably been led into this miserable condition; but that your Lordships would be assisted by some of those pious and learned divines of the Church of England who have constantly borne that infallible mark of sincere Christians, universal charity.*[1] And now, my Lords, nothing remains but that I pronounce upon you (and sorry I am that it falls to my lot to do it) that terrible sentence of the law, which must be the same that is usually given against the meanest offenders in the like kind. The most ignominious and painful parts of it are usually remitted by the grace of the Crown to persons of your quality; but the law in this case, being deaf to all distinctions of persons, requires I should pronounce, and accordingly it is adjudged by this Court, That you, James, Earl of Derwentwater,' &c. &c."[2]

[1] We must recollect that this is the language of the most liberal Judge of that time, who, like Lord Somers, by going such lengths for toleration, had incurred the suspicion of infidelity. The most bigoted Judge of the present age, in passing sentence of death upon a Roman Catholic, would not advise him to prepare for the great change he was to undergo by renouncing that spiritual consolation in the efficacy of which he had been taught to trust.

[2] 15 St. Tr. 796. This performance was loudly praised,—at least to Lady Cowper. She says, in her Diary:—"I am delighted beyond measure to hear

Lord Cowper had now a very arduous and painful task to perform in resisting the application for mercy to those unfortunate noblemen. Most people admitted that, as they believed their cause to be good, they were free from moral guilt; the thought could not be stifled, that if they had succeeded, they would have been celebrated and rewarded as the most loyal subjects; their gallantry and misfortunes excited general sympathy; and many who condemned their conduct, together with all who approved it, attempted to save them. A motion made in their favor in the House of Commons, though powerfully opposed by Walpole, who declared that "he was moved with indignation to see that there should be members of this great body so unworthy as, without blushing, to open their mouths for rebels and parricides," was negatived only by a majority of seven,—and a like motion in the House of Lords was carried by a majority of five. Carnwath, Widdrington, and Nairn were respited; but a warrant was granted, which Lord Cowper signed, for the execution of Derwentwater, Kenmure, and Nithisdale. All know, from the affecting narrative of Lady Nithisdale, that, by her heroic courage and self-devotion, her husband escaped from the Tower in disguise the night before the day when he was to have suffered.[1] Derwentwater and Kenmure died bravely, praying for King James. I must say that I think this was a wholesome severity, and was required by the principles on which penal infliction is to be justified. The power and *eclat* to be gained by a successful attempt to overturn an established government, hold out a temptation which must be counterbalanced by the terrific consequences of failure; and Gibbon

my Lord's speech (at the pronouncing sentence) so commended by every body, but I esteem nobody's commendation like Dr. Clarke's, who says *'tis superlatively good, and that it is impossible to add or diminish one letter without hurting it.*" Horace Walpole thus amusingly alludes to the recollection of Lord Cowper's eloquence on this occasion:—"After the second Scotch rebellion, Lord Hardwicke presided at the trial of the rebel Lords. Somebody said to Sir Charles Wyndham, 'Oh, you don't think Lord Hardwicke's speech good, because you heard Lord Cowper's.' 'No,' he replied, 'but I do think it tolerable, because I heard Sergeant Skinner's.'"

[1] I have often been tickled by George I.'s quaint saying when he heard how Lord Nithisdale had escaped: "It was the very best thing a man in his condition could have done!"—The entry in Lady Cowper's Diary is very amiable: "It's confirmed that Lord Nithisdale is escaped. I hope he'll get clear off. I never was better pleased at anything in my life, and I believe everybody is the same."

has justly observed, " the rebel who bravely ventures, has justly forfeited, his life." [1]

The Earl of Winton having pleaded not guilty, his trial came on shortly after, before the Peers in Westminster Hall, Lord Cowper again acting as Lord High Steward. He thus addressed the noble prisoner when first placed at the bar:—"Your Lordship may be assured that justice will be administered to you, attended not only with the common degree of compassion which humanity itself prompts for persons in your condition, but also with that extraordinary concern for you which naturally flows from a parity of circumstances common to yourself and to them who judge you. On the other hand, you must not hope that, if you shall be clearly proved guilty, their Lordships, being under the strongest obligations to do right that can be laid on noble minds (I mean that of their '*honor*,') will not break through all the difficulties unmerited pity may put in their way to do perfect justice between your Lordship and the public."

Lord Winton was a sort of half-witted person, with a considerable share of shrewdness and cunning, who hoped by delays and accidents to save his life. The Commons made out a very clear case against him, by proving that he had raised and commanded a regiment of horse for the Pretender; that he several times assisted in proclaiming him as James VIII. of Scotland, and James III. of England; that he had actually fought King George's troops at Preston; and that he was taken in arms when that town surrendered. Several times he made frivolous application for the suspension of the trial, on the ground that witnesses whom he expected had not arrived; and he wished his counsel to be allowed to address the House on a point of law, refusing to tell what the point was,—trying to create the semblance of a grievance. The Lord High Steward long kept his temper, but at last overruled a fresh application for an adjournment with some impatience and harshness. Winton, having gained his object, eagerly exclaimed, " I hope, my Lords, I am not to have what in my country we call COWPER JUSTICE—that, is, to *hang a man first and to try him afterwards*." [2] Lord Cowper very prudently took no notice of

---

[1] Decline and Fall, vol. xii. p. 242.
[2] 15 St. Tr. 847. This expression has been familiar to me from infancy,

this sally, although for a short space it discomposed the gravity of the assembly;—and the trial proceeded But such is the effect of party-spirit and of public envy, that the expression was kept alive as long as this great man lived; and when it was desired to question any of his legal positions, there was a cry of "*Cowper Justice!*" or "*Cowper Law!*"

The supposed murderer of the fair Quakeress, now M. P. for Truro, replied on behalf of the Commons, and showed that the trial had been conducted with fairness and kindness towards the prisoner. All the Lords present agreed in an unanimous verdict of *guilty*. A motion was then made in arrest of judgment, and argued by counsel,[1] but properly overruled, and the Lord High Steward pronounced sentence of death upon the prisoner, complimenting and comforting him by these concluding words:— "Being a Protestant, you are likely to become a sincere penitent for having engaged in a design that, had it taken, effect, must have destroyed the holy religion you profess." The prisoner was sent back to the Tower, but (probably with the connivance of the Government) he contrived to escape before the day fixed for his execution.

The conduct of Lord Cowper with reference to these having been born in the town where the Rhadamanthean procedure "castigatque audituque dolos," is supposed to have prevailed. It seems that the same irregular administration of justice was practiced at Lydford, in Devonshire, a burlesque copy of verses on this town begins—

"I oft have heard of Lydford Law,
How in the morn they hang and draw,
And sit in judgment after."
WESTCOTT'S *History of Devonshire*.

My present country residence is in the immediate neighborhood of another town in Scotland, likewise famous for a peculiar mode of enforcing the criminal law. "Jeddart," or "Jedburgh Justice" is, that when several prisoners are jointly put upon their trial, the judge, to save the time and trouble necessary for minutely distinguishing their several cases, puts it to the jury, "Hang all? or save all?"

[1] Sir Constantine Phipps, who had been Lord Chancellor of Ireland in the reign of Queen Anne, and was now again practicing at the bar, being counsel for the Earl of Winton on this occasion, was thus reprimanded by the Lord High Steward for having begun to speak without permission: "I am ordered by the Lords to reprimand you, Sir Constantine Phipps, for having, in a proceeding of this nature, presumed to be so forward as to speak for the prisoner at the bar before a point of law was first stated and you had leave to speak to it; and your fault is certainly the greater for having presumed to do this in a matter which you can not but know is matter of fact, and that the law is not doubtful one way or the other, the fact being supposed."—*15 St. Tr. 875*.

trials was, on the whole, creditable, though not entirely free from blame; and, to mark the improvement which had taken place in the administration of criminal justice, it should be recollected that only thirty years had elapsed since Jeffreys had slaughtered his victims by hundreds at a time, and had made an *aceldama* of the West of England.

I may now finish my view of Lord Cowper as a Criminal Judge with an account of the acquittal of Lord Oxford. The persecuted premier, having lain above two years a prisoner in the Tower, at last presented a petition to the House of Lords, complaining of the delay. In consequence, a day was fixed for his trial; Westminster Hall was fitted up for the solemnity, and Lord Cowper was appointed, by commission under the Great Seal, to preside as Lord High Steward.

When the day arrived, the Peers having assembled, and the King, the royal family, and the foreign ministers being seated round as spectators, the Commons attending as prosecutors, the noble prisoner was brought from the Tower and placed at the bar, the fatal axe by his side, the edge still turned from him. When the articles of impeachment and the answers had been read, the Lord High Steward, holding his white wand in his hand, thus spoke:—" Robert, Earl of Oxford and Earl Mortimer, it has been usual, before the Commons proceed, to say something from this place to persons in your Lordship's present condition; partly by way of exhortation to a reasonable confidence in the great honor, justice, wisdom, integrity, and candor of their judges, their Peers, the House of Lords in Parliament assembled, and partly by way of direction to assist them in their behavior and conduct during the course of their trial. But, considering the many great offices your Lordship has borne in the state, your long experience and known learning in all parliamentary proceedings, I can not but think it would seem improper for me to be speaking to your Lordship in that matter. Wherefore I proceed merely to acquaint your Lordship, and others whom it may concern, with such orders as the Lords have made, which it is fit should thus early be made known." He then stated, that on the articles for high treason counsel could not be heard, but that on the articles for high crimes and misdemeanors, a full defense by counsel might be made, and that, according to a recent statute, all the witnesses for the prisoner would be examined on oath as well as those for the prosecution.

Mr. Hampden then opened the first article, respecting the treaty of Utrecht, and Sir Joseph Jekyll had called his first witness in support of it, when Lord Harcourt, the Tory Ex-Chancellor (it is said from a hint given to him by Walpole, at this time in opposition), interposed and said, "that before the managers proceeded further, he had a motion to make." The Peers having accordingly withdrawn into their own house, he moved "that no evidence should be received on the charges for misdemeanor till the charges for high treason were disposed of." Lord Cowper did not consider it consistent with his duties as Lord Steward to take any part in the discussion. The resolution, though warmly opposed by Lord Sunderland and other ministerialists, was carried by a majority of 88 to 56. It is censured by a great constitutional authority,[1] but, I must say, I think it was very reasonable. The Commons proposed to proceed, on the same trial, for some offenses charged as amounting to high treason, and for others, arising out of entirely different transactions, admitted to be only misdemeanors. Besides the disadvantage under which the prisoner was placed by the length of the inquiry, and his attention and the attention of his judges being distracted by such a diversity of unconnected facts, it seems enough to say that the trial ought to have been conducted on the different charges in a totally different manner, not only as to form—as the accused peer standing outside the bar or sitting within it, —but as to substance—as being allowed or forbidden the assistance of counsel to cross-examine witnesses and to speak upon the merits. The resolution was warmly resisted by the Commons, who pronounced it an infringement of their privileges, and refused to comply with it. Several messages and conferences upon this subject between the two houses only served to widen the breach. The Lords peremptorily named another day for the trial to proceed on the principle which they had laid down, and the Commons resolved that, "being so ill used, and justice being denied to the nation, they would abandon

[1] Hall. Const. Hist. vol. iii. p. 313.

the prosecution." When the day arrived, proclamation was made for "the Commons to appear and make good their charge against Robert, Earl of Oxford and Earl Mortimer;" and no prosecutor appearing, he was acquitted. The Lord High Steward then broke his staff; and the intended victim, having by the harsh treatment he had experienced almost recovered the popularity he enjoyed when his life had been attempted by Guiscard, was, amidst the shouts of the population of London, conducted home by his friends, who had contrived the quarrel between the two Houses.[1] Although this impeachment may be palliated in respect of the violence of the Tories during the four last years of Queen Anne, and of the cry for vengeance raised not only by the vulgar retainers of the Whig party, but by such a veteran as Marlborough, and by such an aspiring youth as Lord Stanhope of Shelford (afterwards the celebrated Earl of Chesterfield), it must be allowed to reflect considerable discredit upon Lord Cowper, with whose sanction it was commenced, and under whose auspices it was conducted. He ought boldly to have declared in the Cabinet, and if necessary, in his place in parliament, at the risk of losing his office and disobliging his friends, that there was no pretense for charging the Earl of Oxford with high treason, and that, whether the treaty of Utrecht was wise or foolish, there was no sufficient ground for prosecuting, as a criminal, the prime minister who had negotiated it, believing it to be for the public good. The impeachment was not only unjust but impolitic, for it caused a strong reaction in favor of the Tory leader,—which, with health and favorable chances, might have restored him to power.[2] The High Steward's personal demeanor towards his old opponents in all these proceedings was allowed to be liberal and courteous. No one then foresaw that before they died they would be sitting on the same opposition

[1] 15 St. Tr. 1046–1195. 7 Parl. Hist. 74-215, 494-498.
[2] If Oxford did not recover the Treasurer's staff, this prosecution at all events secured him the noble tribute of applause from the muse of Pope, which ought to have gratified him more:—

" And sure if aught below the seats divine
   Can touch immortals, 'tis a soul like thine;
   A soul supreme in each hard instance tried;
   Above all pain, all passion, and all pride,
   The rage of power, the blast of public breath,
   The lust of lucre, and the dread of death."

bench, dividing together in the same minorities, and signing the same protests.

A little before this the country was agitated by a measure the responsibility of which, in a constitutional point of view, rested entirely on Lord Cowper; for although Lord Somers is said to have brightened up as it was passing through parliament, and to have approved of it, he was not in a situation to be consulted when it was first brought forward—the SEPTENNIAL ACT. It was in the House of Lords that the battle was to be fought; for little opposition was anticipated among the representatives of the people to a proposal that they should sit on for seven years, having bought their seats for three years, —or been elected after an expensive contest likely soon to recur. To lessen the indelicacy of the trustees by their own authority extending the term of their trusts, the bill was launched in the Upper House, and there it was opposed not only by the great body of the Tories, but by Lord Parker, afterwards Earl of Macclesfield and Chancellor, and by several others who had always supported liberal principles.[1] Lord Cowper seems to have made a masterly speech on the other side, but we have no particulars of it beyond that "he gave a genuine account of the Triennial Act, and by what means it was obtained, and vindicated the Government as to the present dissatisfaction." After a protracted opposition, and furious protests, the bill passed the Lords, and, as had been foreseen, it was received with great favor by the Commons. If it had applied only to future parliaments, the question would fairly have arisen, whether three or seven years be the better term for the duration of parliaments; but when it was to prolong the existence of the actual parliament beyond the period for which the members of the House of Commons were elected to represent the people, little, I think, can be urged for it except NECESSITY—the tyrant's plea, or, in milder language, "the safety of the state." "Nothing," says Mr. Hallam, "can be more extravagant than what is sometimes confidently pretended by the ignorant, that the legislature exceeded

---

[1] The best speech against this bill is by Lord Chief Justice Trevor, who says, "If this House of Commons continued themselves beyond the time for which they were chosen, they were no more the representatives of the people, but a house of their own making."—7 *Parl. Hist.* 298.

its rights by this enactment. or, if that can not legally be advanced, that it at least violated the trust of the people, and broke in upon the ancient constitution."[1] There can be no doubt as to the legal power of the legislature to pass the Septennial Act, but I do think that it was a violation of the trust confided by the people to their representatives. According to ancient constitutional practice, there were frequent renewals of parliaments, and the continuation of the sittings of the same parliament for seventeen or eighteen years was an unconstitutional innovation. The repeal of the Triennial Act, that parliaments might last for seven years, can not be considered a restoration of the old constitution, and this defense would have been equally strong if the members of the House of Commons had enacted that they should hold their seats during the life of the reigning sovereign. However, when we see the names of those who supported the Septennial Act, framed as it was to prolong the parliament which passed it, I by no means presume to condemn the measure, although I can not concur in the arguments by which it is defended. As a *coup d'état* it may be justifiable. There is no doubt that there then existed in the country the "dissatisfaction" to which Lord Cowper refers; that the necessary severity exercised in suppressing the rebellion had cast much odium on the Government; that the classes who were particularly distressed ascribed their sufferings to the King and his ministers; and that all classes were disposed to forget the dangers from which they had been delivered. If a dissolution of parliament had speedily taken place, a Jacobite House of Commons would very probably have been returned, and there might have been another " Restoration," to be followed by another " Revolution;"—whereas the nation was blest with a long course of tranquillity and happiness.

A charge was now brought forward against the Chancellor, which most of his successors have had to encounter —of improperly dealing with the appointment and dismissal of magistrates. We have his own vindication on this subject preserved in the draught of a memorial to his Majesty to prove that he had done enough for the present establishment of the commissions of the peace,

[1] Const. Hist. iii. 316.

as well as that he had not abused his power by oppressing the other side. This he inclosed to Lady Cowper, that she might translate it into French, and render it intelligible to his Majesty:—

"My Dear,

"I hope the above may be quickly turnd into Fr.; I am glad to hear you are pretty well, and upon tryal I thank God I find myself so too.

"Dr Rogue
"Ever and altogether,
"Yⁿ C. C.

"6 Cl. afternoon, going to Cockpit."[1]

The King was satisfied, and the threatened proceedings in parliament against the Lord Chancellor were dropped.

The only other debate in which we have any account of Lord Cowper taking a part while he held the Great Seal was that in February, 1718, on the Mutiny Bill; and here he appears, I think, to very great advantage. It was proposed to keep up a force of 16,000 men for the whole kingdom, and that for any military offenses which they might commit they should be tried by a court-martial. With a view of embarrassing the Government, there was a most heterogeneous opposition to the bill, led by an ex-premier, the Earl of Oxford, who now spoke for the first time since his release from the Tower, and declared "that as long as he had breath in his body he would speak for the liberties of the country; that such a force was wholly useless in the time of profound peace: that the proposal could not but raise apprehensions that something was intended against our happy constitution; and that trial by a court-martial was inconsistent with the rights and privileges of Englishmen." The Duke of Argyle, an ex-Commander-in-Chief, contended, and tried to prove, by various instances drawn from the history of Great Britain, that a standing army in time of peace was ever fatal, either to the Prince or to the nation. And Lord Harcourt, an ex-Chancellor, insisted that this bill, constituting military tribunals without appeal, was an invasion of the rights of the peerage, it being a branch of their Lordships' prerogative to be the supreme court of judicature in all cases, civil and criminal, and that the enactment enabling the King to establish courts-martial, with

[1] This note is addressed "To my Dear Palatine."

power to try and determine any offenses specified in the articles of war, unconstitutionally vested a sole legislative power in the Crown, which was communicated and delegated to a council of war.

Lord Cowper, leaving the woolsack, made a speech which, from the slight sketch we have of it, appears to have been comprehensive and masterly. He said that "he had maturely considered the affair now in agitation, not as a person in a public station, but as a private unprejudiced man, and that he was convinced in judgment and conscience that it was necessary, both for the support of the present happy establishment and the security of the nation, to keep up the force now on foot; he was confirmed in this opinion by considering what thoughts the Pretender and his friends [we may suppose that he here fixed his eyes on Lord Harcourt] had of this matter, and by reflecting that they had nothing more at heart than to procure the disbanding of those forces that had suppressed the late *unnatural*[1] Rebellion: he doubted not but the whole nobility that made up that august assembly [here there must have been a little ironical curl of his lip] was inviolably attached to his Majesty, King George; his Majesty certainly had the best part of the landed, and all the trading, interest; as to the clergy, he would say nothing—but it was notorious that the majority of the populace had been poisoned, and that the poison was not yet expelled; the dangers which seemed to proceed from the army were chimerical, whereas the dangers with which the nation was threatened from the Pretender and his friends, in case there were no army to oppose them, were real, and the mischief that might ensue upon the success of their designs irreparable; if there had been such a small standing force as it was now wished to maintain, timely to suppress the tumult and riots which were raised on his Majesty's accession to the throne, in all probability there had been no open rebellion, and the salutary restraint was really for the safety and advantage of those who exclaimed against it: in his opinion, MAGNA CHARTA was entirely foreign to the present debate; they

[1] I never could understand how this epithet came to be constantly applied to the Rebellions of 1715 and 1745. They might be, and I think they were *wicked* and *foolish*, but there seems nothing *unnatural* in an attempt to drive away foreign rulers, and to recall our native princes.

were now to consider how the Protestant succession was to be supported against vigilant, bold, and restless enemies, and they had the more reason to be on their guard as the advices from Scotland told that sedition and rebellion were again trumpeted forth from the pulpits in that country: as to the courts-martial, they were only to be for the trial of offenses of which common law judges and juries were wholly incompetent to determine upon; objecting to them was objecting to a military force, which without them, could not be kept in a state of discipline; and the argument, that they invaded the rights of the peerage, was not less ridiculous than it would be to contend that shooting a mutineer or a coward in the face of an enemy would be a breach of the privileges of their Lordships' house." The bill passed, but only by a majority of 91 to 77; and a furious protest against it was signed by many Lords, both spiritual and temporal.¹

CHAPTER CXVII.

CONCLUSION OF THE LIFE OF LORD COWPER.

WITHIN two months after delivering this great speech, which must have been so satisfactory to the King and his ministers, Lord Cowper ceased to be Chancellor. The cause of his resignation has been considered a mystery. Addison gave up at the same time the post of Secretary of State, but this was from real ill-health, and a consciousness of official incapacity. There were other partial changes in the Cabinet,—none of them indicating any change in the policy of the Government. We do not know of any personal difference which Lord Cowper had with Sunderland, Stanhope, or any of his colleagues. "Growing infirmity," as usual on such occasions, was talked of, but he had been hitherto able satisfactorily to perform all the duties of his office, and he continued after his retirement to show unabated vigor of body and elasticity of mind. Tindal says, "though it had been reported some months that he desired to retire, yet his resigning his employment at that juncture was a

¹ 7 Parl Hist. 538–548.

great surprise to the public, and no small grief to all unprejudiced persons."[1] In a lively little sketch of his career, published in the "Historical Register," immediately after his death, it is said:—"The great fatigues he had undergone having very much impaired his health, he had some time before entertained thoughts of a retreat. This voluntary resignation was a great grief to the well-affected, and to all dispassionate men of both parties, who knew that, by his wisdom and moderation, he had gained abundance of friends to the King,—kept steady many wavering minds,—brought the clergy into a better temper, and hindered some hot over-zealous spirits from running things to dangerous extremes."[2] The public were called upon to infer that he parted from the Government on friendly terms, by his submitting to an elevation in the peerage.

From original papers still preserved in MS., I think it is clear that his resignation or dismissal arose from the feud in the royal family, and the belief that he took part with the Prince against the King. Lady Cowper's position in the household was at first favorable to her husband's influence. Having been the correspondent, she had become the chief confidant, of the Princess of Wales,[3] who (the wife of George I. being shut up in prison at Zell) already played the part of Queen in England. On the arrival of the Hanoverian mistresses, the most prudish ladies of the Court do not seem to have scrupled to visit them; and Lady Cowper, meeting the King at Madame Kielmansegge's *petits soupers*, attracted his notice by her sprightliness, without any detriment to her character, for, indeed, his Majesty never showed any taste for English beauty.[4]

[1] Tind. Cont. Rap.   [2] Historical Register, 1723.
[3] "I am come into the Court with a resolution never to tell a lie, and I hope I find the good effects of it, for she reposes more confidence in what I say than on any others upon that very account."—*Lady C.'s Diary.*
[4] When Lady Cowper was presented to him on her appointment to the bedchamber, he ought, according to court etiquette, to have kissed her, although she had before received this honor on her first presentation; but "he said five or six times, 'Oh, je l'ay vue; elle est de ma connoissance.' At last the Duke of Grafton told him it was upon my being made a lady of the bedchamber; so then he said, 'Ouy, je le feray avec plaisir.' and I was saluted." Although his Majesty, I presume, at once submitted to kiss the Lady Mayoress, there was a tremendous controversy whether she was to be kissed by the Princess at the banquet given at Guildhall on Lord Mayor's day: "but Queen Anne not having kissed her when she dined in the City, my Mistress did not do it either. My poor Lady Humphreys made a sad figure

Inveighing, in her DIARY, against the Tory Duchess of Shrewsbury, and telling scandalous stories of her, she proceeds:—" Our acquaintance was renewed by supping together at Madame Kielmansegge's, about a month ago, where, speaking of the King of France's eating, she was counting twenty things at least upon her fingers that he had eat at a time, she was saying, ' *Sire, il mange ceci et cela*,' and counting over a number of things. Upon which I said to the King, ' Sire, Madame la Duchesse oublie qu'il a bien plus mangé que cela.' ' Qu'est-ce qu'il a mangé donc?' said the King. ' Sire,' répondis-je, ' il a mangé son peuple, et si le bon Dieu n'avoit pas conduit votre Majesté au trone dans le moment qu'il a fait, il nous auroit mangé aussi.' Upon which the King turned towards the Duchess and said, ' Entendez-vous, Madame, ce qu'elle dit?' and he did me the honor to repeat this to several people, which did not at all strengthen my interest with her Grace."—But from the time when the enmity of the father against the son began, a connection between Lady Cowper and the Princess threw a suspicion on the Chancellor, and the Hanoverian party were desirous of turning him out to make room for Lord Chief Justice Parker, who had been getting possession of the royal ear, and who, it was expected, would be more accommodating in passing grants under the Great Seal.

The following extracts from Lady Cowper's Diary will throw great light on these intrigues. As early as October, 1715, she says,—

" They had done a world of things to force Lord Cowper to quit, who was their superior in everything, because they were afraid of his honesty and plain dealing." . . .

" My Lord was visited by the Duke of Somerset, who repeated all the conversation he had with Lord Townshend upon his dismission. Lord Townshend came to the

---

in her black velvet, and did make a most violent ' bawling for her page to hold up her train before the Princess,' being loth to lose that privilege of the mayoralty. But the greater jest was, that the King and the Princess both had been told that my Lord Mayor had borrowed her for that day only, and I had much ado to convince them of the contrary ; but at last they did agree, that if he had borrowed a wife, it would have been another sort of one than she was."—*Lady C's. Diary.* The Lady Mayoress is said, when dinner was announced, to have roared out to another page, " Boy, carry my *bucket*,"— perhaps meaning her *boquet.*

Duke of Somerset, and, with a sorrowful air, told him he was sorry to tell him that the King had sent him to tell his Grace that he had no further occasion for his services. The Duke of Somerset said, '*Pray, my Lord, what is the reason of it?*' Lord Townshend answers, '*he did not know.*' '*Then,*' says the Duke of Somerset, '*by G—, my Lord, you lie; you know that the King puts me out for no other cause but for the lies which you, and such as you, have invented and told of me.*' Lord Cowper had advised the Cabinet Council against this step, so they did not acquaint him with it when it was done." . . . . " My Lord fell ill again the Saturday following, and continued so a great while, which occasioned a report that he was going out of his place. Some said he had not health to keep in; others, more truly, said the Lords of the Cabinet Council were jealous of his great reputation, and had a mind to have him out, so were resolved to weary him out of it; which last was very true, for they had resolved among themselves, without acquainting Baron Bernstorff with it, to put my Lord Chief Justice Parker into his place." . . .
" I kept house all this time, and saw nobody, and had enough to do to keep my Lord Keeper from giving up, and I'm sure the disputes and arguments we had upon that subject were wholly the occasion of his staying in, and it was at least three weeks before I could prevail. The month ending with the solemnization of the Prince's birthday, which should have been solemnized the 30th, if it had not been Sunday, I went privately to wish them joy, my Lord being very ill; so I saw them alone in the bed-chamber. The Prince asked me what Lord Cowper said to the Duke of Somerset's being put out? I said, 'he knew nothing of it.' He said, '*No more did I, for I opposed it once when it was named, and so they kept it from me.*' I said, '*that was my Lord Cowper's case.*' The Prince said a thousand kind things of my Lord Cowper, and so did the Princess, and the Prince bid me tell him 'he wished he would not lay things so much to heart; that he looked upon him as an old courtier, or else he had imparted some of his experience to him, which was, when the King sided with what he thought not right to endeavor to prevent it, and when he could not, to go on cheerfully; and tell him when I come to be King, all things shall go to his mind, and in the mean time, when-

ever he has a mind to take t'other pull on the Cabinet Council, I'm ready to keep his back hand.' The Princess made as many expressions as the Prince had done; but by some words the Princess let drop, I perceived that she had been talked to by Baron Bernstorff for meddling with what had been doing."—" 14*th* Feb. 1716. The news was confirmed yesterday, the Pretender is gone. My Lord Cowper is so ill that he has a mind to quit office. I have made a resolution never to press him more to keep his place."—" 15*th*. My Lord mighty ill, and still had a mind to quit office. I told him I would never oppose anything he had a mind to do, and, after arguing calmly upon the matter, I offered him, if it would be any pleasure done him, to retire with him into the country, and quit too, and, what was more, never to repine at doing it, though it was the greatest sacrifice that could be made him. I believe he will accept it."—" 16*th*. My Lord still ill. Mr. Woodford wishes I should let him hint to old Mr. Craggs that my Lord Keeper's office was too hard for him, and mention the former offer, that, if my Lord was weary, he might be Privy Seal, and that my Lord Chief Justice Parker would come into my Lord Cowper's place." —" 17*th*. My Lord better, and not talk so much of quitting."—" 18*th*. My Lord better, to my great joy. No talk of quitting to-day, though I fairly laid it in his way." —" *Feb.* 29*th*. M. Robethon spoke to me to propose to Lord Cowper to change Chancellor for President of the Council. I have spoke, and he refuses it, and says if they will have him quit, he'll do it, but he will not change. I represented to M. Robethon it would be a great difficulty to persuade him to be President of the Council, not speaking the French tongue. He replied, '*Pray use all your art to get it done.*' The Princess bade Mrs. Clayton tell me that Baron Bernstorff had been with the Prince, to persuade him to agree to make my Lord Cowper President of the Council, but the Prince absolutely denied going into it, unless my Lord Cowper desired it and insisted upon it, and the Princess bade Mrs. Clayton say that the ministry should never draw them into or force them to give consent to anything that was against my Lord Cowper's inclination. I gave the Princess a thousand thanks, and desired a continuation of her favor, and said it was utterly against my Lord Cowper's inclination, who was ready to quit if they had anybody better to put in his room, but would never change that which he could acquit himself of with honor, for that which he could not perform at all."—"*March* 3. The Princess told me that Baron Bernstorff told her that minute that it was never designed to remove my Lord Cowper; that the change was meant him as a favor, and that it was one of my Lord Cowper's jealousies."—"*July* 7. The King went in the morning and the Prince in the coach with him. Almost all the great officers followed, except the Chancellor, who was obliged to sit in the cause room that morning. In the morning, at Court, the Princess bids my Lord Cowper come to the Prince, for he has confidence in nobody else." —"*July* 8. My Lord Cowper with the Prince almost two hours. He promises to hear him in everything. My Lord Cowper persuades him to live well with all those he thought had not done their duty, because it was for the good of the whole. He promises him to do so; he tells my Lord Cowper he should not have known what to have done without me, who had been very necessary to him, and had done purely."—"*July* 10. The Princess told me that the King had told her that the Prince had as ill an opinion of my Lord Cowper as the rest. But he added, 'he may trust him; he's a very honest, disinterested man; he and the Duke of Devonshire are the only two men I have found so in this kingdom.' Mrs. Clayton said to me one night, she heard that Lord Cowper was going to lay down. I answered, 'he is, they say, to be turned out, and they need not have given themselves that trouble; if they had but hinted to him that they were weary of him, he would have laid down; they know he has done that once already, which is more than ever will be said of them, and upon occasion he can do it again.' She repeated this to the Prince."

The King used to send Baron Bothmar, who could speak English in a certain fashion, to confer with Lord Cowper respecting his differences with the Prince, and the general aspect of affairs.[1] The Chancellor always ex-

---

[1] Lord Cowper prepared himself for these conferences by previously writing down the substance of what he was to say at them. I hold in my hand one of these papers, entitled "Notes for conference with Baron Bothmar, 31st Decr. 1716." It thus begins: "Not fro attachm^t to L T. The contrary. Not for myself, &c. But on this great Crisis on wch King's hap. depends," &c

pressed, and very sincerely, the greatest devotion to the King's service; but there was a want of cordiality between him and the King, and even between him and his colleagues. In a letter to Lord Townshend, in September, 1716, he says:—"Several of the long robe have affected, with some success, to let me see they could find a way to the favors of the Crown without so much as my knowing it. This their practice, I sincerely assure your Lordship, I never thought so much improper on my own account, or from any taste I have of power and dependence, or jealousy, on that head, but purely from an apprehension that the Crown and public can not be so well served if the lawyers are allowed to think their fortunes may be made without the Chancellor's concurrence."

Some of his letters to his wife at this period likewise give a pretty clear insight into his position, and the state of parties. Thus, on the 16th of August, 1719, he says to her :—

" I beg you to present my humble and sincerest duty to the Prince and Princess. I fear I may suffer there by not being more at Court; but you know I went but once a fortnight in the Queen's time, and I am sure 'tis impossible for me to hope to bear the fatigues of the season of public business if the little vacation I have should be most of it spent on the road, or in the inconveniences attending a lodging and court hours. Besides, I assure you, the presence of one of us here is necessary in respect of the children; your sister is prudent, but they don't stand in awe of her, and there was no living *till the birch was planted in my room, where some little action has diminished it.*"—" *1st September,* 1716. I congratulate with you on the good news you send me, that the Prince has given so right a turn to that occurrence which would, any other way, have produced ill effects, and is now likely to do much good. I verily think there is not a surer sign of a mind capable of erecting a solid glory, than its being able seasonably to avoid the frippery appearance of it ; and 'tis plain that, if it be not our own fault, we may often be sensible of the good effects of the Princess's taking part with right reason whenever 'tis in danger of being run down. Her understanding will never let her be deceived if she has an opportunity of hearing both sides of the question. As for her kind expression, that my opinion had some weight in this matter, you know my taste so well as to believe it pleases me above anything the Court can give me, to think I have helped to stem a mischief which was coming upon a cause I have so much at heart. If, encouraged by this, I should appear forward to exert myself, as having H. R. H. favor in a degree above others, it might bring on me such a load of jealousy and envy, as would probably, in a little time, incapacitate me from serving him half as much as I may be able to do by seeming dull and inapprehensive of my advantage; and therefore, if ever that notion be started any more, you may truly, and, I hope, wisely, frame my excuse for not taking more upon me, from what I have above said on this head. They may let a careless, disinterested man perhaps enjoy the Prince's favor in quiet, but an ambitious, busy man they never will. If Providence should call him to the Crown while I have health and any degree of understanding left, I would dedicate them and all my time towards making him great, and would rely on my own integrity and his justice for my support. But, in our present situation, I think I must not only seem not elated with, but scarcely sensible of, his goodness to me."

Notwithstanding Lord Cowper's great anxiety to conceal his anticipations of power in the next reign, his intimacy with the Prince was more and more suspected, and caused him to be looked upon coldly at St. James's, though he was not so imprudent as to show himself at Leicester House.

The proximate cause of his retirement appears to have been his opposition to a bill which, without consulting him, it had been proposed should be brought in, and recommended by a speech from the throne,—to give £100,000 a year to the King, "whereof he was to allot any portion he might think proper for the support of the Prince." The bill and the speech being shown to the Chancellor late at night, he next morning sent the following letter to the King, in bad Latin; this being the only dialect which they understood in common:—

"11 Jan. 1717.

"Hesternâ nocte mandato M. Vræ Billa & oratio designatæ haben in Parl° ostensæ sunt.

"Breve tempus ad perpendend. rem tam arduam.

"Ratio sufficiens tum visa est allegan ad probandum quod M. V. orationem aliqua haberet introductiva; *si Consultu visum foret ut talis Billa introduactur.*

" De Billa ipsa nulla tum tradidi opinionem præterquam quasdam objectiones, genere deliberativo, quæ mihi extempore occurrebant.

" Una observatio fuit (& quæ quodamodo concedi visa est) Qd quamvis Billa paratur *indefinitè*, ad submittendu Regis dispositioni tantu pensionis (£100,000 per an.) quantu ipsi placeret, tamen non plus potest expectari, quam ut pars sufficiens sustentationi Juvenu Princ. ita submitteretur, quonia aliter tota pensio (refigeretur vel) precaria redderetur quod, audivi omni ex parte concedi, hominu animis tentatis, non posse attingi.

" Exposito qd fructus hujus experimenti non alius esse potest quam appropriatio quæda sufficientis partis in educatione Principu, (quam non par est creden Principem unquam recusaturu.)

"Questio huc devenit, An tam parvi comodi causa pretm sit?

"OBJECTIONES.— 1. Minuere quodamodo Majestate Vam appellando Populu; prertim in re adeo tenera versus Filiu etc.

" 2. Dare Licentiam a Throno membris utriusq: Domus loquendi de hoc subjecto quæ velint, et movendi quæstiones non gratas de educatione Principis in Germania.

" 3. Ciere turbas, motusq; animos acerrimos, qui in disputationibus necessarie surgent.

"4. Minuere numeru fideliu amicoru M. Vræ: nam quot ex illis putabunt provisionem illius Billæ, vel impugnare proprietatem vel punire delictu ultrà modum, & ideo, vel aliis rationibus recusabunt dare suffragia cum ministris V. M. exinde putabunt se male acceptos, & consequenter fient malecontenti; fundamentu Throni jam jam nimis arctatur.

" 5. Dare exemplar invadendi Lege lata proprietati subjecti; quod fiat, si plus pecuniæ approprietur, quam sufficit sustentationi Liberoru; & e contra id solumodo efficere, nil valet.

"6. Rem agredi, nullo exemplo comprobatam, quamvis in historia similes offensæ *Casus* non desunt, &c.

"7. Movere novos Sermones de hac materia, pretentis aliquantum sopitis; non tantu in Brit. veru etiam in aliis mundi partibus. Hoc ut puto afficiet authoritatem vram partibus exteris; si in tali subjecto Parl. foret prope equalit divisu:—Cujus unanimitas *hucusq;* tantu ponderis dedit. Itaqu; mea sententia est, QD NON!

"Et qd tanta incurrere mala & pericula, tam exigui, si alicujus, comodi causa, non mihi, submisse dico, prudens futu videtur nec tanti; quod tamen judicio V. M. & potioribus sententiis alior Ministroru humiliter submitto."[1]

[1] The paper is indorsed in Lord Cowper's handwriting: "Latin letter to K. G. 1st. dated 11 Jan. 1707." I attempt a translation:—

"Last night, by your Majesty's order, the bill to be brought forward in parliament, and the Speech, were shown to me.

"A short time is allowed me to consider a matter so weighty.

"The reason alleged then seemed sufficient to prove that your Majesty should make a speech to introduce the bill, *if it should be resolved that such a bill is to be introduced.*

"Respecting the bill itself, I then delivered no opinion, beyond some objections for consideration which occurred to me at the moment.

"One observation was (and which seemed to be conceded), that although the bill is framed *absolutely* to submit to the King's disposal so much of the pension (£100,000 per an.) as he should please, yet no more can be expected, than that a part sufficient for the support of the young Princes should thus be submitted, since otherwise the whole pension would be (annulled or) rendered precarious—which I have heard agreed on all hands, public opinion being sounded, can not be carried.

"The result of this experiment can be nothing else than an appropriation of a sufficient part in the education of the young Princes, (which it is not credible that the Prince of Wales would ever refuse).

"The question comes to this, whether it be worth while to proceed for so small an advantage.

"OBJECTIONS.—1. It would degrade your Majesty in some measure, to call in the people to judge, particularly in so delicate an affair, between you and your son, &c.

"2. It would be to give leave from the throne to the members of both Houses of speaking on this subject what they please, and of stirring disagreeable questions respecting the education of the Prince in Germany.

"3. To collect mobs and inevitably to rouse animosities in debate.

"4. To lessen the number of your Majesty's faithful friends: for so many of them as shall think that the provisions of the bill are generally improper, or in this instance would be an excessive punishment of a fault, and for these or other reasons shall refuse on this occasion to vote with your Majesty's ministers, will henceforth think themselves ill looked upon, and consequently will become discontented; the foundation of the throne is already shaken.

The bill which would have been so offensive to the Prince and his friends was abandoned, but it was resolved that Lord Cowper should no longer remain in office.

On the 15th of April, 1718, at an audience in the royal closet at St. James's, he finally resigned the Great Seal and kissed his Majesty's hand on his elevation to an earldom.[1] His Diary having ceased at the commencement of this reign, and Lady Cowper's MSS. for 1718 being lost, we unfortunately know nothing of the adieus of the Sovereign and the retiring Chancellor.

The same evening he received the following letter from Stanhope, then considered the Prime Minister:—

"Cockspit, April 15.

" My Lord,

" I was extremely concerned to find, at my returning here this evening, the letter your Lordship had done me the honor to send me. If it had been possible to imagine that your Lordship was determined on account of your health, to be eased of the very great fatigue which attends the office you have resigned, I am sure I should have been most intent upon suggesting to the King, and to your Lordship, some expedient that might have kept your Lordship at the head of [2] consistently with more ease to yourself; and I should, I am confident, in that

" 5. To give an example of invading by act of Parliament the property of the subject, which will be the case if more money is appropriated than is necessary for the maintenance of the children; and on the contrary, confined to that, the bill has no operation.

" 6. To undertake a measure, not recommended by any precedent, although in history similar cases of offense are not wanting, &c.

" 7. To stir up new discussions respecting this matter (which had nearly gone to sleep) not only in Britain, but in other parts of the world. This I conceive will lessen your credit in foreign parts, if upon such a subject Parliament should be nearly equally divided, unanimity hitherto having given so much strength to your government.

" Therefore my opinion is, No!

" And with all humility I must say that it does not seem to me prudent nor worth while for so small an advantage (if any may be hoped) to incur so great evils and perils. All these things, however, I humbly submit to the judgment of your Majesty, and the better opinions of your other ministers."

I am not sure that I have always understood the meaning of this epistle. I have only the rough draught of it, with obliterations and abbreviations. I wish there had been preserved a specimen of George's Latinity—which I dare say was quite equal to that of the Chancellor, although his Majesty must have been a good deal puzzled with some of our parliamentary *slang*.

[1] The preamble of the patent was drawn by Hughes in terms of high eulogium   [2] Illegible word.

have had the hearty assistance of my Lord Sunderland, and of every one in the King's service; and I will still hope that your Lordship will so far indulge your servants as to allow them to think whether some happy turn of that kind may not be given. This sudden resolution hath so startled me, that I really do not well know what to write to your Lordship; but as I judge a most honest and necessary maxim to be 'non desperare de republicâ,' so will I not despair of seeing my Lord Cowper soon again in the King's service. I am, with as sincere a respect as possible,

"My Lord,
"your Lordship's
"most humble and
"most obedient Servant,
"STANHOPE."

But, notwithstanding this flummery, Stanhope, to gratify the King's humor, was much delighted with Lord Cowper's retirement, and heartily assisted in smoothing away all difficuties in the way of the appointment of a successor, who by taking a decided part against the Prince had entirely gained his Majesty's confidence.

Parliament having been previously prorogued, the moment that Lord Cowper had got rid of the Great Seal he hurried off to his house at Colegreen, in Hertfordshire, to enjoy his gardens and his woods, which for a time he thought he preferred to all the glittering objects of ambition.

While the ex-Chancellor saw with less regret the fate of some of his officers, he showed his respect for literature by an effort in favor of Hughes, the poet, whom he had appointed one of his secretaries, and for whom he thus implored mercy from Lord Parker, his successor :-

"My Lord,
"Of the many that were losers by my resigning the Great Seal, I shall venture to recommend but one gentleman to your Lordship, the bearer, Mr. John Hughes, who served for some little time in the office of secretary for the commissions of the peace;—and I should not do that but for two reasons: the one, that he had hardly served long enough to make him amends for preparing to execute that trust; the other, that I am convinced from the little time he did serve that your Lordship, if you

continue him in that service, will thank me for having recommended him; and your so doing will be also a great obligation on
"Yours, &c.,
"COWPER.
"I most heartily wish your Lordship much joy."

The application succeeded, and the grateful bard, in an imitation of Horace,[1] thus sung the praises of his patron:—

> 'Let Fame be silent, only tell
> That gen'rous Cowper loves me well;
> Thro' Britain's realms I shall be known
> By Cowper's merit, not my own;
> And when the tomb my dust shall hide,
> Stripp'd of a mortal's little pride,
> Vain pomp be spar'd, and ev'ry tear;
> Let but some stone this sculpture bear:
> 'Here lies his clay, to earth consign'd,
> To whom great Cowper once was kind.'"

Falling dangerously ill soon after, Hughes, in further proof of his gratitude, sent his portrait by Sir Godfrey Kneller to the ex-Chancellor, who thus courteously acknowledged the obligation:—

"Sir,

"I thank you for the most acceptable present of your picture, and assure you that none in this age can set a higher value upon it than I do, and shall while I live; though I am sensible posterity will outdo me in that particular.

"With the greatest esteem and sincerity,
"Your most affectionate Servant,
"COWPER.

"I intend to wait on you very quickly, if I hear you are well enough to be troubled with me."

In an interval of pain, Hughes wrote him another letter, in which he said,—"I congratulate your Lordship on your being so honorably eased from a very great burden, the constant fatigue of which must have made it uneasy, and might have proved prejudicial to your health."[2] The ex-Chancellor received similar felicitations from other friends, and he professed merrily to respond to them:

[1] Lib. ii. Ode 20.
[2] Hughes likewise, a few days before his death, dedicated to Lord Cowper his "Siege of Damascus," the success of which, when first represented, he heard as he expired.

but I strongly suspect that the would have been better pleased to have gone on bearing the "burden," and the "fatigue," from which he was was relieved, if he could have done so without dishonor.

He survived rather more than four years, never returning to office, but still devoting himself to the public service. "Non fuit consilium sorcodiâ atque desida bonum otium conterere; neque vero agrum colendo, aut venando, servilibus officiis intemtum ætatem agere."¹ Nor did he, like some ex-Chancellors, waste his days in listless discontent, or in counting over the money in his chest, or in vain efforts to regain court favor. He attended to his duties in parliament with unabated energy; and when his presence was wanted for the judicial business of the Privy Council, he was always ready to assist.

If he quitted office, having had no quarrel with his colleagues, differences of opinion soon sprung up between them;—and (generally with reason on his side, though sometimes, I fear, actuated by personal pique) he exerted himself to thwart most of the measures which they brought forward. His first display of opposition, though excusable, considering the sentiments which then generally prevailed among enlightened statesmen, tempers our admiration of his regard for religious liberty. The subsisting government was more favorable to true toleration than any England ever knew, prior to that of Earl Grey in the year 1830. Stanhope and Sunderland were at the head of it, with a pretty equally divided power. The former has the merit of originating a measure which, if it had passed as he projected it, would have placed Dissenters and Roman Catholics (as far as all civil rights are concerned) on the same footing of equality which they now happily enjoy with members of the Established Church. He wished not only to repeal the "Schism Act," which had disgraced the close of the reign of Queen Anne, but the "Test and Corporation Acts," passed in the reign of Charles II., in violation of the "Declaration of Breda;" and he actually obtained the consent of the King and the Cabinet to introduce a bill for this purpose. But the novel spectacle was exhibited of a Government being much more liberal than the Opposition, and even than many of its own supporters. The news

¹ Sall. Cat. c. iv.

of such a measure was received with horror by the High Church party, and many good Whigs thought that it went a vast deal too far ; insomuch that the Dissenters themselves soon agreed that the total repeal of the " Test and Corporation Acts," should be deferred, Stanhope pledging himself to move this hereafter at *a more favorable opportunity;* and that the bill to be now brought in should only mitigate some of their more obnoxious clauses, and totally repeal the " Schism Act." A bill so framed, was introduced by Stanhope in the House of Lords as soon as Parliament met. When he had ably explained and defended it, he was zealously supported by Sunderland ; but I am deeply concerned to say that, in as far as it did more than simply repeal the " Schism Act," it was strenuously opposed by Lord Cowper, who said " he had no manner of prejudice against the Dissenters, but rather a tender regard for them ; that as he had been bred in, so he had ever communicated with, the Church of England, which he believed to be the best Protestant church, and the most agreeable to the primitive pattern of Christianity; but that, however, if he had happened to be at Geneva, he would not have scrupled to have communicated with the Protestants there; that he was disposed to afford the Dissenters as much ease as was consistent with the safety of the constitution in church and state, and would readily give his vote for the repealing of the 'Schism Act ;' but that he could not but oppose that part of the bill, which now lay before them, whereby parts of the ' Test and Corporation Acts ' were done away with, because he looked on those acts as the main bulwark of our excellent constitution in church and state, and, therefore, he would have them inviolably preserved." The venerable Hoadly, Bishop of Bangor, in a truly Christian spirit, stood up for the cause of religious liberty, contending that the principles on which the laws to be abrogated rested, would justify all the heathen persecutions of the converts to the religion of Jesus, and all the horrors of the Popish inquisition.' But the Government was obliged to follow the line which Lord Cowper

¹ He was seconded by three other Bishops, Wilson, Gibson, and Kennet, the last of whom warned his brethren against imitating the prelates in the time of Charles I., who, by supporting arbitrary measures and persecution, first brought scandal and contempt upon the clergy, and at last ruin both on church and state.

prescribed, and, when all the clauses had been struck out except the simple repeal of the "Schism Act," the third reading was carried only by a small majority. Stanhope's descendant, inheriting much of his genius and his liberality, remarks, that "the 'more favorable opportunity' promised the Dissenters for the repeal of the Test and Corporation Acts, never came. Those acts remained on the statute book one hundred and nine years more, but remained only like rusty weapons hung in an armory, trophies of past power, not instruments of further agression or defense."[1] This observation is correct with respect to the holding of offices under the Crown, but from municipal offices Dissenters were effectually excluded till Lord John Russell's triumph, in the year 1827.

Lord Cowper ere long redeemed himself from this aberration by his noble stand in the House of Lords, almost single-handed, against a most reprehensible measure, which was very cordially received there,—being brought forward with all the strength of the Government, and being supposed to be favorable to the power and dignity of their Lordships—Sunderland's celebrated PEERAGE BILL—whereby it was to be enacted that the existing number of English Peers should never be increased beyond six, with an exception in favor of Princes of the blood; that for every extinction there might be a new creation; and that instead of the sixteen elective Peers from Scotland, the King should name twenty-five to be hereditary. It is difficult for us to conjecture the real reasons for which this unconstitutional measure was so eagerly brought forward, and so obstinately pressed. Lord Oxford's creation of twelve Peers, to carry a vote in favor of the Peace of Utrecht, was much talked of; but the possibility of abusing a prerogative of the Crown could not weigh much with a minister in whom the exercise of that prerogative was actually vested. The solution is probably to be sought in the enmity of the Heir Apparent to the present Government, and Sunderland's hope that by insuring the continuance of a majority at his command in one chamber of the parliament, he might thereby perpetuate his own power.

The country seems to have been nearly as much agitated by this measure for altering the constitution of the

[1] Lord Mahon, vol. i. p. 494.

House of Lords, as it was in our time by the " Bill for reforming the Representation of the People." Addison plausibly defending it in the " Old Whig," and Steele successfully assailing it in " The Plebeian," it was the cause of a breach in the friendship between those two eminent and amiable men. In the House of Lords it was highly extolled on account of its supposed oligarchical tendency, although, by stopping the infusion of fresh blood, it must, in another generation, have reduced that House to utter imbecility and insignificance. Lord Cowper, from the first, and during its whole progress, most strenuously opposed it. In his earliest speech against it, he appears to have made the greatest impression by attacking what I should have thought its least vulnerable enactment,—to make Scotland be represented in the Upper House by hereditary instead of elective Peers,—but he was much applauded while he denounced the change as a violation of the Union, and he pointed out the deplorable condition of the excluded Scotch Peers, who would be reduced to a worse condition than any other subjects, since they would neither be electors nor elected, neither representatives nor represented.[1] In consequence of this opposition, when the bill stood for a third reading, it was dropped,—on the alleged ground that, from being so misrepresented and misunderstood, its merits were not likely to be fairly considered in the Lower House.

But in the new session, which began in the autumn of the same year, it was again introduced, when Lord Cowper again vigorously opposed it, throwing out some dark hints as to the motives of its supporters, and concluding with the observation, that, " for his own part, he could not help being of opinion that if there were no secret meaning in this bill, some men would not be so pressing for it."[2] He met with so little support, that he did not venture to divide the House against it in any of its stages. But the Peers were saved from the effects of their own infatuation by the unanimous abhorrence of the measure which animated all the wives and daughters of members of the House of Commons, and by the most rhetorical speech ever delivered by Sir Robert Walpole, beginning with these memorable words, " Among the Romans, the

---

[1] 7 Parl. Hist. 591.   [2] Ibid. 607.

wisest people upon earth, the Temple of Fame was placed behind the Temple of Virtue."[1]

In the following year Lord Cowper showed his sagacity by strenuously, though ineffectually, opposing the South Sea Bill,—which excited a spirit of gambling unequaled till the speculations in railway shares,—which in the result brought ruin on thousands of families and almost subverted the national credit,—but which was expected to produces riches and prosperity till then unknown in the world. He compared it to the Trojan horse, ushered in and received with great pomp and acclamations of joy, but contrived for treachery and destruction:—

> ———"Scandit fatalis machina muros,
> Fœta armis. Pueri circum, innuptæque puellæ
> Sacra canunt, funemque manu contingere gaudent,
> Illa subit, mediæque minans illabitur urbi.
> Instamus tamen immemores cœcique fuore,
> Et monstrum infelix sacratâ sistimus arce."

When the bubble burst, Lord Cowper concurred in the punishment of the Directors of the South Sea Company, but animadverted with severity upon the Government that had enabled them to commit such frauds, and to create such mischiefs.[2]

I mention his next appearance in the House as the earliest instance I find recorded of the practice, now so prevalent, of putting questions in parliament to the Ministers of the Crown. There being a report that a gentleman of the name of Knight, against whom the House of Lords wished to take some proceedings, and who had absconded, had been arrested in Brussels, upon the application of the English resident there, Lord Cowper, rising in his place, mentioned the report, " which being a matter in which the public was highly concerned, he desired those in the administration to acquaint the House whether there was any ground for that report?"[3] Lord Sunderland then stated that the report was true, and informed the House in what manner Mr. Knight had been apprehended and secured—taking credit to the Govern-

---

[1] The bill was rejected in the Lower House by 269 to 177.; Lord Cowper's brother, Spencer, voting with the majority. 15 Parl. Hist. 624.

[2] 7 Parl. Hist. 693.

[3] I know not when the existing form of commencing the question was established:—" Seeing the R^t Ho^{nble} gentleman (or the noble Lord) in his place," &c.

ment for the promptitude and energy they had exhibited.¹

It appears by a proceeding the same year, which Lord Cowper strenuously supported, that a wholesome practice then prevailed in the Lords and Commons, which has unfortunately now fallen into desuetude,—being merely talked of in one House, and being absolutely forgotten in the other,—of fixing a day for calling over the House, and actually compelling the attendance of all members during the debate and the division.²

The idea that law Lords are only to discuss questions of laws was scorned by Lord Cowper, and he now introduced a bill for relaxing the regulations respecting quarantine, which he represented as ineffectual, unnecessary, vexatious, odious, and basely copied from the arbitrary law of France. The bill being thrown out by the Government, he was joined by many Peers in a spirited protest, describing its merits, and exposing the motives for its rejection.³ He likewise took a very active part in a debate and a protest, respecting the management of the navy.⁴

A few days after there was a scene in the House which showed the existence of considerable ill will between him and his "noble and learned friend" who succeeded him. The House had been adjourned to the 3rd of February, at eleven o'clock, then the usual hour to meet for business, instead of seven or eight as in the good old times. A considerable number of Lords assembled, but no Lord Chancellor appeared, and Lord Chief Justice Peter King, commissioned to sit in his absence, was likewise absent. At last, Lord Cowper, in the exercise of the undoubted right of the Lords, in default of the Lord Chancellor, or a Speaker specially authorized by the Crown, to choose a Speaker for themselves, moved, first, that the Duke of Somerset, as the Peer of highest rank, and then, that the Duke of Kingston, should take the woolsack as Speaker; but they successively ran out of the House as soon as their names were mentioned. Lord Cowper then made the same motion with respect to a law lord, Lord Lechmere, who had been made a Peer without having held any higher office than that of Attorney General and Chancellor of the Duchy of Lancaster, and is long ago

¹ 7 Parl. Hist. 709.   ² Ibid. 921.   ³ Ibid. 933.   ⁴ Ibid. 939.

forgotten, though he moved the impeachment of the Rebel Lords, led the opposition against Walpole, and was famous in his day. After a short debate, the question was about to be put, when the Mace and the Great Seal presented themselves to the House, and were followed by the Lord Chancellor. "Puffing and blowing, he took his seat on the woolsack;" and, having observed some uneasiness among the Lords, he acquainted their Lordships "that he having been summoned to attend his Majesty at St. James's, had accordingly waited upon his Majesty there, where he was detained longer than he could foresee by his Majesty's command; and that as soon as he was at liberty he came hither with the utmost expedition; and asked pardon for his stay of the Lords, who had been so long kept in expectation of him." But several opposition Lords declared this excuse to be wholly insufficient; and one of them, prompted by Lord Cowper, moved "that the House, to show its indignation at the affront offered to it, should immediately adjourn to Monday without transacting any further business." But the motion being put, it was negatived by a majority of 49 to 31. Lord Cowper thereupon drew, and, with other Peers, signed a protest, which, after reciting the facts,—with the Lord Chancellor's excuse,—thus proceeded:—"which excuse, though it might in great measure free the Lord Chancellor from the imputation of willful neglect of duty, yet it seemed to us in no degree to justify the indignity which we think was upon the whole matter done to the House, which is undoubtedly the greatest council in the kingdom, and to which all other councils ought to give way; and therefore the business of any other council ought not to have detained the Speaker of this House after the hour appointed for its meeting, and during the time of the day the House has usually of late spent in business; and as we venture to say the dignity of this House has not of late years been increasing, so we are unwilling that anything we conceive to be a gross neglect of it should pass without some note on our records—which we thought would have been in some measure attained by an immediate adjournment."[1]

Bitterness of feeling between Lord Cowper and his late colleagues becoming more intense, they spread reports

[1] 7 Parl. Hist. 960.

that he had coalesced with the Tories, and was even plotting with the Jacobites,—for which there was not the slightest color, except that, in opposing some of the measures of the Government, he had found himself dividing with the Earl of Oxford and Bishop Atterbury. Most preposterous hopes were entertained by the exiled royal family that Lord Cowper might be brought to espouse their cause; insomuch that the Earl of Mar, and James himself, wrote him letters filled with solicitations and promises; but these he treated with neglect and contempt. However, Layer, when a discovery was made of his conspiracy to restore the Stuarts by a French invasion, and he was examined in the Tower by a ministerial committee of the House of Commons, thought to ingratiate himself with the Government by implicating some of the discontented Whig lords, and he said, "he had been told by one Plunket, a friend of the Pretender, that Lord Cowper had sent in his adhesion to that Prince, and that, along with seven other lords and six commoners, he formed a cabinet, under the name of BURFORD'S CLUB, for carrying on the government in his name." This improbable and incredible information was eagerly caught at by the committee, and conspicuously blazoned forth in their Report, which was twice read aloud in the House, printed in the votes, recorded in the Journals, and industriously circulated over the kingdom.

Lord Cowper thereupon made a formal complaint upon the subject in the House of Lords. He said, "that little regard had been shown to divers members of that illustrious assembly, whose honor and reputation had been attacked by the Report from the Secret Committee of the House of Commons,—being represented on mere hearsay, as privy to treasonable designs against the Government. Having been raised, however unworthily, to the dignity of a Peer, he considered himself bound to defend the rights and privileges of the peerage of England, which they held by the fundamental law of the land, and which were confirmed to them by MAGNA CHARTA. After having, on so many occasions, and in such difficult times, given undoubted proofs of his hearty zeal and affection for the Protestant succession, and of his attachment to his Majesty's person and his dynasty, he had just reason to be offended when he saw his name bandied about in a list of a chimerical club of disaffected persons, on the hearsay evidence of an infamous man charged by the committee themselves with having, to magnify the number of the Pretender's friends, inserted in lists of his supporters the names of well-affected persons, without having the least authority for so doing." Having attempted to throw some doubts on the whole of the conspiracy, he concluded by moving, "that the persons supposed to have given the information to Layer should be sent for, and examined at the bar of the House respecting the truth of this charge."

Lord Townshend, on the part of the Government, insisted that "as the noble and learned Earl's name was mentioned in the examination of Layer, there was an absolute necessity that it should be introduced into the Report, but the committee had declared their entire conviction of his Lordship's innocence, so that his reputation could not have suffered in the manner he had supposed: further inquiry was therefore unnecessary. But the House must have been much surprised to find that a noble and learned Peer, whose abilities and merit had justly so great weight in that assembly, should upon a trivial circumstance ridicule as a fiction a horrid and execrable conspiracy supported by so many concurring proofs."—The motion was negatived by a majority of 81 to 26. Lord Cowper having entered a protest in the Journals against this decision, signed a solemn declaration, "upon his HONOR, that the statement was false." [1] Layer, notwithstanding this service, was convicted and executed.

It may well be believed that Lord Cowper would vigorously oppose the bill of pains and penalties against Atterbury, however much he might condemn his principles. This bill did not affect the life of the party accused, going no further than to deprive him of all his ecclesiastical preferments, to banish him, and to make it felony to correspond with him without the King's license. No one doubted that, by overt acts to bring in the Pretender, he had actually been guilty of high treason, yet there was no sufficient legal evidence against him upon which he could be convicted judicially before a criminal

---

[1] This document, which was printed and extensively circulated, was thus entitled:—"The Declaration of William, Earl Cowper, showing that the matters contained in some heresays relating to him in the examination o Christopher Layer are false and groundless." See 8 Parl. Hist. 204.

court, and reasonable men regarded with disapprobation and alarm the precedent of legislating penally against a political enemy. We have a fuller account of Lord Cowper's speech on this occasion than of any other he ever delivered. A few extracts from it will display its character and merit:—" I am, my Lords, against this bill, not only because I think nothing has been offered sufficient for the support of it, but because I think the honor and dignity of the Crown, of this House, and of the House of Commons, concerned in the event of it. That House began by voting the Bishop, without hearing him, guilty of high treason, and then, instead of impeaching him, or leaving him to the ordinary course of law, they make themselves his judges as well as his accusers, and pass sentence of condemnation upon him. Your Lordships' privileges are invaded, for in you is vested the supreme judicial power. And in what a situation does this course of proceeding place his Majesty, who is to be called upon to give his royal assent to a bill for the utter ruin of one of his subjects, without any means of knowing the evidence on which it rests!¹ Where is now the necessity for this unconstitutional interference? The alleged culprit stands at your bar, and has never attempted to fly from justice. If there be legal evidence against him, let him be legally convicted; without legal evidence he must be wrongfully condemned. I expected to have heard from the Right Reverend Bench, that to make or deprive bishops is no part of the business of the state; and it must be owned that if the Parliament can properly deprive this bishop, we are equally authorized to make another in his room. I can guess at no advantage which the Church can derive from this bill, except that it will cause a vacancy in the Deanery of Westminster and in the See of Rochester."² After a very minute and masterly analysis of the evidence adduced

¹ This is a sophistical subtlety, for the King may be present and is supposed to preside in the High Court of Parliament. Besides, he is to act by the advice of his ministers.

² Pretty well!—but not equal to the sarcasm of Lord Bathurst in the same debate on the Bishops about a vote against Atterbury:—" I can hardly account for the inveterate malice that some persons bear to the learned and ingenious Bishop of Rochester, unless they are possessed of the infatuation of the wild Indians, who fondly believe they will inherit not only the spoils but even the abilities of any great enemy they kill "

in support of the bill, he thus concludes:—" My Lords, I have now done; and if upon this occasion I have tried your patience, or discovered an unbecoming warmth, your Lordships will impute it to the concern I am under lest, if this bill should pass, it should become a dangerous precedent to after ages. My zeal as an Englishman for the good of my country, obliges me to set my face against oppression in every shape ; and wherever I think I meet with it (it matters not whether one man or five hundred be the oppressors), I shall be sure to oppose it with all my might; for vain will be the boast of the excellency of our constitution, in vain shall we talk of our liberty and our property secured to us by law, if, when it suits the purpose of a vindictive majority in parliament, without law or evidence we may be deprived of both. There is a boast in this case that life is spared ; but that mercy is very equivocal which bids a man live after depriving him of all for which life is desirable." The bill, however, was carried by a majority of 83 to 43, and the Bishop was banished. The impolicy of this proceeding was rendered more flagrant by the fact that Bolingbroke, an infinitely more dangerous man, who had been openly in the service of the Pretender as Secretary of State,—at the same time, by means of a bribe to the Duchess of Kendal, received a partial pardon, and was allowed to return to England. Atterbury, when landed at Calais, finding him ready to embark there, said, with a smile,—" Then I am exchanged!" [1] I can not find that Bolingbroke and Lord

[1] Pope, the friend of both, exclaimed,—" This nation is afraid of being overrun with too much politeness, and can not regain one great genius but at the expense of another." But the Poet had partly contributed to this catastrophe by being such a shocking bad witness for Atterbury, when called at the bar of the House of Lords to prove his character and habits. He afterwards tried to make compensation by the couplet,—
" How pleasing Atterbury's softer hour !
How shines his soul unconquer'd in the Tower !"
Atterbury's best defense is by Swift, who most happily ridicules the evidence of the horrid conspiracy chiefly relied on—of the dog Harlequin, who
" Confess'd as plain as he could bark ;
Then with his forefoot set his mark."
To this conspiracy the relentless satirist afterwards alluded in Gulliver's Travels, " as the workmanship of persons who desire to raise their own character of profound politicians ; to restore new vigor to a crazy administration ; to stifle or divert general discontents, and to fill their coffers with forfeitures."
Gay joined the tuneful throng in singing the praise of the banished man :—
" See Rochester approving nods his head,
And ranks one modern with the mighty dead."

Cowper afterwards met. The former, however, now had an interview with the King; while the latter, although as steadily attached as ever to the Protestant succession and the House of Hanover, seems no longer to have been admitted at Court.

Before he closed his honorable career, there was only one other occasion of his appearing before the public,—when he displayed the same liberal principles and sound judgment which had almost invariably distinguished him. Stanhope and Sunderland were now no more, and the reins of government were in the firm grasp of Walpole, who, although far from being of a cruel or bigoted temper, had by no means their enlightened views of religious toleration, and who was willing, for the quiet march of civil government, to foster religious prejudice. Those implicated in the late Jacobite plot were chiefly Roman Catholics, and great odium was incurred by all adherents of the Roman Catholic faith, in the belief that, because James had refused to renounce it to mount a throne, they were all zealously devoted to his cause. Walpole, therefore, as well to gain popularity as money, came forward with a proposal to raise £100,000 a year upon the estate of Roman Catholics. The tax was much approved of in the House of Commons, and was extended to all non-jurors.

When the bill to impose it came up to the House of Peers, it was vigorously opposed by Lord Cowper, who contended that whatever gloss religious and party zealots might put upon the measure, those who were to suffer by it must regard it as persecution; they must feel that they were unjustly made to suffer for the crimes of others, and they must be rendered hostile to the Government which could sanction such an outrage. He desired their Lordships to consider whether they were not themselves injuring the Protestant cause; for Protestants abroad might have severe hardships inflicted upon them by reason of our persecuting Roman Catholics at home. He said he was informed that the King of Spain and the Regent of France had used their good offices in behalf of those of their own religion amongst us; and as those two powerful princes had given undoubted proofs of their friendship to his Majesty in discovering and quashing the late conspiracy, so they could not but think themselves but indifferently requited if this bill, marking indiscriminately all Roman Catholics for vengeance, should pass into a law. His Lordship added, that no government ever got any advantage by persecuting a portion of its subjects, of which he gave several instances; and he particularly dwelt upon the ill consequences to France from the revocation of the Edict of Nantes, "whereby many of her wealthiest merchants and most skillful artificers had been driven away to exercise their industry in rival states; and the object seemed to be that there should be *English Roman Catholic refugees* enriching France and Spain, and plotting against their native country, by whom they had been treated so unjustly." He carried with him a glorious minority of 55 against the ministerial majority of 69 —showing very clearly that the measure was condemned by the real sense of the House. Lord Cowper's last act as a Peer was to record a protest against it.[1] In a few days afterwards, the session, which proved to be his last, was terminated by a prorogation.

But we must view him after his resignation in private life. He divided his time between Colegreen and London;[2] like most well-educated men, relishing the beauties of nature, but preferring the intellectual pleasures of a great metropolis. Although not unacquainted with gardening and farming,[3] he left the management of his

[1] 8 Parl. Hist. 363. I am much surprised to find Archdeacon Coxe saying, —"Whatever opinions may be formed of this measure according to the strict rules of theoretical justice, *the policy was unquestionable*," when he himself publishes an admirable letter from Speaker Onslow, in which that sound and practical politician, giving an account of the people going to take the oaths that they might avoid the tax, says,—" It was a strange as well as a ridiculous sight to see people crowding to give testimony of their allegiance to a Government, and cursing it at the same time for giving them the trouble of so doing, and for the fright they were put into by it; and I am satisfied more real disaffection to the King and his family arose from it than from anything which happened in that time. It made the Government appear tyrannical and suspicious, than which nothing can be more hurtful to a Prince or lessen his safety." He adds some admirable observations on the general inutility of political oaths.—*Coxe's Mem. of Sir R. Walp.* vol. ii. p. 93-555. This bill explains a line in Pope which has puzzled unlearned critics:—
" Fortune not much of humbling me can boast;
Tho' double taxd, how little have I lost !"

[2] His town house was latterly in Great George Street, Westminster, erected on the building of Westminster Bridge, and then the most fashionable residence for the high nobility, since appropriated to railroad committee rooms. Having had many Chancellors living in the City of London and Borough of Southwark, I shall soon transfer them to Grosvenor Square.

[3] I give a specimen of his directions:—" The weeds in the orchard to be mowed. The little kitchen-garden in the corner to be cleaned. The goose-

country affairs to his "VILLICUS;" and when not engaged in the public service, to which we have seen he still devoted himself, he employed his leisure in the education of his children, and in the society of his professional, political, and literary friends.

From a kindly feeling for him, I could wish that he had been more given to philosophy, and that, after the example of several of his illustrious contemporaries, he had mingled the *belles lettres* with politics. He had before his eyes *politicians* like Bolingbroke and Chesterfield, who were making themselves distinguished as *fine writers;* and *fine writers*, like Addison and Prior, who, with less felicity of amalagamation, had risen to distinction as *politicians*. What an interesting and instructive work he might have left us—ranking him with the most illustrious of his order—if, on his retirement from office, he had sat down and written the "History of his own Times," an undertaking for which he has shown, by several of his compositions, particularly by his "Impartial State of Parties," presented to George I., that he was singularly well qualified! His style is more accurate and flowing than that of his friend, the Bishop of Salisbury; he took larger views of constitutional questions; his insight into the character of public men was truer; he had a better opportunity of knowing the real springs of action in parties and individuals, and he was infinitely better qualified to weigh evidence and to detect falsehood. Had he begun with the Trial of the Seven Bishops, given us an account from personal observation of the Defendants, the Judges, the Council, the Jury, and the feelings of the spectators, till the shout of applause arose on the acquittal —and had gone on with his narrative, introducing the sensation produced in the metropolis when the news arrived of William's landing—his own march at the head of a little military band to meet the deliverer—the opinions and wishes of the lawyers in general at this great crisis[1]—the speedy reaction in favor of the banished despot—the writer's first introduction into the House of

berry and currant bushes trimmed. The fig-trees, mulberry-trees, and such as seem decaying but not desperate, watered. Stir and clean the borders. Remove trees which are to be removed."

[1] I am afraid he would not have added much to the reputation of our profession; for my investigations lead me to think that they were very slavishly inclined, and that the CHURCH did more for the Revolution than the LAW.

Commons—his rise to be the leader of the Whigs there—the state of the borough representation when he proposed to bribe Totness and took refuge in Berealstone—the bitter disappointment of the Tory party when their leaders betrayed them and became Whiggish in the beginning of the reign of Anne—the cabals in the cabinet after he was her Chancellor—the deliberations on the prosecutions of Sacheverell—the dismay of the Whig leaders when they discovered the fatal error they had committed—the revolution in the public mind respecting the continuation of the war—the real views of different parties as to the succession on the Queen's death—the exultation of the Jacobites on the arrival of King George's German favorites, and the rapacity they displayed—the dissensions in the royal family, with which the Chancellor was so much mixed up—the feelings at Court when the Earl of Mar's rebellion broke out, and the old Pretender landed in Scotland—the intrigues for saving the lives of the Rebel Lords—the growing favor of Lord Macclesfield with the King—the true circumstances of the historian's own resignation—his motives for opposing the Bill to repeal the Test and Corporation Acts—the manner in which he was regarded when all his prophecies respecting the South Sea scheme had been more than realised—and the ultimate safety of the Revolution settlement, and of the new dynasty, by the appointment of Walpole as Prime Minister,—he would have left us a work far more interesting than the gossip of Burnet,—to be placed by the side of the "History of the Grand Rebellion." But he despised authorship, and he is comparatively obscure.

He now composed nothing of greater magnitude than familiar epistles to his wife. The Countess continuing in the household of the Princess of Wales, was frequently separated from him while in waiting. Thus he from time to time addressed her:—

"As for your present condition, I hope, now the regret at parting is over, it is not only easy to you, but delightful; it can not be otherwise while you are with so good a mistress, and from whom you have received such proofs of kindness to you as can not be counterfeit, whatever some would make you believe: if everybody would have counterfeited with me at that rate, I should not have had any cause to complain. If you discern that any are sowing seeds in your Court that may raise strife, I hope you will use your best endeavors to root 'em out, and when you have so done your duty, you will have more reason to be unconcerned at the event, if it should be unfortunate, than if you had endeavored nothing. Though when you have done so well, I would not have you so much as hope that there are not those who will represent you as a most intolerable mischief-maker. Slanders which are no more than expected are the easier borne, which makes me foretell this."[1] "I thank you for your endearing, and, I depend, very sincere expressions; but considering all things, I think 'tis but reasonable that at least, for variety of living, you should find something more satisfactory in a Court than you can in a retired minister (who you know is always a peevish creature), and so solitary a place."[2] "The Attorney General puts me in mind of the choice by which they usually try idiots; 'tis to see if they will choose an apple before a piece of gold; the practice of the Attorney General (well performed) is not only of great profit and substantial honor, authority, and credit in the state, whereas being in the list of Privy Councillors is the very emptiest and lightest food for vanity that I know of."[3] "I am just come from the House at eight o'clock at night, and therefore you'll excuse me if I write the shorter. The debate turned on this, whether the address to the King should contain an approbation of the stroke given Spain, or that part be left to a further and more mature consideration, before the House engaged their advice in it. The immediate approbation was carried by 59 against 45. I was of the losing side."[4] "I am mighty full of business from morning to

---

[1] 24th June, 1718. [2] 29th June, 1718.
[3] 4th July, 1718. This refers to Lechmere, then Attorney General, who then took good advice; but was afterwards, in May, 1720, silly enough to retire on a peerage.
[4] 11th Nov. 1718. This was the first day of the session, and the debate was on the address. According to the Parliamentary History (vii. 361), the division was 83 to 50; but, I presume, this included proxies. Earl Cowper himself spoke, although he does not mention this to his wife; but Lord Stanhope's, on the ministerial side, is the only speech in the debate of which a fragment is preserved.

That I may not break the series of his letters to his wife, I will here copy a letter from him to the Princess of Wales, and another to the Prince, which are worth preserving, to show the terms on which he lived with them :—

night, and sufficiently weary before that comes. It is cruelty in you to tantalize a poor countryman with the life of state and pleasure you describe. I could be content as I am if I did not hear of such fine doings."[1] "Since we neither beat our servants, nor fine them, the only way to govern them is to make them so content with their places, that they shall fear turning away. John's drunkenness seems a tertian, having one sober day between two drunken ones, except that on Friday it proved quotidian."[2] "The country is excessively pleasant, but I am sensible while it pleases, it dulls me, and in these

> "Madam,
> "I do myself the honor to write to your Royal Highness for my poor wife, who is not able to do it for herself, being taken with a violent diarrhœa on Friday morning last, which, though yesterday, and thus far of this day, it hath in some degree abated, has rendered her so very weak, that 'tis impossible for her to stir from the place she is in without the greatest hazard of her life. I am far from thinking her safe with all the care she can take. Her real and earnest desire and hope to wait on your Royal Highness have caused her not to consent to my writing this true excuse till the last moment allowed, which has also hindered her from trying to get another lady to wait for her, so that she has nothing to rely on but your goodness; of which she has had, on former occasions, so great proofs, as it is impossible we should not both ever acknowledge with the utmost gratitude.
> "I am, with perfect fidelity and devotion,
> "Madam,
> "Your most dutiful and most obedient Servant,
> "19th July, 1719. "COWPER.
> "My wife desires her most humble duty may be presented to your R. H.; and we beg our most humble duty may be presented to his R. H."
> "Sir,
> "I was concerned that y^r messenger had ye trouble to come so far as this place, wch I hop'd was prevented by my ordering y^t y^r R. H.'s l^{re} should be receiv'd at my house in town, and sent by my packet of this night to me; but I was coverd with confusion when I found in it ye goodness and most oblidging manner wth wch you had granted my request, least I should not live to deserve it. I assure you S^r, y^t what is left me of life shall be principally applyd to that end.
> "I am, wth perfect constancy and truth,
> "Your much obliged, and most dutifull and most obed^t servant,
> "18th July, 1720. "COWPER."
> [1] 2nd June, 1720. I am much afraid that the ex-Chancellor, notwithstanding his affected pleasantry, was really at this moment in his retreat sighing for the woolsack with all the anxieties and labors which induced him to resign it. Perhaps I may say of most of my ex-Chancellors:
> "Quam vellent æthere in alto
> Nunc . . . . duros perferre labores!
> Fas obstat, tristique palus inamabilis unda
> Alligat, et novies Styx interfusa coercet."
> I remember old Judge Heath observing to me soon after I was called to the bar, "I have known many ex-Chancellors in my time, but I have never known a contented one yet." [2] 5th June, 1720.

few days I have contracted a great degree of indolence, and an aversion to all cares but the little ones of this place. Would to God our leaders would need no observation, or that they would effectually take it up. I am far from thinking it pleasant, or indeed wise, to set up for a Reformer; but somebody must endeavor to prevent things from running to an excess of ill."[1]

The following is the only remaining letter in my possession of Lord Cowper to the Countess, and it will be read with great interest, as it is the last he ever sent to her, and was written exactly one week before he died. She was then at Colegreen, he being detained by some private business in London. Having dispatched this, he hoped to join her immediately. The handwriting is considerably altered, indicating infirmity or nervousness. I am not able to offer any further explanation of the letter or its allusions:—

"George Street, Thursd. 3 Oct.

"My D^{rst} Life,

"I recd your lre here last night, dated on Tuesday last: it is very hard a man and wife can not correspond wth innocent & proper freedom, without its beeing a diversion to a third person. To-day I hope to finish wth ye D. of K., who is gone somewhatt ill to Rest by the D^{rs} advice; but then I have 3,000 dead to dispose of, w^{ch} 'tis worth staying one day longer for; so I can't be wth you till Sat. next. I am,

"Dr M.,

"Yours wth perfect affection,

"C."

He reached Colegreen on Saturday, as he expected, but, being exposed to severe cold on his journey, he was taken violently ill immediately after his arrival at home, and his disease soon assumed a very alarming aspect. He received all the attentions which the fondest affection could bestow from his wife and from his children. When informed of his danger, he received the intelligence with firmness, and with becoming resignation and composure he prepared to meet his end. He expired on Thursday, the 10th of October, 1723, in the sixtieth year of his age.

He was buried in the parish church of Hertingfordbury, in Hertfordshire, the resting-place of his immediate an

[1] 13th April, 1722.

cestors, and of many of his descendants. The sexton shows a splendid marble monument as his, but, in reality, it was erected in honor of his brother, Spencer, the Judge. In the same church there is a beautiful small mural monument (I think by Roubillac) which may be the monument of the Lord Chancellor.

Brass and marble may be reserved for those who, without their aid, would soon sink from the memory of mankind. Lord Chancellor Cowper achieved for himself a permanent place in the public annals of his country. He retains a high reputation as a lawyer, as a statesman, and as an orator. He was a consistent and most honorable politician, fully understanding, and ever acting upon, the true principles of the English Constitution. He must likewise be considered, upon the whole, a friend to religious liberty, although he had not, like Lord Stanhope, so far outrun the prejudices of the age as to perceive that, for the sake of true piety, and to rescue the Established Church from unmerited odium, civil privileges ought not to depend upon any religious test.

It is now my duty deliberately to examine the grave imputation cast upon his moral character. When he was rising to eminence as the leader of the Whigs in the House of Commons, the rumor to which I have alluded originated, that he had married a second wife while the first was still alive, and this was industriously circulated during his first chancellorship. On the change of government, (as we have seen) it was eagerly seized on by Swift, become Tory, who, in his contrast between the then late and present ministers, did not scruple to charge the ex-Chancellor Cowper with having not only practiced, but deliberately defended, polygamy. Then came Swift's associate, the infamous Mrs. Manley, who, in the NEW ATALANTIS, under the names of "HERNANDO and LOUISA," gave a most detailed and inflammatory account of the guilty loves of Lord Cowper and a young lady, supposed to have been his ward,—with a representation that he had persuaded her of the lawfulness of a plurality of wives—and a broad assertion that his brother, Spencer, disguised as a French refugee priest, performed the ceremony of marriage between them. The charge was so often repeated that it gained credit, and the nickname of "Will Bigamy," by which the Tories designated the

Keeper of Queen Anne's conscience, afterwards stuck to him. When Voltaire visited England, to inspect our customs, he found the story very rife. Believing, or affecting to believe it,—when he published his "PHILOSOPHICAL DICTIONARY," and, under the word "Femme," discussed the subject of *Polygamy*,—in the section entitled " De la Polygamie permise par quelques Papes et par quelques Réformateurs." he boldly introduced this sentence:—" Il est public en Angleterre, et on voudroit le nier en vain, que le Chancellier COWPER épousa deux femmes, qui vécurent ensemble dans sa maison avec une concorde singulière qui fit honneur à tous trois. Plusieurs curieux ont encore le petit livre que ce Chancellier composa en faveur de la Polygamie."[1]

After an impartial investigation, I am bound to say that the charge rests on no authority, and is contradicted by strong circumstantial evidence. I suppose Voltaire's testimony will have as little weight with respect to the fact of the *polygamy*, as to the " petit livre " in favor of the practice.

The jumble of obscenity and falsehood, entitled the NEW ATALANTIS, was treated with scorn by all sensible men when it appeared, and can now mislead no one acquainted with its infamy. Swift, a notorious slanderer of private character, is to be placed in the same category with Mrs. Manley. Indeed, he himself expresses great respect and sympathy for her, and shows that there can be no injustice in classing them together. " Poor Mrs.

[1] The same statement is made by Voltaire, in his "Essai sur les Mœurs," c. 130. I have heard it asserted, that Voltaire declares elsewhere, that, "according to the laws and usages of England, the Lord Chancellor is privileged by his office to have as many wives as he pleases, whence one of his titles is that *Lord Keeper*." I should not have been at all surprised to have seen such a statement in the " Lettres sur L'Angleterre," but I have not been able to meet with it there, or in any of the other writings of the Philosoper of Ferney which I have ventured to consult. It may perhaps be worth mentioning, as a parallel case, that Socrates was in antiquity accused of bigamy; the names of the two wives being Xanthippe and Myrto. Modern critics have however rejected the story as fabulous. A separate treatise to refute this story has been written by a Dutch Scholar: Luzac de Digamiâ Socratis. See Smith's Dict. of Ancient Biog. and Myth., art. Socrates, vol. iii. p. 850; also Boeckh's Economy of Athens, b. i. c. 20.

It is rather curious to observe how strictly the Greeks from the earliest times adhered to the institution of monogamy. All the Oriental nations, including the Jews, permitted polygamy, and it is difficult to understand what was the origin of the strictness of the Greeks and all their cognate races on the subject.—*4th Edition.*

Manley," he writes to Stella, "is very ill; the printer tells me he is afraid she can not live long. I am heartily sorry for her; she has very generous principles for one of her sort,[1] and a great deal of good sense and invention."[2] General rumor can go for nothing where such arts are used to poison the public mind. The charge is never glanced at in parliamentary conflict, although the vices of the Duke of Wharton frequently are; and it is not mentioned in any publication with the slightest claim to respectability.

On the other hand I have had access to documents in which, had the story been true, there must have been some trace of it. Lord Cowper actually was married to two wives—but—successively—not simultaneously. I have seen his correspondence with both these ladies from before the time when he wedded the first, till he left the second a widow to lament his loss, and I can find nothing in it but sentiments of warm, mutual, and undivided affection. He seems to have been a true and a tender husband—of which I may give a touching proof by an extract from the diary of the second Lady Cowper:—

"April 7th, 1716. After dinner we went to Sir Godfrey Kneller's to see a picture of my Lord which he is drawing, and is the best that was ever done for him; it is for my dressing-room, *and in the same posture that he watched me so many weeks in my great illness.*"

Upon the whole I think we may safely set down the charge, that Lord Chancellor Cowper advocated and practiced polygamy, to party malignity, which in his time raged among men and women to a degree of which we can form no notion without studying the libelous publications which then disgaced the press.[3]

[1] Her most creditable position was as mistress to Swift's old friend, Alderman Barber. The Dean was well acquainted with her history from the moment of her birth, as we know by his lines to "CORINNA." Most of these are unfit to be transcribed, but I may copy the stanza celebrating her precocity in slander:—

" Her talents she display'd betimes,
    For in twice twelve revolving moons
She seem'd to laugh and squall in rhymes,
    And all her gestures were lampoons."

What she did at six and twelve must not be told.
[2] Journal to Stella, 1712. 26th January.
[3] The fable of the " Treatise," is evidently taken from the panegyric on " a

Having paid such attention to Lord Cowper's detractors, it will be bare justice to mention some of the eulogies pronounced upon him by contemporary writers in verse and in prose. Ambrose Philips, secretary to a Lord Chancellor, as well as a poet, and therefore competent to judge of his merit, not only praises his disinterestedness in sacrificing "New Year's Gifts," but, in the Pindaric ode to his memory, ascribes to him every public and private virtue. A few extracts from it may please:—

"Wake the British harp again
To a sad melodous strain
* * *
Here we come, and hence we go,
Shadows passing to and fro,
Seen awhile, forgotten soon,
But thou to fair distinction born,
Thou, Cowper, beamy in the morn
Of life, still bright'ning to the pitch of noon;
Scarce verging to the steep decline,
Hence summon'd, while thy virtues radiant shine,
Shall be remember'd with a fond applause
So long as Britons own the same indulgent laws.
* * *
Hear him speaking, and you hear
Reason, tuneful to the ear!
Lips with thymy language sweet,
Distilling on the hearer's mind
The balm of wisdom, speech refin'd
Celestial gifts! Oh, when the nobles meet
When next, thou sea-surrounded land,
Thy nobles meet at Brunswick's high command,

---

plurality of wives," which Mrs. Manley puts into the mouth of Lord Cowper, in a speech supposed to be addressed by HERNANDO to LOUISA. Much of it is too gross to be read; but an innocent specimen of it may be given:—"The law of nature, as well as the custom of many nations, and most religions, declare for polygamy. The ancient Hebrews indulged in plurality of wives and unlimited use of concubinage. The Turks, and all the people in the world, but the Europeans, still preserve the privilege. It is to be owned, their manner in all things is less adulterated than ours; their veracity, morality, and habit of living less corrupted. In pretending to reform their abuses, Europe has only refined their vices." Some of the scenes between HERNANDO and LOUISA, which Swift thought displayed Mrs. Manley's "good sense and invention," are most flagitiously indecent.

A similar story was told (and perhaps with as little foundation) of another eminent lawyer who then flourished. Instead of the two wives agreeing so well together in the Voltaire fashion, it was said that they did not know of each other's existence; and that he passed a part of every night in the house with each of them, telling the one whom he visited first that he was obliged to leave her to go very early in the morning to his chambers in the Temple; and the other, whom he then visited, that he was obliged to remain at chambers till so late an hour.

> In vain they shall the charmer's voice desire,
> In vain those lips of eloquence require,
> That mild conviction which the soul assails,
> By soft alarms and with gentle force prevails!"[1]

In Pope's imitation of Horace, where he introduces his two brother Sergeants complimenting each other, he makes Cowper their model of grace:—

> "'Twas, 'Sir your wit,' and 'Sir, your eloquence.'
> '*Yours, Cowper's manner;*' and 'yours, Talbot's sense.'"[2]

He is likewise celebrated in the poem ascribed to Sir Charles Hanbury Williams, in which offerings are supposed to be made to Sir Hans Sloane to enrich his Museum;—

> "Some strains of eloquence, which hung
> In ancient times on Tully's tongue,
> But which conceal'd, and lost had lain,
> Till COWPER found them out again."

"Who," says Steele, in describing the characters of the Whig ministers, "is not pleased to see a person in the highest station in the law, who was the most eminent in his profession, and the most accomplished orator at the bar?"[3] The same writer, in his Dedication of the 3rd volume of the "Tatler" to Lord Cowper, thus speaks of him: "It is our common good that your admirable eloquence can now no longer be employed but in the expression of your own sentiments and judgment. The skillful pleader is now forever changed into the just judge; which latter character your Lordship exerts with so prevailing an impartiality, that you win the approbation even of those who dissent from you, and you always obtain favor because you are never moved by it. The graceful manner, the apt gesture, and the assumed concern, are impotent helps to persuasion, in comparison of the honest countenance of him who utters what he really means. From whence it is, that all the beauties which others attain with labor, are in your Lordship but the natural effects of the heart that dictates."

While he was excluded from office in the latter end of the reign of Queen Anne, and never likely again to have

---

[1] I wish that Ambrose had tried to celebrate in him a "Pastoral," instead of an "Ode."

[2] "Frater erat Romæ consulti rhetor; ut alter
    Alterius sermone meros audiret honores."

[3] Tatler, 7th Feb. 1710.

the distribution of public patronage, Hughes devoted to his praise an entire paper of the "Spectator," with this motto from Tibullus:

> ..."Quodcunque meæ poterunt audere Camœnæ
> Seu tibi par poterunt; seu quod spes abnuit, ultra;
> Sive minus; certeque canent minus: omne vovemus
> Hoc tibi; ne tanto careat nihi nomine charta." [1]

I extract the passages which I consider the most characteristic:—

"In his private domestic employments he is no less glorious than in his public; for it is in reality a more difficult task to be conspicuous in a sedentary, inactive life than in one spent in hurry and business. There are many who are acceptable to some particular persons, whilst the rest of mankind look upon them with coldness and indifference: but he is the first whose entire good fortune it is ever please and to be pleased, wherever he comes to be admired, and wherever he is absent to be lamented. His merit fares like the pictures of Raphael, which are either seen with admiration by all, or at least no one dare own he has no taste for a composition which has received so universal an applause. It is below him to catch the sight with any care of dress: his outward garb is but the emblem of his mind. He is still the principal figure in the room. He first engages your eye as if there were some point of light which shone stronger upon him than on any other person. Nothing can equal the pleasure that is taken in hearing him speak, but the satisfaction one receives in the civility and attention he pays to the discourse of others. His looks are a silent commendation of what is good and praiseworthy, and a secret reproof to what is licentious and extravagant. He knows how to appear free and open without danger of intrusion, and to be cautious without seeming reserved." [2]

The following character of him appeared in the "True Briton," a few days after his death, and was afterwards transferred into the "Historical Register" for the year 1723:—

"He was the most accomplished lawyer, civilian, and statesman that England bore for many ages past; being consummate in the knowledge not only of the common and statute law, and of the constitution of his country,

[1] Tibull. 1 Carm. iv. 24.   [2] Spectator, No. 467, vol. vi. 386.

but also of the law of nations, imperial institutes, and canon law; and he had received from nature, and cultivated by polite literature, excellent endowments, that gave a luster to his great learning; a bright, quick, penetrating genius; an exact and sound judgment; a fruitful yet unluxuriant and agreeable imagination; a manly and flowing eloquence; a clear, sonorous voice; a gracious aspect; an easy address; in a word, all that's necessary to form a complete orator."

The Duke Wharton, writing after Lord Cowper's death, says,—

"He came not to the Seals without a great deal of prejudice from the Tory party in general, among whom I believe there was not one but maligned him. But how long did this scene continue? He had scarcely presided in that high station one year, before the scales became even with the universal applause and approbation of both parties. There was not the least mark of party rage, rashness, rigor, or impatience to be seen or traced throughout all his conduct in this critical branch of his high office; for which he showed such a masterly genius and uncommon abilities, that made easy to him the great task of dispensing justice, which, like the sun, he dispensed with equal luster on all without regard to quality or distinction."

The most valuable testimony to his powers of speaking, although mixed with a little sarcasm, is from Lord Chesterfield:—

"The nature of our Constitution makes eloquence more useful and more necessary in this country than in any other in Europe. A certain degree of good sense and knowledge is requisite for that as well as for everything else; but beyond that, the purity of diction, the elegancy of style, the harmony of periods, a pleasing elocution, and a graceful action, are the things which a public speaker should attend to the most; because his audience does,—and understands them best,—or rather, indeed, understands little else. The late Lord Chancellor Cowper's strength as an orator lay by no means in his reasonings, for very often he hazarded very weak ones. But such was the purity and elegancy of his style, such the propriety and charms of his elocution, and such the gracefulness of his action, that he never spoke without universal applause. The ears and the eyes gave him up the hearts and the understandings of the audience." [1]

After all, perhaps, the very high opinion entertained of his talents in his own time may best be understood by the extorted praise, mixed with gratuitous abuse of him, to be found in the NEW ATALANTIS itself—

"All the great success he has met with is due to the brightness of his own genius; he owed much more to his natural than acquired parts. His memory was good, so was his luck; to those were joined a great deal of wit; volubility of tongue; ready sentiments, and a most plausible address; religion in pretense, none in reality. He held it lawful for a man to obtain, by any methods, either pleasure or riches; he was violent in the pursuit of both; quitting his interest for nothing but pleasure, and his pleasure for nothing but interest." [2]

I am sorry that I am not able to record any of his happy sayings, and that so few genuine personal anecdotes of him are preserved; but I have great pleasure in doing justice to his good feeling and good taste on an occasion which tested both. After the Revolution, the tone was to treat all that had happened during the time of the Commonwealth with equal horror as when the sons of the Blessed Martyr were misgoverning the kingdom. But it happened that Richard Cromwell, in his old age, had to appear in Westminster Hall before Lord Cowper when Chancellor, and his Lordship ordered him a chair in respect of the high station he had once held. This was different treatment from the ex-Protector's rude ejection from the House of Lords by the door-keeper as one of the mob, when he exclaimed, "The last time I was in this place I sat upon the throne."

From his practice at the bar, and the fair emoluments of his offices, Lord Cowper honorably raised a large fortune. He purchased the manor of Hertingfordbury, and built upon it his country house, Colegreen, which afterwards made way for the more stately Panshanger, the residence of his descendants.[3] He collected a fine gallery

[1] Lord Chesterfields Letters, ccv.   [2] Vol. i. 195.
[3] While in office, besides his town house, in Lincoln's Inn Fields, or Great George Street,—that he might be the near the Court, he had a lodging at Kensington, then considered as far from London as Windsor now is. To this Lady Cowper refers in her Journal in a manner which strikingly shows the state of the police 142 years ago:—

of paintings, still preserved in the family, among which the most valued are portraits of himself, by Kneller, strikingly representing the very handsome and intelligent countenance admired by his contemporaries.

Lord Cowper, by his second wife, left both sons and daughters; and his family, illustrated by the great poet of his blood and name, still more than by the title of Prince of the Roman Empire, conferred on his grandson, is now one of the most distinguished in the Peerage of England.[1]

I may, perhaps, be pardoned if I conclude this memoir with a valueless, but sincere, tribute of admiration and gratitude to Peter Leopold, the late Earl. He had too much delicacy of sentiment to take a leading part in public life, but to the most exquisitely pleasing manners he joined a manly understanding and a playful wit. From him I received kind and encouraging notice when I was poor and obscure; and his benevolent and exhilarating smile is one of the most delightful images in my memory of pleasures to return no more.

CHAPTER CXVIII.

LIFE OF LORD CHANCELLOR HARCOURT FROM HIS BIRTH TILL HE RECEIVED THE GREAT SEAL.

I NOW enter upon the life of a Chancellor who was not only a very zealous Tory, but a Jacobite; and it gives me sincere pleasure to think that I shall be able, almost uniformly, to speak of him with respect and with kindness. He was a tolerably good lawyer, an accomplished orator, and an ardent lover of polite learning. His mind was early imbued with the doctrines of high prerogative; but he may fairly be said in very difficult times to have preserved his consistency and his character. I do not consider his efforts to restore the exiled Stuarts morally inconsistent with the engagements into which he

---

"October, 1715. I was at Kensington, where I intended to stay as long as the camp was in Hyde Park, the roads being so secure by it that we might come to London at any time of the night without danger, which I did very often."—This encampment was previous to the march of the army to put down the rebellion in Scotland.   [1] Grandeur of the Law, p. 52.

had entered to the existing Government; and although there were loud complaints against him for at last sending in his adhesion to the House of Hanover, it should be recollected that the cause of the Stuarts had then become desperate, and that, instead of betraying, he did everything in his power to screen, his old associates.

Upon Lord Cowper's first resignation of the Great Seal —after it had been a short time in the custody of the Lords Commissioners, Trevor, Tracy, and Scrope, it was delivered with the title of Lord Keeper, to SIR SIMON HARCOURT. This individual, who had qualities to raise himself from the humblest origin, was descended from a very ancient and distinguished family.[1] His ancestor is said to have been a younger brother of a Saxon king, and second in command to Rollo, when the band of northern adventurers, in the year 876, invaded France, and got possession of the province to which they gave the name of Normandy. For the services of this chief there was assigned to him the signory of Harcourt, on the banks of the Seine, from which his family took their name. Here they were seated in the middle of the eleventh century—when a younger son of the then chief accompanied Duke William in his memorable expedition to claim the crown of England, fought with him at Hastings, and, having many manors granted to him for his bravery, became the founder of the English Harcourts. Robert, his great-grandson, by marriage with Isabel de Camvile, obtained the estate of Stanton, in the county of Oxford, which thenceforth received the name of Stanton-Harcourt, and has for a period of above seven hundred years remained the property of his descendants.[2] The elder branch flourished in

---

[1] Coll Peer. iv. 428; Noble, i. 14.

[2] This Robert was sheriff of Leicester and Warwickshire in the years 1199, 1201, 1202, and the manor of Stanton-Harcourt was confirmed to him and Isabel, and their heirs, by King Stephen and King Henry II. It was held of the Crown by the following service; namely, " That the Lord of Stanton-Harcourt should find four browsers in Woodstock Parke in winter time, when the snow shall happen to fall, and tarrye, lie, and abide, be the space of two days; and so to find the said browsers, there browsing, so long as the snow doth lye; every browser to have to his lodging every night one billet of wood, the length of his ax helve, and that to carry to his lodgings upon the edge of his ax. And the King's bailiff of the demesnes, or of the hundreds of Wootton, coming to give warning for the said browsers shall blow his horn at the gate of the mannor of Stanton-Harcourt aforesaid, and then the said bailiff to have a cast of bread, a gallon of ale, and a piece of beef, of the said Lord of Stanton-Harcourt aforesaid; and the said Lord, or other for

Normandy, as a great ducal house, down to the time of the French revolution, producing many distinguished warriors and statesmen. The *cadets* in England maintained the reputation of the race for gallantry and loyalty. In the war of the Roses they sided with the House of York, as the true heirs to the throne; and one of them particularly signalizing himself under the banner of Edward IV. was by him created a Knight of the Garter. When the troubles began in the reign of Charles I. they were all devoted royalists. Sir Simon, the then Lord of Stanton-Harcourt, and grandfather of the Chancellor, fell in the first conflict which took place with the troops of the Parliament in Ireland. Sir Philip, the Chancellor's father having married the daughter of Sir William Waller, the parliamentarian general, is said to have embraced the Presbyterian religion; but he abhorred the Independents, who had gained a decided superiority, and he refused to submit to Cromwell, even after resistance had ceased to offer any prospect of success. In consequence, a great part of his property was seized and confiscated. When the monarchy was at last re-established, like many other loyal men, he was doomed to the disappointment of all hopes of preferment and even of indemnity, and to struggle with penury during the rest of his days.

His son Simon, the subject of this memoir, was born the very year of the Restoration, and was obliged to submit to some early hardships, which perhaps invigorated his character and sharpened his intellect. I have not been able to ascertain anything of his early education, and it is probable that till he was fit for the university he remained under private tuition at home—imbibing a proper hatred of Roundheads and Puritans, and hearing the praises of the Blessed Martyr—intermixed with some grumblings at the ingratitude of the restored monarch.[1]

the time being, to have of custom yearly out of the said parke, one buck in sumer, and one doe in winter. And also the Lord of Stanton-Harcourt must fell, make, rear, and carry all the grasse growing in one meadow within the parke of Woodstock, called Stanton and Southly mead; and the fellers and the makers thereof have used to have of custom, of the King's Majesty's charge, six pence in money, and two gallons of ale."—*Account of Stanton-Harcourt, by George Simon, Earl Harcourt, 1808.*

[1] I have since seen a statement that he was at a private school, kept by a Presbyterian minister, at Shelton, Oxfordshire; having for his schoolfellows, Harley, afterwards Earl of Oxford, and Trevor, Chief Justice of the Common Pleas.—*Townsend's Hist. of the House of Commons,* i. 88, 3rd ed.

When fifteen years of age, he was sent to Pembroke College, Oxford, where he was strengthened in his faith in the divine right of kings, and the wickedness of all resistance to their authority. At the same time he occupied himself diligently in classical studies, and he acquired a taste for poetry and polite literature, which stuck by him through life.[1]

Having resided three or four years at Oxford, he was removed to the Inner Temple, and began the study of the law.[2] Aware that it was with great difficulty his family could defray the expense of maintaining him at the university and the inns of court, and that any patrimony to which he could look forward was exceedingly slender, he applied himself assiduously to "Finch," "The Doctor and Student," and other institutional books then fashionable; and though he was never famous for Black Letter, he made himself pretty fairly master of his profession. He at least learned where the law upon different subjects was to be found, so that, as the occasion required, he could get up an argument well on any question *pro re natâ*, and appear more learned than others who had laid in a larger stock of law over which they had less command. From his family connections he had access to the best society, and he kept up an intimate acquaintance with poets and dramatists. His person was handsome, and his manners were prepossessing.

He was called to the bar in Michaelmas, 1683, when Jeffreys was Chief Justice of the King's Bench, and Guilford was Lord Keeper. There had been great anticipations of his success, and these were not disappointed. "He was scarce sooner admitted to plead than admired for his pleading."[3] He had occasional fits of dissipation, and he very soon spent all the fees he received; but he was generally very attentive to the affairs of his clients, and at the age of thirty he was rising rapidly to the top of his profession. He now obtained his first professional dignity,

---

[1] The Registers of Oxford have been in vain searched for any entry of his Bachelor's or Master's degree, and there seems reason to think that, for some cause not explained, he left the university without graduating. In 1702, when made Solicitor General, attending the Queen and her consort on a visit to Oxford, he being then re-admitted of Christ Church, was created LL.D., and in the entry of this proceeding he is merely described as "*nuper Coll. Pembrok.*"

He had been admitted May 17, 1676.   [3] Gent. Mag. vol. lxv.

which he probably valued at the time more highly than he ever did any that followed it; he was elected Recorder of Abingdon, and had to act the Judge in the presence of the villagers among whom he gamboled when a boy.

Not blind to the errors of the reign of James II., he had viewed with extreme aversion what he had long continued to designate "the usurpation of the Dutch Stadtholder,"—but seeing the irresistible combination of churchmen and dissenters to expel the Popish king, he perceived that all opposition to the national will must be vain and mischievous, and he therefore resolved " to bide his time."

He would have nothing to do with the Convention Parliament, although he might have had a seat in it if he had pleased; but seeing the reaction so speedily begin,— when a new parliament was summoned he got himself returned for Abingdon, in the hope of doing something for King James, and at all events, resolved to embarrass the new Government. He took the oaths of allegiance to William and Mary, upon the maxim which guided the conduct of "downright Shippen," and many other adherents of the Stuarts, who were considered "honorable men,"—that such oaths were not binding, and that the sin of taking or breaking them lay upon those who imposed them.

He made his maiden speech on the 9th of April, 1690, in the debate on the bill for recognizing the new Sovereign, and confirming the Acts of the Convention Parliament, which had sat without any royal summons. He could not directly oppose the bill, but he tried to disparage it, from the manner in which it was framed, and he boldly said, " I have ever thought the monarchy hereditary; and by this, what becomes of your entail?"— (meaning the settlement of the Crown). " I am not satisfied that the acts of the Convention of 1660 were binding till confirmed by a parliament summoned by a lawful king."[1]

When the bill came to be considered which required an oath to abjure King James and his descendants, Harcourt, feeling that this might be very harassing to some of his friends with tender consciences, manfully and ably

---

[1] 5 Parl. Hist. 582.

opposed it as unnecessary, tyrannical, and ineffectual for its object. He said, "You have already the oath of allegiance; and if that is equivocated, what security have you in an oath of abjuration? I often hear that we have a powerful enemy abroad, and that there is a necessity to unite at home. This will endanger fomenting and increasing jealousies. I will discharge my conscience, however I may be mistaken. Such an unprecedented oath will give occasion to think there is some radical defect in the Government, which is to be so supported by such extraordinary expedients. You will gain no ground by it; you will make enemies. I hope there will be no reflection upon me as against the Government because I am against this bill." Sir John Mainwaring, the next speaker, seems to allude to some indiscreet declaration of Harcourt in private company. "Suppose you have a member within these walls who should say, *'If you will do as I would have you, send away King William, and send back for King James.'*"[1] The bill passed, which remaining unmodified, I am ashamed to say, still compels us to abjure upon oath, any allegiance to the descendants of King James long after these descendants have become extinct.[2]

He next stoutly resisted the suspension of the Habeas Corpus Act,—which was proposed on the ground of plots against the Government, and he showed how speedily and aptly Tories and Whigs could change their language as they were in opposition or in office. "As we are sent here," said he, "to preserve the liberties of England, so there is no greater security for them than this act, and I think I have acquitted my trust very ill if I give it up. You struggled many years for it: you obtained it in times which we are taught to look back upon as oppressive, and we are now to be deprived of it. Suspending it thus, on every frivolous pretense, amounts to a repeal. At this particular time, now we have an army of foreigners in our bowels (William's Dutch guards), we should rather increase our liberties than diminish them."[3]

[1] 5 Parl. Hist. 596.
[2] It is a reproach to all the successive Administrations which have governed the country since the death of the Cardinal of York, that the abjuration oath has not been repealed or new-modeled. As we are living happily under the sixth Sovereign of the House of Brunswick, and there is no longer a disputed succession, I think it would be more for the dignity of the Crown to return to the ancient practice of testifying the duty of the subject by simply taking the oath of allegiance.   [3] 5 Parl. Hist. 606.

He was presently in such keen opposition, and so little afraid of flying in the face of the Court, that when the "Assassination Plot" broke out, he was one of the small minority of commoners who refused to sign the voluntary association for the defense of William's person, although Lord Chancellor Somers erased from the commission of the peace the names of all magistrates who imitated Harcourt's example.

I do not find any further notice of his speeches in the House of Commons till his gallant opposition to the iniquitous bill for the attainder of Sir John Fenwick:[1]—

"This general charge of treason," said he, "seems a great hardship. There is nothing by which so many have been unjustly taken off, as such vague allegations in indictments; and the grievance was justly considered so great, that in your bill lately passed for regulating trials for high treason, you have provided that the overt acts shall be specifically laid, with time, place, and circumstances. This is a bill to deprive an individual of the benefit of a general law, which you allow to be necessary for the protection of innocence. This is called a trial, and we are said to be the judges. I know no trial for treason but what is confirmed by MAGNA CHARTA—*per judicium parium*, by a jury, which is every Englishman's birthright, and is always esteemed one of our darling privileges: but if it be a trial, it is a pretty strange one, where the person who stands upon his trial hath a chance to be hanged, but none to be saved. I can not tell under what character to consider ourselves, whether we are judges or jurymen: I never before heard of a judge, I am sure, nor of a juryman, but he was always upon his oath: I never yet heard of a judge, but had power to examine witnesses upon oath: I never heard of a judge but had power to save the innocent as well as to condemn the guilty. Have we this power? If you were satisfied of the innocence of the accused, you must remand him to Newgate to be subject to another trial, if his prosecutors so please. Again, if I am a judge in this case, ought I not to be governed by the rules of evidence, which are the rules of law? and the very foundation of the bill is that by the rules of evidence and of law, he can not be lawfully convicted. It is said we have a discretion; but

[1] See ante, p. 149.

my Lord Chief Justice Coke says, 'a judge's discretion is *discernere per legem:*' and on another occasion, 'that a judge is to be guided by the straight line of law, and not by the crooked cord of discretion.' The practice of Westminster Hall is talked of with some disdain, as if there they only look for reason in what is the rule : but let me tell you, there the rule is laid down because it is reason—reason approved by long experience : and therefore it is a rule. To tell me the Government is in danger, and that the fate of England and of Europe depends upon this bill, is certainly rather offered to amuse than to convince. Although I have no acquaintance of Sir John Fenwick, from the account I receive of him, he can not, from his capacity, be very formidable to any government. At any rate, he is your prisoner, and you have the power of detaining him as long as you please in close custody. God forbid we should live under a government which can not subsist without taking away the life of an unfortunate gentleman contrary to the rules of law! You say you are of opinion he is guilty, and that is enough. If the opinion of those who condemn will justify the condemnation, let us no longer call the verdicts against Cornish, Sydney, and Russell, murders by a perversion of the rules of law in violation of the principles of justice."[1]

The only other occasion on which Harcourt is recorded as having made a great display in the House of Commons during the reign of King William, was upon the impeachment of Lord Somers, which seems to have been entirely under his direction. He conducted it at first very skillfully. The ex-Chancellor having made his powerful speech in his own defense in the House of Commons, the Tories were in great apprehension that there might be a division soon after he had concluded; and Harcourt, starting up, made a most taunting, stinging attack on the Whigs and their leader. Walpole, wary, though inexperienced, avoided the snare, and was for an immediate division. But "Cowper's indignation moved him to reply, which occasioned the prolongation of the debate,—at the end of which, what had been significantly and fully urged by Lord Somers was in a great measure forgotten. But had the impetuous zeal of his friends been restrained, and his enemies been permitted to proceed without interrup-

[1] 5 Parl. Hist. 1016, 1032, 1067, 1135.

tion as long as they thought fit, Walpole apprehended they would not have ventured to divide the House."[1] The impeachment being carried, after a very protracted debate, by a majority of ten, it was ordered that Mr. Simon Harcourt should present it at the bar of the House of Lords, in the name of the House of Commons and of all the Commons of England.

I think he is much to be censured afterwards in framing the articles—that, instead of confining himself to the blank commission clandestinely sealed, for negotiating the Partition Treaty, and the clandestine ratification of that Treaty, he introduced a number of frivolous and groundless charges. I likewise think that although he knew he should bring the case before a hostile tribunal, there being a Whig majority in the Lords, and that there would probably be an acquittal, whatever evidence he might adduce,—he acted injudiciously in allowing the case to go off upon the quarrel between the two Houses, as to the manner in which the trial should be conducted. By the unprecedented demand which he made at the conference of "a joint committee to arrange the preliminaries" he put the Commons in the wrong, and gave ground for contending that he was unwilling to proceed because he felt that no part of the charges was maintainable, and that the prosecution was instituted merely from party malevolence. Nevertheless he was higher in favor than ever with his own party; and as at this time they had a complete ascendency in the House of Commons, and the unfortunate result of the Partition Treaties had brought a load of unpopularity on the Whigs, it was expected that he would on the first vacancy be made Attorney or Solicitor General, or be promoted to some higher office. He had contrived to remain on friendly terms, and to be trusted by both sections of the Tories,— by those who were engaged in active correspondence with St. Germain's, and those who were willing to serve under William, they themselves having as ministers to take charge of the church and the prerogative.[2]

[1] Coxe's Sir R. Walpole, i. 22; 5 Parl. Hist. 1246.
[2] It is clear, from Vernon's correspondence, that there was at this time a great desire to bring Harcourt into office. May 21, 1700: "Some press for Mr. Harcourt being made Solicitor General." May 25, 1700. "It is certain that my Lord Coningsby would be glad to see Mr. Harcourt, and I know not whom besides, brought into places." Jan. 13, 1701. "The King has been

All his hopes were dashed by the reaction in favor of the Whigs, when Louis XIV., on the death of James II., proclaimed the Pretender—undertaking to restore him by a French force;—and a Whig House of Commons being returned, the King's speech was written by Lord Somers, about to be restored to the Great Seal. But there was a still more sudden change in his favor when, on the death of William III., Anne chased all the Whigs from her Court, and put herself into the hands of Marlborough and Godolphin, believing that they would ever be true to the High Church cause. Still his good fortune continued when her first House of Commons was ready to second her in putting down the Dissenters, and doing everything that might tend to crush the Whig party for ever.

It is believed that Harcourt might now have had the Great Seal if he had liked; but he had been very careless about money matters, and he was not rich enough to sacrifice his practice at the bar and run the risk of speedily losing his office. He therefore preferred waiting till he might become a law officer of the Crown; and old Sir Nathan Wright was continued in office, to the great joy

pressed that Mr. Solicitor should be brought upon the bench to make room for Mr. Harcourt to succeed him." Jan. 22, 1701: "We talked, likewise, about Mr. Harcourt, whom they would make Solicitor by removing Sir John Hawles to be a Judge. I desired him to consider what they would again by such a step; that I always understood it was his opinion that the Whigs should not be made desperate; and I asked him if any one act could go further towards it than by giving the first preferment to Mr. Harcourt; and that not in a very natural way, since the Solicitor had no inclination to be removed."

Shortly before, he had been exposed to great peril, having fallen among thieves (whether they were Whigs is not stated); but he had the good luck to escape with his life, and to recover his property. The adventure is thus graphically related in the "London Post" of 1st June, 1700:—"Two days ago, Mr. Simon Harcourt, a lawyer of the Temple, coming to town in his coach, was robbed by two highwaymen on Hounslow Heath of £50, his watch, and whatever they could find valuable about him; which being perceived by a countryman on horseback, he dogged them to a distance, and they taking notice thereof, turned and rid up towards him; upon which he, counterfeiting the drunkard, rid forward, making antic gestures; and being come up with them, spoke as if he had clipped the King's English, with having drunk too much, and asked them to drink a pot, offering to treat them if they would but drink with him; whereupon they, believing him to be really drunk, left him and went forward again; and he still followed them till they came to Cue (Kew) ferry, and when they were in the boat discovered them, so that they were both seized and committed; by which means the gentleman got again all they had taken from him."

of the Queen and the Church,—the Ministers having the satisfaction to know that he could be removed at any time when it might be convenient to make a vacancy.

On the 2nd of June following, Harcourt was made Solicitor General in the room of Sir John Hawles, and received the honor of knighthood, the Queen expressing great satisfaction that she had in her service a lawyer whose principles she so much approved.[1] She was not unaware of his Jacobitish propensities, which in private society he was at no great pains to conceal; but she, too, was a great admirer of the doctrine of "divine right," if she could have reconciled it with her own title, and she secretly wished that it might prevail, after the single deviation in her favor during her own life. As a mark of her special good will, she invited Mr. Solicitor to attend her on a visit she immediately after made to the University of Oxford, where they rapturously received her as the daughter of James II., forgetting for the moment that she had a "brother over the water." Sir Simon, for having so strenuously advocated the doctrines of the High Church, both ecclesiastical and political, now received, amidst tremendous applause, the honorary degree of Doctor of Laws.

He continued, under Godolphin and Marlborough, Solicitor General five years, and Attorney General for a year and a half longer;[2] but he had the mortification to see the Administration become gradually more Whiggish, till at last, in 1708, he resigned, with Harley and St. John. During the early part of this period he zealously supported Government measures in the House of Commons, though latterly he with sulkiness confined himself to the discharge of his official duties. The bill against occasional conformity had his eager support; and when the conference upon the subject took place between the two Houses, he was the chief manager on the part of the Commons—contending, "that if a national Church be necessary, which the Lords did not venture to deny, the only effectual way to preserve it is by keeping the civil

---

[1] Burnet says, "Harcourt, and several others, who had during the last reign expressed the most violent and unrelenting aversion to the whole administration, were now put into good posts."—iv. 433.

[2] He was appointed Attorney General 25th April, 1707.

power in the hands of those whose practice and principles are conformable to it."¹

In the following year he conducted a prosecution, of which the High Church party have the chief disgrace, although, strange to say, it was applauded by a considerable section of bigoted Dissenters. Sacheverell, beginning to preach the course of sermons which at last brought him into such notoriety, had lately, with great applause, announced from the pulpit to the enlightened University of Oxford, that the priest could not be a true son of the Church who did not hang out "the bloody flag and banner of defiance" against all who questioned her doctrines or her discipline. This discourse, being hawked about in the streets for two pence, was very generally read, and was making a deep impression on the public mind. The celebrated Daniel De Foe, one of the greatest literary geniuses the island of Great Britain has ever produced, at this period of his checkered career carrying on a prosperous trade and keeping his coach, was roused by the love of civil and religious liberty, which ever burned in his bosom, and, saying that "he would make an effort to stay the plague," wrote and published anonymously his celebrated tract entitled "The shortest Way with Dissenters." It affected to personate the opinions and style of the most furious of the ultra High Churchmen, and to set forth, with perfect gravity and earnestness, the extreme of the ferocious intolerance to which their views and wishes tended. A finer specimen of serious irony is not to be found in our language, and it may be placed by the side of Swift's "Argument against the Abolition of Christianity." "'Tis in vain," said he, "to trifle in this matter. We can never enjoy a settled, uninterrupted union in this nation till the spirit of Whiggism, faction, and schism is melted down like the old money. Here is the opportunity to secure the Church, and to destroy her enemies. I do not prescribe fire and faggot, but, '*Delenda est Carthago.*' They are to be rooted out of this nation if ever we will live in peace and serve God. The light, foolish handling of them by fines is their glory and advantage. If the *gallows* instead of the *comper*, and the *galleys* instead of the *fines*, were the reward of going to a conventicle, there would not be so many sufferers. The

¹ 6 Parl. Hist. 73.

spirit of martydom is over. They that will go to church to be chosen sheriffs and mayors,[1] will go to forty churches rather than be hanged."—Such was the existing state of society, that for some time both sides were taken in. Timid nonconformists were struck with the dread of coming persecution; valorous supporters of the divine obligation of imposing episcopacy on all Christians loudly shouted applause. A Cambridge fellow wrote to thank his London bookseller for sending down such an excellent treatise, which was considered in the combination rooms, there, next after the Holy Bible and the Church Liturgy, the most valuable book ever printed! But when the hoax was discovered, both parties were equally in a rage against the unlucky author; and when his name was discovered, there was a general cry that he should be pilloried. In this the Presbyterian fanatics joined, because they owed him a grudge for having on former occasions ventured to laugh at some of their absurdities. They pretended to say that such a pamphlet was a scurrilous irreverence to religion and authority, and they would have none of it. Nay, a puritanical colonel said, "he'd undertake to be hangman rather than the author should want a pass out of the world." Lord Nottingham, the head of the High Church party, rejoiced in this opportunity to punish a man who had been their constant assailant since the beginning of William's reign, and Godolphin being unable to resist a proposal so agreeable to the Queen (although at the instigation of Harley she afterwards took the same man into favor) a reward of £50 was offered for the apprehension of "Daniel De Foe, suspected of publishing a blasphemous libel." The Attorney General was ordered to prosecute him.

It would well have become Harcourt (himself a wit) to have refused to treat as a criminal for penning a mere *jeu d'esprit*, one who, although he had not yet laid the foundation of his immortality by writing "Robinson Crusoe," or "The History of the Plague of London," had, in his "Review," and other publications, given proof of the most lively invention, and of great mastery over the English language; but I am sorry to say that Mr. Attorney engaged in the prosecution with great zeal and animosity.

[1] This refers to occasional conformity, which had given rise to the controversy.

Daniel surrendered himself to save his printer and bookseller, who had been cast into prison; and in July, 1703, he took his trial at the Old Bailey, being placed like a felon in the dock. Speaker Onslow (I think rather harshly) describes Harcourt as "a man very able, but without shame." On this occasion he deserved that character. He attended in person, made a most inflamed statement of the case to the jury, and tried to stir up their religious prejudices against the defendant, insinuating that the man who could so play with sacred things could be little better than an infidel. But the legal crime charged was an attack upon the Queen's ministers, whose conduct, it was pretended, was evidently censured by this libeler, and whom he must be taken to have wished to bring into disrepute. Mr. Attorney brought forward his favorite doctrine, that "he was entitled, and in duty bound, to prosecute every man who should assert any power in the people to call their governors to account," —a doctrine sanctioned by what was laid down by the great Holt, in Tutchin's case, "that no man might lawfully publish a writing reflecting on the government, or even upon the capacity or fitness of any one employed in it."

In proving *publication* there was a difficulty, which was surmounted by a stratagem (I hope and believe) without the privity of Harcourt; for though eager to obtain a conviction, to please the High Church party, of which he was considered the champion, he was not, like the *Riches* of a former century, ready to resort to any dishonorable means to rescue the law officers of the Crown from the disgrace of failing in a state prosecution. But as De Foe afterwards declared (and there can be no doubt of the fact) he was induced to admit the publication of the alleged libel by a private assurance given him in court, "that a high influence was not indisposed to protect him," —by which he was to understand that if he were found guilty, any punishment awarded against him would be remitted by the Queen. Short work was then made of it; for the Judge said "there could be no doubt that the pamphlet was a wicked libel," and the jury, without leaving the box, found a verdict of *guilty*. Mr Attorney instantly prayed judgment, and the judges, who, happily for them, are forgotten, sentenced him whose name will be remembered with affection as long as our nation or language remains, "to pay a fine of 200 marks, to be imprisoned *during the Queen's pleasure*, to stand three times in the pillory, and to find sureties for his good behavior for seven years." He returned to his cell in the firm belief that he was forthwith to be pardoned and liberated, but he was told next day that he must prepare to undergo his punishment. Undismayed, he sat down and composed his most felicitous poetical effusion, entitled "A Hymn to the Pillory," with a view to be revenged on his prosecutors. The following stanza is evidently aimed at the Attorney General, whom he suspected, however unjustly, of having deceived him:—

> "Tell them the men that placed him here
> Are scandals to the times;
> Are at a loss to find his guilt,
> And can't commit his crimes."

This was published, and sold in thousands, the day he stood in the pillory before the Royal Exchange; and it was in everybody's mouth the two following days, when he stood in the pillory in Cheapside and at Temple Bar. The mob drank the health of De Foe, and cursed the Attorney General. The culprit was pelted with roses, and covered with garlands. "The people were expected to treat me very ill," he tells us, "but it was not so. On the contrary, they wished those who had set me there, placed in my room, and expressed their affections by loud shouts and acclamations when I was taken down." There was no foundation for the report that his ears were cut off; and I believe that there had been no instance of mutilation or branding, as a punishment for libelers, since the abolition of the Star Chamber—at any rate, none since the Revolution; yet Pope, himself the most vindictive of libelers, chose to introduce this most benevolent man, as well as fine writer, into the Dunciad, coupled with a rascal who lived by lying, in the well known distich—

> "*Earless* on high stood unabash'd DE FOE,
> And *Tutchin* flagrant from the lash below."

I have been reluctantly obliged to mention this prosecution, and to censure Harcourt's share in it: but we must chiefly blame the spirit of the age in which he lived, and we should remember, in mitigation, that more than a century afterwards, and in our own generation, sentence of the pillory was pronounced upon Leigh Hunt, a poet admired by many, and on Lord Cochrane, admitted by all to be one of the most gallant and skillful officers who ever adorned the naval service of England,—neither of whom had committed any offense deserving punishment.

The only state trial in which Harcourt was engaged was that of Tutchin for publishing the "Observator,"—a trial discreditable to several of the parties concerned in it —I am sorry to say, including Chief Justice Holt, who on this occasion laid down law which, if acted upon, would be fatal to the press, and indeed to public liberty. The defendant's counsel having attempted to put an innocent construction on some parts of the alleged libel, Mr. Solicitor Harcourt thus interposes:—" But Mr. Montague says nothing of *the prerogative the people have that the representatives are the judges of the maladministration of their governors; that they can call them to account, and can appoint such to wear the crown who are fittest for government,*'—he passes by all this scandalous matter."—*Montague.* "I did so, Mr. Solicitor, and I did it on purpose, because I look upon it as a matter not proper for you and me to talk about as advocates in this place. I think the rights of the prince and the power of the people too high topics for me to meddle with."—*Northey, A. G.* "I am surprised to hear it justified here by a counsel that the people have power to call their governors to account. I will always prosecute any man that shall assert such doctrines."[1]—*Holt, C. J.* (to the jury). "This is a very strange doctrine, to say it is not a libel—reflecting on the government—endeavoring to possess the people that the government is maladministered by corrupt persons. To say that corrupt persons are appointed to administer affairs is certainly a reflection on the government. If writers should not be called to account for possessing the people with an ill opinion of the government, no government can subsist. Now you are to consider whether those words I have read to you do not tend to beget an ill opinion of the administration of the government? To tell us that 'those who are employed know nothing of

---

[1] 4 St. Tr. 1122.

the matter, and those who do know are not employed,—that men are not adapted to offices, but offices to men out of a particular regard to their interest and not to their fitness for the places,'—this is the purport of these papers."[1] The defendant was found guilty, but, on account of some informality, the verdict was set aside, and the prosecution caused such public indignation that by Harcourt's advice it was dropped.[2]

When the great case of privilege arose out of the Aylesbury election, the House of Commons was chiefly guided by the advice of Harcourt, and to enable the Tory majority, which then bore tyrannical sway, to dispose of seats as they thought fit, he very improperly proposed the resolutions "that no action could be brought against a returning officer by an elector," and "that the judgment of the House of Lords determining that such an action was maintainable, amounted to a breach of the privileges of the Commons,"—by which extravagant resolutions those privileges received the deepest wound ever inflicted upon them. Yet I can not but admire the spirit with which he conducted the whole affair—not hesitating to come into direct collision with the Judges and the House of Lords, whatever might be the consequence. Some of his sentiments respecting actions brought in violation of the just privileges of either House I entirely approve of, and I wish that they had been, and that they may be, acted upon:—"*Principiis obsta* ; never let your disease grow to such a head as to put you on the necessity of complaining of a judgment of the Lords, but rather check it in its infancy, If an action should be brought against the Speaker or the Sergeant-at-arms for obeying your commands, ought we to sit still here to see what they will do in the Courts below, and afterwards wait for the event in the House of Lords by writ of error? The law of Parliament is above the Judges of the Common Law; it is *alieni fori*. If you will induce any person to go into Westminster Hall and to bring an action to question your rights, a jury may find a verdict that you have no such rights and judgment shall be given accordingly. Does not this submit your proceedings to the

[1] 14 St. Tr. 1128.
[2] But Lynch Law was more effectual against Tutchin. For another libel, he was cruelly beaten by ruffians, and lost his life. 14 St. Tr. 1200.

examination and censure of inferior Courts, and may it not soon confine you to such privileges as the other House of Parliament, as the Supreme Court of Error, may be pleased to accord to you?"¹ But in this controversy I am bound to say that I think Somers, Cowper, and the Whig lawyers, upon the whole, deserved more praise than those who for party purposes brought such odium upon parliamentary privilege.

Harcourt acquired much credit by the manner in which, to cut off long debates, he framed the Bill for the Union between England and Scotland,—whereby all the articles which the Commissioners had agreed upon were recited in the preamble, and enacted by a single clause. "This put those upon great difficulties who had resolved to object to several articles, and to insist on demanding some alterations in them, for they could not come at any debate about them; they could not object to the recital, it being merely matter of fact, and they had not strength enough to oppose the general enacting clause, nor was it easy to come at particulars and to offer provisos relating to them. It passed through the House of Commons before those who intended to oppose it had recovered themselves out of the surprise under which the form it was drawn in had put them."² He did not speak upon the subject himself, and his name does not occur in the parliamentary debates, after the discussions which arose out of the case of *Ashby* v. *White*, till he was once more an opposition leader.³ When, upon the death of Prince George, Lord Somers was made President of the Council, and the Cabinet became entirely Whig, Harcourt justly thought it inconsistent with his dignity to serve them, and he resigned the office of Attorney General,⁴ being

---

¹ 6 Parl. Hist. 264–267.   ² 4 Burnet, 176.
³ However, there seems reason to think that in this interval he delivered speeches which are lost, sometimes against the measures of the Goverment. Swift, in his "Memoirs relating to the Change in Queen Anne's Ministry," when speaking of the Whigs who joined the Government in 1705, says: "Upon the admission of these men into employment, the Court soon ran into extremity of Low Church measures; and although in the House of Commons Mr. Harley, *Sir Simon Harcourt*, Mr. St. John, and some others, made great and bold stands in defense of the constitution, yet they were always borne down by a majority."
⁴ "As Harley laid down, both Harcourt, then Attorney General, Mansel, the Comptroller of the Household, and St. John, the Secretary at War, went and laid down with him"—*4 Burnet, 220.*

succeeded by a good Whig, Sir James Montague, brother of Lord Halifax.¹

While Solicitor and Attorney General, he had tried to prop up the existing Administration in a manner that seems strange to a modern law officer of the Crown. He acted as chairman of the Quarter Sessions for the county of Bucks, and quarterly, in charging the grand jury, delivered a panegyric upon Tory rule. His MS. notes of several of these addresses are preserved in the British Museum, and a few sentences from one of them may be amusing:—" How much happier are we, gentlemen, than our neighbors, who groan under insupportable miseries even to the last degree of slavery, while we live in ease and hospitality, and eat the fruit of our own vine! As, gentlemen, we are blessed with such good laws, so we are under the most auspicious reign of the best of Queens (whom God long preserve)—a Queen who will impartially put them in execution—a Queen who is a zealous professor of the religion of the Church of England as established by law, and will always be a promoter of its honor and interest, and a Queen who wishes from the very bottom of her breast there were no separatists from it in her dominions."

He was now to be the victim of such a faction as in a former parliament he had led on to acts of injustice and violence. At the general election which followed the late changes, the Whigs gained a decided majority. Sir Simon Harcourt, however, was again returned for Abingdon, the borough which he had long represented, and in which his interest was still unshaken. But Mr. John Hucks, the beaten Whig candidate, trusting to the blind support of his friends, presented a petition claiming the seat. The case, according to the usage which prevailed till the passing of the Grenville Act, was heard at the bar of the House, the debate lasting till past two in the morning, as there was an intense desire on the one side to oust the sitting Member, and on the other, to save him. Before the division, he himself thus spoke :—

" Whatever the determination of this House may be, I know, and all impartial men will believe, that I am entitled to sit as representative for Abingdon in this parliament.

---

¹ This change took place 21st October, 1708. Harcourt's resignation was enrolled in Chancery, being the only instance of that nature in our records.

The just construction of the charter, as it has been understood and acted upon for 150 years, deprives my competitor of the shadow of a right, and, even upon his construction of it, I have still a majority of votes. He himself, at the close of the poll, declared that he had not offered himself with any hope of success, and it was not till he had seen that his party had fared better in other places, that he thought of petitioning. But what a mean and contemptible notion must he entertain of this House! He must suppose that you are to be awed by the word of command which he thinks may be given to expel me, and to substitute himself in my place against the will of the electors, and after his own confession that he was fairly defeated. If it should indeed be declared that I am not duly elected, I shall leave this House feeling deep compassion for the unfortunate friends who stay behind me, for they must be destined to make a constant but ineffectual struggle against fraud and folly. Whoever suggested this petition, believing there is such a parliament, must be the most abandoned wretch in the world, who has long quitted all notions of right and wrong, all sense of truth and justice, all regard for honor and conscience. But I trust it will be found he makes a most calumnious estimate of a British House of Commons. The Petition charges me personally with many indirect practices; but not an attempt has been made to prove any part of these charges, and all who know me know that they must be false. As to the indirect practices of my agents—I had no agents. Till the morning of the election, I knew of no opposition, and I had made no preparation for a contest. I had every reason to believe that my former services in six parliaments had met with the approbation of the great bulk of my constituents, and that they were willing again to confide to me the high trust of representing them.[1] The electors of Abingdon were not influenced by the solicitations, menaces, and promises used against me, and I trust their example will be imitated by the Members of this House, who are expected to be patterns of purity, independence, and honor." He then bowed and withdrew, and the division took place—when the resolution was carried by a considerable majority, that

[1] He was Recorder of Abingdon, and seems to have been a great favorite there.

"John Hucks, Esq., was duly elected, and ought to have been returned a burgess to serve in the present parliament for the borough of Abingdon; and that the return for the said borough be amended by substituting the name of the said John Hucks, Esq., for that of Sir Simon Harcourt, Knight."[1]

This ceremony was accordingly performed next day by the Clerk of the Crown, but Harcourt had soon ample revenge on the Whigs by becoming leading counsel for Dr. Sacheverell, and by inflaming the nation against them as the enemies of the Church. If he had continued a member of the House of Commons, his mouth would have been closed as soon as the impeachment was voted.

When this most preposterous and ill-fated prosecution came to a hearing in Westminster Hall, the chief part assigned to Harcourt was to answer the first article, charging the defendant with having, in his sermon at St. Paul's, traduced the Revolution, and denied the lawfulness of resistance. The ground of defense taken, very ably, and, I think, very satisfactorily, was, that both the Church of England and the municipal law of the country inculcate obedience to the civil magistrate, and that cases of justifiable resistance are exceptions to the rule, which are implied, and can not possibly be anticipated or defined. Harcourt introduced a little false and sophistical reasoning, by saying that "there was no resistance at the Revolution, as the supreme power supposed to be resisted is in this country vested in the legislature, and that the Revolution took effect by the Lords and Commons concurring and assisting in it." But he goes on to show that his client had only used the language of great divines and great lawyers, and to ask, "whether, when the general rule of obedience is taught, the particular exceptions out of that rule which may arise are always to be expressed? or whether, when the general rule is laid down, the particular exceptions out of that rule which might arise are not more properly to be understood or implied?" He decently dissembles so far as to speak respectfully of the Revolution, although in his heart he abhorred it: "Such an exception, no doubt, the Revolution was, when our late unhappy Sovereign, then upon the throne, misled by evil counselors, we are told, endeavored to subvert and

[1] 6 Parl. Hist. 778.

extirpate the Protestant religion, and the laws and liberties of the kingdom." He then argues very forcibly in support of his position: " Every minister of the Gospel is sufficiently instructed, from law and religion, to press the general duty of obedience, but such extraordinary cases wherein resistance is lawful, wherein it becomes an indispensable duty, are nowhere laid down. The same Apostle who enjoins obedience to the higher powers, and non-resistance, commands also servants to obey their masters, and children their parents, in all things; notwithstanding which general precepts, many cases may happen wherein it may be not only unfit, but sinful, for servants to obey their masters, or children their parents. And yet the Apostle contents himself with pressing the duty of subjection in general, leaving such cases, when they happen, to justify themselves. The cases of resistance to the supreme power of the state are nowhere fit to be considered but in Parliament, and the Parliament itself hath never yet thought fit otherwise to consider them than, retrospectively, to sanction what had of necessity been done contrary to the general rule; but never went so far as to enumerate the cases in which, for the future, it might be lawful for the subject to resist. The danger of prospectively introducing an exception is well illustrated by the late Mr. Pym, in his speech on the impeachment of Dr. Mainwaring : ' The inhabitants of the duchy of Normandy, being much oppressed by the King's officers, petitioned him for redress, and he granted them a charter, whereby they were, for the future, to be free from all subsidies and talliages imposed by him and his successors, *unless when great necessity required*,—which small exception devoured all their immunities.' In the same manner, all allegiance would be devoured by the express exception of lawful resistance. Surely none can show themselves truer friends to the Revolution than those who prove that it may stand without impeaching the doctrines of our Church, or any fundamental law of the kingdom. Suppose that on the day in question, when the rubic requires the reading of one of the homilies on the duty of obedience, or a sermon to the like effect, the Doctor had chosen to praise the Revolution, and to inculcate the duty of resistance, would he not have been told by his ecclesiastical superiors that he ought to have imitated the example of the Apostles and the fathers of the Church? and if he had been indicted for his sermon, might not the judges have said to the jury, 'It is easy to discern what spirit he is of, what party he belongs to, and what he aims at; he has not been preaching in defense of the late Revolution to show the justice of it; he was covering the treason of his heart, and, under pretense of praising one revolution, a friend of the Pretender, was laboring to bring about another?'"[1]

Just as Harcourt concluded this address, it was publicly announced that he had been returned to parliament for the borough of Cardigan. The Whigs asserted that he was privately in possession of the intelligence while he was inveighing against the impeachment, but they did not venture to bring forward any charge against him for breach of privilege. When he took his seat in the House of Commons, he was loudly cheered by the Tories, and there were clear indications of their speedy triumph.

A wit in 1710 might have anticipated Sheridan's observation on the Whigs in 1806: "I have heard of men knocking their heads against a brick wall, but now we see men building up a brick wall to knock their heads against."[2] One of the earliest official changes in consequence of the cry of the Church being in danger, was the removal of Sir James Montague, who had opened the case against Sacheverell, from the office of Attorney General, and the appointment of the leading counsel for Sacheverell to succeed him.[3] For prudential reasons he was desirous to have continued some time longer a law officer of the Crown, in which situation he might accumulate more money for his family, and in case of any political reverse he had his profession to fall back upon.[4] This

[1] 15 St. Tr. 196-213.
[2] Harcourt himself ascribed the change in the government entirely to this prosecution. Swift, in his "Journal to Stella," 24th April, 1711, speaking of Sacheverell, says—"He hates the new ministry mortally, and they hate him, and pretend to despise him too. They will not allow him to have been the occasion of the late change,—at least some of them will not,—*but my Lord Keeper owned it to me the other day.*"
[3] Swift's "Journal to Stella" at this time is curious as to the reports about Harcourt,—*Sept. 14:* "We hear the Chancellor is to be suddenly out, and Sir Simon Harcourt to succeed him." *15th:* "We hear Sir Simon Harcourt is made Lord Keeper; so that now we expect every moment that the parliament will be dissolved." *17th:* "Sir Simon Harcourt is made Attorney General, and not Lord Keeper."
[4] The custody of the Great Seal as Lord Keeper was privately offered to

was the reason for the pressing solicitations that Lord Cowper would retain the Great Seal. But as this high minded man was inexorable, and actually forced it into the hands of Queen Anne, Harcourt had no choice; for the Tories had no other great lawyer in whom they could confide, and he himself would not have liked to have seen put over his head a member of his own party whom it might have been difficult to remove. He therefore agreed with Harley and St. John to hold the Great Seal under them; but, to give time for the necessary preparations for the change, it was for a short time put into commission, the Commissioners being Lord Chief Justice Trevor, Mr. Justice Tracy, and Mr. Baron Scrope. It was now vacation time, and the Lords Commissioners never sat in court, for in three weeks the Great Seal was demanded from them, and it was delivered to Sir Simon Harcourt.

CHAPTER CXIX

CONTINUATION OF THE LIFE OF LORD HARCOURT TILL THE DEATH OF QUEEN ANNE.

THE ceremony of transferring the Great Seal took place at Hampton Court.[1] We have no account of the speeches made on the occasion, but we need not doubt the Queen expressed her high satisfaction at having, for the Keeper of her conscience, a champion who had been so instrumental in procuring for the Church its present triumph, and that he dexterously contrived to reconcile his devoted attachment to her throne with his

Sir Simon Harcourt; who, besides his eminent adherence to the Church party, on many other occasions had exerted his parts, in a very distinguishing manner, in the defense of Dr. Sacheverell. But he declined that trust for the present, and in the mean time contented himself with the place of Attorney General, which he formerly discharged with great reputation. He appeared the first time in that quality at the Council held on the 21st of September, at which time the Earl of Rochester, the Duke of Buckingham, and Mr. St. John were sworn of that most honorable assembly."—*Boyer's Polit. State*, vol. i. p. 7.

[1] Lond. Gaz.—" Hampton Court, Oct. 19, 1710. Her Majesty was pleased to deliver the Great Seal to Sir Simon Harcourt, Knt., who was thereupon sworn one of her Majesty's most Honorable Privy Council, and Lord Keeper of the Great Seal of Great Britain; and he accordingly took his place at the board."

belief in the indefeasible rights of royalty. He was at the same time sworn a member of the Privy Council. On the first day of the ensuing Term, he was duly installed in the Court of Chancery, after a procession to Westminster Hall, in which the Tory Peers mustered in great strength, as well as the heads of the law. These venerable sages, with few exceptions, being strongly inclined to Tory principles, could not conceal their exultation when they saw at the head of the profession one of whom they were justly proud for his learning, for his abilities, and for his honorable career.[1]

He was now almost overpowered by letters and addresses of congratulation in prose and in verse, and his illustrious client, Dr. Sacheverell, presented to him a magnificent piece of plate, in the form of an altar, for washing after dinner, bearing the following inscription:

" VIRO HONORATISSIMO,
UNIVERSI JURIS ORACULO,
ECCLESIÆ ET REGNI PRÆSIDIO ET ORNAMENTO,
SIMONI HARCOURT, EQUITI AURATO,
MAGNÆ BRITANNIÆ SIGILLI MAGNI CUSTODI,
ET SERENISSIMÆ REGINÆ E SECRETIORIBUS CONSILIIS,
OB CAUSAM MEAM CORAM SUPREMO SENATU,
IN AULA WESTMONASTERIENSI
NERVOSA CUM FACUNDIA ET SUBACTA LEGUM SCIENTIA
BENIGNE ET CONSTANTER DEFENSAM ;
OB PRISCAM ECCLESIÆ DOCTRINAM,
INVIOLANDAM LEGUM VIM,
PIAM SUBDITORUM FIDEM,
ET SACROSANCTA MAJESTATIS JURA
CONTRA NEFARIOS PERDUELLIUM IMPETUS
FELICITER VINDICATA ;
VOTIVUM HOC MUNUSCULUM
PERPETUÆ GRATITUDINIS PIGNUS,
D. D. D.
DEVINCTISSIMUS CLIENS
HENRICUS SACHEVEREL, S. T. P.
ANNO SALUTIS MDCCX."[2]

" 19th October, 1710.—The Lords Commissioners for the custody of the the Grt. Seal of Grt. Britain having delivered the Great Seal to the Queen on Wednesday, the 18th of October, 1708, her Ma^{ty} was pleased to deliver the same to Sir Simon Harcourt, Knt., her Att. Gen. on the day following at Hampton Court, with the title of Ld. Keeper of the Grt. Seal of G. B., on who Monday the 23rd day of the same October, being the 1st time of his sitting in Westm. Hall, was accompanied to the Chancery Court by the Earl of Rochester, Ld. President of the Councill, the Duke of Ormonde, Ld. Lieutenant of Ireland, the Earls of Scarsdale, Anglesey, and Orrery, the Lord Hyde, and several other persons, and in their presence did then and there take the oaths of allegiance and supremacy, and the oath of Ld. Keeper

[2] Sloane's MS. Brit. Mus. 4292.

Lord Harcourt's administration of justice in the Court of Chancery seems to have given contentment to the public, although lawyers sometimes sneered at him, and he did not leave behind him the reputation of a profound Equity Judge. Swift, become the trumpeter of the new ministers,—in his celebrated parallel between them and their predecessors, ventures to set him above Lord Somers and Lord Cowper: " Was any man more eminent in his profession than the present Lord Keeper, or more distinguished by his eloquence and great abilities in the House of Commons? and will not his enemies allow him to be fully equal to the great station he now adorns?" Then ironically acquitting him of the charges of immorality, which he wishes to fasten on the Whig Chancellors, he says, "after all, to speak my private opinion, I can not think these such mighty objections to his character as some would pretend."[1] The Whig writers, to their credit, not having retaliated by the invention of calumny, Harcourt is allowed to have been untainted by corruption or any other vice. He was not only free from the imputation of taking money from suitors, which after Lord Bacon's impeachment was almost unknown, but he was not liable to be accused of trafficking in the sale of offices in his gift, which could be said of very few Chancellors till after the impeachment of Lord Macclesfield. Although he issued no general orders to improve the practice of the Court, and proposed no bills for the amendment of the law, the cases which came before him, generally speaking, were satisfactorily disposed of. He had been, when at the bar, the most eminent counsel in the Court of Chancery,[2] and his experience, combined with his reading and his admirable manner, enabled him to occupy his new seat with ease and dignity.

of the Grt. Seal of Gt. Britain the Ma^r of the Rolls holding the book, and the Clerk of the Crown reading the oaths; after which the Lords departed, and left the Lord Keeper in the said Court."—*Cr. Off. Min. Roll, 1710-1714.*

[1] Examiner, No. 27.

[2] The rarity of Equity reports prevents me from proving this assertion by a reference to "the books;" but I have for it what may be called "evidence of reputation." J. Philips's Poem on Cyder, addressed in 1706 to the younger Harcourt, then abroad, contains this invocation:—

"Return, and let thy father's worth excite
Thirst of pre-eminence; see how the cause
Of widows and orphans he asserts
With winning rhetoric——."

The chief herald of his judicial fame is PEERE WILLIAMS, from whose Reports a few interesting cases decided by him may be selected. In England, our modified system of "substitutions," or "entails," rests mainly on the appointment of "trustees to preserve contingent remainders," whereby a father may have only an interest for life in land, although there be no one *in esse* in whom any ulterior beneficial interest is vested,—and the land can not be alienated till a son has been born, and has reached the age of twenty-one. An attempt was made in the beginning of the reign of Queen Anne to break through this by inducing the trustees to join with the father in conveying before the birth of a son: but the attempt was crushed by Lord Keeper Harcourt, who held that such a conveyance, though it would carry the legal estate, was a breach of trust, saying, "It is so very plain and reasonable, that if there be no precedent I will make one."[1] He first established the important doctrine, that if money is directed, either by deed or will, to be laid out in land, the money shall be taken to be land, even as to collateral heirs.[2] He held, that where by a family settlement a provision is made for younger children, the eldest child of the marriage, being a daughter, shall be deemed a younger child in equity, if there be a son, or the estate by the settlement goes to a remainder man.[3] On an application for a writ of "ne exeat regno," the question arose whether, since the Union, Scotland was for this purpose to be considered in or out of the kingdom. *Lord C. Harcourt.*—"Scotland, being out of the jurisdiction of this Court and consequently out of the reach of the process thereof, the defendant's going into Scotland is equally mischievous to the suitor here as if he went actually beyond the seas."[4] The writ was awarded—with an intimation that it should be worded "not to go out of the realm, *or to Scotland*."[5] On points of practice he

[1] *Pye* v. *Gore*, 1 Peere Williams, 128, afterwards affirmed by the House of Lords, 1 Br. P. C. 359; and see *Mansel* v. *Mansel* 2 P. W. 678.
[2] *Lingen* v. *Sowray*, 1 P. W. 172.   [3] *Beale* v. *Beale*, 1 P. W. 244.
[4] Done's Case, 1 P. W. 263.
[5] Harcourt seems to have given mortal offense to Vernon, the reporter, who practiced as a counsel regularly before him, but spitefully suppresses his best decisions, amd gives doubtful ones. See 2 Vernon, 664–688. I suspect that the reporter may have been a Whig, and copied the Tory blacksmith, who in shoeing the horse of a Whig always lamed him. When I was a nisi prius reporter I had a drawer marked "BAD LAW," into which I threw all the cases

very openly admitted the superior knowledge of Sir John Trevor, the Master of the Rolls—as in the instance where he altered his ruling upon the opinion of that Judge, respecting the regularity of process issued against a wife during her husband's absence abroad.[1]

I am afraid that he was seduced by the excitement of politics, and by the *agrémens* of the " Brothers," the " October," and other clubs of which he was a member, from paying devoted attention to the business of his Court, and that I can hold him up for imitation as a Judge only for impartiality and integrity.

We must now view him in the Senate, where he appears to greater advantage. At the general election, shortly before his promotion he had been returned to the House of Commons for his old borough of Abingdon, and he would no longer have been in danger of being ousted by a Whig majority; but he received the Great Seal before parliament met, and although it seems to have been formerly thought that a Lord Keeper might sit in the House of Commons, although a Lord Chancellor could not, the Great Seal, with whatever title, was clearly a disqualification to act as a representative of the people, after the statute giving the same rights and privileges to the holder of the Great Seal under either appellation.[2] It seems most unaccountable that a whole year was allowed to elapse before he was raised to the peerage, as the Ministry was very weak in the Upper House, both in numbers and debating power,—and, without a single law Lord to support it, was daily assailed by the ex-Chancellors Somers and Cowper. There never hitherto had been an instance of a gentleman being taken from the bar, to hold the Great Seal, being immediately made a Peer, but Harley and St. John were not very scrupulous about precedent in their peerage promotions—insomuch that, having afterwards made Harcourt a Baron by himself—when they at last came to their famous batch of a dozen, they included in it Trevor, the Tory Chief Justice of the Common Pleas, that the law Lords might be equally balanced.

which seemed to me improperly ruled. I was flattered to hear Sir James Mansfield, C.J., say, " Whoever reads Campbell's reports must be astonished to find how uniformly Lord Ellenborough's decisions were right." My rejected cases, which I had kept as a curiosity—not maliciously—were all burnt in the great fire in the Temple when I was Attorney General.

[1] Ante, Vol. IV. p. 455.   5 Eliz. c. 18.

Whatever might be the reason for the delay, during the whole of the session which began in Nov., 1710, Harcourt had only to sit as Speaker.[1] On one interesting occasion, however, he was suddenly called upon for an exercise of his oratorical powers. After long and angry discussions respecting the conduct of the war in Spain, a vote of thanks to the Earl of Peterborough was carried; and as he was present, and was to set off next morning on foreign service, the Lord Keeper was ordered to return him the thanks of the House forthwith.

Lord Keeper Harcourt.—" My Lord Peterborough, I am commanded by my Lords to return their thanks to your Lordship for your many eminent and faithful services to your Queen and country during your command in Spain. My Lord, the thanks of this illustrious assembly is an honor which has been rarely paid to any subject; but never after a stricter inquiry into the nature of any service, upon a more mature deliberation, or with greater justice, than at this time to your Lordship. Such is your Lordship's known generosity and truly noble temper, that I assure myself the present I am now offering to your Lordship is the more acceptable, as it comes pure and unmixed, and is unattended with any other reward which your Lordship might justly think would be an alloy to it.[2] My Lord, had more days been allowed me than I have had minutes, to call to mind the wonderful and amazing success which perpetually attended your Lordship in Spain (the effect of your Lordship's personal bravery and conduct), I would not attempt to enumerate your particular services, since I should offend your Lordship by the mention of such as I could recollect, and give a just occasion of offense to this House by my involuntary omission

[1] During this interval he is said to have got into a scrape at Court by presenting there a batch of Scotch representative peers to her Majesty. The rule being, that a peer could only be presented by a peer, the Earl of Rochester, the Queen's uncle, the President of the Council, pointed out the enormity of which he had been guilty; but ex-Chancellor Lord Cowper good-naturedly came to his rescue, and insisted that this being a question of precedence, and the Lord Keeper, though a commoner, having precedence of all peers, there had been no breach of etiquette. The most absurd rule of this sort still subsisting is,.that upon a division in the House of Lords the tellers on opposite sides must be of equal rank. A proposal that a baron should tell against a duke, or even against a viscount would be received with horror —although all there are supposed to be *pares.*

[2] This is a sarcasm upon the alleged covetousness of the great Whig general, who was loaded with riches as well as honors.

of the far greater part of them. Had your Lordship's wise counsels, particularly your advice at Valencia, been pursued in the following campaign, the fatal battle of Almanza, and our greatest misfortunes which have since happened in Spain, had been prevented, and the design upon Toulon might have happily succeeded. I shall detain your Lordship no longer than, in obedience to the order I have received, to return your Lordship, as I do, the thanks of the House for your eminent and remarkable services to your Queen and country during your command in Spain."

Although the Lord Keeper had ventured to touch on party politics, and to show his party propensities, the address was approved of, and ordered to be entered in the Journals.

A few months afterwards, Harley having acquired immense popularity from the attempt of the Marquis de Guiscard to stab him, before the Privy Council, and having been created Earl of Oxford and Earl Mortimer, and having received the staff of Lord High Treasurer,—when he was to be sworn into his new office, the Lord Keeper thus addressed him :—

"My Lord Oxford: The Queen, who does everything with the greatest wisdom, has given a proof of it in the honors she has lately conferred upon you, which are exactly suited to your deserts and qualifications. My Lord, the title which you now bear could not have been so justly placed on any other of her Majesty's subjects. Some of that ancient blood which fills your veins is derived from the Veres: and you have showed yourself as ready to sacrifice it for the safety of your Prince and the good of your country, and as fearless of danger on the most trying occasions, as ever any of that brave and loyal house were. Nor is that title less suited to you as it carries in it a relation to one of the chief seats of learning; for even your enemies, my Lord (if any such there still are), must own that the love of letters, and the encouragement of those who excel in them, is one distinguishing part of your character. My Lord, the high station of Lord Treasurer of Great Britain, to which her Majesty has called you, is the just reward of your eminent services. You have been the great instrument of restoring public credit, and relieving this nation from the heavy pressure and ignominy of an immense debt, under which it languished; and you are now intrusted with the power of securing us from a relapse into the same ill state out of which you have rescued us. This great office, *my Lord*, is every way worthy of you, particularly on the account of those many difficulties, with which the faithful discharge of it must be unavoidably attended, and which require a genius like yours to master them. The only difficulty, which even you, *my Lord*, may find almost insuperable, is how to deserve better of the Crown and kingdom, after this advancement, than you did before it."

This custom of ministers of state extravagantly praising each other, has surely been well laid aside; and no one would think the better of Sir Robert Peel or his policy for a panegyric pronounced upon them by Lord Chancellor Lyndhurst.[1]

Lord Keeper Harcourt's next subject of eulogy was, according to the custom of the age,—himself. He was soon after raised to the peerage by the title of Baron Harcourt, of Stanton-Harcourt, in the county of Oxford; and the preamble of his patent celebrated the splendor of his Norman ancestors, commemorated the Harcourts who had particularly distinguished themselves under Edward IV. and Charles I., averred that there never had been one of that race who had not been eminent for his love to his country and loyalty to his prince, and thus spoke of Sir Simon: " Descended from such noble ancestors, he suffered indeed in his paternal inheritance, which was diminished by the fury of the civil wars, but their glory acquired by military virtue descended upon him unimpaired: and this he, having assumed the gown, increased by the force of his genius and his eloquence; so various are his powers, that many doubt whether he most excels in pleading causes at the bar, or in debating the affairs of the nation in the senate, but all agree that he is the most eloquent of lawyers, and the most learned of orators." After praising his private virtues in the same strain, the Queen is made to say,—" Him whom, endowed with such high qualities, all clients have wished to defend their causes,—not without reason we preferred to be our Attorney General; and finding other employments unsuitable to his extraordinary capacity, we have advanced to

[1] Written in 1845.

the highest pitch of forensic dignity, and made him our supreme Judge of Equity. Still his conduct is more and more meritorious in proportion to his elevation." Having mentioned his dispatch and his anxiety to furnish cheap as well as speedy justice to the suitors, she proceeds: "Such services being grateful to us, honorable to himself, and beneficial to the state, we think deserving of higher rewards: therefore, that our most able Judge may not be without a voice in our supreme Court, that he who can think and speak so well should not be silent in an assembly of the eloquent, we grant him a place among the Peers of our realm, that he may add splendor to that order from which he and his posterity will derive so much; and we desire that he take his title from that place which, for six hundred years, has borne the name and been the patrimony of the family of Harcourt."

There can be no doubt that Lord Harcourt now took a leading part in the debates in the House of Lords. Supported by Lord Trevor (made a Peer as Chief Justice of the Common Pleas, while Holt, Chief Justice of the King's Bench, being a Whig, had died a Commoner), he manfully stood up to Lord Somers and Lord Cowper, and although he was often in danger of being beaten in the division, he did not quietly allow his party to be vilified —not content to do the routine business of his office, and to receive its emoluments. Yet there is not the slightest scrap remaining of any of his speeches, nor is his name even mentioned in the "Parliamentary History" during the rest of this reign. The two chief Ministers of the Crown, following the practice which prevailed till the premiership of Sir Robert Walpole, had come from the House of Commons to the House of Lords; but there, in the last years of Anne, was the chief battle-field of the opposite factions, and on the Tory side, Harcourt was considered the third man in debate as well as in counsel.[1] The circumstance of his not being noticed by any reporter is no argument against his celebrity in his own time, for Bolingbroke, allowed to be easily the first orator

[1] About this time in England the House of Lords seems to have had the same superiority in knowledge, talent, and moderation over the House of Commons, which in America the Senate now has over the House of Representatives. Our House of Commons gained its ascendency in the reign of George II. under Walpole, who was the first Prime Minister who chose to remain there.

in either House during the present reign, in this respect shared his fate.

When the treaty of Utrecht had been agreed upon between the English and French negotiators, and was about to be formally signed—to add to Harcourt's dignity and weight in defending it, he had the title of Lord Chancellor conferred upon him, instead of that of Lord Keeper. A long congratulatory poem[1] was on this occasion addressed to him, from which I shall make a few extracts, to show how it was then thought that Chancellors were to be pleased :

> "Th' enraptur'd Muse to a glad nation sings
> First the great race from which our Harcourt springs,
> Noble his blood, and ancient his descent,
> E'er since to Norman yoke Britannia bent."

Harley and he are then represented as attacking the poor Whigs in the House of Lords, and utterly destroying them :—

> "From such united hearts, and hands, and tongues,
> Well might we hope redress of all our wrongs,
> These, these are they who stemm'd th' impetuous tide
> Of factious boldness and rebellious pride.
> Thus when two Lions from the forest roar,
> And shake the neighboring hills and distant shore
> Tigers and Wolves, and all the beasts of prey,
> Draw in their dastard tails and sneak away.
> Thus when a brace of Eagles, towering high,
> Purge of rapacious fowls the darken'd sky,
> The stork, the vulture, and the chattering daw,
> Kites, buzzards, bitterns, hawks, and rooks withdraw."

---

[1] It is a folio of thirty-five pages. The title, with the four mottoes, may be amusing :—

A
POEM
On occasion of the Promotion of the Right Honorable
THE LORD KEEPER HARCOURT,
TO BE
LORD HIGH CHANCELLOR OF GREAT BRITAIN,
The 7th of April, 1713.

"Tum pietate gravem ac meritis si forte virum quem
Conspexere, silent, arrectisque auribus astant :
Ille regit dictis animos, et pectora mulcet."—VIRG.

————"Et quid facundia posset
Tum patuit."—Ov.

"Ille Deæ donis, et tanto lætus honore."—VIRG.

"Quid facit interea qui nil nisi prælia noscit."—Ov.

By Mr. H. Crispe.

Next comes a testimony to our Chancellor's judicial excellence :—

> "Thou, Harcourt, o'er our laws art bid preside,
> Most learn'd expounder, most unerring guide,
> To thee the poor, to thee the friendless fly,
> To thee the widow and the orphan cry.
> Each suit a just and speedy judgment ends,
> And cheap success the honest cause attends."

His Peerage is thus celebrated :—

> "Thy title great without exchange of name,
> Harcourt could only answer Harcourt's fame;
> The noblest style, and sweetest could be found,
> All hearts retain it, and all tongues resound."

Finally the poet anticipates immortality for his patron and himself ;—

> "Some loftier Muse shall yet in deathless lays
> Sing first our Anna's, next our Harcourt's praise,
> Your matchless virtues will sure credit bring
> To all the wonders poets e'er can sing,
> Their names with yours, as prophet, I divine
> In British annals shall for ever shine;
> Perhaps, not quite forgot this humble muse of mine."

The Chancellor might have reasonably expected long to enjoy his new dignity. The peace being approved of by both Houses, the Government seemed firmly established; Tory measures were sure to pass the Commons by acclamation, and in the Upper House the Whigs found themselves in a lessening minority. The Queen was more than ever adverse to them on account of the ingratitude and rudeness of the Duchess of Marlborough, and as her Majesty was still in middle life, their prospects appeared most dreary. But from this time Harcourt found only discord and distraction in the Cabinet, and he was obliged to make his election between the two great chiefs of the Tory party, who, from their struggle for superiority, and the different views which they took respecting the succession to the Crown, soon became mortal enemies. He had hitherto been on equally good terms with both, and, with the assistance of Swift,[1] had con-

---

[1] Swift first made Harcourt's acquaintance on coming to England, as the change of government was taking place in the autumn of 1710 :—*October 10.* "I dined with Mr. Harley to-day, who presented me to the Attorney General, Sir Simon Harcourt, with much compliment on all sides."—*Journal to Stella.*

A few more extracts from Swift, with reference to the Lord Keeper, may prove interesting :—

"It was Mr. Harley's custom, every Saturday that four or five of his most

trived, notwithstanding occasional differences, to keep them on decently good terms. Being one of the club of sixteen, composed of Cabinet Ministers and leading supporters of the Government, who called each other "Brother," and dined weekly at each other's houses, he selected the *mollia tempora fandi;* and when champagne intimate friends among those he had taken in upon the great change made at Court, should dine at his house, and after about two months' acquaintance I had the honor always to be one of the number. The company at first consisted only of the Lord Keeper Harcourt, the Earl Rivers, the Earl of Peterborough, Mr. Secretary St. John, and myself; and here, after dinner, they used to discourse and settle matters of great importance."—*Memoirs relating to the Change in Queen Anne's Ministry.*

"I dined with Mr. Harley to-day. Every Saturday, Lord Keeper, Secretary St. John, and I, dine with him, and sometimes Lord Rivers, and they let in none else. I stayed with Mr. Harley till nine, when we had much discourse together after the rest were gone; and I gave him very truly my opinion when he desired it."—*Journal to Stella.* 3rd March, 1711.

"After dinner, we had coarse Doiley napkins, fringed at each end, upon the table to drink with. My Lord Keeper spread one of them between him and Mr. Prior; I told him I was glad to see there was such a fringeship (friendship) between Mr. Prior and his Lordship."—*Ibid.* p. 287.

"I went in the evening to see Mr. Harley; and, upon my word, I was in perfect joy. Mr. Secretary was just coming out of the door, but I made him come back; and there was the old Saturday club, Lord Keeper, Lord Rivers, Mr. Secretary, Mr. Harley, and I."—*Ibid.* p. 249.

"I am sometimes talked into frights, and told that all is ruined; but am immediately cured when I see any of the ministry. My comfort is, they are persons of great abilities, and they are engaged in a good cause. And what is one very good circumstance, as I told three of them (Harley, St. John, and Harcourt) the other day, they seem heartily to love one another in spite of the scandal of inconstancy which Court friendships lie under."—*Swift's Letter to Lord Peterborough.* Feb. 1711.

July 5, 1711. "I dined to-day at our society, and we are adjourned for a month, because most of us go into the country. We dined at Lord Keeper's with young Harcourt, and Lord Keeper was forced to sneak off and dine with Lord Treasurer, who had invited the Secretary and me to dine with him; but we scorned to leave our company, as George Granville did, whom we have threatened to expel. However, in the evening, I went to Lord Treasurer, and, among other company, found a couple of Judges with him. One of them, Judge Powell, an old fellow with grey hairs, was the merriest old gentleman I ever saw; spoke pleasant things, and laughed and chuckled till he cried again."

"I was to have dined to-day with Lord Keeper, but would not, because that brute, Sir John Walter, was to be one of the company. So I dined with Lord Treasurer, where there was none but Lord Bolingbroke."—*Journ. to Stella,* 13th Jan. 1713.

Lord Harcourt showed as much deference as Harley and St. John to Swift, and used to say of him, "Dr. Swift is not only our favorite, but he is our governor." The Dean was, in fact, a leading member of the Government. He had a seat in the cabinet, without office, and was of great use to his colleagues, not only by his pen, but by his advice. If the Reverend Sydney Smith had assisted at Earl Grey's cabinet dinners, he might have supplied them not only with wit, but with wisdom.

and tokay, of which they freely partook, had dissipated for a season the animosities of rivalry, he tried to impress upon them the importance of their mutual cordiality to their country, to their party, and to themselves.[1] He was likewise a member of the smaller club which dined every Saturday with the Treasurer, and to which hardly any others but St. John and Swift were admitted, and there, while they planned the peace of Europe, he pointed out the necessity of peace in the Cabinet. Decency was so well preserved that even Swift for a time was not aware of the jealousies which had subsisted from the very formation of the Tory government. " There could hardly be," he says, "a firmer friendship in appearance than what I observed between those three great men, who were then chiefly trusted; I mean the Lords Oxford, Bolingbroke, and Harcourt. I remember, in the infancy of their power, being at the table of the first, where they were all met. I could not forbear taking notice of the great affection they bore to each other, and said, ' I would venture to prophesy that, however inconstant our Court had hitherto been, their ministry would certainly last, for they had the Church, the Crown, and the people entirely on their side:' then it happened that the public good and their private interest had the same bottom, which is a piece of good fortune that does not always fall to the share of men in power: but principally because I observed they heartily loved one another, and I did not see how their kindness could be disturbed by competition, since each of them seemed contented with his own district; so that, notwithstanding the old maxim which pronounces Court friendships to be of no long duration, I was confident theirs would last as long as their lives. But it seems the inventor of that maxim happened to be a little wiser than I, who lived to see this friendship first degenerate into indifference and suspicion, and thence corrupt into the greatest animosity and hatred, contrary to all appearances, and much to the discredit of me and my sagacity."[2]

While imminent peril hung over the Administration from the risk of a rupture of the negotiations for peace,

[1] Young Harcourt, the Chancellor's son, was the secretary to this club, under the directions of his father.
[2] " Inquiry into Behavior of the Queen's last Ministry.

and the risk of the treaty being condemned by parliament, the difficulty of preventing dissensions in the Cabinet was comparatively small; but now the party seemed secure of power, and the question arose, Who was to be at the head of it? Bolingbroke, greatly excelling his rival in eloquence and in energy of character, would bear no superior; while Oxford confident from his higher rank, longer experience, and better moral character, was for centering all power and patronage in his own hands, wished to keep Bolingbroke under subjection as if still only Secretary at War,—and treated his pretensions as presumptuous and preposterous.[1]

The breach between them was hastened by the declining health of the Queen. From the attacks of illness to which she was subject, and her enfeebled constitution, those who had access to her were aware that her life was very precarious, and could not be long protracted. Who was to rule in her stead? Oxford, although accident had placed him at the head of a Tory government, had Whiggish propensities. While he was a member of the House of Commons, he had himself brought in the act by which the Crown was limited to the House of Hanover; and although he had carried on a correspondence with St.

---

[1] Swift now writes thus to Lord Peterborough: "Our divisions run further than, perhaps, your Lordship's intelligence has yet informed you of; that is, a triumvirate of our friends I have mentioned to you; I have told them more than once, upon occasion, that all my hopes of their success depended on their union; that I saw they loved one another, and I hoped they would continue it, to remove that scandal of inconstancy ascribed to Court friendships. I am not now so secure."—*May, 1711.* So in his Journal to Stella, he says, "I do not much like the posture of things. I always apprehended that any falling out would ruin them, and so I have told them several times."—*21st Aug. 1711.*

About the same time, Swift composed "The Faggot," applying to the quarreling ministers the fable of "the Old Man and the Bundle of Sticks," and deals a hard blow to the Lord Chancellor:

> "Come, courtiers, every man his stick;
> Lord Treasurer for once be quick;
> And that they may the closer cling,
> Take your blue ribbon for a string.
> Come *trimming Harcourt*, bring your mace.
> And squeeze it in, or quit your place;
> Dispatch, or else that rascal Northey *
> Will undertake to do it for thee."

---

* Northey was Attorney General, and supposed to be a candidate for the Great Seal.

Germain's, and had held out hopes to the supporters of divine right, this was only to soothe the Jacobite party, and he was fully resolved, in his heart, to stand by the Protestant succession. He trusted that his services might be favorably considered by the new family; and, at any rate, he was not without some little regard for religion and liberty. Bolingbroke, utterly unprincipled, saw that for him there was no hope on the accession of the Hanoverian family, as they would either entirely throw themselves into the arms of the Whigs, to whom chiefly they owed their summons to the throne, or, if they favored any Tory, would prefer him who had assisted the Whigs in bringing about this settlement. He, therefore, devoted himself to the cause of the Pretender. Though, in his public professions, he was furiously High Church, in private he was a scoffer at all religion. He cherished the hope of prevailing on James to follow the example of his ancestor, Henry IV. of France, and, out of policy, to change his creed; but, if this could not be accomplished, he would not have scrupled to try to make the nation conform to the faith of the Sovereign, and he would have set them the example. As to the constitution he was indifferent, for he intended that the prerogatives of the Crown should be exercised by himself.

Harcourt, a very different man, engaged in the same enterprise from very different motives. It is impossible to deny that in Queen Anne's reign there might have been conscientious, disinterested, aye, and *enlightened* Jacobites,—and I reckon this eminent lawyer in the number. Looking to the conduct of James II. and considering what might be expected from his bigoted son, I myself, for the sake of the reformed religion and civil liberty, should have been still for breaking the line of hereditary succession, and placing another family on the throne, notwithstanding all the objections to which this proceeding was liable. But Harcourt reasoned very differently. He questioned, on plausible grounds, the power of parliament to change the succession to the Crown,—urging that by the fundamental law of the monarchy, given by God, and assented to by the whole body of the people before parliaments existed, this succession was hereditary, and that the Lords and Commons were only summoned to advise the King *de arduis regni*—to carry on the existing constitution—not to subvert it,—which, if the wild notions of liberty propounded in modern times were to prevail, could only be done by a general convention of the whole people, or by some scheme for ascertaining the opinion of the majority. At all events, he pronounced the resolution of the two Houses to alter the succession, without the consent of the reigning monarch, in point of law, a nullity;—and the Revolution was nothing more. If the misdeeds of James would justify resistance to his authority, and the setting him aside for his life, as if he were deprived of reason,—his innocent son might exclaim, "*ubi lapsus? quid feci?*" On grounds of expediency, as well as right, it would be proper to adhere to the ancient line of our kings. The true heir was an Englishman born, and, though unfortunately reared in a foreign land, he spoke our language, and had been bred with a familiar acquaintance with our literature, our laws, and our habits,—ever looking to England as his home, and having nothing to divert his affections from this country when he should have been placed on the throne of his ancestors. He would be ready to consent to all the limitations on the royal authority which had been recently introduced; and, indeed more had been offered in the reign of Charles II., rather than violate the law of succession by the Exclusion Bill. Religion was a difficulty, but there was great reason to hope for the conformity of the true heir to the Church of England. Having promised security for Protestantism, why should not he enjoy liberty of conscience as well as his subjects? and where was the justice in saying he had forfeited the Crown by adhering to the faith of our great law-giver, Edward I., and of the heroes of Cresci, Poictiers, and Agincourt, from whom he was descended? Then regard was to be had to the foreign family to be invited to rule over us. The Princess Sophia, herself an amiable and accomplished princess, was now in her eightieth year; and her son George, the reigning Elector of Hanover, had nothing but the vulgar virtue of personal courage to recommend him. Though fourteen years had elapsed since the passing of what was called the "Act of Settlement," under which he was to claim the Crown, he had not yet paid his future subjects the compliment of learning the first rudiments of their language; he had an utter contempt for all literature, and for the fine arts, having shut up his lawful wife in a castle on an unjust suspicion of infidelity, he lived with mistresses, who were to be transferred to this country to squander our money, and to corrupt our morals; he himself was deeply involved in petty German politics, from which his mind never could be extricated; to add a few acres to his hereditary dominions, he would be ready lavishly to waste British blood and treasure; utterly ignorant of our constitution and form of governing, he would be a mere puppet in the hands of others, and his accession would be a usurpation of the government by the odious Whig faction, who pretended a love for civil and religious liberty that they might reign in his name. English history proved that the true heir to the throne had always recovered his rights, and as long as a stranger was on the throne, there would be a constant succession of conspiracies and rebellions, incompatible with public peace or public prosperity. The royal line of James II. would be perpetuated by his two grandsons, and if it were extinct, there were still all the descendants of Henrietta, daughter of Charles I., and there were all the descendants of the elder children of the Queen of Bohemia, descended from James I., before the Princess Sophia of Hanover, or her descendants, could have the slightest color of claim.

Accordingly, under the secret sanction of Harcourt, various treatises were now published in England to support the imprescriptible claim of the Stuarts to the Crown, and the invalidity of the Act of Settlement. One of these, which had been composed, it was believed, from materials furnished by him, and which had been advertised in the London Gazette, advocated, in the boldest and most explicit terms, the cause of the Pretender; and when the indignation of the Whigs, and the clamor of the press, had compelled the commencement of a prosecution against the publisher, this was rendered abortive by the interference of the Government in remitting the sentence.[1]

There is no direct evidence to show how far the Queen concurred in these views. She would not listen to the proposal that her brother should come to England on an

---

[1] Letter to Bothmar, 25th May, 1714; Political State, vii. 488.

understanding that she should sit upon the throne during her life, and that he should succeed her; but there seems no reason to doubt that, entertaining the greatest abhorrence of the Hanoverian family, she would have been pleased with any plans to insure his succession which were consistent with the continuance of her own rule. In answer to an address from the Lords, who were alarmed by the aspect of affairs, and prayed that she would issue a proclamation against the Pretender,—by Harcourt's advice, and with the strong approbation of Bolingbroke,—against the remonstrances of Oxford—she said, " I do not at this time see any occasion for such a proclamation : whenever I judge it to be necessary, I shall give my orders for having one issued."[1] She likewise agreed to the new modeling of the army by the dismissal of a great many Whig officers—a measure which she was perhaps told was only for the safety of the Church, but which Bolingbroke and Harcourt certainly recommended for the purpose of defeating the Hanoverian succession.[2] They made another attempt, which might have been much more effectual—by imploring the Pretender to change, or dissemble, his religion ; but James, who is to be praised at least for his sincerity, wrote an answer solemnly declaring that "he would neither change nor dissemble his own religion, but that he would show indulgence to the religious errors of his subjects;" and this was injudiciously made public by some of his partisans, in the vain hope of assisting him by raising his character for honesty.[3] But, upon the whole, things looked so favorably for the Stuart family, and such confidence was reposed by their party in the Lord Chancellor, that a bill was filed in the Court of Chancery by Mary of Modena, claiming arrears of her dowry to the amount of £650,000. An objection being made that she styled her-

[1] 7 Parl. Hist. 1340.
[2] Macpherson's Pap, ii. 412 ; Com. Jour. xvii. 293.
[3] At this time Bolingbroke in a great rage declared to Iberville, that "if the Elector of Hanover ever did mount the throne of England, it would be entirely through the fault of the Pretender in refusing to do what was quite indispensable to gain the hearts and to allay the apprehensions of the nation ;" and several leading Catholics concurred in the same advice, saying, that "the delay of his conformity at this dangerous crisis of the Queen's health they thought could only arise from his requiring assurances that on taking that step he would be acknowledged as heir."—*Letters of Iberville to Torcy*, June and July, 1714.

self "Queen Mother," he was obliged to order it to be taken off the file—but having reformed her title to "the Most Illustrious Princess Maria, relict of James II. King of England," it was received, and although no formal decree was pronounced upon it, a sum of £50,000 was remitted to France for her use.

The friends of the Protestant succession were not inactive, and they now recommended a move for which the Chancellor was little prepared. In the year 1706 a patent had passed the Great Seal creating the Electoral Prince of Hanover, afterwards George II., an English peer, by the title of "Duke of Cambridge;" but no writ of summons had ever been issued to him, and there was no apprehension that such a thing would ever be proposed, as the Whigs themselves, when in office, out of tenderness to the feelings of the Queen, had resisted the application that a member of the electoral family should be invited to reside in England. But having been naturalized by act of parliament—*de jure*, he was entitled to a writ as much as any other peer, and it was thought that his presence would not only embarrass the ministers, but in case of a demise of the Crown might essentially further the accession of his family. On the 10th of April the Whig Lords held a consultation at Lord Halifax's, to which Baron Schutz, envoy from Hanover, was admitted; and it was resolved that, without any address to the Crown, or parliamentary discussion, and without any previous notice, the writ should be demanded as a mere matter of course from the Lord Chancellor, whose official duty it was to have issued it under the Great Seal. Accordingly Baron Schutz, as the agent of the Duke, paid a visit to the Lord Chancellor, and, after the ceremony of salutation had passed in due form, and they were both seated, the following amusing dialogue was held between them: —*B. S.* "I wait upon your Lordship to acknowledge, in the name of the Elector, my master, the affection your Lordship has shown on various occasions to the Most Serene Electoral House of Hanover."—*L. C.* "I am extremely sensible of the honor which your Excellency does me by this visit, and this compliment, and I beg you will assure his Most Serene Highness, the Elector, of my entire devotion to his service, and I hope his Most Serene Highness gives no credit to the false reports which are industriously spead abroad in order to excite jealousies in the minds of his Most Serene Highness against myself and others of her Majesty's present Ministers."—*B. S.* "My Lord, I shall not fail to discharge such an agreeable commission. But, in the mean time, I have a small favor to ask from your Lordship on behalf of the Electoral Prince—that your Lordship would be pleased to make a writ for his sitting in the House of Peers as Duke of Cambridge."—*L. C.* (*much astonished, puzzled, and perplexed.*) "It is not usual to make out writs for Peers who are out of the kingdom. However, I will forthwith apply to her Majesty for directions in this case."—*B. S.* "I doubt not that your Lordship will duly perform what you know to be the duty of your office. But I can relieve your Lordship from all difficulty on the score of the Duke of Cambridge being out of the kingdom, for I can assure your Lordship that his Electoral Highness will come over very speedily, and he may probably have landed before the writ is made out. And now, my Lord, I respectfully take my leave of your Lordship."—*L. C.* (*in some confusion and trepidation, and perhaps recollecting that this scene might be the foundation of a future impeachment.*) "Your Excellency will be pleased to remember that I do not refuse your demand, but only think it proper to acquaint the Queen, my mistress, with it— which I will forthwith do."—*B. S.* "Your Lordship will also be pleased to remember that I, by the authority and in the name of the Duke of Cambridge, do demand that a writ of summons may be made out to him to sit in this present parliament according to the rights and privileges of the peerage of England."

The Chancellor immediately called a Cabinet Council, which sat on this subject from 9 o'clock till midnight, and then resolved "that a writ should be made out for the Duke of Cambridge." Bolingbroke was convinced, although with great difficulty, that the Lords would immediately take up the refusal of the writ as a breach of privilege, and that the nation would be on their side. Next day the Hanoverian Minister addressed the following letter to the Lord Chancellor:—

"My Lord,

"I hope your Lord^p will be pleased to send me an answer concerning what I had the honor to entertain you with yesterday, that I may this evening acquaint the Princess Sophia with the same by my letters

"I am, with great respect,
"My Lord,
"Your Lord^p most obed^t
"humble Servt
"Gsyr Schutz,

"London, the $\frac{1}{1}\frac{3}{4}$ April, 1714,
in the afternoon."

Without again consulting his colleagues, the Chancellor returned an answer in the spirit of the resolution which the Government had adopted:—

"13th April, 1714.

"S^r,

"When you came to me yesterday, and told me that by order of the Princess Sophia you demanded a writ of summons for the Duke of Cambridge, I let you know that I thought it my duty to acquaint her Ma^y therewith.

"I have accordingly layd this matter before the Queen, who was pleased to say, that not having received the least intimation of this demand from you, or in any other manner whatsoever from the Court of Hanover, she could hardly persuade herself that you acted by direction from thence; that she, therefore, did not think fit to give any other answer than this, that I would do what the law required.

"The writ for the Duke of Cambridge was sealed of course, when the writs of summons to all the other peers were sealed, and lyes ready to be delivered to you whenever you call for it. I am,

"S^r,
"Your most humble Servt,
"Harcourt, C."[1]

The statement that the writ had been sealed "of course," the Chancellor considered himself at liberty to make, on the well-known doctrine of his Court, that "Equity considers what ought to be done as actually done." However, it was secretly determined that measures should be taken to counteract this project; that the journey of the Electoral Prince should be delayed; that if the Queen survived, measures should be taken to repeal the Act of Settlement; and that if she should suddenly

---

[1] Lans. MSS. Brit. Mus. 1236, fo. 257, 259.

die, the Pretender should be proclaimed.¹ Oxford, at the head of a party called the "Hanoverian Tories," remained true to the Protestant succession; but he was left almost alone in the Cabinet. Mrs. Masham, who had made him Prime Minister, had now conceived a most mortal enmity to him, because he had prevented her from recovering a large sum of money from the Assiento contract. As a consequence, she warmly sided with Bolingbroke and Harcourt, and took up the cause of James III.² We likewise find from the Memoirs of the Marshal Berwick, that the Court of St. Germain's, through the channel of the Duke of Ormond and Lady Masham, had intimated to the Queen a wish that the Lord Treasurer should be removed.³

The Chancellor having, on the 9th of July, the last time Queen Anne was ever seen in public, prorogued parliament by her command, retired into the country to enjoy a short repose after the labors of a protracted session; but he was immediately summoned to town by Bolingbroke, who was impatient to break up the existing Cabinet, and added the following:—" P. S. Pray, my Lord, be punctual, and bring back with you a more sanguine disposition than you left town with; at least don't fancy that the Queen and all the rest of us are to be slaves of him who was raised by the favor of the former, and the friendship of the latter."⁴

On the 27th of July came the long expected crisis, when Oxford fell. After a renewal of his personal altercations with his rival, often repeated in the royal presence, and a tumultuous scene, which was continued till two in

¹ Anne's real sentiments on this subject may be gathered from the narrative of Lockhart, of Carnwath, a zealous Jacobite, of his presenting to her a "high monarchical," or Jacobitish address from the county of Edinburgh. Being told by the Queen that "she did not doubt his affection to her person, and that she hoped he would not concur in any design to bring over the Prince of Hanover during her lifetime," somewhat surprised at this mark of confidence,—"I told her," says he, "that her Majesty might judge from the address I had read, that I should not be acceptable to my constituents if I gave my consent for bringing over any of that family, either now, *or at any time hereafter.*" "At this," adds Lockhart, "she smiled, and I withdrew; and then she said to the Duke of Hamilton she believed I was an honest man and a fair dealer."—*Lockh. Corr.* 317.

² "The Lord Chancellor, Lord Bolingbroke, and Lady Masham, openly declared against him," &c.—SWIFT, *Inquiry into the Behavior of the Queen's last Ministry.* ³ Ber. Mem. ii. 133.

⁴ Bolingbroke to Harcourt, 19th July, 1714; MSS. of G. G. Vernon Harcourt, Esq., M.P.

the morning, Anne summoned up resolution to resume the White Staff, and the whole power of the state was left in the hands of Bolingbroke, with orders to form a new administration.[1] For a few hours the cause of the Pretender seemed triumphant. The new Premier, of course, intended that Lord Harcourt should continue to hold the Great Seal as Chancellor. He announced that he would put the Treasury in commission, and, retaining the office of Secretary, which at such a juncture was the most important under the Crown, he named for the other departments of the government stanch Jacobites, several of whom showed their sincerity by afterwards going into exile, and openly espousing the falling cause of the Stuarts. In the wantonness of his exultation, he next day gave a grand dinner to the Whig leaders at his house in Golden Square, as if, while determined to rule in the name of James III., he had intended to make overtures to them to assist him in securing the Protestant succession, to which he declared himself a devoted adherent.

But his ambitious plans, when seemingly so near their consummation, were for ever blasted by the mortal illness of the Queen, which she ascribed to her agitation on the night she vested all power in his hands. While she lay in a state of stupor, the friends of the Protestant succession seized the government; she was made to go through the form of appointing Shrewsbury Lord Treasurer, and as soon as she expired George was peaceably proclaimed King.

[1] The letters of Erasmus Lewis to Swift give a lively picture of the behavior of Harcourt and Oxford to each other just before the breaking up of the Cabinet: *July 17, 1714.* "The great Attorney (Harcourt), who made you the sham offer of the Yorkshire living, had a long conference with the Dragon (Oxford) on Thursday, kissed him at parting, and cursed him at heart."—*July 22.* "They eat and drink and walk together, as if there were no sort of disagreement; and when they part, I hear they give one another such names as nobody but ministers of state could hear without cutting throats."—*July 24.*——" Intelligence that the Dragon has broke out in a fiery passion with my Lord Chancellor, sworn a thousand oaths he would be revenged," &c.

CHAPTER CXX.

CONCLUSION OF THE LIFE OF LORD HARCOURT.

HARCOURT had been deliberating with the other ministers of Anne, when Somerset and Argyle burst into the council chamber. If these two noblemen had been committed to the Tower, if a messenger had been immediately dispatched to Loraine for the Pretender, and if the Duke of Marlborough, who had just then landed from the Continent, and who personally bore no good will to the Elector, could by immense offers have been gained over,—the Stuart dynasty might have remained on the throne. But Bolingbroke, Harcourt, and the Jacobites were stunned and bewildered by the sudden blow; they did not make the slightest effort to resist the measures of the Whigs, and they seem all to have fallen into passive despair, except Atterbury, who, when his offer that he would head the procession to proclaim James at Charing Cross, was rejected, exclaimed, "The best cause in Europe is lost for want of spirit."

However, I think all reasonable men—even those who concurred in Harcourt's political principles—must approve, in point of policy, of the course which he now adopted. The Jacobites were considerably outnumbered in the Council, and there was reason to believe that, from the prevalent horror of popery, the great majority of the officers in the army and navy, and the majority of the population of the country, would have declared for the Protestant line. To resist the Act of Settlement would have been another revolution—which, for the sake of the cause and of those who were to be engaged in it, was not to be attempted under circumstances which afforded no reasonable hope of success.

In reality, Harcourt acted as if he had never in any degree plotted against or disapproved the change of dynasty. At the meeting of the Council which took place as soon as the Queen had breathed her last, he produced the sealed paper which had been deposited with him as Lord Chancellor, containing the names of those appointed Lords Justices by George on his mother's death. Being himself, under the Act of Regency, officially a Lord Justice, he immediately took the oath of allegiance to the new Sovereign, together with the oath of abjuration of James, which he had so strenuously opposed, and he administered these oaths to his brother Lords Justices, as well such who were official, as those who had been personally nominated. They then all signed the formal recognition of the title of the new Sovereign, and ordered the Heralds to proclaim "that the high and mighty Prince George, Elector of Brunswick Lunenburgh, is, by the death of Queen Anne of blessed memory, become our lawful and rightful liege Lord, King of Great Britain, France, and Ireland, Defender of the Faith."

Lord Harcourt's authority as Chancellor under his appointment by Queen Anne was gone, but he was reappointed by the Lords of the Regency, in the name of the new Sovereign, and was again sworn in.[1]

The House of Lords having assembled in pursuance of the Act requiring parliament to meet immediately on the demise of the Crown, the Chancellor hastened to the woolsack, and, to give time for taking the oaths to the Government, moved an adjournment till the 5th of August. On that day, the Commons being summoned to the bar, the Chancellor, in the name of the Lords Justices, now invested with royal authority, thus spoke:—
" My Lords and Gentlemen, it having pleased Almighty God to take to himself our late most gracious Queen of blessed memory, we hope that nothing has been omitted which might contribute to the safety of these realms, and the preservation of our religion, laws, and liberties in this great conjuncture. As these invaluable blessings have been secured to us by those acts of parliament which have settled the succession of the Crown in the most illustrious House of Hanover, we have regulated our proceedings by the rules therein prescribed." After stating the constitution of the new government by the

[1] "Anno Primo Georgii Regis, 3rd August, 1714.—Simon, L⁴ Harcourt, Lord High Chancellor of Great Britain, went afterwards (*i. e.* swearing of the L⁴ Chief Justice Parker, the Attorney and Solicitor General, etc.) into Court at his house aforesaid (Lincoln's Inn Fields), attended by the Maʳ of the Rolls, some of the Masters in Chancery, Six Clerks Registers, and his Lordship's officers and servants, and there took the oaths appointed to be taken by the Act primo Willi. et Marie, and the oath of Chancellor; the oath being read by the Deputy Clerk of the Crown, the Master of the Rolls holding the book."—*Min. Roll, 1714.*

Lords Justices under the Regency Act, he proceeds: "We are persuaded you will bring with you so hearty a disposition for his Majesty's service and the public good, that we can not doubt of your assistance in everything which may promote those great ends." Having asked supplies from the Commons, he thus concluded: "My Lords and Gentlemen, we forbear laying before you anything which does not require your immediate consideration, not having received his Majesty's pleasure; we shall therefore only exhort you with the greatest earnestness to a perfect unanimity and a firm adherence to our Sovereign's interest, as being the only means to continue among us our present happy tranquillity."

On the 13th, Lord Harcourt made another speech, as the organ of the Lords Justices, to both Houses, announcing his Majesty's approach "to employ his utmost care for putting these kingdoms into a happy and flourishing condition." On the 21st of August, the Speaker of the House of Commons having delivered a long address to the Lords Justices when presenting a money bill for the royal assent, Lord Harcourt in their name made a suitable reply, thus concluding—"You may be assured that the unanimity, the cheerfulness, and the dispatch with which you have proceeded in granting these aids, will render them yet more acceptable to his Majesty, and you may depend upon our making a faithful report thereof to him." A few days after, he put an end to the session by a prorogation.[1]

Bolingbroke was eager to enter the service of the new King. Whether if an offer of the Great Seal had been made to Lord Harcourt it would have been accepted, I can not positively say; but my opinion is, that it would without hesitation have been rejected. He was still devotedly attached to the exiled family; and there was a movement going on in Scotland, with a manifestation of favorable sympathies in the south, which might have led to their restoration. He never would voluntarily have accepted office with the intention of betraying his employer.

But he was not exposed to any temptation, for George on his arrival declared for an exclusively Whig cabinet, and treated the Chancellor with particular neglect, and

[1] 7 Parl. Hist. 3-11.

even rudeness on account of the rumors which had got abroad of his machinations at the end of the late reign to bring in the Pretender. When the new King landed at Greenwich, Harcourt attended with the other Lords Justices to receive him; but while his Majesty loaded the two ex-Chancellors, Somers and Cowper, with civilities, he would not even speak to the present Lord Chancellor, who had exercised the royal authority in his name. In three days, his Majesty, without having admitted him to an audience, took the Great Seal from him by Townshend the new Secretary of State, who was fortified by a warrant under the sign-manual to demand it, and exercised his authority very offensively

It seems rather surprising that ,when bills of attainder were passed against Bolingbroke and Ormond—and Oxford, who had always supported the Protestant succession, was impeached for high treason,—Lord Harcourt was allowed to remain unmolested, although it was well known that, being a Jacobite in principle, he had done everything in his power to obstruct the King's accession, and that, "biding his time," as soon as a favorable opportunity arose he would be ready to risk everything for the Stuarts. But he had spoken and acted with much more caution than Bolingbroke—so that there might have been great difficulty in adducing any evidence against him; and, from his courteous manners and the prevalent opinion of his honesty, there was a general wish to treat him with lenience.

For the first three years of the new reign, Harcourt did not openly take any part in politics. He professed to have withdrawn from public life. Of his two most distinguished colleagues, one was a prisoner in the Tower of London, and the other, having fled, and being attainted, was openly in the service of the Pretender. He himself, while the cause was desperate, retained his former principles and wishes with respect to the Crown; but no opportunity occurred for his interfering actively, with any prospect of advantage to displace the family who he considered had usurped it. He remained in a state of extreme excitement and suspense during the rebellion in the north. When the news reached London, of the fight at Sheriffmuir, and James's arrival at Scone, he was for a short time much elated, and amidst his family he sang

"The King shall have his own again;" but still the English Jacobites, when sounded, were adverse to any open manifestation, till it should be justified by more decisive success; and ere long the Earl of Mar and the Prince were obliged to fly from Scotland, Preston was taken, and the heads of the rebel Lords were stuck over Temple Bar. The ex-Chancellor, though a tolerably steady politician, was not an enthusiast, and, when he looked up as he passed into the city, did not wistfully exclaim—

"Forsitan et nostrum—miscebitur istis." [1]

The Government had a keen eye upon him during these transactions, but he was not committed to the Tower along with Lord Lansdowne, Sir William Wyndham, and other suspected adherents of the Stuarts, and he had acted so cautiously that no evidence could be discovered to justify any proceedings against him. Nevertheless, when the act of grace passed he was expressly excluded from it.[2]

He professed to dedicate himself entirely to literature, and he was much in the society of literary men. Now, indeed, he had great reason to rejoice that he had continued to mix elegant pursuits with business, and that he had not been "a mere lawyer." He found constant agreeable occupation in reading and in conversing with men of genius. Swift had gone to his Deanery of St. Patrick's, but the ex-Chancellor assisted in forming the celebrated Quincunx, and improving the Grotto at Twickenham. He himself was a worshipper of the Muses, and was not despised by them. His productions were chiefly *vers de société*—but we have one poetical effusion of his, of which I am rather proud, for the honor of the Great Seal. When Pope published a collection of his works, Harcourt, according to the fashion of the time, supplied an encomiastic poem, to be prefixed to the volume, along with Sheffield, Duke of Buckingham, Parnell, Wycherly, and Lord Lyttelton: and the lawyer's lines will bear a comparison with those of the more elaborate pieces of the professed poets:—[3]

[1] See Bosw. Johnson, ii. 243.
[2] In spite of this and several other exceptions, a contemporary pamphlet carries its adulation to such a pitch of blasphemy as to say that "the clemency of King George was not only great, but even extended further than that of God himself."—*Tindal*, vii. 160.
[3] "To Mr. Pope, on the publishing his Works."

"He comes! he comes! bid every bard prepare,
The song of triumph and attend his car.
Great Sheffeld's Muse the long procession heads,
And throws a luster o'er the pomp she leads ;
First gives the palm she fir'd him to obtain,
Crowns his gay brow, and shows him how to reign.
Thus young Alcides by old Chiron taught,
Was form'd for all the miracles he wrought:
Thus Chiron did the youth he taught applaud,
Pleas'd to behold the earnest of a god.
But hark! what shouts, what gathering crowds rejoice!
Unstain'd their praise by any venal voice,
Such as the ambitious vainly think their due,
When prostitutes or needy flatterers sue.
And see the chief! before him laurels borne;
Trophies from undeserving temples torn;
Here Rage, enchain'd, reluctant raves, and there
Pale Envy, dumb and sickening with despair;
Prone to the earth she bends her loathing eye;
Weak to support the blaze of majesty.—
But what are they that turn the sacred page?
Three lovely virgins, and of equal age!
Intent they read, and all enamour'd seem,
As he that met his likeness in the stream:
The Graces these: and see how they contend,
Who most shall praise, who best shall recommend.
"The chariot now the painful steep ascends,
The pæans cease, thy glorious labor ends.
Here fix'd the bright eternal temple stands,
Its prospect an unbounded view commands:
Say wondrous youth, what column wilt thou choose,
What laurel'd arch for thy triumphant muse?
Though each great ancient court thee to his shrine,
Though every laurel through the dome be thine,
(From the proud epic, down to those that shade
The gentler brow of the soft Lesbian maid).
Go to the good and just, an awful train,
Thy soul's delight, and glory of the fane;
While through the earth thy dear remembrance flies,
' Sweet to the world and grateful to the skies.' "

The first occasion of Lord Harcourt again appearing upon the political stage was in the year 1717, when, by his management, an end was put to the long impending impeachment of the Earl of Oxford, and that nobleman was restored to liberty. It happened that at this time Walpole was out of office, and disposed to show to the Court his powers of annoyance. It is very rare that two leaders are in the opposition to a government, however different their past course and principles may have been, without a mutual good understanding, if not a coalition, being speedily established between them. Walpole had assisted in instituting the prosecution against the author of the Peace of Utrecht; but, out of spite to Stanhope, and those on whom the conduct of it now devolved, he wished that it should be terminated with some disgrace to the accusers. Among the articles of impeachment there were several of the character of "high crimes and misdemeanors" (such as secret orders given to generals and negotiators), for which there was some foundation; but there were others for alleged "high treason," which were entirely false or frivolous. Seeing the chance of bringing about a quarrel between the two Houses, which would be annoying and discreditable to the Administration, he advised Harcourt to try to make the Lords irritate the Commons by the mode of fixing the trial, and, when the trial came on, to move that no evidence be received upon the articles charging *misdemeanor* till those charging *treason* should be disposed of. Thereupon, Lord Harcourt, supported by Lord Trevor, got a committee appointed to search for precedents as to the mode of conducting the trial of impeachments, and, the report being that it was the undoubted privilege of the Lords to fix a day for the trial at their discretion, the 24th of June was peremptorily fixed for the commencement of the trial of the Earl of Oxford. On that day, when the managers for the Commons had opened, and were beginning to prove the first article, Lord Harcourt moved the adjournment of the Lords from Westminster Hall to their own chamber; and after a long speech to show the cruel manner in which the prosecution had been conducted, " urging that it would be a great hardship upon a Peer, who had already undergone so long a confinement, to stand every day at their bar like a traitor, and be at last found guilty only of high crimes and misdemeanors, or entirely absolved," he proposed the resolution " that the Commons be not permitted to proceed on the articles for high crimes and misdemeanors till judgment be first given upon the articles for high treason." I have already narrated, in the Life of Lord Cowper, how the expected quarrel which arose between the two Houses speedily produced the desired acquittal.[1] Lord Harcourt conducted the conferences on the subject, and wrote the reasons on the part of the Lords,—still communicating with the wary Walpole in every stage. This

[1] Ante, p 240

affair established an intimacy between them which, by-and-by, when Sir Robert was Prime Minister, induced him who had been such a determined opponent of the Protestant succession *sincerely* to " abjure " King James, and to send in his adhesion to King George.

But for several years longer he continued a bitter enemy of the Government, and did all in his power to disgust the nation with Hanoverian rule. Thus, in the debate on the " Mutiny Bill," in 1718, he made a very factious speech against standing armies and courts-martial ; and in " South Sea Year " he attempted to prove that all the follies, frauds, and sufferings of the nation were to be imputed to the Government.

Lord Harcourt continued to attend diligently in parliament, and to take an active part in disposing of the judicial business of the House of Lords.[1]

His conversion did not take place till the summer of 1721, when, on the deaths of Stanhope and Sunderland, Walpole, being undisputed Prime Minister, began an administration the longest and most prosperous of the 18th century. It was a great object with him to gain over a Jacobite leader. Bolingbroke, dismissed from the service of the Pretender, now importunately offered to support the Government on having his attainder reversed, and being allowed to resume his seat in the House of Lords. Walpole did not much doubt the sincerity of his purpose to change sides, but dreaded his ambition and his talents, and foresaw that he would soon struggle to be Prime Minister to King George. He therefore sounded the ex-

---

[1] There now lies before me the original of a letter written to him by Sir Richard Levinz, an Irish Judge from Dublin, showing that his voice was considered potential in the decisions of appeals and writs of error, and that canvassing the Lords in such matters was not considered at all indecent :—" My very good Lord,—Mr. Thomas Acton, who is chirographer of the Court of Common Pleas here, has a cause depending before your Lordship upon an appeal from the Chancery here, and has desired me to write to your Lordship. I was very unwilling to give your Lordship this trouble, and told him that if he had justice on his side he might be assured of a full measure of it from your Lordship ; and if that were wanting, nothing could supply the defect. But he being very importunate, and known to me to be a very honest man and a good officer in the court in which I sit, and it being the custom here with great diligence to seek for letters from persons to such of the Lords as they have the honor to be known to, I hoped your Lordship would not take it ill if I took this opportunity of expressing the great respect I have ever had for your Lordship, and desiring the favor of your Lordship to be present at the hearing this gentleman's cause."—*16th Jan. 1721-2.*

Chancellor, with whom he had kept up a private intimacy since Oxford's acquittal, and who, enjoying a fair reputation, was less aspiring and more trustworthy.[1]

Harcourt is generally considered as having forfeited his character by listening to the overtures made to him, but I think without sufficient reason. The government *de facto* established was supported by a vast majority of the English nation, and, notwithstanding plots entered into by some few from principle, and by others from the hope of personal advantage, there was no reasonable chance of overturning it. The conduct of the true heir had been so excessively indiscreet, and he seemed so impenetrable to all good advice, that there appeared an absolute impossibility of serving him effectually, and any attempt to restore him was only likely to lead to the wanton shedding of blood and the utter ruin of the families of those who might engage in it. I therefore can see no culpable inconsistency in a man who, in the reign of Queen Anne, strove to prevent the succession of the Hanoverian family, and upon her death continued to oppose them till the opinion of the people should be manifested on the grand question, afterwards for the sake of the national tranquillity and prosperity, agreeing to support them. I must allow that he might have shown better taste in his mode of going over, and that he ought to have avoided the suspicion of mercenary motives by rejecting all favors that might be proffered to him by the Court; but to give weight to his adhesion, and to prove that he could never *resile*, he agreed to accept of an increase of his pension as ex-Chancellor, with a rise in the peerage to the degree of a Viscount. In the following year he was sworn of the Privy Council, and thenceforth attended when any judicial business was before the Board. However, unlike Murray of Broughton, who justly incurred eternal infamy by his treacherous change of sides in 1745, he never betrayed any confidence that had been reposed in him, and he was always pleased to do a good-natured turn for an old Jacobite friend. Notwithstanding strong solicitations and temptations, he ever

---

[1] About this time there was a suspicion of other Jacobites going over. Prior writes to Swift: "The Bishop (Atterbury) can not be lower in the opinion of men than he is, and I wish our friend Harcourt were higher than he is."—*April, 1721.*

after remained true to the new engagements into which he had entered. Atterbury's plot, which might have proved very formidable, soon afterwards arose, but he refused to be concerned in it, though united to the bishop by the closest ties of private friendship.

When the bill of pains and penalties against Atterbury was brought in, the Opposition Peers wished to carry a resolution in the House of Lords that he should be forbidden to appear to plead against it at the bar of the House of Commons. This Lord Harcourt opposed, alleging "that in such a proceeding the Commons did not act as a court of judicature, but as a part of the legislature, and that they had as much right to decide as the Lords themselves." So far he was surely right, although Lord Cowper, with a view to defeat the measure by any means, took the other side. When the bill came up to the House of Lords, I could wish for Lord Harcourt's fame that he had actively opposed it. However, he did not vote for it—taking care to be absent when it passed through its several stages there.[1] In the debate on the third reading, a sarcasm was leveled against him by Duke Wharton, who said,—"There is a noble and learned member of this House who made the greatest figure in opposing the bill for the attainder of Sir John Fenwick. I am sorry that I do not see him in his place, as we should no doubt have his assistance to defeat a bill equally obnoxious."[2]

We next find Lord Harcourt exerting himself for his old colleague, Bolingbroke, who had sent over his second wife, the Marquise de Villette, to solicit his restoration. The ex-Chancellor, finding that he himself could make no impression upon Walpole, introduced her to the Duchess of Kendal, who, for a bribe of £11,000, promised that the favor should be granted, and he afterwards supported the passing of a free pardon when that step was proposed by the King at a council where he was present. Walpole still strongly opposed any concession, concealing his apprehensions for his own supremacy, but contending that

---

[1] As the Lords' Journals daily gives the names of all the peers present, the absence of a peer on any particular day can be proved satisfactorily. The Journals of the Commons now show the names of the members in every division (an improvement not adopted by the Lords), but do not mention the names of members present without dividing.

[2] Parl. Register, 1723, p. 380.

such a restless and faithless man, if replaced in parliament, would poison the minds of the people, and soon alienate them from the happy establishment to which they were at present so much attached. Harcourt proposed a middle course, which was adopted,—that Bolingbroke should be restored in blood, so that he might live unmolested in England and enjoy his property, but that all the other civil disqualifications of his attainder should still continue. Walpole would rather have resigned than agreed to more,—certain that Boligbroke's eloquence in the senate would soon have been fatal to the existing Administration, and might have disturbed the public tranquillity.[1] Bolingbroke was sensible that more could not then be accomplished for him; and, soon after his restoration, being about to revisit the Continent to settle his affairs there, thus addressed Lord Harcourt: "If by any accident, your return should be deferred, I must beg leave to wait on you in the country, or desire you to give me a meeting, where it may be least inconvenient to your Lordship, on the road; for I can not think of leaving England without embracing the person to whom I owe the obligation of having seen it once more."

During the remainder of this reign, Harcourt continued steadily to support the Government. He was not put into office, but an honorary mark of distinction was conferred

[1] Letter, Bolingbroke to Harcourt, 26th January, 1723, concluding thus: "I am, and shall be in all circumstances of life, and in all the countries of the world, "My Lord,
"Your most faithful and obedient Servant,
"BOLINGBROKE."
However, Bolingbroke felt more and more deeply the privation he suffered from being disqualified to sit in parliament; and in a letter to Lord Harcourt, dated Dawley Farm, 22nd March, 1725, strongly urges his complete pardon, and denies the report that he had been caballing with Pulteney against the Government. "I have very much esteem for Mr. Pulteney. I have met with great civility from him, and shall, on all occasions, behave myself towards him like a man who is obliged to him. But, my Lord, I have no private correspondence or even conversation with him; and whenever I appeal to the King, and beg leave to plead my cause before him, I will take care that his ministers shall not have the least pretense of objection to make to me in any part of my conduct I will only say upon this occasion, that if I had caballed against them, there would have been other things said, than were said, and another turn of opposition given."—*MSS. of G. G. Vernon Harcourt, Esq., M.P.* Lord Harcourt gave Bolingbroke fair words, but does not seem to have interfered further for him—which he could not have done without breaking with Walpole.

upon him, to testify reciprocal confidence and good will. George, having obtained a repeal of the clause in the Act of Settlement which forbade him to leave the realm without the consent of the two Houses of Parliament, was in the yearly habit of spending some months in Hanover; and after his quarrel with his son, whom he at first appointed Guardian of the Kingdom in his absence, he always named Lords Justices to exercise the royal authority in his name and under his directions. Lord Harcourt, from 1723, was one of these, and he was actually a representative of royalty, in June, 1727, when King George expired, on his journey to Hanover, between Ippburen and Osnabruck.

When the news arrived in London, Harcourt repaired to Leicester House, was present at the first council of George II., and took the oaths of allegiance to that sovereign. He attended in the House of Lords on the 27th of June, when the King made his first speech from the throne, and thence regularly till the 17th of July, when parliament was prorogued.

But his own end approached. His constitution had been much enfeebled by the fatigues of business and by convivial indulgence, so common in that age. As he was traveling in his coach, on Sunday, the 23rd of July, to visit Sir Robert Walpole, at Chelsea, he was seized with a violent fit of paralysis, and was immediately carried home to his house in Cavendish Square. He rallied so far as partially to recover the use of speech, and to be considered by his physicians out of immediate danger; but a fresh attack supervened on the following Friday, when he expired in the sixty-seventh year of his age. His remains were deposited, with those of his long line of ancestors, in the family cemetery at Stanton-Harcourt,[1] but no monument was erected to him, and none of his poetical friends contributed a stanza to his memory. He had so lived as not to stand in need of such memorials after death.

Upon the whole, I consider him an ornament to the profession of the law. Those who lament that he had

[1] "There are twenty of *Harcourt's* Barons bold,
    Lie buried within that proud chapelle;"
—of which a very interesting account was written by George Simon, Earl Harcourt, 1808.

not the liberal political principles of Somers and Cowper, should bear in mind his Tory descent, and the rigorous High Church principles which were early instilled into him. Swift had vainly tried to fix upon him the nickname of "Trimming Harcourt," but this was merely because the lawyer thought the divine went too great lengths in libeling his old friends and patrons—in accusing Marlborough of cowardice, and Somers of irreligion. Great allowance must be made for public men who live in revolutionary times; and, till Harcourt's adhesion to the House of Hanover, I know not that any serious objection can be made to his conduct. Others must determine upon the apology I have attempted for the part he took on that occasion.

Lord Chancellor Brougham says, "Though a respectable lawyer, he is certainly not to be ranked with the Finches, the Parkers, and the Hardwickes."[1] What will generally be more admired than black-letter law, he had a taste for polite literature, and (as I have shown) was himself no contemptible poet. "The Advice to the October Club," written and much read in 1711, was ascribed to him, but, I believe, erroneously; and I am not acquainted with any prose publication which can be certainly traced to him.

Like the most illustrious statesmen of his time, on both sides in politics, he was a patron of learning. When he received the Great Seal, he waived the contingency of his presentation to the first preferment that should fall vacant in the Queen's gift, that he might get a prebend in the cathedral at Norwich annexed to the mastership of Katharine Hall.

He was ever ready to assist men of genius in distress. J. Philips, the author of "The Splendid Shilling," and the poem in praise of "Cider," he liberally patronized while living, and he erected, at his own expense, a monument in Westminster Abbey to his memory, obtaining for it an inscription by Atterbury.[2]

Both while he was in office, and after his fall, he lived

[1] *Jones* v. *Scott*, 1 Russ. and Mylne, 269.
[2] "SIMON HARCOURT Miles
Viri benè de se, de literis meriti,
Quoad viveret fautor,
Post obitum piè memor
Hoc illi saxum poni voluit."

on terms of the greatest intimacy, not only with Pope, but with Gay, Prior, Parnell, Arbuthnot, the Philipses, and most of the other wits of the time. Addison he occasionally met,—when there was perfect courtesy, but, on account of politics, no cordiality between them. Pope and Gay he treated as brothers. The old family mansion at Stanton-Harcourt had been untenanted since the death of Sir Philip, in 1688, but a few rooms continued furnished Of three of these, each thirteen feet square, one above the other in an antique turret, Pope, that he might be sequestrated from the world, took possession in the summer of 1718, and here he devoted himself to the translation of the Iliad. The uppermost retains the name of "Pope's Study," he having, with his own hand traced upon a pane of red stained glass, in one of the casements still preserved, the following inscription :—

"In the year 1718,
Alexander Pope
finished here
the fifth volume of Homer."

Lord Harcourt himself then lived at Cockthorpe, a place in Buckinghamshire, at no great distance,—having Gay for his inmate ; and they were allowed occasionally to intrude upon the inspired translator.

It was during one of these vists, that they witnessed the melancholy end of John Hewet and Sarah Drewe, two rustic lovers, of which we have the following account from the pen of Gay, within a few days after :—

"They had passed through the various labors of the year together with the greatest satisfaction : if she milked, 'twas his morning and evening care to bring the cows to her hand. It was but last fair that he bought her a present of green silk for her straw hat, and the posy on her silver ring was of his choosing. Their love was the talk of the whole neighborhood : for scandal never affirmed that they had any other views than the lawful possession of each other in marriage. It was that very morning that they had obtained the consent of her parents, and it was but till the next week that they were to wait to be happy. Perhaps in the intervals of their work they were now talking of their wedding-clothes, and John was suiting several sorts of poppies and field flowers to her complexion, to choose her a hat for the wedding-day.

While they were thus busied, (it was on the last of July, between two and three in the afternoon,) the clouds grew black, and such a storm of lightning and thunder ensued, that all the laborers made the best of their way to what shelter the trees and hedges afforded. Sarah was frightened, and fell down in a swoon on a heap of barley. John, who never separated from her, sat down by her side having raked together two or three heaps, the better to secure her from the storm. Immediately there was heard so loud a crack, as if heaven had split asunder. Every one was now solicitous for the safety of his neighbor, and called to one another throughout the field. No answer being returned to those who called to our lovers, they stepped to the place where they lay. They perceived the barley all in a smoke; and then spied this faithful pair, John with one arm about Sarah's neck, and the other held over her, as to screen her from the lightning. They were struck dead, and stiffened in this tender posture. Sarah's left eyebrow was singed, and there appeared a black spot on her breast; her lover was all over black, but not the least sign of life were found in either. Attended by their melancholy companions, they were conveyed to the town, and the next day were interred in Stanton-Harcourt churchyard."

Lord Harcourt, Pope, and Gay, attended the funeral; and the peer, at the request of the poets, caused a stone to be laid over the grave of the lovers, and a mural tablet to be placed in the outward south wall of Stanton-Harcourt church, with the following inscription:—

> "Near this place lie the bodies of
> John Hewet and Sarah Drewe,
> An industrious young Man
> and virtuous Maiden of this Parish,
> who being at harvest work
> (with several others)
> were in one instant killed by Lightning
> the last day of July, 1718."

Pope and Gay, in fulfillment of a promise to Lord Harcourt that they would join in composing a poetical epitaph to be subjoined, proposed to him the following lines:—

> "When Eastern lovers feed the funeral fire,
> On the same pile the faithful pair expire;

> Here pitying Heaven that virtue mutual found,
> And blasted both that it might neither wound.
> Hearts so sincere, th' Almighty saw well pleas'd,
> Sent his own lightning, and the victims seiz'd."

Lord Harcourt candidly confessed that he did not much like this composition, and said the country people would not understand it. "Well, then," said Pope, "I will make one with something of Scripture in it, and with as little of poetry as Sternhold and Hopkins." He next day produced the lines still to be read in passing through this country churchyard, which Lord Harcourt allowed were equally distinguished for sublime piety and exquisite poetry—equally calculated to touch the heart of the refined critic, and of the peasant who required assistance to spell them out :—

> "Think not by rig'rous judgment seiz'd,
>   A pair so faithful could expire ;
> Victims so pure, Heaven saw well pleas'd,
>   And snatch'd them in celestial fire.
> Live well, and fear no sudden fate ;
>   When God calls virtue to the grave,
> Alike 'tis justice soon or late,
>   Mercy alike to kill or save,
> Virtue unmov'd can hear the call,
> And face the flash that melts the ball."

Soon after this, Lord Harcourt had the heavy misfortune to lose his only son, a most accomplished and promising young man, who was so much in the confidence of Harley, St. John, and Swift, as to be appointed by them secretary to the famous society of "BROTHERS," and who was expected himself to turn out a distinguished statesman and wit.[1] The afflicted father sought to mitigate his grief by recording the virtues of the deceased in an epitaph, but, after many efforts, he found that his feelings overpowered him when he tried to express them according to the rules of metrical composition. In this extremity he applied to his friend Pope, who, having long honored the father, had formed an acquaintance with the son, and readily undertook the mournful task. The lines as at first

---

[1] The young man not only resembled his father in genius, but very strikingly in looks—a circumstance to which Gay refers in his address to Pope on the completion of the far-famed translation of Homer, in which he supposes all the poet's friends assembled to welcome his return from Greece :—

> "Harcourt I see, for eloquence renown'd,
>   The mouth of justice, oracle of law !
> Another Simon is beside him found,
>   Another Simon, like as straw to straw."

proposed were not quite relished, and a correspondence took place with a view to their amendment. Of this, one letter has been preserved, which proves the critical acumen as well as the paternal tenderness of the ex-Chancellor:—

"December 6, 1722.

"I can not but suspect myself of being very unreasonable in begging you once more to review the inclosed. Your friendship draws this trouble on you. I may freely own to you that my tenderness makes me exceeding hard to be satisfied with anything which can be said on such an unhappy subject. I caused the Latin epitaph to be as often altered before I could approve of it.

"When once your epitaph is set up, there can be no alteration of it: it will remain a perpetual monument of your friendship, and, I assure myself, you will so settle it that it shall be worthy of you. I doubt whether the word *deny'd*, in the third line, will justly admit of that construction which it ought to bear, (viz.) renounced, deserted, &c. *Deny'd* is capable, in my opinion, of having an ill sense put upon it, as too great uneasiness, or more good nature, than a wise man ought to have. I very well remember you told me you could scarce mend these two lines, and therefore I can scarce expect your forgiveness for my desiring you to reconsider them.

"Harcourt stands dumb, and Pope is forc'd to speak."

I can not perfectly, at least without further discoursing with you, reconcile myself to the first part of that line; and the word *forc'd* (which was my own, and, I persuade myself, for that reason only submitted to by you) seems to carry too doubtful a construction for an epitaph, which, as I apprehend, ought as easily to be understood as read. I shall acknowledge it as a very particular favor if at your leisure you will peruse the inclosed, and vary it, if you think it capable of being amended, and let me see you any morning next week. I am," &c.

These suggestions were attended to, and the exquisite epitaph was produced which is now to be read on the monument erected in the church of Stanton-Harcourt to the memory of the son of the Chancellor:—

"To this sad Shrine, whoe'er thou art, draw near!
Here lies the Friend most lov'd, the Son most dear;
Who ne'er knew Joy, but Friendship might divide,
Or gave his Father Grief but when he died.

> "How vain is Reason, Eloquence how weak!
> If Pope must tell what Harcourt can not speak.
> Oh! let thy once lov'd Friend inscribe thy Stone,
> And, with a Father's sorrows, mix his own!"[1]

Lord Harcourt was likewise on terms of intimacy with the celebrated Dr. Mead, who not only took care of his health, but was of great service to him in collecting his library. The following is an original letter from the physician to the peer:—

"Ormond Street, July 25, 1723.

"My Lord,

"I do myself the honor to acquaint your Lordship that of the books expected from France, the TRACTATUS TRACTATUM, and one of those that belong to the King of France's collection, are come. The TRACTATUS is a fine copy. I have ordered my bookseller to collate it very carefully, and if it proves perfect, I shall purchase it for fourscore guineas, which is the lowest price, and I believe not dear. The book belonging to the French King's collection I shall take, and your Lordship shall not pay for it till the other volumes are sent over, which I hope will be quickly.

"Our friend, my Lord Bolingbroke, was seized yesterday with a violent fit of his ague, and I expect will have another to-morrow, and no more. I have advised him to hasten his journey to Aix, and I believe he will set out in a few days after your Lordship's coming to town. He desired me, with his humble service, to excuse his not writing by this post to your Lordship, upon the account of his indisposition.[2] I am, always with the greatest respect," &c.

I can only gratify any curiosity which may be felt respecting Lord Chancellor Harcourt's personal appearance by the following description of him a few years before his death, from the pen of a contemporary who knew him well: "He is a fair, lusty man; has been handsome; he has so much learning and eloquence, and so sweet a delivery, that he may not improperly be styled a second

---

[1] "This epitaph is principally remarkable for the artful introduction of the name, which is inserted with a peculiar felicity, to which chance must concur with genius, which no man can hope to attain twice, and which can not be copied but with servile imitation."—JOHNSON.

[2] It is supposed that Bolingbroke was shamming illness as a pretense for going abroad—a supposition contradicted by the letter, unless Mead was his accomplice.

Cicero; is extremely generous and good-humored; has been extravagant, but is now grave, and lives within bounds; hard study, and too much fatiguing himself in his business, have both spoiled his eyes and his constitution. He is about sixty years old."[1]

From the same authority we learn, that if he was not always very strict in the observance of outward religious duties, he was ready to atone for any irregularity into which he might have fallen:—" Ld. Chancellor Harcourt, traveling on Sunday through Abingdon in time of divine service, was stopped by the constables, by whom a humble apology was made to his Lordship for doing what they understood to be their duty; in consequence of which, his Lordship ordered his coach to the church-door, and joined in the public worship till the conclusion of it."[2]

He exercised a splendid hospitality in London, and at his country-house in Buckinghamshire. From his honorable savings he purchased large additions to his hereditary property—among others, the manor of Nuneham Courtenay, in Oxfordshire, where his successor built and laid out the splendid mansion and park, which became the chief residence of the family.

When a very young man, with little to live upon, he most imprudently contracted a private marriage with the daughter of his father's chaplain, who had nothing but beauty and an unspotted character to recommend her. With her he lived very happily, notwithstanding the pecuniary difficulties with which they had to struggle, and she brought him the son whose untimely end he had to weep. After her death, he married Elizabeth, daughter of Richard Spencer, Esq., of the county of Derby; and being again a widower, he married Elizabeth, daughter of Sir Thomas Vernon, Bart., but he had no issue by either of his last two wives.

He was succeeded in his titles and estates by his grandson, who, in the year 1749, was raised to an Earldom. In 1830, the male line of the Chancellor failed by the death of the third Earl without issue,—when the honors of the family became extinct, and the estates came to the venerable Archbishop of York[3]—who is descended from the Chancellor through a female, and, by royal license, has taken the name of Harcourt in addition to his own dis-

---

[1] Gent. Mag. vol. lxv. 467.   [2] Ibid.   [3] Dr. Vernon.

tinguished name of Vernon. The heir male of the English Harcourts, is George Simon Harcourt, Esq., of Ankerwyke, some time M.P. for Bucks, descended from Sir Philip Harcourt, the father of the Lord Chancellor, by his second wife, Elizabeth Lee.[1]

CHAPTER CXXI.

LIFE OF LORD MACCLESFIELD FROM HIS BIRTH TILL HE RECEIVED THE GREAT SEAL.

WE next come to a Chancellor, who, instead of "fetching his life and being from men of royal siege," and boasting of an illustrious pedigree for a thousand years, was the son of an obscure village lawyer, but who inherited from nature a most acute and vigorous intellect, who raised himself by unwearied perseverance and a stupendous store of acquired knowledge to the highest offices in the state, who, though precipitated from power by the judgment of his peers, was more unfortunate than criminal, and whose descendants, now flourishing and distinguished in the peerage of England, ought, notwithstanding the sentence pronounced upon him, to be proud of the founder of their house.

It might have been more interesting to have traced his career through difficulties and discouragements than if it had been the easy result of birth and fortune; but unluckily he has suffered more from biographical neglect than even Somers or Cowper, and the materials have perished from which it might have been hoped that tardy justice would still have been done to his memory. Unless when he was actually mixing in public transactions, little can be known of him by this age or by posterity.[2]

[1] From the information of my friend Mr. Pulman of the Herald's College.
[2] His venerable representative, the present Earl of Macclesfield, in a very kind answer to my inquiries respecting him, says—"I regret extremely that I can not give you any information as regards the early life of my ancestor, the Lord Chancellor Macclesfield, or after his retirement from public to private life. In the large collection of MS. letters I possess at Shirburn Castle there are very few of his, and I am sorry to add, *none* that would be of use to your Lordship for the valuable work you are now publishing. Had it been otherwise, I should with pleasure have forwarded them to you."—*30th April 1846.*

Thomas Parker, afterwards Lord Chief Justice of England, Lord High Chancellor of Great Britain, and Earl of Macclesfield, was born on the 23rd of July, 1666 (the "annus mirabilis"), at Leeke, in Staffordshire, where his father carried on the business of an attorney, and by the savings of a long life, accumulated a fortune of nearly £100 of annual rent. Having been taught to read by his mother,[1] he was put for two or three years to a free grammar school, in the neighboring town of Newport, in Shropshire. The two cleverest boys there were Tom Parker, and Tom Withers, the son of a shoemaker. They were in the same form, and friends, though rivals. The prognostications with respect to the latter were the most favorable, and he displayed such parts and application, that there was an attempt made to send him to the University by a subscription among the neighboring gentry. This failing, he was bound apprentice to his father, and flourished for many years as a shoemaker; but, not observing the maxim, "ne sutor ultra crepidam," he kept up his classical learning, quoted Homer and Virgil to his

After the publication of the first edition of this work I received from the Earl of Macclesfield a pedigree representing his ancestor as descended from the ancient family of the Parkers of Park Hall,—which may be correct, although, from an unfortunate fire at Park Hall, the documents to prove it were destroyed. I have most unintentionally, and to my great mortification as well as surprise, given offense to some of the Chancellor's descendants by my Life of him. As he was a good Whig, I had every desire to do him honor, and I really thought I should be accused of showing a bias in his favor. All the authentic accounts of him which have appeared represent that he was of obscure origin, that he was brought up as an attorney under his father, and that by extraordinary energy of character he conquered the difficulties of his early career. Therefore, I could not, and can not, narrate that, being the son of a wealthy father, as well as of high connections, he was early destined to the bar; that, after being at a public school, he went through a regular course of academical education at Cambridge; that he was then transferred to the Inns of Court, and that he advanced to eminence in the commonplace progress of a high-born university-bred barrister.

[1] She was of a respectable Cheshire family of the name of Venables. In the Diary of "Oliver Heywood, an ejected minister, and one of the founders of the Presbyterian congregations in the county of York," there is a curious notice respecting her, indicating that her marriage with the Leeke lawyer was considered a *mésalliance*:—"July, 1666. Went to Leeke, in Staffordshire, and visited one Mrs. Parker, Colonel Venable's daughter, who married against her father's consent. The thing is sadly aggravated, and he wonderfully exasperated against her. She weeps bitterly. Hath buried two children."—*Life of Heywood, by Hunter*, p. 179. This must have been immediately before the birth of her son Thomas. Little did the Cheshire squire think that he was to be grandsire to an earl, and placed in the pedigree of an illustrious house.

clerical customers, and fell into misfortunes in his old age. It is pleasant to think that the two schoolfellows socially met when the one occupied a stall at Newport, and the other was Lord Chief Justice of England,—and that they afterwards renewed their correspondence when the one, having lost all his customers, was reduced to penury, and the other had been precipitated with disgrace from the highest station a subject can hold in this kingdom.

Young Parker, although he picked up a smattering of Greek and Latin while at school, then knew little more than the peasantry among whom he was reared, and he may be considered as in a great measure self-taught. But he had acquired a taste for reading and a habit of steady application, to which all his future greatness must be ascribed. While still a boy he was placed in his father's office, and was articled as a clerk—to become himself an attorney. It is said that he displayed from the tenderest years most wonderful diligence and steadiness, and that, not contented with making himself perfect in the routine of his father's business, he read all the books of amusement and instruction on which he could lay his hands—spending the perquisites which came to him as clerk in the purchase of a little library of his own.

The father about this time removed from Leeke to Newcastle-under-Lyne; and the dutiful son following him, still displayed, we are told, the same attention to business and desire of self-improvement.

While he was so engaged, there is respecting him, in the admission book of the Inner Temple, the following perplexing entry:—

"Thomas Parker, Gent., sonne and heir apparent of Thomas Parker, of New Castle under Lyme, in the county of Stafford, Gent. Admitted 14th February, 1683[4]."

No explanation can be given of his admission to an Inn of Court when he was only in his eighteenth year, and in the middle of his apprenticeship. It may be conjectured that his father had humored his ambitious designs of being one day a counselor; or that, being sent up to do some law-business during the term in London, he had got himself admitted without his father's knowledge. Still greater perplexity arises from the following entry, to be found in the books of Trinity College, Cambridge:—

"Thomas Parker, Fil. Thomæ natus Newcastle under lime, Com. Stafford. E schola Derbiensi M^ro Ogden ludimagistro. Ætat. 18 Octob. 9. 1685. pens. M^ro Tho. Boteler Tutore."

The same Thomas Parker appears to have been matriculated on the 17th of December following. The first question is, whether this individual was Lord Macclesfield, who certainly was born at Leeke, not at Newcastle-under-Lyne; who certainly had been educated at the free grammar school of Newport;[1] and who, at the above date, was in his twentieth year. I have likewise ascertained that at the end of the 17th century there was another family of the name of Parker residing at Derby. I am inclined, however, to believe that Lord Macclesfield was the Thomas Parker here designated, for at some period or another his name had been inscribed as a member of Trinity College; and no other entry that can refer to him can be found in the books of that society. The probability is, that, ambitiously contemplating a call to the bar at some future period, he wished to have the *éclat* of being a Cambridge-man, and that a year and a half after he had entered himself of the Inner Temple he thus entered himself of Trinity College, not being very scrupulous as to the particulars which he gave of his place of birth and of his age.

It is certain, that he went on working in his father's office till, having regularly served his time, he was placed on the roll of attorneys, in the year 1686.

To prosecute his profession with more advantage, he established himself at Derby, a flourishing town, in which a wealthy client of his father had lately settled in trade, and promised to patronize him. Here he prospered beyond his most sanguine hopes, and, from his great skill and diligence, in a year or two his business, in point of extent and respectability, was equal to that of any attorney in the county. We know no further particulars of his history while he remained in this department of the profession, except that his house in Derby was in Bridge Street, at the foot of the bridge next the Three Crowns. We may imagine that, when the assizes came round, he was at first struck with immense awe at beholding the Judges in their scarlet robes, and could scarcely venture

[1] This education at Newport has been stoutly denied, but is placed beyond all doubt by his letter to Lord Chancellor King.

to speak to the leaders of the Midland Circuit on delivering them briefs in the causes which he had entered for trial; that his reverence for these dignitaries gradually dwindled away; that he began sometimes to think he himself could have examined witnesses quite as well as the barristers employed by him, and even, by making a better speech to the jury, have won verdicts which they lost; that he was likewise hurt by the distance at which he was in public kept by all members of the superior grade of the profession, while some of them were intensely civil to him in private; that he thought it hard, having with great labor prepared a case of popular expectation so as to insure victory, another should run away with all the glory; that he measured himself with those who were enjoying high reputation as advocates and had the prospect of being elevated to the bench; that, possessing the self-respect and confidence belonging to real genius, he felt himself superior to them; and that he sickened at the thought of spending the rest of his days in drawing leases, in receiving instructions from country bumpkins to bring foolish actions, in preparing briefs, and in making out bills of fees and disbursements which any discontented client might tax before the Master. Whatever his train of feeling or of reasoning might be, he soon resolved that he would quit his position of an attorney for that of a barrister.

Not having been at any public school or resided at a university, and having started in life so very early on his own account, he was still quite a young man when he had laid by enough decently to support him for some years to come. Instead of going on to accumulate a large fortune, which was easily within his reach, he nobly put all to hazard, that he might invest himself in the long robe. He is said to have had that presentiment of future greatness which sometimes springs up under very adverse circumstances, and leads to victory over all obstacles. He accordingly renounced his profitable business as an attorney at Derby, and removed to complete his terms as a student of law in the Inner Temple.

I regret exceedingly that I can find no particulars whatever of the next period of his life; and I am quite ignorant of the course of study he pursued, and the companions with whom he associated. That he was very diligent we need not doubt—still, mingling professional acquirements with an attention to more liberal pursuits.

Some have supposed that he now fixed himself at Cambridge, but no trace of him can be found in the books of Trinity College after his admission in 1685, and there seems great reason to doubt whether he ever revisited this celebrated seat of learning. Yet when he became Lord High Chancellor of Great Britain, his flatterers, while they discovered that he was descended from "Reginald Le Parker," who had accompanied Edward I., when Prince of Wales, to the Holy Land, asserted that he had gained great academical distinction on the banks of Cam. Thus wrote Eusden, the Poet-laureate—expecting a good sinecure in the Court of Chancery:—

> "Prophetic Granta, with a mother's joy,
> Saw greatness omen'd in the manly boy,
> Who mad'st her studies thy belov'd concern,
> Nor could she teach so fast as thou couldst learn,
> Still absent, thee our groves and muses mourn,
> Still sighing echoes the sad sound return;
> And CAM, with tears, supplies his streaming urn."

Parker was called to the bar on the 24th day of May, 1691.[1] And doubtless he began his new career with greater advantages—with a far better chance of getting on—than if he had been the younger son of an earl, and had taken a high degree at Oxford or Cambridge. Many attorneys and attorneys' clerks, whom he had known on a footing of familiar intimacy, were now desirous of pushing him forward; and from his former experience he was, when consulted, better able to assist them in the conduct of suits than barristers who, after graduating at the University, had merely gone through the usual curriculum at Lincoln's Inn or the Temple. The danger is, that a man who begins with the less liberal department of forensic procedure may not be able to enlarge his mind so as to perform the duties of a great advocate, and that when pleading before a special jury, or at the bar of the House of Lords, he may dwell earnestly on small and worthless

---

[1] "Interius Templum } Parliament tent 24º Die
   Willus Farrer, Arm^r { Maij Anno Dñi 1691, &c.
   Sob Dne Regine
   Thesaurarius ibm. }

"At this Parliament, Mr. Thomas Parker (and others) are called to the Bar and to be utter Barristers of this Society."

points. This may be the reason why, with splendid exceptions, attorneys turned barristers are generally unsuccessful. But it is quite certain that, whatever was Parker's course of study, he acquired a profound and scientific knowledge of the most abstruse branches of the law—that he rendered himself a most accomplished jurist, and that he became a consummate advocate.

His progress at the bar was rapid and steady. Of course he chose the Midland Circuit, and in a few years he was at the head of it. Yet he passed others without exciting envy or ill will; and his brother circuiteers, acquitting him of making any improper use of the advantages he derived from the early part of his career, candidly ascribed his extraordinary success to his extraordinary merit. He was now designated the "silver-tongued Parker," and the "silver-tongued counsel." It was some time before he had much business in Westminster Hall, but by degrees his circuit fame extended to the metropolis, and he was retained in most of the great causes which came on in the Court of Queen's Bench, sitting either in London or in Middlesex.

He first attracted the attention of the public as counsel for the defendant in the great case of *Regina* v. *Tutchin*, tried at Guildhall, before Lord Holt, November 4, 1704.[1] This was an information by the Attorney General against the publisher of a journal called the "Observator," for various alleged libels upon the Queen's Ministers, charging them with incapacity and an unskillful managment of the navy. Parker, who was throughout life a consistent politician, had strongly attached himself to the Whigs, and had been noticed by Somers, Cowper, and the leaders of that party as a rising lawyer. Along with Montague, the brother of Lord Halifax, he was now selected to defend their partisan. The alleged libels contained no reflection on the private characters of the Ministers, and the defendant's counsel contended that their public conduct was a fair subject of observation; but, to our surprise and mortification, we find that enlightened Judge, Lord Holt, telling the jury they were to consider "whether the alleged libels did not tend to beget an ill opinion of the administration of the government?"[2] The defendant

[1] 14 St. Tr. 1095.
[2] Some have supposed that Holt, who was a decided Whig, was subject to the

was found guilty; but he was saved from punishment by an objection afterwards taken to the regularity of the jury process. Parker's argument on this question (too technical for the general reader) is most masterly, and by genuine lawyers is perused with enthusiasm.[1]

His appearance in this case acquired him such *éclat* that his promotion was considered certain if ever the Whigs should come into office.

There was a partial change in the Administration in the following year,—when, taking the degree of the coif, he was made a Queen's Sergeant, and was knighted. He gave rings on this occasion to Queen Anne and Prince George of Denmark, with the complimentary motto, "MORIBUS, ARMIS, LEGIBUS."[2]

From strong local connection, he had been before appointed Recorder of Derby, and at the general election, which soon followed, he was returned to parliament as member for that borough, along with Lord James Cavendish. We know that he made a most favorable impression on the House, and that he frequently took part in debate, being a terror to the High Church party, and a praise and protection to such as supported religious and civil liberty; but, unfortunately, there is not to be found the smallest fragment of any of his speeches in parliament till the impeachment of Sacheverell.

Not being in the Cabinet, he is not answerable for this foolish measure. He probably regretted and condemned

weakness of a great mind, and that, to avoid the suspicion of partiality, he showed a leaning in favor of the Tory Ministers; but I believe that this doctrine was then considered to be law, and it will continue to be occasionally brought out till there is (as there ought to be) a statutable definition of the limits of free discussion.

[1] The admiration which has been expressed of Parker's argument on the "*Distringas*," reminds me of a saying of my deceased friend DUVAL, the greatest conveyancer of his day, who being asked by me "whether the constant perusal of abstracts of title was not weary work?" answered me, "Why, it is sometimes a little dull; but every now and then one meets with a *brilliant deed*, which is a reward for all one's labor!!!"

[2] He had a few months before been made a Bencher of the Inner Temple, —whether by ballot I know not:

"Interius Templum ⎫ Parliament tent decimo Octavo die
    Thomas Walker, Arm<u>r</u> ⎬   Maij, 1705, &c.
      Thesauraribus ibm. ⎭

"At this parliament, Mr. Thomas Parker (and others) are called to the Bench."

He does not appear ever to have been "Reader," or "Treasurer."

it, along with Somers and the other Whig lawyers; but when it was commenced, he did his best to bring it to a fortunate conclusion. He was appointed one of the managers on the part of the Commons. Burnet, giving an account of the trial, says, "Jekyll, Eyre, Stanhope, King, *but, above all, Parker*, distinguished themselves in a very particular manner: they did copiously justify both the Revolution and the present Administration." I must confess, however, that I have perused the report of his two long harangues at the bar of the House of Lords, on the 4th article, which was assigned to him, with considerable disappointment; and I can extract little from either of them to interest us in these times. He contended that the defendant had falsely and maliciously charged her Majesty's Administration, both in ecclesiastical and civil affairs, as tending to the destruction of the constitution.

Why those who entertained such a bad opinion of her Majesty's Administration should not have been at full liberty to express it, we are rather at a loss to understand. But Sergeant Parker, in the name of the Commons of England, upbraids "the Doctor" for his rudeness in assailing the character of the Ministers and the measures of their government. He is rather happy in contrasting the defendant's incitements to insurrection with his doctrine of non-resistance. "Not in terms of lamentation," said Sergeant Parker, "not as grounds of humiliation, or in a language that might become one that thought the only arms of the Church to be prayers and tears, does he assail the Government; but with all malice, bitterness, reviling, insolence,—endeavoring to raise in his auditors the passions himself puts on, and pointing out (as far as he dares) to arms and violence for a cure: On his own principles, he ought to have taught the people to do their duty, submitting wholly to the Queen and those in authority under her, and to leave the rest to God: But, following his advice, they would instantly rise in a mass, and if they did not at once restore the Pretender, they would forcibly expel from office, and utterly crush all who, on the doctrine of resistance to tyranny, were concerned in the Revolution: Is this sermon an exhortation to piety and virtue? or is it not manifestly a trumpet to rebellion? Does the preacher show his congregation their own faults that they may amend their lives, or attempt to expose the faults of the Government with a view to a forcible change? The duty of passive obedience is so warmly inculcated to cause the destruction of those who deny it: The whole discourse exhorts to insurrection and not to submission." He thus concluded:—" My Lords, the Commons have the greatest and justest veneration for the clergy of the Church of England, and it is with regret and trouble that they find themselves obliged to bring before your Lordships, in this manner, one of that order. But when we find Dr. Sacheverell stripping himself of all that peaceful and charitable temper which the Christian religion requires of all its professors, deserting the example of our Lord and Master, and of his holy apostles, and with rancor branding all who differ from him (though through ignorance) with the titles of hypocrites, rebels, traitors, devils; reviling them, exposing them, conducting them to hell, and leaving them there; treating every one who falls in his way worse than Michael the Archangel used Satan; despising dominion, speaking evil of dignities: like raging waves of the sea, foaming out his own shame; then laboring to sap the establishment, and railing and declaiming against the Government; crying *to arms!* and blowing a trumpet in Sion to engage his country in seditions and tumults, and overthrow the best constitution, and betray the best Queen that ever made a nation happy, and this with Scripture in his mouth; the Commons looked upon him, by this behavior, to have severed himself from all the rest of the clergy; they thought it their duty to bring to justice such a criminal; and they are in no fear of being thought discouragers of those who preach virtue and piety because they, in the supreme court of justice, prosecute him who preaches sedition and rebellion, or to have any design of lessening the respect due to the clergy by bringing to punishment him who disgraces that sacred order."[1]

Sergeant Parker afterwards replied to the speeches of the counsel for the defendant, and of the defendant himself, and obtained loud applause for the unsparing manner in which he assailed them:—"My Lords," said he, "I am amazed that a person in holy orders, in his distinguished habit, before this awful assembly, should dare to take the tremendous name of God into his lips, and appeal to the

[1] 15 St. Tr. 186.

Supreme Being for the sincerity and integrity of his heart at the very time when he stands under such a charge, and is neither able to repel it, nor has the sincerity and honesty to repent—to take shame upon himself in the most public way, and to ask pardon of God and of the world for the sin and the crime of which he is guilty. I hope the clergy will be instructed not to preach the doctrine of submission in such manner as to prepare the way for rebellion." But by far the finest part of the reply was the felicitous quotation from Scripture:—" In what moving and lively colors does the holy Psalmist paint the crafty insidiousness of such wily *Volpones!* 'Wickedness is therein; deceit and guile go not out of their streets. For it is not an open enemy that hath done me this dishonor, for then I could have borne it: neither was it mine adversary that did magnify himself against me, for then, peradventure, I would have hid myself from him. But it was even thou, my companion, my guide, and mine own familiar friend. There is no faithfulness in their mouths, their inward parts are very wickedness: their mouths are open sepulchres, and their words are smoother than oil, yet be they very swords! Like Joab they pretend to speak peaceably, and smite us mortally under the fifth rib.'"[1]

Whatever we may think of the Sergeant's performances on this occasion, they gave the highest possible satisfaction to the true VOLPONE, whose the impeachment was; and Lord Chief Justice Holt having died while the proceeding was pending, Sergeant Parker was instantly appointed to succeed him,—the Attorney and Solicitor General, who had been less zealous in the prosecution, being passed over.[2] According to Burnet, an inference was drawn from " this great promotion "—that the Queen, who had attended during the whole of the trial, favored the prosecution, " for none of the managers had treated Sacheverell so severely as he had done;"[3] but, in reality, she had only constitutionally taken the advice of her ministers while she employed them, though she was eagerly desirous to get rid of them.

[1] 15 St. Tr. 454.
[2] This appointment took place on the 13th of March, and judgment was not given on Sacheverell till the 23d of the same month.—*2 Lord Raymond, 1309.*
[3] Burnet, iv. 285. De Foe thus jeeringly addressed the High Churchmen on this appointment: " You are desired to take particular notice of her

Parker remained Chief Justice of England for eight years, and it could not be said of him, as of some popular lawyers, who, upon their elevation to high judicial office, have disappointed public expectation," Omnium consensu capax imperii nisi imperasset." His fame as a common law chief is not quite equal to that of his immediate predecessor; but this probably arises from there not having been in his time any controversies between the two Houses of Parliament, or any questions of great political interest coming before him for judicial decision. He was during this part of his career never suspected of any sort of corruption, and the only charge I find brought against him is of having been sometimes rather discourteous to the bar. This is not enough to lower him much in our estimation. Although I can conceive no more striking proof of a mean spirit than for a barrister, when put upon the bench, really to behave with insolence or ill temper to his former competitors at the bar, it is rather difficult for a Judge altogether to escape the imputation of discourtesy if he properly values the public time; for (according to a dictum of the great Lord Lyndhurst) one of his duties is "to render it disagreeable to counsel to talk nonsense."[1] Chief Justice Parker's judgments show an accurate acquaintance with his subject, a logical mind, and great power of illustration.

He began his judicial career with the trial of Damaree and Purchase for being concerned in the Sacheverell riots and assisting to pull down dissenting meeting houses. Although this prosecution was, I think, exceedingly discreditable to the Whig Government, I know not that the Lord Chief Justice of the Queen's Bench can be much blamed for it, as we can not suppose that he was consulted respecting the manner of shaping the offense; and if it was charged as high treason, there were distinct authori-

Majesty having severely punished Sir Thomas Parker, one of the managers of the House of Commons, for his barbarous treatment of the Doctor in pretending in a long speech to show, as he called it, the impatience and superficial jingle of the Doctor's speech. Her Majesty being, as you know, heartily concerned for this prosecution, hath testified her care of the Doctor's character in most justly punishing that forward gentleman, having condemned him for his boldness to perpetual confinement, being appointed to the constant drudgery of Lord Chief Justice of the Queen's Bench, a cruel and severe sentence indeed!"

[1] I wrote this when I had no prospect of becoming a Judge. Having now been a Judge near seven years, I adhere to the sentiment, hoping that the duty may be performed without the imputation.—*Sept. 1856.*

ties for holding it to be so, although most lawyers probably now think that thereby the statute of Edward III. was overstrained, if not perverted. He would have acted a nobler part if he had summed up for an acquittal; but he pressed for a conviction. In commenting upon the evidence in favor of the character of the prisoners, he said "There is another unfortunate circumstance I must observe, that we are in a time when many people were led into a belief that doing these actions was a commendable thing; that it was a showing their zeal to the Queen and the Church. And if that be the case, reputation and previous good behavior are of no avail, and raise no presumption against guilt. Dr. Sacheverell (I would not reflect upon him; he has undergone a censure elsewhere) fell foul of the Toleration Act, and these people, thinking him a confessor for the Church, thought they could do no less than pull down meeting houses, which they considered the seminaries of schism. The doctrine of non-resistance, pronounced to be the doctrine of the Church, is to be propagated by resistance; these people will resist, to show they are not for resisting. The Queen's guards are to be attacked, to illustrate the rule of passive obedience. When a madness has got among the people, many unaccountable things will be done by men of reputable character. Those who honor Dr. Sacheverell for the things which parliament was condemned, might think it honorable to demolish meeting houses, and to raise seditions and riots which are not to be borne in a civilized country." Upon the law of the case he was clear and explicit: "A brothel," said he, "is a nuisance, and may be punished as such; and being a particular nuisance to any one, if he enters to abate it, he may only be guilty of a riot; but if he will presume to pull down all brothels, he has taken the Queen's right out of her hand, and has committed high treason by compassing her death, and levying war against her in her realm.—Of brothels, so of meeting houses." Let us hope that the Lord Chief Justice was ashamed to feel himself obliged to talk such nonsense, although backed by the other Judges; and that it was through his merciful interference that the prisoners, though found guilty, and sentenced to a cruel death, were reprieved and pardoned.[1]

[1] 15 St. Tr. 522-703. No other Crown case of any importance came before

When the change of government took place in the autumn of the same year, Harcourt wishing to continue in the office of Attorney General, and Lord Cowper declining to remain Chancellor, the Great Seal was offered to Lord Chief Justice Parker, and even pressed upon him. He is much lauded for his virtuous self-denial, and it is sarcastically observed that "he is the first lawyer who ever refused an absolute offer of the Seals from a conscientious difference of opinion."[1] I am very sorry to appear to detract from his merit; but, principle not considered, he would have acted very foolishly to have given up his place of Chief Justice, which he held for life, in exchange for an office the tenure of which would have been very insecure; for, till after Guiscard's desperate attempt, Harley expected almost daily to be turned out;— and, at any rate, such a sudden change to the High Church party by the most distinguished manager of the late impeachment, would have reasonably led to the conclusion that he would give his first piece of preferment to the "Doctor," and would have covered him with such infamy that he must have been treated contumeliously by his colleagues, and kicked out by them whenever they wished to get rid of him. The wonder, therefore, is that the offer should have been made—not that it was rejected.

Parker was out of parliament for the rest of this reign, and he devoted himself exclusively to the discharge of his judicial duties. In prosecutions for libels during the Tory Government, he was supposed to bear very hard upon those who attacked the Whigs. He had caused some alarm to Swift, the most virulent of libelers[2]—as we

him while Chief Justice; and his only opinion as a Common Law Judge in a civil case which attracted much notice was on the question whether the word "purchase," in 11 & 12 W. 3, c. 4, against Papists acquiring property, was confined to the acquisition of property by "purchase" in common parlance, or meant every acquisition of property except by "descent." Being called in to assist Lord Chancellor Harcourt, he was for giving the word its largest sense, although occurring in a penal statute, that he might effectuate the intention of the legislature in putting down Popery. The Chancellor decided the other way; but his decree was reversed by the House of Lords.—*Roper* v. *Radcliffe*, 9 Mod. 167; 1 Br. P. C. 450.

[1] Parke's "Court of Chancery," 291.
[2] Morphew, the publisher of Swift's "Conduct of the Allies," had been summoned before the Chief Justice, threatened with severe punishment if he persisted in concealing the author's name, and bound over to appear next term to plead to an indictment for a seditious libel.

learn from the following anecdote related in the "Journal to Stella:" "I was to-day at a trial between Lord Landsdowne and Lord Carteret, two friends of mine. It was in the Queen's Bench for about £6,000 a year. I sat under Chief Justice Parker, and his pen falling down I reached it up. He made me a low bow; and I was going to whisper him that 'I had done good for evil, for he would have taken mine from me.' I told it Lord Treasurer and Bolingbroke. Parker would not have known me if several Lords on the Bench and in the Court, bowing, had not turned everybody's eyes and set them a whispering. I owe the dog a spite, and will pay him in two months at farthest if I can."[1]

This threat Swift afterwards executed, by inserting the following passage in his famous pamphlet, entitled "The Public Spirit of the Whigs," denouncing the Chief Justice as a favorer of publications which attacked the Tories, while he punished High Church publications with relentless severity, and as having become a keen supporter of the Protestant succession after having been a rank Jacobite:—"I look upon it as a great evil to see seditious books dispersed among us, apparently striking at the Queen and her Administration, at the constitution in church and state, and at all religion; but whether this remissness may be imputed to Whitehall or to Westminster Hall, is other men's business to inquire. As for the poor nonjuring clergyman who was trusted with committing to the press a late book on the subject of hereditary right, by a strain of *summum jus,* he is now, as I am told, with half a score children, starving and rotting among thieves and pickpockets in the common room of a stinking jail. However, I would fain ask one single person in the world a question—'Why he has so often drank the abdicated King's health upon his knees?' But the transition is natural and frequent, and I shall not trouble him for an answer." If the taunt against Parker as against Somers had been that he was "sprung from the dregs of the people," however ungenerous it might have been, there would have been some color for it; but the reckless invention of a falsehood seems necessary to give full gratification to Swift's malignity. Well might the renegade Whig say that "transitions were natural, and fre-

[1] 28th October, 1712.

quent."—The Chief Justice wisely took no notice of this libel; and the Scotch nobility would have acted a more dignified part if they had imitated his example, instead of whiningly going in a body to Queen Anne and insisting that a reward should be offered for the discovery of the author, because it likewise attacked them saying that "their whole revenues before the union would have ill maintained a Welsh justice of peace, and that some of them had since gathered in England more money than ever any Scotchman who had not traveled could form an idea of."[1]

De Foe, who had celebrated Parker's elevation to the bench, had recently been gained over by the personal civilities of Queen Anne; and, being brought before him on a charge of libel, the Chief Justice is said to have expressed satisfaction "that so notorious a libeler was about to be punished for going against his old friends and principles." This story is highly improbable; but the Chief Justice certainly somehow had offended the Journalist very deeply, for he was now violently vituperated in the "Review," a periodical in which Daniel for a time assailed the Whigs under pretense of going beyond them in liberality.

The Chief Justice was sworn of the Privy Council at the time when he was raised to the bench, and he was summoned to give his advice upon the Recorder's report of capital convictions at the Old Bailey. As he was not a member of the Cabinet, and he still avowedly adhered to the party opposed to the Government, we should have thought this the only occasion when he would have attended on being summoned; but I am perplexed by meeting in Swift's "Journal to Stella," under date April 7, 1713, with the following entry: "At a council held to-night the Lord Chief Justice Parker, a Whig, spoke against the peace; so did Cholmondeley, another Whig, who is Treasurer of the household." I can only conjecture that a general meeting of the Privy Council had been held for formal business, when these two individuals, without being asked, took this opportunity to express

---

[1] This seems to have been the notion of the Earl of Salisbury, who, to cure the extravagance of James I, caused to be exposed upon a table in silver, for the King's inspection, a sum of money for which his Majesty had given a written order on the Exchequer.

their opinion on the great question of peace and war in the Queen's hearing.¹

The last instance I have discovered of the interference of the Chief Justice of England as a magistrate of police was by Parker, in Queen Anne's time,—to counteract the plot that was going on shortly before her death to bring in her brother to succeed her. An information being laid before him as Chief Justice respecting the unlawful enlistment of soldiers, he granted a warrant, under which one Kelly was arrested a few days after at Deal, with five men he had enlisted, bearing a pass from the Earl of Middleton, Secretary of State to James III.,—whereupon Bolingbroke was reluctantly obliged to issue a proclamation offering a reward for the apprehension of the Pretender, if he should land in England.²

Under the Regency Bill the Chief Justice of the King's Bench had important functions to perform on a demise of the Crown, being one of the seven official Lords Justices who, together with those personally appointed by the successor, were to carry on the government till his arrival. Upon the summons of all Privy Councillors to attend, after the Queen with a dying hand had delivered the Treasurer's staff to the Duke of Shrewsbury, Chief Justice Parker immediately repaired to Kensington, and joined in the measures which were taken to secure the succession of the House of Hanover.

When George I. landed at Greenwich, Chief Justice Parker was on the beach along with the other Lords Justices, and met with a very flattering reception from the new Sovereign, who had been told that he was a good Whig, and a warm friend to the Revolution settlement. He, who had started as an attorney's clerk in a small provincial town, and had got on by a vigorous intellect joined with stupendous application to business, now showed in a marvelous manner the versatility of his powers, by becoming a courtier and making himself personally agreeable to George I. and the German attendants who accompanied him, male and female. Whether, like Sir Robert Walpole, he conversed with the King in bad Latin, or how he made himself intelligible to the others,

¹ Cholmondeley for this impertinence was immediately turned out of the household—*Journ.* April 8, 1713. Parker luckily held "quamdiu se bene gesserit." ² 6 Parl. Hist. 1358.

I have not been able to ascertain, but he certainly was early a great favorite with them, and they wished to give him the Great Seal,—probably from an expectation that a new Chancellor, entirely of their own making would pass whatever grants they chose to ask.

There were intrigues for this purpose on foot so early as the spring of 1715, although I can not say that Parker was himself privy to them, and they gave rise to reports of Lord Cowper's speedy resignation. Subsequently an ineffectual attempt was made to induce him to exchange his office for that of President of the Council—from a pretended regard for his health, but from a real dislike of a Chancellor who had objected to improper grants of honors and money. Meanwhile, Parker was raised to the peerage by the title of Baron Parker, of Macclesfield, in the county of Chester; and, the better to enable him to support this dignity, a pension for life was bestowed upon him of £1,200 a year.

Being now legitimately restored to politics, he was very diligent in his attendance in the House of Lords, and took an active part in debate, although still we have to lament that we have hardly any remains of his oratory. His maiden speech as a Peer is said to have been *against* the Septennial Bill, which surprises us much, as the measure was supported by almost all Whigs and courtiers; but he had either been influenced by the grave objections to it on constitutional grounds, or had thought it convenient to show that he could make himself formidable. He called up Lord Cowper, from whose defense (as reported) it might be inferred that the Chief Justice had made a violent attack upon the King's Ministers, and had even reflected upon the severity exercised towards those engaged in the late rebellion.¹

But Lord Parker warmly supported the Government, when, after long delays, the Earl of Oxford's impeachment at last came to a hearing. Lord Harcourt having moved, on the dexterous suggestion of Walpole, that evidence should not be received respecting " high crimes and misdemeanors " till the articles charging " high treason " were disposed of, our law Lord answered, " that in all courts of judicature it is the usual and constant method to go through all the evidence before judgment be given

¹ 7 Parl. Hist. 305, 306.

upon any part of the accusation; that though the House of Peers be the supreme court of the kingdom, yet it has ever a regard to the rules of equity, and even to the forms observed in the courts below—which rules and forms required that the trial should be conducted as the Commons proposed—and thus only could the conduct of the prisoner be satisfactorily investigated and justice done between him and the country." He concluded with the following unfeeling sentiment—little foreseeing that he himself was one day to stand disgracefully at the same bar as a convicted culprit: "As for the noble Earl appearing at the bar in the abject condition of a traitor, it is but a piece of formality, which does him no manner of hurt, and to which persons of the highest rank have ever submitted to clear their innocence."[1] But the opinion had become very general that the prosecution was oppressive, and many of Oxford's former opponents supported the motion which put an end to it.[2]

Nothing ingratiated Lord Parker with the King so much as the opinion which he himself gave, and in which he prevailed on a great majority of the Judges to concur, respecting the power of the reigning Sovereign over his grandchildren. There was now such open enmity between his Majesty and the Prince of Wales that Lord Carteret declared prophetically, "This family will quarrel from generation to generation."[3] The Prince's numerous children were all in England except Frederick, the eldest, left behind in Hanover; and the King, to annoy his son, asserted the power by his prerogative to direct their education, and prospectively to dispose of them in marriage. The Prince *contra* maintained that, by the law of nature and by the law of the land, this power belonged exclusively to himself, as their father and the heir apparent to the Crown. Lord Chancellor Cowper would not take upon himself to decide the question, and wrote a letter to Lord Parker signifying the King's pleasure, that all the Judges should meet, and give him their opinion, "Whether the

---

[1] 7 Parl. Hist. 486   [2] Ante, p. 242.
[3] "There have been four Princes of Wales since the death of Anne, and all the four have gone into bitter opposition."—*Lord Mahon*, i. 314. The scandalous St. Simon thus accounts for the dislike of the first to the second George: Jamais le Père n'avoit pu souffrir ce fils, parcequ'il ne le croyait point à lui."—*Mem.* xxviii. 197. But the prevailing opinion now is, that Sophia of Zell was ever a true wife.

education and the care of the persons of his Majesty's grandchildren, now in England, and of Prince Frederick, eldest son of his Royal Highness the Prince of Wales, when his Majesty shall think fit to cause him to come into England, and the ordering the place of their abode, and appointing their governors, governesses, and other instructors, attendants, and servants, and the care and approbation of their marriages, when grown up, do belong of right to his Majesty as King of this realm?" The truth was, that as no King of England had lived to have grandchildren in the male line since the time of Edward III., when the Black Prince was allowed to have the care of his son Richard,—and as no institutional writer had discussed the subject, the Judges had no materials for giving a judicial opinion upon the first branch of the question; and with respect to the second, although the reigning Sovereign had exercised a control over the marriages of the royal family, and the contracting of a marriage with any of the blood royal without his consent was considered a contempt of the Crown, such marriages were undoubtedly valid in law, and the only mode of punishing those concerned in them was by a prosecution in the Star Chamber,—so that when this Court was abolished, the alleged prerogative was without any means of vindication or redress. However, Lord Parker, having assembled all the Judges at his chambers in Sergeants' Inn, read the Lord Chancellor's letter to them, and intimated his own opinion strongly to be that the whole of the question was to be answered absolutely in the affirmative. He was able to bring forward nothing in support of the grandfather's right to have the care of his grandchildren, except that "the law of God and law of nature are *rather* with the grandfather." But he showed by various instances, beginning with the match made by Henry III. between his sister Joan, without asking her consent, and Alexander, King of Scots, that the Kings of England had assumed to themselves, and had generally been allowed to exercise, the right of disposing in marriage of those who, being of the blood royal, were in the succession to the throne. He prevailed upon nine of the Judges to agree with him; but two, Baron Price, and Baron Eyre, the Prince of Wales's Chancellor, differed— returning for answer, that though the approbation of the marriages of the royal family belonged to the King, there was no instance where a marriage had been treated by the King for any of the royal family without the consent of the father, and that the case of the Prince of Wales was no exception to the general rule by which the father has a right to the custody and education of his children. George I. was exceedingly delighted with having so large a majority of the Judges in his favor, and he ordered their opinions to be recorded in the Books of the Privy Council, as a warrant for the authority which he was resolved to maintain. He attributed this triumph over his son mainly to the exertions of Lord Chief Justice Parker, which may possibly account for the transfer of the Great Seal which so speedily followed.[1]

CHAPTER CXXII.

CONCLUSION OF THE LIFE OF LORD MACCLESFIELD.

EARL COWPER, from whatever cause, having on the 18th of April, 1718, resigned his office, the Great Seal was, for a short time, put into commission,—the Commissioners being Mr. Justice Tracy, Mr. Justice Pratt, and Mr. Baron Montague. The general expectation was that the "good old Whig," Sir Joseph Jekyll, who was Master of the Rolls, with great reputation as an Equity Judge, and enjoying his faculties unimpaired, though well stricken in years, would have been appointed to succeed him,—the then Attorney and Solicitor General not being very eminent in their profession.[2] But on the 12th of May, to the great surprise of Westminster Hall and of the public, it was announced that Lord Parker, from being Lord Chief Justice of England, had become Lord High Chancellor.[3] Lord Holt, Lord Mansfield, and Lord Ellenborough refused the offer which

---

[1] 15 St. Tr. 1195. Things remained on this footing till the year 1722, when the Royal Marriage Act passed, 12 Geo. 3 c. 11. Some legislation was probably necessary; but the provisions of that Act have produced serious evils, and will require modification.

[2] Lechmere, the Attorney, accepted a peerage and was soon forgotten. Thompson, the Solicitor, was dismissed for a false charge of corruption against his colleague. [3] Cr. Off. Min. 140 b.

he accepted, and it would have been well for him if he had adopted the same course, as thereby he would have escaped the temptations and perils which proved his ruin. But I can not condemn the choice which he made. He felt that he could creditably perform the duties of his new office, and he might think that he was likely to do more in it for his own reputation, and for the public advantage than if he had remained a Common-Law Judge. He made an excellent bargain for himself and his family —according to which, beyond the £2,000 usually granted with the Great Seal for equipment, and £4,000 a year salary, and beyond other profits and presents, he actually received the sum of £12,000 in ready money from the King,—and a tellership of the Exchequer was bestowed upon his son. Three days after his appointment, he led a grand procession from the Inner Temple to Westminster, and he was installed in the Court of Chancery with the usual solemnities. Afterwards,[1] probably in performance of a promise made to him, he was created Earl of Macclesfield; and it will be convenient that henceforth I should give him his new title, by which, as Chancellor, he is historically known.

Trinity College was now eager to claim the dispenser of church patronage as an *alumnus*, and the following address was voted to him :—

"My Lord,

"As the great and eminent virtues and abilities whereby you have been long distinguished, and by which you have filled and adorned so many and so important stations, have been lately called to a further advance, and to display themselves in a yet more exalted sphere, so that we now behold your Lordship invested with supreme dignity, and entering on the custody and conduct of the most arduous as well as the most illustrious province of the Law; and as we have this peculiar happiness and glory belonging to us, that, together with those great ornaments of the profession, the Lord Chief Justice Cook, and the Lord Chancellor Bacon, *your Lordship's name is recorded among us*,[2] and that so noble a triumvirate were all members of our Society; we, therefore, the Master and

[1] 15th Nov. 1721.
[2] This language seems rather to corroborate the conjecture that he had never resided at College as an undergraduate.

Senior Fellows of Trinity Coll., esteeming it a duty we owe not only to y^r Lordship, but to our Society, not to be silent upon so great an occasion, have appointed two of our Fellows, D^r. Baker and D^r. Rudd, personally to wait upon y^r Lordship in our names and behalf; being with all veneration and respect may it please y^r Lordship,

"Y^r Lordship's most devoted
"Humble Servants,
"&c. &c. &c."[1]

Notwithstanding his high reputation, the old Equity practitioners grumbled at his appointment, because he had not been trained to draw bills and answers, and had never regularly practiced at their bar. Although occasionally he had been called in to assist them in cases of importance, his regular routine had been to ride the Midland Circuit, and to sit first in the Court of Queen's Bench, and then in the Court of Common Pleas, till he was made a Judge. Never having been Attorney or Solicitor General, he had never, even for a single term, transferred himself to the Court of Chancery. The consequence was, that although he was regarded generally as a "dungeon of law," yet, by those who knew little beyond the technical rules of Chancery pleading, it was thought he never could be made to understand them, and, therefore, that he was quite unfit for his office.

He turned out to be one of the greatest Equity Judges who ever sat in the Court of Chancery; and not only is he entitled to the equivocal compliment that none of his judgments were reversed, but his authority upon all points, whether of a practical or abstruse nature, is now as high as that of Nottingham, Somers, or Hardwicke.

I am sorry I can not praise him for any correction of abuses in his Court. Well would it have been, not only

---

[1] One of the deputation was the Rev. Dr. Rudd, and in his MS. Diary is to be found the following curious account of their reception :—" 1718, May 27. Dr Baker & I were sent by ye M^r & Sen^{rs} to wait upon my Ld Parker wth a Letter & a complem^t from ye Coll : upon his beg prefer'd to be Ld High Chan : because He was formerly of o^r Coll : we delivered ye letter on ye 29 & w^{re} invited to dine wth his L^{d}sp on June 2^d. beg Whitson-Monday, & bring wth us such of o^r Fellows as we c^d meet wth in Town. Accordgly we went ab^t a doz: of us to Kensington, w^{re} we w^{re} entertain'd very nobly & very kindly by His L^{d}sp till ab^t 7 in ye Even^g. I return'd to Coll : on ye 4th."

for his fame, but for his fortune, had he begun with making regulations against the sale of offices, and for securing the money of the suitors. Alas! he was under the dominion of a vice which was an effectual bar to all such improvements—AVARICE. This never seduced him to receive a bribe, but drove him as long as he could consider himself protected by existing usages, however objectionable, to regard the accumulation of wealth as the great object of his existence. Hence, he not only proposed no Bill in Parliament, and issued no General Order for remedying the evils which must forcibly have struck him when he first examined the Master's offices, and saw how the interests of the suitors were sacrificed by the prevailing system; but, for his own benefit, he carried venality in the disposal of offices to a pitch before unknown. When he must have been aware that the South Sea madness had taken possession of the functionaries acting under his control, to the peril of those who were entitled to his protection, he would not interfere,—from the dread of touching his own emoluments,—till, in the midst of his sordid infatuation, he was suddenly precipitated from power, and (what he probably felt as a greater misfortune) he was stripped of a large portion of his illgotten gains.

There were loud complaints of his discourtesy to some counsel, and his partiality to others, particularly to Philip Yorke, afterwards Earl of Hardwicke, which gave deep offense to the bar and hastened his own fall.

In deciding on his own tribunal between litigating parties, however, he displayed in every other respect the high qualities of a consummate magistrate. We are not told, and it would be idle to conjecture, the course of study he pursued for making himself master of Equity, or the method he adopted in thoroughly comprehending and preparing satisfactorily to decide the important cases which came before him. His leading judgments must have been the results of much labor and anxiety applied to each of them, as well as of profound learning and an extraordinary share of logical acuteness. They are chiefly to be found in the first and second volumes of Peere Williams, who is an accurate and skillful reporter, but unfortunately is too succinct in stating the *rationes decidendi*, and does not do justice to the methodical arrangement and nervous language for which Lord Macclesfield was celebrated.

I shall select a few of his decisions which I may hope to make intelligible to non-professional readers. An ancestor of the late Sir Francis Burdett devised his estates " in case he should leave no son at the time of his death " to his cousin, Francis Hopegood, and died leaving his wife pregnant without his knowledge [*privement ensient*]. She gave birth to a son—and the question was, which should have the estates ?—the devisee contending that the testator had *left no son at the time of his death,* as it was then doubtful whether any child would be born of the widow, and what the sex might be, so that the estates vested in the devisee, and could not be devested by the son's subsequent birth. But Lord Macclesfield, after consulting the Judges of the Court of Common Pleas, held that the infant, Sir Robert Burdett, though not actually born at the death of his father, yet in the eye of the law had existence in his mother's womb [*ventre sa mere*],—as if a pregnant woman takes poison to kill her child, and the child being born alive, dies of the poison, she is guilty of murder ; an unborn child therefore may take as heir or devisee, and here it could not be imagined that the testator ever intended to disinherit his own son.[1] So the estates remained with the Burdetts. There being a bequest, however, by the Duke of Devonshire, of a sum of money " to all the natural children of his son by Mrs. Heneage," and the question arising whether natural children born after the will should share, Lord Macclesfield held that even a child of which Mrs. Heneage was pregnant at the time of the will, was excluded, for a bastard can only take by its name of reputation, which it can not acquire till after its birth.[2]

An act was passed in the reign of Queen Anne,[3] " to oblige the Jews to maintain and provide for their Protestant *children,*" whereby it was enacted, that " if any Jewish parent, in order to compel his Protestant *child* to change his or her religion, shall *refuse* to allow such Protestant *child* fitting maintenance suitable to the degree or

---

[1] *Sir Robert Burdett* v. *Hopegood,* 1 P. W. 486.
[2] *Metham* v. *Duke of Devon,* 1 P. W. 529. This decision was followed by Sir W. Grant, M. R., in *Earle* v. *Wilson,* 17 Ves. 528 ; and in *Arnold* v. *Preston,* 18 Ves. 288. [3] 1 Anne, c. 30.

ability of the parent, and to the age and education of such *child*, it shall be lawful to the Lord Chancellor to make such order for the maintenance of such Protestant *child* as he shall think fit." A Jew had a daughter, Jessica, who turned Protestant. The rich father left the whole of his great wealth to charity. The daughter having reached the mature age of forty-four years, and being married to a Christian, petitioned for a maintenance under this statute. There were great difficulties in her way, for supposing her to be still a *child*, it was objected, how could her father be said to have *refused* to allow her a maintenance, when she did not allege that she had ever asked him to do so? *Lord Chancellor:* "I strongly incline to think this case within the act. The petitioner is the Protestant child of a Jewish parent, though the parent be dead. Suppose the child of a Jew turns Protestant, and the Jew by will gives his estate to trustees upon a secret trust that if the child turn Jew, the child shall have the estate, and not otherwise: as this would be clearly within the mischief, so every one must wish it to be within the meaning of the act. It is not said that the complaint shall be against the *father*, nor that the order shall be made upon or against the *father*, so that this case fits every word made use of by the legislature. Suppose, a petition being exhibited, the Jew had died pending the suit, having given all away from his Protestant child for having become Protestant, doubtless the order might be made against the *executor*. Then, as to the *refusal* of the parent, it is not to be intended that the Jew must make an actual refusal in words, for by that construction the statute might easily be evaded. If the Jew does by his will dispose of all his estate from his child, this is in law a *refusal;* and, unless some other reason appear, it shall be understood, *because the child was a Protestant*. The obligations of nature plead so strongly on behalf of a child, that when such a case happens, some great provocation must be supposed to have occasioned it, and, in the absence of any other, the Court will consider the true reason to be this difference in religion."[1]

Lord Macclesfield, reversing the decree of Sir Joseph

---

[1] *Vincent* v. *Fernandez*, 1 P. W. 524. See other orders made under this statute for the maintenance of the children of Jews, by Lord Macclesfield and Lord King, 1 Sand. Orders, 457, 524.

[1718.]

Jekyll, decided the famous case of *Forth* v. *Chapman*, holding, that though a devise over of real property on the first devisee "dying without leaving issue" is too remote, the construction being, "*if there should be a failure of descendants at any time, however distant,*" the same words, when applied to personal property, shall be construed to mean, "*if the first taker die, leaving no issue at the time of his death,*" and therefore the bequest over is good.[1]

A general pardon coming out, according to the fashion of that age, on account of some auspicious event in the royal family, with an exception of "all contempts and offenses for which any prosecution was then pending, and which had been prosecuted at the charge of any private person," the question arose, whether gentlemen committed to the Fleet for running away with wards in Chancery were entitled to the benefit of it? Lord Macclesfield liberated them all, saying that their contempt, or offense, ended only in the punishment of the party offending, and not in relieving or redressing the prosecutor,—as the marriages, though irregularly contracted, could not be dissolved, and the wards could not be restored to their former condition.[2]

Lord Macclesfield established an important rule in favor of the female sex—that, although the wife's paraphernalia [jewels and personal ornaments] are subject to the debts of the husband, she shall be entitled to her paraphernalia where those debts are a charge on the real estate of the husband. *Lord Chancellor:* "*Paraphernalia* are not devisable by the husband from the wife any more than heir-looms from the heir. Though the creditor may subject a specific legacy to his debt, yet the legatee shall, in equity stand in the place of the bond creditor or mortgagee, and the legacy is relieved. If the legatee shall have this favor in equity, much more shall the wife be privileged with respect to her *parapher-*

---

[1] 1 P. W. 664. Lord Kenyon, in *Porter* v. *Bradley*, doubted the soundness of the rule laid down by Lord Macclesfield (3 T. R. 143); but Lord Eldon, in *Crooke* v. *De Vandes*, said that Lord Kenyon's dictum in *Porter* v. *Bradley* went to shake settled rules to their very foundation ; and Lord Macclesfield's distinction must be supported 9 Ves. 203. This distinction will hereafter be rendered immaterial by the "Wills Act," which enacts that "dying without issue" shall always mean *at the death of the first taker*, so as to give validity to the devise over; 7 W. 4, and 1 Vic. c. 26, s. 29.

[2] *Phipps*, son of *Sir Constantine Phipps* v. *Earl of Anglesea*, 1 P. W. 696.

nalia, which are preferred to legacies. Wherever the creditors are sure of being paid, the *paraphernalia* shall be retained by the wife."[1]

In the case of *Mr. Justice Eyre* v. *the Countess of Shaftesbury*, in which Lord Macclesfield held, that where the guardianship of children is left to several persons, without saying, "and the survivor of them," the survivor shall be guardian,—he entered most elaborately into the whole law of guardian and ward, and the jurisdiction of the Chancellor over infants even in the lifetime of their parents, expressing opinions which have materially guided the decisions of the court on this important subject down to our own time.[2]

Commercial law in England was still in its infancy, and the contract of insurance was so little understood that a court of law would have allowed a merchant to recover on a policy, although at the time when he effected it he had intelligence, which he concealed from the insurers, that the ship had encountered a storm, and was probably lost. *Lord Chancellor:* "The merchant has not been guilty of any express misrepresentation, but he has not dealt fairly in this case. He ought to have disclosed to the insurers the intelligence he had of the ship being in danger; he feared that she was lost, though he had no certain account of it. The concealment is a fraud." *Decree for the policy to be delivered up, with costs.*[3]

Lord Macclesfield laid down doctrine with regard to Ireland that would now raise a rebellion in that country; saying that he would grant a sequestration to be executed there, "as the courts of justice here have a superintendent power over those in Ireland, and a writ of error lies in the Court of King's Bench in England to reverse a judgment of the Court of King's Bench in Ireland."[4]

When *Dr. Martin and Lady Arabella Howard, his wife*, v. *Nutkin*, came before Lord Macclesfield, he must have been in a great agony, for this was the last day he sat in court,

[1] *Tipping* v. *Tipping*, 1 P. W. 729; *Puckering* v. *Johnson*, Ib. 730.
[2] 2 P. W. 102.   [3] *De Costa* v. *Scandret*, 2 P. W. 169.
[4] *Fryer* v. *Bernard*, 2 P. W. 261. I never could understand how this writ of error could have originated; for if Ireland were a colony, or a conquered country, the appeal would have been not to the King's Bench in England, but to the King in council. Mollyneux accounts for it by an Irish act of parliament not extant (p. 111): it was abolished by 23 Geo. 3, c. 28. Lord Coke says, that on a judgment given at Calais a writ of error lay returnable into the Court of King's Bench in England. (4 Inst. 281.).

and he well knew the disgrace which was impending over him. Yet he had self-possession to examine the case deliberately, and to dispose of it so as to make it a valuable precedent, which has been frequently quoted and acted upon. The plaintiffs lived at Hammersmith, very near the church, and were much disquieted by the ringing of a peal of bells at five o'clock every morning. They were about to remove to a distance, when it was agreed between them and the parish, at a vestry meeting, that, in consideration of their erecting a new cupola, clock, and bell, the five o'clock peal should not be rung during their lives or the life of the survivor. The new cupola, clock, and bell were erected, and for two years the agreement was observed by the parish; but at the end of that time, there being a revolution in Hammersmith, an order was made by the vestry that a peal should be rung every morning at five o'clock, according to ancient usage, and the churchwardens executed the order, the peal being rendered louder by the present of the plaintiffs. The Lord Chancellor granted an injunction against the ringing of any bells, at that hour, on the ground that there was a meritorious consideration executed on the plaintiffs' side; that the churchwardens were a corporation, and might sell the bells or silence them; that the ringing of a peal of bells at five in the morning did not seem to be of any use to others, though of very ill consequence to the Doctor and Lady Arabella; and that the agreement which was beneficial to the parish, was binding on the parishioners and their successors.[1]

I ought to mention here, that while Lord Macclesfield was Chancellor the long protracted controversy arose between the celebrated Dr. Bentley and the fellows of his college, and that an application was made on their behalf by Dr. Colbatch for the interposition of a royal visitor to be appointed under the Great Seal. Of this affair we have the following amusing account of Bishop Monk, in his "Life of Bentley," showing that such applications to the "Keeper of the King's conscience," though judicial, were then dealt with rather on the principles of policy than of justice:—

"With the Lord Chancellor, Colbatch had several personal interviews, and, at his desire, laid before him a de-

[1] 2 P. W. 266.

tailed statement of the College grievance, and heard from him with great delight that it was intended to advise the King to grant the full visitatorial power to the Bishop of Ely, and that the patent for this purpose would pass the Great Seal. At other times his Lordship intimated his opinion that the Bishop was already authorized to execute those functions. His chaplain, Zachary Pearce, who had daily opportunities of conversing with the Chancellor, encouraged Dr. Colbatch with the same constantly repeated hopes of his taking some decisive step in this business. But Lord Macclesfield was a politician, and an adept in the subtlest arts of political management. It appears to have been the feeling of the Ministry that Bentley, being a professed and active partisan of the Whigs, must not be abandoned in the hour of his necessity: at the same time it was seen that, if an absolute refusal were given to those who only prayed for common justice, the odium of the Master's proceedings would be transferred from himself to the Government. The Lord Chancellor continued for at least three years to amuse Dr. Colbatch with expectations that the prayer of the petitioners was immediately to be complied with. It may appear surprising that a man of sense, who knew the world, should have suffered himself to be so long deceived; but the candor and frankness of the language held by the great man, and the confidence reposed in his designs by Pearce, his chaplain, will account for the credulity of the Doctor and his confederates."[1]

We must, for the present, take leave of Lord Macclesfield in the character of a judge, and view him acting avowedly as a statesman. Though a member of the cabinet, and a great personal favorite of the King, I do not think that he ever possessed much political influence. Stanhope and Sunderland seem to have brought forward the "Dissenters' Relief Bill," and the "Peerage Bill," without consulting him. Walpole, entertaining a little jealousy of his personal interest with the King and the Hanoverian ministers, reposed no confidence in him, and when trouble came made no effort to save him. Yet the Chancellor appeared very secure in his place; and being in no danger from ministerial crisis or formidable rival, had it not been for the storm which unexpectedly

[1] Vol. ii. 79, 80.

arose from the abuses of the Court of Chancery, his Chancellorship would probably have been one of the longest, as well as most distinguished, in our annals.

He took his seat on the woolsack at the first meeting of parliament after his appointment, when he had to read the King's speech to the two Houses, his Majesty having as yet made no progress in acquiring the language of his new subjects.[1] Lord Cowper soon went into smart opposition, and Lord Macclesfield is said to have supported the measures of the Government with great vigor; but still the published Parliamentary Debates are so defective, that we know little of his style of eloquence. The London Magazine and the Gentleman's Magazine were shortly after established,[2] in which, under feigned names, we have the speeches of the most eminent debaters on both sides, by Samuel Johnson and other distinguished men, who began their career by this exercise. Till then we are confined to the meager notices of speeches to be found in the "Historical Register," "Boyer's Political State of Europe," and "Timberland's History and Proceedings of the House of Lords."

Macclesfield appears to have done himself much credit by defending the "Quakers' Affirmation Bill" against the Bishop of Rochester, who endeavored to prove that none but Christians should be admitted as witnesses, and that Quakers are not Christians.[3] When Atterbury's case came on, he successfully counteracted a scheme, supported by Lord Cowper, that to create a seeming grievance the Bishop should be forbidden, under a standing order of the House of Lords, to make any defense against the Bill of Pains and Penalties in the House of Commons;[4] but soon after, I am afraid, he behaved ungenerously and disingenuously to his defeated predecessor. A committee of the House of Lords, appointed to inquire into the "Plot," presented a report insinuating that Lord Cowper was implicated in it, and he, in vindicating himself, had altogether denied its existence. A resolution being now carried, that the Lord Chancellor, in the name of the House, should return thanks to the Committee for

---

[1] I do not find any statement as to the manner in which the ceremony was conducted when the King had to deliver an answer to the address of the House of Lords. It must have appeared rather ridiculous if the Chancellor first read the address and then the answer.—See 8 Parl. Hist. 502.

[2] In 1731 and 1732.   [3] 7 Parl. Hist. 942.   [4] 8 Ibid. 210.

their services, Macclesfield pretty plainly repeated the insinuation of Lord Cowper's complicity: said he, "Your application in going through so many papers of affected and studied obscurity, your candor and exactness in examining the persons concerned, and in representing what they said [this was what Lord Cowper had most bitterly complained of [1]], the accuracy and judgment of your remarks, *though subject to the cavils of those who are loth to have the truth found out,* must give a sensible pleasure to every Lord who has heard your report read, by enabling him to form a satisfactory judgment concerning this abominable work of darkness which the actors have endeavored to surround with impenetrable obscurity."

The extreme enmity now subsisting between these two great men, is very strikingly proved by the advantage taken of the Lord Chancellor's detention at St. James's when he ought to have been present in the House of Lords, and the attempt to fix a stigma upon him for an unintentional irregularity.[2] After a diligent search, I really can discover nothing more respecting Macclesfield's proceedings in the House of Lords for the seven years which elapsed between his being appointed Chancellor and his impeachment.

During this period, as often as the King went abroad (which he did several months every year) the Chancellor was appointed a Lord Justice, and was at the head of those who acted in the regency. The Prince had been at first appointed sole guardian of the realm, no precedent being found for associating the heir apparent with others in a commission of regency; but he was now excluded from the appearance as well as the reality of power.

The only political measure in which I find the Chancellor personally mixed up, arose out of these unhappy disputes between the father and the son. The resentment of the King was at last carried so far that, out of spite to his successor, he proposed, under pretense of consulting the good of the nation, that hereafter no one should be allowed to be Sovereign of this country without renouncing any foreign dominions to which he might be entitled—not held in right of the crown of England.

[1] Ante, p. 267.
[2] Ante, p. 266. 7 Parl. Hist. 960. I am glad to think that there is a better feeling among law Lords at the present day.

The proposal seems to me very fair and salutary, and agreeable to well-established constitutional as well as international law; but we are told that the opinion of Lord Macclesfield being demanded in a conference on the subject, "the answer given by the Chancellor fully put a stop to the measure as inexpedient and impracticable, and liable to be followed by dangerous consequences."[1] Had it been adopted, it would have saved England much perplexity and expense, and some discredit, in the two following reigns. Happily, there is little danger of the recurrence of such a state of things; but for this reason, perhaps, now is the time to pass the law which was projected by the founder of the Hanoverian dynasty in England.

When parliament met, in the month of November, 1724, Lord Macclesfield seemed at the height of worldly success, with the prospect of a long continuance of his greatness. From the union of genius for legal distinctions and unwearied industry he had acquired with the public the highest possible reputation as a Judge, and, except by a few acquainted with the mysteries of the Court of Chancery, he was supposed to be immaculate.[2] His levees were crowded by laity and clergy. At his newly-acquired country seat, Shirburn Castle, he exercised a splendid hospitality; and he had been appointed Lord-Lieutenant not only of Oxfordshire, in which it stood, but likewise of the adjoining county of Warwick, in which also he had acquired large possessions.

Walpole, now the undisputed Prime Minister had by his dexterous management in the last session almost annihilated opposition, and, for a time, Whigs, Tories, and Jacobites, without show of resistance, submitted to his rule. The Great Seal, under such a minister, was consid-

[1] Cor. Sir R. W. 13.
[2] No attention is to be paid to the line in Duke Wharton's satire on the lawyers,
"When Parker shall pronounce one right decree,"
as one of the impossibilities on which he says,
"Then shall I cease my charmer to adore,
And think of love and politics no more."
For though he is right with respect to PAGE, and one or two more, he scatters his arrows at random among political opponents, and there can not be a doubt that, till the very eve of Parker's disgrace, he was as much respected as any man who had ever sat in the marble chair. The Duke went so far to prove his personal enmity as actually to sign a protest against the leniency of the sentence pronounced by the Peers on his victim.

ered free from all the perils and anxieties which generally surround it. For a time all went well, and another very smooth session was anticipated. The Chancellor might himself have been thought an emblem of the joyous conjuncture which he described when, in the King's name, he pronounced these words—" My Lords and Gentlemen, I am persuaded you share with me in the satisfaction I feel at the prosperous situation of affairs : peace with all powers abroad ; at home, perfect tranquillity, plenty, and an uninterrupted enjoyment of all civil and religious rights,—are most distinguishing marks of the favor and protection of Divine Providence. And these, with all their happy consequences, will, I doubt not, by the blessing of God upon our joint endeavors, be long continued." [1]

Whether Macclesfield had any misgivings or fatal anticipations respecting himself, I know not, but his ruin was at hand. In a few days the storm of public indignation arose against him ; in a few weeks he was deprived of his office, and in a few months he was a prisoner in the Tower, under sentence to pay a heavy fine, by the unanimous judgment of the House of Lords,—while the vulgar insulted him with the oft-repeated saying that " Staffordshire had produced the three greatest rogues ever known in England,—*Jack Sheppard, Jonathan Wild*, and TOM PARKER!"

Soon after the bursting of the South Sea Bubble, voices —at first ambiguous—were heard whispering that great frauds had been committed on the suitors in the Court of Chancery, and that their money had been made away with by the Masters to whose custody it had been intrusted till the interminably delayed decree should be pronounced. Rumors became louder and louder, and the Chancellor's name was proclaimed as having caused or connived at all the abuses which had been discovered. The whole Government was next involved in the obloquy, and the ever-watchful opponents of the Minister were ready to say that such enormities could only be sanctioned under Hanoverian auspices, under Whig rule, and under that section of the Whigs which had now usurped supreme power. Walpole, with his usual shrewdness and decision, immediately appointed a committee of the Privy Council, in whom the public would place confidence, to investigate

---
[1] 8 Parl. Hist. 396.

the subject, and to make a report to be laid before parliament. Assisted by three Judges and the Attorney and Solicitor General, the Privy Councillors selected, after an examination of many witnesses, did make a report which showed that there were serious defalcations in the Masters' offices, and that there was a grave case of suspicion against the Lord Chancellor. His Lordship thereupon, in the hope of setting himself right with the public, immediately issued a very stringent order, by which every Master was required to send all the trust-moneys and securities in his hands to the Bank of England, in a chest under three locks, one to be kept by the Master himself, another by the Six Clerks of the Court of Chancery, and the third by the Governor of the Bank.[1] But this was considered rather an acknowledgment of past misconduct; the storm of indignation rose higher against the Lord Chancellor, and loud declarations were made that he could not decently occupy the judgment-seat longer till the charges against himself were investigated. The Ministry becoming afraid of being suspected of a wish to screen a guilty colleague, Lord Macclesfield was compelled to surrender the office of Lord Chancellor. Sir Peter King, Chief Justice of the Court of Common Pleas, was appointed to officiate as Speaker of the House of Lords, and the Great Seal was put into commission. When the Lords Commissioners—Sir Joseph Jekyll, Sir Geoffrey Gilbert, and Sir Robert Raymond—were sworn in before the Council, it was published to the world that the King thus addressed them :—" I have had such experience of your integrity and ability that it is with pleasure I now put the Great Seal into your hands. You are fully informed of the state of the accounts of the Masters in Chancery. I earnestly recommend to you the taking effectual care that entire satisfaction be made to the suitors of the Court, and that they be not exposed to any dangers for the future ; and I have such confidence in the faithful discharge of the trust I now repose in you, that I am persuaded you will look narrowly to the behavior of all the officers under your jurisdiction, and will see that they act with the strictest regard to justice, and to the ease of my subjects."[2]

Hopes were entertained that this proceeding would

[1] 17th December, 1724.   1 Sanders, 465.   [2] 8 Parl. Hist. 417.

tranquillize the public mind, and that it would be left to the Lords Commissioners to grant relief for past wrongs, and to make regulations to guard the property of the suitors for the future. But it was found that the deficit could not be made up without the interference of Parliament, and many were of opinion that exemplary punishment should be inflicted on him who was considered the chief delinquent.

Proceedings were originated in the House of Commons by a petition from the Earl of Oxford and Lord Morpeth, guardians of Elizabeth, Duchess Dowager of Montague, a lunatic, stating that large sums paid to a Master in Chancery on her account had been embezzled, and praying such relief as the House should think fit. A debate arising, it was adjourned, in the expectation of obtaining more information before any resolution should be passed. In a few days the following royal message was brought down:—

"GEORGE R.

"His Majesty having reason to apprehend that the suitors of the Court of Chancery were in danger of losing a considerable sum of money from the insufficiency of some of the Masters, thought himself obliged, in justice and compassion to the said suitors, to take the most speedy and proper method the law would allow for inquiring into the state of the Masters' accounts, and securing their effects for the benefit of the suitors: and his Majesty having had several Reports laid before him in pursuance of the directions he had given, has ordered the said Reports to be communicated to this House, that this House may have as full and as perfect a view of this important affair as the shortness of the time, and the circumstances and nature of the proceedings, would admit of."[1]

Soon after, Sir George Oxenden,[2] having made a long speech upon the enormous abuses which had crept into the Court of Chancery, chiefly occasioned by the magistrate who was at the head of that court, and whose duty it consequently was to prevent them, concluded by moving, "That Thomas, Earl of Macclesfield, be impeached of

[1] 8 Parl. Hist. 415.
[2] He was said to belong to the Leicester House party; and, certainly, the Prince's friends were eager in the prosecution, from the recollection that Parker had taken a strong part against the Heir Apparent of the King.

high crimes and misdemeanors." The motion was seconded by Mr. Doddington, who said, "the misconduct of the late Chancellor was of the most dangerous consequence, since most of the estates in England, once in thirty years, pass through the Court of Chancery." Mr. Pulteney and Sir William Wyndam took the opposite side, chiefly on the ground that the Reports laid on the table were no sufficient ground for an impeachment, and that the Commons were bound themselves first to institute an inquiry. But an immediate impeachment was voted by a majority of 273 to 164, and Sir George Oxenden was ordered forthwith to present it at the bar of the House of Lords.

When he had performed this duty, he brought in a bill to indemnify witnesses who should give evidence respecting the sale of offices in the Court of Chancery, and it speedily passed both Houses. Sir Philip Yorke and some of Lord Macclesfield's private friends made a feeble stand for him in the House of Commons, on a motion respecting the framing of the articles of impeachment, but were defeated, being bitterly opposed by Sergeant Pengelly, Sir Clement Wearg and other Chancery lawyers, who considered that they had been personally ill-used by the late Chancellor.

In the Lords there was a smart debate on the question, whether the trial should take place at the bar of their own House, or in Westminster Hall? and a majority preferring the former, there was a strong protest signed by several Peers, on the ground that all possible publicity and solemnity should be given to a proceeding of such national importance. Those who wished to render the prosecution effectual, wisely contrived to make it appear as much as possible a judicial inquiry instead of a theater for rhetorical display.

The trial excited intense interest, and although very few could be within hearing, great crowds assembled in Palace Yard daily while it lasted. The charge not being capital, there was no Lord High Steward appointed. Sir Peter King, Lord Chief Justice of the Common Pleas, acted as Speaker of the House of Lords, giving directions to the managers for the Commons and the counsel for the defendant, and he afterwards pronounced sentence. The Peers wore their robes. The defendant was every morning called upon to appear, and had a stool placed for him within the bar.[1]

The trial began on the 6th of May, and lasted thirteen days, the House generally sitting from ten in the morning till nine in the evening, with adjournments, during pleasure, for refreshment. The principal managers for the Commons were Sir Clement Wearg, Solicitor General, Mr. Doddington, Mr. Onslow, and Lord Morpeth. Lord Macclesfield was defended by Sergeant Probyn, Dr. Sayer, and Mr. Strange. He himself took an active part in cross-examining the witnesses, and arguing points of law, and, after his counsel had been fully heard, he addressed the House on the whole of the case.

The twenty-one articles of impeachment, in substance, charged him with selling masterships in Chancery when the office, being vacant, was in his own gift; with receiving large sums of money for agreeing to the sale and transfer of masterships from one Master to another; with receiving a large sum of money for agreeing to a sale and transfer of the office of clerk of the custodies; with conniving at the fraudulent practice of Masters paying for their places out of the suitors' money in their hands; with trying to conceal the delinquencies of an insolvent Master who had absconded; with encouraging the Masters to traffic with trust-money, and with advising them to conceal the frauds they had committed.

The formal "Answer," put in by the defendant disclaimed all corruption, and relied on law and usage. I present to the reader a little specimen of the opening of the managers:—

"Will example plead for him? Surely, my Lords, there are none such: or if there were, what would that be but to defend crimes by their own blackness and malignity? as if a distemper were not to admit of any remedy because it is general and contagious. But supposing, for argument's sake, there have been great persons, his predecessors, who have ventured upon small presents and gifts on such occasions, does it follow, with any color or pretense of reasoning, those having been confined within the bonds of moderation, that the ex-

---

[1] When referred to during the trial, he was designated "The noble Earl within the bar." Peers on trial for treason or felony are placed outside the bar.

tortion of exorbitant sums to connive at outrageous oppressions, exceeding almost the fears of the oppressed themselves, should take shelter under the poor plea of precedent? Whence comes it, that example should have all the beauty of an angel where it should be shunned, and all the deformity of a fiend where it should be followed? Happy had it been for him who now excites our pity as well as our indignation, happy for the widow and fatherless whom his misconduct has reduced to want, had he copied his renowned predecessors in their wise and upright administration of justice. To what a low ebb would the virtue and reputation of this nation be reduced, if impunity could justify offenses, and bribery should be called the fashion of the age! His Lordship, in his answer to the articles of impeachment, says, 'he did not sell offices; and that he only received presents from the persons on whom the offices were conferred.' There probably may be a difference between a present and a price; if there is, it is the latter his Lordship is charged with taking; a price fixed by his Lordship, insisted upon, haggled for, and unwillingly paid by the purchaser. Unfortunately, the price was greater than could possibly be given by one who was to be contented with the fair profits of the office, as was well known by the recipient, who, to make amends to the purchasers, connived at their paying that extravagant price from the money of the suitors with which they were intrusted; and indulged them, and encouraged them, and compelled them, to hazard the rest of that money in speculations which turned out to be disastrous. Against apparent extortioners and robbers we guard ourselves with a caution proportionable to the infamy of their characters; but when the sanctity of the laws and the ensigns of authority, designed to defend and protect us, are made use of to invite us into ruin, how sure and extensive must that ruin be! My Lords, the Commons have beheld with the deepest concern such corrupt practices in this high Court—such as have deformed the beauty of justice. The first magistrate in the state, who is invested with an extraordinary power to detect and punish fraud, becomes himself its fabricator and its patron. The guardian of orphans has proved their oppressor. The Keeper of the King's conscience prostitutes his own. He who ought to reform abuses and amend the laws spends his days and nights in an ignominious traffic with the best bidder. He who ought almost to be revered as a superior being above human frailty, and only presented to the imagination as dealing out blessings, is actually beheld employing the scales of justice in the business of a usurer."

The evidence was very long, and clearly established that Lord Macclesfield had sold masterships through his agent, Peter Cottingham; that he had received sums for consenting to the transfer of others; that this mode of disposing of the office of Master led to great abuse; that in several instances the suitors had suffered from the Master becoming insolvent, and that Lord Macclesfield had taken great pains to conceal these abuses and losses from the public.

From the examination of one or two of the principal witnesses, I will give a specimen of the manner in which, in days of yore, such negotiations were conducted: Master Bennet had agreed with Master Hiccocks to buy his office from him on obtaining the necessary consent of the Lord Chancellor to the transfer. Being now compelled under the Indemnity Act to disclose all that passed, he said,—

"I applied to Mr Cottingham, and desired him to let me know my Lord Chancellor's thoughts, whether he approved of me to succeed Mr. Hiccocks? Soon after that, he told me he had acquainted my Lord with the message, and my Lord expressed himself with a great deal of respect for my father, and was glad of an opportunity to do me a favor and kindness, and that he had no objection in the world to me—but that 'there was a present expected, and that he did not doubt but I knew that;' I answered, 'I had heard there was, and I was willing to do what was usual;' I desired to know what would be expected; he said 'he could name no sum, and I might apply to my brother, a Master, and Master Godfrey, who had recommended me, and they would tell me what was proper to offer.' I returned to Mr. Cottingham, and told him 'I had talked with them about it, and their opinion was, £1,000 was sufficient for me to offer, but I would not stand for guineas.' Upon this, Mr. Cottingham shook his head, and said, 'That won't do, Mr. Bennet, you must be better advised.' 'Why,' said I, 'won't that do? I think it is a noble present.' Says he, 'a great deal more has been given.' Says I, 'I am sure my brother did not give so much, and I desire you to acquaint my Lord with the proposal.' Says he, 'I don't care to go with that proposal; you may find somebody else to go.' Says I, 'I don't know whom to apply to.' Says he, 'Mr. Bennet, sure, you won't go to lower the price; I can assure you Mr. Kynaston gave 1,500 guineas.' Says I, 'only acquaint my Lord with it, and if he insists on more, I will consider of it.' Says he, 'there is no haggling with my Lord; if you refuse it, I don't know the consequence; he may resent it so as not to admit you at all.' Then I began to consider, and was loth to lose the office, and told him 'I would give £1500.' He said, 'Mr. Kynaston had given guineas.' Then I asked 'whether it must be in gold?' He said, 'in what way you will, so it be guineas.' On the 1st of June he desired me 'to come immediately, and to come alone and bring nobody with me, for my Lord would swear me in that morning.' Accordingly I went, and the first question Mr. Cottingham asked me was, 'if I had brought the money?' I told him 'to be sure, I should not come without it.' He asked me 'what it was in?' I told him 'in bank bills, one of £1,000, and the other of £575.' He took them up and carried them to my Lord: he returned and told me 'my Lord was ready to admit me.' I was carried up stairs, and in his bed-chamber was I sworn as Master."

The witness admitted that he neither should nor could have bought the place if he had not been to pay for it with the money of the suitors as he did.

A still more amusing scene is presented to us by the evidence of Master Elde, who was to pay the Lord Chancellor a much larger sum, as the office was vacant by death, and who was imprudent enough to carry a considerable portion of it in specie. In this instance the brokership of Cottingham was at first dispensed with, and the Chancellor in person saw and dealt with the purchaser, who swore as follows:—

"His Lordship said 'he had no manner of objection to me; he had known me a considerable time, and he believed I should make a good officer.' He desired me '*to consider of it*, and to come to him again.' I came again in a day or two, and told him '*I had considered* of it, and if his Lordship would admit me, I would make him a present of £4,000, or £5,000;' I can not say which of the two, but I believe it was £5,000. My Lord said, 'Thee and I,' or 'you and I' (my Lord was pleased to treat me as a friend) 'must not make bargains.' He said, ' if I was desirous to have the office, he would treat with me in a different manner than he would with any man living.' I spoke to Mr. Cottingham, meeting him in Westminster Hall, and told him 'I had been at my Lord's, and my Lord was pleased to speak very kindly to me, and I had proposed to give him £5,000.' Mr. Cottingham answered, —'GUINEAS ARE HANDSOMER!!!' I immediately went to my Lord's, being willing to get into the office as soon as I could. I did carry with me 5,000 guineas in gold and bank notes. I had the money in my chambers, but did not know how to convey it;—it was a great burden and weight, but recollecting I had a basket in my chambers, I put the guineas into the basket, and the notes with them. I went in a chair, and took the basket with me in my chair. When I came to my Lord's house, I saw Mr. Cottingham there, and gave him the basket, and desired him to carry it up to my Lord. I saw him go up stairs with the basket, and when he came down he intimated to me that he had delivered it. When I was admitted, my Lord invited me to dinner, and some of my friends with me, and he was pleased to treat me and some Members of the House of Commons in a very handsome manner. I was after dinner sworn in before them. Some months after, I spoke to my Lord's gentleman, and desired him, if he saw such a basket, that he would give it me back. He did so, *but no money was returned in it.*"

Next, I will give an extract from the evidence of *Master Thurston.*—He had agreed with Cottingham to buy a mastership for 5,000 guineas, and, being introduced to the Lord Chancellor, had a promise that he should be admitted in a few days, but a difficulty arose from an inquiry into his character and sufficiency for the office, insomuch that his admission was postponed, and the Lord Chancellor entered into a treaty for disposing of the office to another purchaser,—

"Which," said he, " gave me an uneasiness and put me upon an expedient that, since I could not have ready access to so great a person as his Lordship, I went to

Kensington one morning to wait upon the Countess of Macclesfield, and upon sending up my name and that I desired to speak with her, in a short time I had the honor of seeing her, and acquainted her that I was the person that my Lord had promised the office to, and I desired her to intercede with my Lord that I might be speedily sworn in. Her Ladyship said, 'She never did meddle in any affairs of a public nature.' I used several arguments with her, as 'the thing was now public and in print, and it would be a great disappointment to me and might affect my character if my Lord did not think fit to admit me,' and I acquainted her Ladyship that ' I did not expect or desire to come in without the due present that is always esteemed the perquisite of the Great Seal.' Her Ladyship was prevailed upon to promise 'she would write a letter and acquaint my Lord Chancellor with it.' Before I went away from the room where I had the honor to be with the lady, I did leave upon the table bank-notes to the value of £5,250."—*Q.* " How were they directed?"—*A.* " I directed them to the COUNTESS OF MACCLESFIELD." —*Q.* " How soon after were you admitted?"—*A.* " Within two or three days at farthest I was admitted and sworn in." The witness then goes on to state that, from the misconduct of his predecessor, Master Borret, which could not have been unknown to the Lord Chancellor, he found the office in a state of the most dreadful confusion, the money of the suitors for which he had became responsible having been abstracted, and he says, that if he had been fully aware of the whole truth, "instead of giving 5,000 guineas for the appointment, he he would have given 5,000 guineas to avoid it." He added, however, "that some months after, and shortly before the complaints against the Lord Chancellor broke out, Lady Macclesfield sent for him, and returned him £3,250, saying 'she did not know he had left so large a present,— that it was too large a present,—that she was afraid my Lord Chancellor would come to the knowledge of it,— that the largest part of it must be taken back, and that she would appropriate the rest to her own use.'"

Godfrey, another witness, gives a most lamentable account of the state in which he found the office of Master Borret, who seems to have died suddenly:—" We found his papers in great confusion, lying without any method or order. We collected them as well as we could, and what things we found of value or belonging to the suitors, as goldsmiths' notes, we put them on a file, and that file, together with other little movables we found belonging to him, as rings and a watch, were all put in a bag, and we put them into a trunk, and locked them up, and they are now at my house." Master Borret had speculated deeply in the South Sea, with the suitors' money in his hands, and, thinking at one time to increase the amount twenty fold for his own benefit, the whole of it was lost. Master Dormer and other Masters had followed his example with the like hopes and the like result.[1] When the defalcations were first discovered, it was proved that the Chancellor compelled all the Masters under a threat of depriving them of the use of the suitors' money, to contribute to make them up; but, from the increasing amount, reparation and concealment became impossible.

The managers having finished their evidence on all the articles, and summed up at great length, the counsel for the defendant thus addressed the House:—

"The greatest respect must be shown for a prosecution by the Commons of Great Britain, but (with all respect be it spoken) they have in this instance mistaken their course, and instead of proceeding legislatively to remedy a defective state of the law, and asking your Lordships to concur with them in prospectively amending a system which is supposed to lead to abuse, they have been misled by public clamor to appeal to this House as a court of justice, and to call for punishment where there has been no offense. The managers have utterly failed in making out the inflamed and exaggerated case which they opened, and we might well contend that the moderate sums which were spontaneously given to the noble Earl within the bar, by the competent and respectable persons who were appointed by him to be Masters in Chancery, were 'presents' only. Yet, assuming that they were the 'price' received upon the sale of offices, he must be acquitted, unless the sale of these offices was forbidden by the common law, or is contrary to an act of parliament. There is no pretense for saying that it is *malum in se*,—that the

[1] It is well for the Masters that they are no longer exposed to such temptations, or it might have been suspected that they engaged in " Railroad speculations "—as seducing as the " South Sea."

practice is so much against morality and sound policy that it can not be endured in any well regulated state. He that has an office in his gift, if he takes care that the duties of it are faithfully performed, may dispose of it as he may of anything else that is valuable on such terms as may be agreed upon between himself and the person on whom it is to be bestowed. The receiving of money for it is no act of injustice to the person appointed, for he had no right to it, and his advancement is owing to the favor of him who has the power of nomination. If the office be valuable, so is the right of nomination to it,—which may be considered part of the estate of that person to whom it belongs. Of whatever nature the office may be, the consequence does not follow that its duties will not be adequately performed because a consideration has been paid for it. The Roman Civil Law, the great fountain of justice which humanized the barbarous hordes of the North, permitted the sale of offices. In France justice is administered with great purity, and her parliaments boast of magistrates equal in learning and integrity to any that have ever graced the bench in Westminster Hall; yet in that country the highest judicial offices may be transmitted to heirs, or may be resigned during life to a purchasing successor. Our own records present many instances of the highest offices in the administration of justice being exposed to sale, and openly, and avowedly, and without censure or scandal, purchased from the Crown. With us the distinction has always been preserved between the sale of justice and the sale of judicial offices; and while the former has been condemned, the latter has been tolerated. In the time of King Stephen, 'Richard Fitz-Allured fined fifteen marks of silver that he might sit with Ralph Basset, the King's Justiciar, to hold the King's Pleas,' or, as we should say, 'to be a puisne Judge of the Court of King's Bench,—and an entry is made of the receipt of the money as part of the ordinary revenue of the State. So in a subsequent reign there is an enrollment in the public records still extant, showing that the office of Lord Chancellor itself was sold: *Gualterus de Gray dat Domino Regi* 5,000 *marc. pro habendâ Cancellariâ Domini Regis totâ vitâ suâ, et pro habendâ inde chartâ Domini Regis.*[1] Lord Coke has censured this transaction;

---

[1] Mad. Exch. 743.

but Walter de Gray enjoyed the office, and the open announcement of the price he paid for it shows that there was no horror excited by the sale of offices in the times when the common law took its origin. The very dictum to be found elsewhere against the sale of the Chancellorship, proceeds on the ground that, being partly of an ecclesiastical nature, the sale of it might savor of simony,—and being treated as an exception, it proves the rule. But the statute 6 Ed. VI. c. 16, to inflict a penalty upon the sale of certain offices concerning the administration of justice—so much relied upon by the managers—is decisive against them with regard to their argument on the common law; for it provides that 'this act shall not extend to any contract made before the 1st of March then next,'—and further that 'this act shall not extend or be prejudicial to any of the Chief Justices of the King's courts, commonly called the King's Bench or Common Pleas, or to any Justices of Assize, but that they, and every of them, may do in every behalf, touching and concerning any office or offices to be given or granted by them, as they or any of them might have done before the making of this act.' By virtue of this proviso, the offices of Master in the King's Bench, of Prothonotary in the Common Pleas, of Clerk of Assize, are at this day openly and avowedly sold by the ermined sages who now sit upon the woolsacks in your Lordships' house to advise you whether the sale of offices be a misdemeanor by the common law of England. It comes then, my Lords, to the construction to be put upon the enacting clause of that statute. Now this being a penal statute, it is not to be extended by implication, and as it creates a new offense, no punishment can be inflicted for that offense, except of the nature—to the degree—and in the manner which the statute specifies: it contains no general prohibition of the sale of offices—but merely inflicts a particular penalty on those who buy or sell offices which are not excepted from its operation. The contract made between the buyer and seller is declared void; the party selling loses his estate and interest in the office, and the party buying is rendered incapable to hold and enjoy it. There is no maxim of English law better established, that when a statute appoints a penalty for doing a thing which before was innocent, and points out how the penalty is to be imposed, the offense is to be punished in that way and no other.¹ We deny that this office comes within the purview of the statute, or that the noble Earl has sold it; but at all events, the statute only inflicts upon him the penalty of forfeiting the nomination to it for the future;—and that he has already suffered by the loss of the Great Seal;—so that he is liable to no other punishment, and the present impeachment can not be supported. But it is painful, and humiliating, and unnecessary, and improper to resort to such technical reasoning, for neither morally nor legally has the noble Earl committed any offense. The best proof that the practice is neither against common law nor statute law is, that it has been invariably, and confessedly, and notoriously followed by all his predecessors—which we do not urge to palliate violation of duty, but to show that no duty has been violated. Many most pure and upright men have sat in the marble chair since the statute passed, and all of them without any public censure, and without any self-reproach, have received gratuities on disposing of these offices—and with as little hesitation, and as little secrecy, as they have received their fixed fees or their annual salary. Nay more, where Chancellors have been impeached in factious times (as in the instances of Lord Clarendon and Lord Somers), and there was the most eager desire to bring them to shame—among all the frivolous charges preferred against them, no political opponent, no furious zealot, no private enemy ever thought of accusing them of corruption because they had conformed to the usage of selling offices in their court. Should this now be adjudged criminal, what numbers of good and just men now sleeping in their honored graves are to be exhumed and put upon their trial, and condemned as criminals! Your Lordships are called upon to spread an universal cloud of reproach and infamy over venerable sages of the law, some of them the ancestors of illustrious Peers now present —men whose memories have hitherto been considered sacred, and have not only been fondly cherished by their descendants, but have been dear to their country—men who despised riches and hated covetousness, who would have shrunk with abhorrence from every appearance of corruption, and who, without ostentation, were famous in

¹ Castle's case, Cro. Jac. 644.

their day for acts of benevolence and charity. Till within a few short months the noble Earl within your bar was equally respected, and every one believed that he too would go down to the tomb regretted and revered. His public services require no panegyric. We might appeal to those gentlemen who are now managers against him, whether they have not often applauded him with warmth, whether they have not loudly commended his zeal and intrepidity in the cause of liberty and our country—his steady adherence to the Protestant succession—his disinterested and patriotic conduct in moments the most trying? Did they not love as well as praise him? Have they not celebrated his noble refusal of the Great Seal itself when the acceptance of it would have been inconsistent with his principles? and when they saw him honorably placed in the high station which he lately adorned, did they not rejoice in his elevation as their own security and happiness? This once was the Earl's character; this once his merit. What has he since done to have his name branded to all posterity as guilty of judicial corruption? He has administered justice between party and party as Chancellor (all allow) in a manner as able and as upright as the most distinguished and most virtuous of his predecessors. He has not introduced a new system with respect to the disposal of offices in his court. Consider the difficulties which beset such attempts at reform—the vested interests which must be affected—the hardships which must be inflicted on individuals and families—the misconstruction to which the reformer is exposed, and the odium which he is sure to incur. But, my Lords, if the noble Earl be thought wanting in energy, if he ought to have been more active in improving our institutions, is not this rather matter for the criticism of the historian or biographer, than to be made the foundation of an indictment before a grand jury, or an impeachment before this august assembly for high crimes and misdemeanors? Then, my Lords, remember how the noble Earl has employed the wealth he has acquired, and consider whether so to employ it he would acquire it by the commission of a crime. It was a cruel application by one of the managers of a well-known maxim, that 'a man may be profuse of his own while he greedily grasps the property of others. But how has the noble Earl been profuse?—in relieving the needy and the oppressed,—in assisting poor scholars, —in patronizing obscure merit wherever he could find it out,—in liberally contributing wherever a benevolent object was to be gained by the joint efforts of the charitable. Are you necessarily to infer that he was 'unsatisfied in getting' because 'in bestowing he was most princely?' Hard indeed is the condition of the Earl, when his very virtues, when his most commendable actions, are turned to his disgrace—are wrested into instruments to achieve his ruin. He who has 'a hand open as day for melting charity' you are required to believe must necessarily be guilty of corruption and extortion. Such is the reasoning of his accusers, but he has your Lordships for his Judges."

The noble defendant, during the disputes about evidence, retorted on the managers rather contemptuously, and at last drew forth this remonstrance from Onslow: "The managers can not but observe the indecent behavior of this Lord, and his unworthy manner of treating us. We do not think the Lord at the bar should be directing the managers as if he sat in his place as Judge. We are here advocates for all the Commons of Great Britain, to demand justice against him." I must acknowledge that the whole trial was conducted by them in a good spirit, and in a very business-like manner—while every now and then the sharp country attorney could be discovered under the disguise of the Earl.

Witnesses were called to make out the usage relied on. However, only three instances of the sale of the office of Master were established—one in Lord Cowper's time, and two in Lord Harcourt's—the largest amount received being £800, and the money having been paid in every instance out of the private funds of the parties, before their admission, without any meddling with the money of the suitors. To account for the larger sums paid to the defendant for Masterships, he proved that other offices in the Court of Chancery, particularly those of the sworn and waiting clerks, had greatly risen in price of late years. He further proved that he had himself contributed £1,000 to make up the deficiencies of a Master, and that he had given away large sums in charity.

Before the Commons replied, he begged permission himself to address the House, and several days were given to him to prepare. His speech was a very masterly performance, but was confined to a minute analysis of the evidence, which would now be uninteresting and unintelligible. He went over all the twenty-one articles of the impeachment, and tried to show that they were all unsupported. He thus concluded, perhaps with more dignity and a better chance of a favorable result than in the most labored peroration:—

"My Lords, having thus gone through all my observations, it may be expected that I should close them by offering something in general: but I think it proper to forbear. I am not conscious myself that it is necessary in this case to apply to the passions, which is a common artifice to assist a weak defense. If I have done any public or private good (of which last some specimen has been laid before your Lordships), it will, I am confident, have its full weight. I submit my whole life and conduct to your Lordships' judgment; and rely entirely on your justice for my acquittal."

At last, on the 25th of May, ninety-three Peers being present, the Earl being placed at the bar, and the Commons attending, Lord Chief Justice King put this question severally to every Peer, beginning with the junior, "Is Thomas, Earl of Macclesfield, Guilty of High Crimes and Misdemeanors charged upon him by the impeachment of the House of Commons, or Not guilty?" and the unanimous answer of all was, "Guilty, upon my honor." *Lord Chief Justice King:* "My Lords, your Lordships have unanimously found Thomas, Earl of Macclesfield, guilty of high crimes and misdemeanors charged upon him by the impeachment of the House of Commons." The defendant was then called upon to appear at the bar to hear the verdict, but the Duke of Devonshire, the Lord President, signified that he was so much indisposed that he was unable to attend. He appeared at the bar the following morning, when the verdict was solemnly intimated to him. He then attempted to make a speech in exculpation of his conduct, but, being interrupted by the managers, he threw himself on the mercy of the House. He was immediately ordered into the custody of the Gentleman Usher of the Black Rod; and the Lords proceeded to consider what sentence should be passed upon him.

A friendly motion was made, that the opinion of the Judges be asked, " whether the sale of an office that hath relation to the administration of justice be an offense against the common law ?" but it met with no encouragement, and was negatived without a division. All then agreed that he should pay a heavy fine, to be applied towards the relief of the suitors who had suffered from the insolvency of the Masters in Chancery, and the sum was fixed at £30,000.

The grand question was, whether he should not likewise be disqualified to hold any place or employment in the state or commonwealth, upon which there was a long and animated debate : one side insisting that the loss of his office of Lord Chancellor, the heavy costs of his defense, the anxiety he had suffered, and the disgrace cast upon him, together with the proposed fine, would be punishment enough, considering the example set him by his predecessors ; while the other contended, with vehemence, that, according to invariable precedent and clear reason, a person who, upon an impeachment by the Commons, had been convicted of corruption in a high judicial office, should, for the protection of the present generation, and as a warning to posterity, be effectually prevented from filling the seat of judgment which he had dishonored ; and they pointed out many circumstances to show that this was an aggravated case, which would be most inadequately punished by a mere pecuniary fine. On a division, the numbers were equal, 42 to 42,—so, according to the rule of the House of Lords *præsumitur pro negante* —the motion was lost. Then violent protests were drawn up and numerously signed against this decision. Still, the sentence was not to be pronounced till judgment was prayed by the Commons.

The managers immediately received the unanimous thanks of their House by Speaker Compton, who said to them—" You have maintained the charge of the Commons with a strength of reason, and beauty of expression, which would have gained you the highest applause in the most flourishing Grecian commonwealths:

――' Nec dignius unquam
Majestas meminit sese Romana locutam.'

You have stopped the cries of orphans, and dried up the

tears of the widow; even those who must ever be insensible of the benefits they receive—idiots and lunatics (and such only can be insensible of them)—will be the partakers of the fruits of your labors." He went on more particularly to thank them for having shown that the power of impeachment vested in the Commons might be practically used for the good of the people, and that "the sword of vengeance, which, when drawn by party rage, when directed by the malice of faction, or wielded by unskillful hands, has too often wounded that constitution it was intended to protect, had, by their able management, turned its edge to its proper object, and had struck down a great public offender."

There was a party in the Commons, however, disposed to a mild course. They said that enough had already been done for the public by exposing the long-established abuses of the Court of Chancery, and that the Earl of Macclesfield ought not to be made a scapegoat. They therefore resisted the motion that the Speaker be ordered to go to the bar of the House of Lords and demand judgment; but, upon a division, this motion was carried by a majority of 136 to 65.

Accordingly, on the 27th of May, Speaker Compton, attended by many members of the House of Commons, presented himself at the bar of the House of Lords to demand judgment. The Lord Chief Justice King thereupon directing the Gentleman Usher of the Black Rod to produce his prisoner, the Earl of Macclesfield was marched in, and, after low obeisances made, knelt until the Lord Chief Justice told him he might rise.[1] The Speaker of the House of Commons then, having recited the impeachment and the proceedings, thus concluded:—
"I do, therefore, in the name of the knights, citizens, and burgesses in parliament assembled, demand judgment of your Lordships against Thomas, Earl of Macclesfield, for the said high crimes and misdemeanors." *Lord C. J. King:* "Mr. Speaker, the Lords are now ready to give the judgment you demand. Thomas, Earl of Macclesfield, the Lords having unanimously found you guilty of high

[1] The Commons' Journals most studiously record, that the Sergeant at Arms attending the House of Commons stood at the bar on Mr. Speaker's right hand, with the mace on his shoulder; and that the Earl of Macclesfield, being placed at some distance on his left hand, was ordered "to kneel in the presence of the Commons."

crimes and misdemeanors charged on you by the impeachment of the Commons, do now, according to law, proceed to judgment against you, which I am ordered to pronounce. Their Lordships' judgment is, and this high Court doth award, that you, Thomas, Earl of Macclesfield, be fined in the sum of £30,000 unto our Sovereign Lord the King, and that you be imprisoned in the Tower of London, and there kept in safe custody until you shall pay the said fine." The Earl of Macclesfield was immediately carried off by the Gentleman Usher of the Black Rod, and delivered into the custody of the Constable of the Tower of London. Here he was confined in the room which had last been occupied by his opponent, the Earl of Oxford. Three days after, the King (it is said, *with a sigh*) ordered his name to be erased from the list of Privy Councillors.

There has been a disposition in recent times to consider that Lord Macclesfield was wrongfully condemned. " The unanimity of his Judges," says Lord Mahon, "might seem decisive as to his guilt; yet it may perhaps be doubted whether they did not unjustly heap the faults of the system on one man; whether Parker had not rather in fact failed to check gradual and growing abuses, than introduced them by his authority, or encouraged them by his example."[1] I must say, that although it is impossible not to pity a man of such high qualities when so disgraced,—and although, with good luck, notwithstanding all he had done, he might have escaped exposure and preserved an untarnished fame,—yet, in my opinion, his conviction was lawful, and his punishment was mild. There can be no doubt that the sale of all offices touching the administration of justice (with a strange exception in favor of Common-Law Judges) was forbidden by the statute of Edward VI., and every Chancellor who afterwards sold a Mastership in Chancery must have been aware that he was thereby violating that statute. It is a fallacy to say that he was fully justified by the example of his predecessors. Lord Cowper had abolished " New Years' Gifts " from the officers of the court as well as from the bar, and had been followed in the same course by Lord Harcourt,—both Chancellors showing a desire to conform to the improving spirit of the age. In Lord

[1] Vol. ii. 106.

Macclesfield's time, from the speculations caused by the South Sea mania, the abuses in the Masters' offices had become more flagrant. But, instead of trying to redress them, he increased their enormity by raising the price which the Masters were to pay for their places, and rendering it still more necessary that, for their own indemnity, they should traffic with the trust-money in their hands. Whoever takes the trouble of perusing the whole of the evidence will see that he was rapacious in his bargains, and that, with the view of bolstering up a system which was so profitable to him, he resorted to very arbitrary means to keep the public in ignorance of its consequences. His contemporaries could form a more correct opinion of his conduct than we can, and we should be slow to accuse them of harshness.

There is no pretense for saying that he fell a sacrifice to party resentment. It so happened that, at the time of his impeachment, party had actually disappeared in both Houses of Parliament. The two law lords, Lord Harcourt and Lord Lechmere, were present, and concurred in the verdict. High Churchmen must, no doubt, have rejoiced to see disgrace fall upon him who had gained distinction as the prosecutor of Sacheverell; but many zealous Whigs actively, though sorrowfully, joined in the prosecution. The Prince's friends were exasperated against him, but the King's friends joined in the sentence. Walpole certainly did gain great credit by allowing the prosecution fair play; but he neither originated nor unduly encouraged it. Macclesfield had been a useful and submissive ally of the existing Government, and there was no rival whom they desired to elevate in his place. Of all the impeachments recorded in our annals, I find no one marked by more honesty of purpose, more practical ability in the manner in which it was conducted, or more benefit to the public in its result.

The mob were most highly delighted—and would have been still more pleased if, in his procession to the Tower, he had been attended by an axe with its edge turned towards him. In his way thither his ears must have been saluted with ballads which were sung in the streets, comparing him to Jack Sheppard, Jonathan Wild, and other famous freebooters, and giving him the preference over all in infamy, as, instead of rich travelers and stout wayfaring men, he robbed widows and orphans who were put under his care.[1]

He remained a prisoner six weeks, while he made arrangements for the payment of his fine. The money was at last raised, and, in pursuance of an address from the House of Commons to the Crown, was paid into the Court of Chancery, to be applied towards making good the losses of the suitors from the misconduct and insolvency of the Masters.

The King being told that it was chiefly for fidelity to himself, in taking part with him against the Prince, that the Chancellor had been prosecuted, had signified to him by Sir Robert Walpole his intention to repay him the amount of the fine out of the privy purse as fast as he could spare the money, accompanying the message with gracious expressions of his sympathy and continued favor. One installment of £1,000 was thus actually paid to him soon after, and the following year he received an intimation that he might receive £2,000 more from the royal bounty whenever he chose to apply for it. Not wishing to appear too eager to avail himself of such generosity, he had abstained from making the application till the sad news arrived of the death of George I. in Germany Lord Parker, his son, then hurrying to Sir Robert Walpole to clutch the money, received for answer, " that his late

[1] The best apology I have met with for Lord Macclesfield is by Oldmixon—which, lest I should be supposed to have treated a great man harshly, I, in fairness, subjoin :—" There had been for some time a murmuring against the insufficiency of the Masters in Chancery to answer the great sums lodged in their hands by the suitors in that court ; and it was suspected, that the large sums they paid for admission into their places made their way more easy than it ought to have been, and very much lessened the inquiry into their qualifications for them. 'Tis true, this abuse had been long growing up to this enormity, and there was hardly any commodity in a market bought and sold more freely and openly than a Master in Chancery's place. The suitors' money, with which they paid no interest, brought them in great interest from the funds ; and the profits of the place being consequently doubled and trebled at least to what they were before, there was such an opportunity to enrich themselves by the advantage they made of the money they had in their hands, 'tis no wonder the Lords Keepers and Lord Chancellors doubled and trebled the price they were to pay for admittance, which had risen from £1,000, to £3,000 in my remembrance ; who, being intimate with several of of them, have heard this matter frequently discoursed of before there was any whisper of imputing it as a crime to the Lord Chancellor. But from a complaint in general, it came to a charge in particulars ; and the Earl finding it was impracticable for him to prevent it, or keep the Great Seal under it, he resigned his high office."—Vol. iii. 758.

Majesty and his Minister had a running account which had not been settled, and, as there was no saying on which side the balance was, it would be too great a risk to pay the £2,000 at present." Some shrewdly conjectured that Sir Robert expected to ingratiate himself with the new King by thus treating the man who had rendered himself so obnoxious to his Majesty when Prince of Wales. However that may be, not another farthing from the funds of the late King could be extorted towards the payment of the fine.

The very day after Lord Macclesfield's commitment to the Tower, he wrote the following letter to Lord Chief Justice King, who had presided as Speaker of the House of Lords during his trial, and was now designated as his successor:—

"My Lord,

"Will y^r Ldp have ye goodnesse to forgive me if, to ye trouble I have already given, I addê this more in favor of Mr. Thomas Parker, of New Inne, who served me as Deputy Purse-bearer severall y^{rs}. He is a very sober, honest, and sensible man, and who I am sure will serve y^r Ldp very diligently and faithfully if you have occasion to employ him in any of ye offices belonging to ye Great Seal. If these are all provided for, give me leave to recommend him to be one of ye Comm^{rs} of Bankrupts. He was in one of ye lists, and behaved himself very well, but when I made him Deputy Purse-bearer, I put an^r in ye list of Comm^{rs}, by wch means his name stands not now amongst those Comm^{rs}. There is another Thomas Parker of y Temple, whom y Lords Comm^{rs} have been pleased to continue in, and I beg y^r Ldp still to allow a place amongst them. I ask pardon for this presumption, and I heartily wish y^r Ldp all happiness and satisfaction in an office w my want of discretion has made so fatall to me, but wch I am sure, by y^r Ldps great prudence and caution, will, in y^r hands, be an honor to yourself and a blessing to y^e King and his people, and I wish it may long continue so happily placed.

"I am with the greatest respect,
"My Lord,
"Y$_r$ Ldps most humble and most obed^t Servt,
"MACCLESFIELD."[1]

[1] From the MSS. of the Earl of Lovelace. The letter is without date, to

A letter written under such circumstances, to intercede for two dependents, and probably poor relations, places him in a very amiable point of view; and as he had not committed any black crime for which he could be expected to feel deep remorse, he may be forgiven if he imputes his fall to "want of discretion," and intimates that, along with the qualities for the office which he himself possessed, "prudence and caution" only were required to insure a glorious career to his successor.

I have no further means of judging of the manner in which the fallen Chancellor bore his reverse of fortune, or how he spent his time in the Tower. He could have had none of the sympathy felt for political martyrs which had often made a commitment to its cells a triumph rather than a disgrace, and few visitors, besides his near relatives and dependents, could have come to relieve his thoughts from sad retrospects and anticipations.

When restored to liberty, he had not the courage to try to recover his position as a public man or in private society. Although he had still a vigorous constitution of body, and his faculties were unimpaired, he could not face political opponents or friends under whose unanimous verdict he had dropped on his knees to receive sentence as a fraudulent criminal at the bar of that House in which he had long presided with dignity and splendor. He considered the last division on his case, although the motion was lost by an equality of votes, as tantamount to sentence of civil death. He never resumed his seat in parliament, or appeared in public, or took any interest in party struggles.

As soon as his private affairs were settled in London he hurried to bury himself in obscurity in the country He selected as his retreat a small house near Derby, which had belonged to him when he carried on business as an attorney in that town. Here he entirely shut himself up from society, neither mixing with his former intimates in the lower or middle ranks of life, nor with the aristocracy—to which, in point of rank, he now belonged.[1]

---

avoid any reference to the writer's "doleful prison in the Tower;" but it is indorsed by Sir Peter King, "28th May, 1725."

[1] Although the above account of the ex-Chancellor's retreat seems to rest on authentic evidence, I have recently received a statement from the present Earl of Macclesfield, that he resided sometimes at Shirburn Castle, and there

Some years afterwards he made occasional visits to his son, who had a house in London, in Soho Square: but on these occasions he still shunned all intercourse with the world. His old age, I fear, was very cheerless. "Obedience," and "troops of friends," which he had enjoyed, he could look to have no longer.

Unfortunately he was unable to imitate the conduct of his predecessor, Bacon, who, under similar circumstances, devoted himself to science, and the extension of his literary fame. Macclesfield, when educating himself, had acquired an adequate knowledge of the Latin classics, and had read the most popular English authors; but he had no high value for literature, and he had no taste whatever for philosophy. He now probably regretted that he ever left the profession of an attorney, in which, if he had been contented to continue, he might have lived and died respected, though obscure. But the mind wonderfully adapts itself to circumstances, and in the saddest condition solace is found. As he had hastened to be rich, a large fortune remained to him after the payment of his fine, and his latter days may have been rendered tolerable by the pleasures of avarice.

exercised great hospitality; in proof of which I am furnished with the following extracts from his CELLAR BOOK:—

"June 20th 1725.   Bottles.
   Sent to *the Tower* French Claret from Lord Ch. B. Hale's Hhd. No 1   12
                        Red Port   10

May 25th 1726.   . . . . .   Latour   . . .   6
                             Port   11
June 8th 1726, the family went to Shirburn. Ale   15
                             Cyder . . .   15
Novr 1726, came to town from Shirburn, being Tuesday.

Jany 1st 1727.   . . . . .   French Claret . . .   13½
                             Red Port . . .   4
                             White Port . . .   1
                             Champagne . . .   1
                             Burgundy . . .   1
   The family went to Shirburn, July 20th. Shirburn Ale . . .   14½
   My Lord Macd was in town twice. Cyder . . .   3

Jany 1st 1728.   . . . . .   French Claret . . .   3
                             Red Lisbon . . .   10
                             Stafford Ale . . .   1
                             Shirburn Ale . . .   7
                             Cyder   . . .   2

N. B.—These extracts are taken, first, when at Shirburn, and secondly, on leaving Shirburn for London."—*Note to 2nd Edition.*

At the commencement of his seclusion he took interest in superintending the education of his son, afterwards so famed for scientific acquirements, and, for his sake, he maintained in his house a mathematician of great eminence, but little wealth, the father of Sir William Jones, the celebrated lawyer, orator, poet, classical scholar, and orientalist.

In this state of listless existence, Lord Macclesfield languished nearly seven years. At last, on the 28th day of April, 1732, he was relieved from his sad reflections on the sale of masterships, and from the wretchedness of non-official life. While at his son's house in Soho Square he had a severe access of stranguary—a complaint from which he had before often suffered, but which was now so violent and painful, that he was immediately impressed with the conviction that it would prove mortal. His mind being weakened to superstition, he foretold that "as his mother had died of that disease on the eighth day, he should do the same." On the morning of the eighth day he declared that he felt himself "drowning inwardly, and dying from the feet upwards." He is said to have received in a very exemplary manner the consolations of religion, and to have taken leave of his family and household with the same calm cheerfulness as if he had been setting out upon a journey with the prospect of a speedy reunion with those he loved. A little before midnight, being informed that the physician was gone, he said faintly "and I am going also, but I will close my eyelids myself." He did so, and breathed no more. Thus, in the sixty-sixth year of his age, he piously closed a career long eminently prosperous—at last deeply disastrous. Who can tell whether he would have made so good an end if cut off without having experienced any reverse?

> —— "To add greater honors to his age
> Than man could give him, he died fearing God."[1]

---

[1] In the Diary of his son-in-law, Sir William Heathcote, who bears testimony to the resignation and piety he displays on his death-bed, it is said, "He bore his great change of fortune and station with an uncommon firmness of mind ; and, upon his retreat from public business, was so well satisfied with private life, that he both said and showed that he had never enjoyed true happiness till then."

There now lies before me, in the handwriting of Lord Chancellor Macclesfield, a collection of Prayers prepared by him for his private devotions,—

He had constructed a family vault in the church of Shirburn in Oxfordshire, and there he lies interred without monument or epitaph.

The subject of this memoir is a striking instance of the scope afforded by our constitution to talent and energy. He was not suddenly elevated by the caprice of a despot from a servile condition to rule the state. The possibility of such a promotion shows an arbitrary form of government, and a barbarous state of society. The power of rising to distinction in a free country ought to be by the possession of useful qualities, and the performance of public services. The government that employs and rewards the meritorious aspirant, ought merely to ratify the opinion of his fellow-citizens, and to carry into effect the wishes of an enlightened community. Parker got on in the world first by diligence in his father's little office at Leeke, and rendering services to the wealthy manufacturer who translated him to Derby;—then by showing himself superior in intelligence and activity to the other attorneys of that place;—then by being the greatest winner of verdicts of all the barristers on the Midland Circuit;—then by proving the most formidable opponent which Westminster Hall could supply to oppressive prosecutions of the press by the Attorney-General;—then by becoming in the House of Commons a most efficient member of the political party to which he attached himself;—then by gaining the chief glory in a great parliamentary prosecution, having for his competitors the most eminent lawyers and statesmen of the day;—then by being acknowledged equal as a Judge to those who had filled with the loudest applause the most important magistracies;—then by taking a leading part in the Upper

giving striking proof of a Christian frame of mind. I copy an extract from the last of these, which seems to have been written shortly before his fatal illness.

"Also I thank thee for any sanctified chastisement and affliction. O my God, as long as I live will I magnify thee. [Probably alluding to his trial and sentence.]

"Thou hast granted thy loving kindness in the day time, and in the night season will I make my prayer unto the God of my life. And now, O Lord my God, as the day is vanished and gone, so doth my life vanish and wear away. The end of the day is arrived, the end of my life is at hand; how near, thou alone knowest. Remembering this, O Lord! I beseech thee that the end of my life may be Christian and acceptable to thee, without sin, without shame, and if it please thee, without grievous pain; gathering me together with thine elect, when thou wilt, and as thou wilt."

House of Parliament when he was elevated to the peerage;—and finally by making it appear for the interest of the Sovereign on the throne to place him in the highest civil office which a subject could hold—at a time when he had established such a reputation with all ranks, that his promotion caused general joy.

He achieved greatness; but for solid glory he wanted a contempt of riches, a love of literature, and a desire of improving the institutions of his country. He could occasionally part with money for charitable purposes, but, beyond the laudable desire of providing decently for his family, he certainly displayed an inordinate desire to accumulate wealth, and this was the remote cause of his downfall.

While Somers, and Harcourt, and Cowper were familiar with the greatest contemporary poets, and are immortalized in their verses, Macclesfield preferred the conversation of judges and sergeants, and his name is to be found in doggerel ballads recording his disgrace. He had a noble opportunity of serving the state and enhancing his own fame by law reforms which were loudly demanded; but in neither House of Parliament did he ever introduce any measure to supply a defect or to correct an abuse in the administration of justice, and for his personal advantage he aggravated crying evils, which in his time had brought such obloquy on the Court of Chancery that suitors were said to be "inveigled and delayed there that they might be plundered."

As a politician he deserves unqualified praise, for he was the steady, zealous, and consistent friend of civil and religious liberty. I am afraid he intrigued with the Hanoverian party against Lord Cowper; but when he had gained his object, and was placed on the woolsack, notwithstanding the grants of money and honors for which he struggled, I know not that he said or did anything at variance with his former principles or professions.—On one occasion he appears in favorable contrast with his predecessor, for he warmly supported the Government bill for placing churchmen and dissenters on an equal footing with respect to civil rights; while Lord Cowper defended the Test and Corporation Acts, and was the cause of their being continued on the statute book for a century.

He despised authorship, and not only never contributed

a paper to the "Tatler" or "Spectator," but never even wrote a political pamphlet in an age when almost every one engaged in party strife sought to influence public opinion by pamphleteering—daily newspapers not being yet established, and the publication of parliamentary debates being not only forbidden but prevented. As far as we know, he did not even keep a Diary, like Lord Cowper and Lord King. His autobiography would have been one of the most curious ever given to the world, both in his rise and in his fall.

One publication was imputed to him while he held the Great Seal—but not on sufficient grounds—"A Memorial relating to the Universities;" the author of which sets up for a great reformer of academical education—with a view less to scholarship, than to cure the Heads of Houses and Fellows of the Jacobitism by which they were almost all supposed to be then tainted. According to his plan, they were to be appointed by the great officers of state and some bishops, and were to be enticed into the world by a liberal dispensation from their residence in college. He likewise recommended, after the model of the Scotch Universities, professorships of logic, moral philosophy, experimental philosophy, and chemistry, which all the students should be compelled to attend. Thus were those seats of learning to be made more useful to the nation, and the men who frequented them were to become better affected to their King and country.

Although Lord Macclesfield had no relish for literary society, and was never admitted of the Kit-Cat, looking with far more admiration on nisi prius leaders and equity draughtsmen than on the wits at Button's, yet, to comply with the fashion of the age, he rather affected the reputation of being a patron of literature. We have seen that, at the request of Lord Cowper, he retained Hughes in his employment as one of his secretaries, and he showed him further kindness—for which he was thus on his birthday saluted by the poet:—

> "Not fair July, tho' plenty clothe his fields,
> Tho' golden suns make all his mornings smile,
> Can boast of aught that such a triumph yields,
> As that he gave a Parker to our isle.
>
> "Hail, happy month! secure of lasting fame!
> Doubly distinguish'd thro' the circling year!

> In Rome a hero gave thee first thy name,
> A patriot's birth makes thee to Britain dear."

The very learned Zachary Pearce, when wholly unknown beyond the walls of his college, dedicated to Lord Macclesfield, when Chief Justice of the King's Bench, an edition of "Cicero de Oratore," displaying much learning and ability, and by his recommendation rose successively from a Fellow of Trinity to be Chaplain to the Lord Chancellor, Rector of St. Martin's in the Fields, Chaplain to his Majesty, and Bishop of Rochester. Indeed, Lord Macclefield's distribution of church patronage is represented as always disinterested and judicious.

He is placed in a very amiable point of view by the following letter written by him, after his fall, to his successor, Lord Chancellor King, in favor of his old schoolfellow, Tom Withers:—

"My Lord,

"I have received a letter from one Thomas Withers, of Newport, in Shropshire, to desire your Lordship to appoint him master of the English school in that town, in the room of Thomas Sanbrook, lately deceased. At his request I formerly obtained the place of my Lord Chancellor Cowper for this Thomas Sanbrook, who was his nephew; but he himself is now fallen into misfortune, and begs the place for himself. And indeed he deserves much better. He was my schoolfellow, and in the same form with me, in the Latin school, and was a very good scholar, and went quite through the school; but his father not being able to send him to the university, nor to get the assistance of friends for that purpose, took him to his own trade, which was that of a shoemaker, wherein he succeeded very well, and had the general esteem of the neighboring gentlemen, and was a great favorite of the late Lord Bradford, who, if living, would have saved your Lordship this trouble. Just before I was made Chancellor I lay at Newport, and sending for the Master who had been usher when I was at the school, he told me of Tom Withers, my old schoolfellow, who was then in good circumstances, and gave me an extraordinary good character of him in all respects. I sent for him, and found he retained pretty well his Greek and Latin, though he made no show in conversation of either. He has since his misfortunes officiated sometimes for his nephew, whose health did not permit him to attend the school; and he has ample certificates of his very good behavior, which he (imagining me to be in London) tells me he will order one to wait upon me with, and I will order to be laid before your Lordship if you care to be troubled with them. I beg pardon for taking up so much of your time, but I think the case so compassionate, and him so much the best man that can possibly be proposed for this place, that I could not forbear laying before your Lordship some of these particulars, as the opportunity I had of knowing so much of the person.

"I am with great respect,
"My Lord,
"Your Lordship's most faithful
"and obedient Servant,
"MACCLESFIELD."[1]

I have not been able to ascertain whether the application succeeded. It would have been pleasant to have known that Tom Withers reached the dignity of Head Master of Newport school, and that the ex-Chancellor visiting him there, they both for a time forgot all past misfortunes, looking at their names cut out on the old desks, and talking over their battles and boyish adventures.

I know hardly anything more of Lord Macclesfield in private life. It is said that he was warm in his friendships, and generally accessible and affable. We read a good deal of his faults of temper; his manners appear to have been rough, both in society and on the bench; and I suspect that in his highest elevation he occasionally forced the bystanders to recollect his origin and his want of early education.

He married Janet, daughter and coheir of Charles Carrier of Wirkworth, in the county of Derby, Esq., and by her had issue, a son George, who survived him, and a daughter Elizabeth, married to Sir William Heathcote. The second Earl of Macclesfield was a celebrated mathematician, and became President of the Royal Society.

[1] Lord Lovelace's MSS. The original, in Lord Macclesfield's handwriting now lies before me. In spite of this letter, a certain class of Lord Macclesfield's admirers, who think that he is disgraced by the imputation of having practiced as an attorney much more than by being found guilty upon the charges of having corruptly sold judicial offices, deny that he was ever at Newport school.

He it was that, in the year 1751, so ably assisted in carrying through the bill for the reformation of the Calendar,[1] which made the Parkers for some time very unpopular, although it is now one of their greatest boasts.[2] The present respectable representative of the family is Thomas, the fifth Earl of Macclesfield.

CHAPTER CXXIII.

LIFE OF LORD CHANCELLOR KING FROM HIS BIRTH TILL HIS APPOINTMENT AS LORD CHIEF JUSTICE OF THE COURT OF COMMON PLEAS.

WE now come to a Chancellor, not of the highest genius, but of most respectable talents, and, what is of more consequence, of unblemished virtue. Neither the wantonness of scandal, nor the virulence of faction, could ever invent anything to the discredit of his morals or of his principles, and he descended to the tomb one of the most consistent and spotless politicians who have ever appeared in England.

The subject of this memoir was the son of a grocer and salter at Exeter. His father, though carrying on a wholesale and retail trade, is said to have been of a genteel family, long settled at Glastonbury, in Somersetshire, and he was certainly of good substance, and highly respectable character. In religion he was a Presbyterian dissenter, and he was inclined to the tenets of the Puritans. He had married a sister of John Locke, the philosopher. Peter King, the only fruit of this union, was born in the year 1669, but not being baptized by a clergy-

---

[1] "Lord Macclesfield, who had the greatest share in forming the bill, and who is one of the greatest mathematicians and astronomers in Europe, spoke afterwards with infinite knowledge and all the clearness that so intricate a matter could admit of; but as his words, his periods, and his utterance were not near so good as mine, the preference was most unanimously, though most unjustly, given to me."—*Lord Chesterfield's Letters*, CCXLVII.

[2] The Chancellor's grandson, some time after, standing a contested election for the county of Oxford, the mob insultingly called out to him—" Give us back, you rascal, those eleven days which your father stole from us."

man of the Established Church, the day of his birth is not ascertained by the parish register.

The sensible and worthy tradesman intended that his son should "increase his store" by likewise dealing in figs and hams, and, having given him a school education suitable to this mode of life, placed him, while still a lad, behind the counter. For some years the future Chancellor continued to serve customers in the shop, or to go on errands about the city of Exeter. But, from nature, or more probably from some unknown accidental circumstances, he cherished a most enthusiastic love of learning, which disadvantages and difficulties only served to inflame. Having exhausted his father's little library, consisting chiefly of a few books on divinity, for which he ever after retained a great relish, he spent all his pocket money and perquisites in buying treatises on the profane sciences. He even contrived to initiate himself and to make considerable proficiency in the learned languages; and this application to study was so secret, that, in the language of one of his biographers, "he was an excellent scholar before any one suspected it." But he was detected by his uncle Locke, who, after a long separation, paid a visit to his parents, and who, astounded at the progress he had made by self-tuition, foresaw that it would be vain to try to force him to submit much longer to the drudgery of a shop or warehouse, and anticipated his fitness to succeed in a learned profession.

Instead of going to a public school or university in England, where his past occupations would have been known, and foolishly made a reproach to him, by the kind and judicious advice of his uncle, he was sent to the University of Leyden, rarely frequented by Englishmen, but which, for its excellent professors, and for its cheapness, continued the resort of Scottish youths down to the time of James Boswell, the biographer of Johnson. Here young King continued some years, and addicted himself to the studies of the place with an ardor and perseverance of which there are few examples. Besides perfecting himself in classical lore, he ran round the whole circle of the sciences as there taught; but theology was still his favorite pursuit, and under a Calvinistic professor of Church history, he thoroughly established himself in the belief that, in the New Testament, and in the earliest ages of Christianity, the words $E\pi\iota\sigma\kappa o\pi o\varsigma$ and $\Pi\rho\varepsilon\sigma\beta\upsilon\tau\varepsilon\rho o\varsigma$ are used indiscriminately, and that those to whom the terms were applied formed one and the same grade in the Church. He was very orthodox in concurring in all the *doctrine* of the Church of England, and did not consider it sinful that there should be a separate order of bishops; but he preferred the Genevese model of church government, founded on Presbyterian parity, and, strongly denying the necessity for episcopal ordination, he maintained that the sacraments from the hands of a presbyter ordained by presbyters were equally efficacious as if administered by one who could prove his ecclesiastical pedigree through a succession of bishops from the Apostles. He, therefore, warmly supported the plan which had been promised by Charles II. in his Declaration from Breda,—which Clarendon, for a time, pretended to sanction, and which there had been a renewed attempt to carry at the Revolution,—for a revision of the Articles and Liturgy of the Church, whereby Presbyterians as well as Episcopalians might be comprehended within her pale. With this view he wrote, and on his return to this country published, a most learned and profound treatise on the subject, entitled, "An Enquiry into the Constitution and Discipline of the Primitive Church." This work made a great sensation, passed through several editions, and called forth many learned and able answers, particularly one by a nonjuring clergyman of the name of Sclater, which is said (I believe without authority) to have made a convert even of King himself.

I know not that he ever thought seriously of going into holy orders. If he had, he must soon have perceived that, to be recognized by the Church of England, he must submit to episcopal ordination; for his treatise did not a bit advance the scheme for a comprehension, and, on the contrary, there was a strong inclination by bills against "occasional conformity," and against "schism," to draw a broader and more offensive distinction between churchmen and dissenters.

Locke could not instil into his nephew his own love for medicine. Of the learned professions, law alone remained, and to this King had no aversion, having with much satisfaction attended at Leyden a course of lectures on the Pandects. Accordingly, with the full approbation of his uncle, within a year after his return to England he was entered as a student at the Middle Temple.[1]

"Moots," and "readings," and "exercises," at the Inns of Court, had now fallen into decay; and the existing practice of pupilage under special pleaders, conveyancers, and equity draughtsman having hardly begun, I know not by what appliances a practical knowledge of the law was obtained, beyond reading in the chambers, and note-taking in the courts at Westminster. Of King's habits during this period of his life, I have been able to obtain no authentic account; but, from the result, his devotion to juridical study must have been intense and unremitted. He was never supposed to have become quite familiar with Equity practice; but, before he had put on his gown, he was allowed to be a consummate master of the Common Law, having studied it scientifically and historically, and knowing thoroughly its foundations and its principles, as well as the procedure by which it was administered. His study of the English Constitution, and of political sciences, on which at the same time he bestowed much attention, was conducted under the advice of his uncle, who had become tenderly attached to him, and regarded him as a son.

After keeping Terms for seven years he was called to the bar in Trinity Term, 1698.[2] A few days after, he received the following letter, containing good wishes and good advice from his kinsman:—

"Oates, 27th June,—98.

"Dear Cousin,[3]

"Your company here had been ten times welcomer

---

[1] "Octobris 23°, 1694°.—Mr. Petrus King filius et heres apparrens Jeronimi King de Civitat-Exon-gen-Admissus est in Societatem Medij Templi Spealiter et obligatur una cum Et dat ₧ fine . . . . . . } 04.00.00"
—*Books of Middle Temple.*

[2] "Ad Parliamentu-tentu-Junij 3°, 1698°.—Mr. Armory H., Ffloyne J., Gardner G°., Pyne W., Nelson H., Thomson W., Rutter E., Partridge, H., Brockett J., Junr. Salkeld W., Hurdis H., Edwards H. Jun. are called to the Degree of the Utter barr; Weldon W., and Nutley R., ex gratia King P., upon the recommendation of ye Lord Cheife Justice Treby, and Clarke, J. upon the recommendation of Mr. Baron Lechmere, are also called to the same degree."—*Books of Middle Temple.* On the 31st of May, 1698, King had been admitted to a set of chambers in Elm Court.

[3] From this appellation some have contended that they could not have been so nearly related as I have supposed; but, in the English language,

than any the best excuses you conld send. But you may now pretend to be a man of business, and there can be nothing said to you. I wish you good success in it, and doubt not but you have the advice of those who are better skilled than I in the matter. But yet I can not forbear saying this much to you, that when you first open your mouth at the bar, it should be in some easy, plain matter that you are perfectly master of."

Our young barrister sent to Oates an account of having successfully made his maiden motion, and of having a prospect of a little business. Still he was cautioned against presumption :—

"Oates, July 3,—98.

"Dear Cousin,

"I am glad that you are so well entered at the bar; it is my advice to you to go on quietly, and to speak only in things that you are perfectly master of, till you have got a confidence and habit of talking at the bar. I have many reasons for it, which I shall discover to you when I see you."

King chose the Western Circuit, and there his own merits were seconded powerfully by the Dissenters, and the laudable Devonian disposition to push forward a young countryman well qualified to succeed at the bar. His success was rapid; he was soon eagerly retained in causes of all sorts, particularly in *quo warrantoes* respecting borough elections, which, till the Reform Bill, were the great source of profit in the West,—and the attorneys contended among themselves which of them had the chief credit of having brought him into business.

He was ere long ripe for the next step in the progress of a successful lawyer—being introduced into the House of Commons. The Whigs, whose principles he approved of, were at this time very low. The Tory reaction had been so strong as to compel King William to dismiss Lord Somers, and to transfer the Great Seal to Sir Nathan Wright. According to a very common professional course followed before and since—so often as to be free from last-

---

"cousin" means "any one collaterally related more remotely than a brother or sister;" and it is often applied to a *nephew*.

"Tybalt, my cousin! O, my *brother's child!*
Unhappy fight! Alas! the blood is spilled
Of my dear cousin."—*Shaks.*

ing disgrace—the ambitious young lawyer should have *ratted*,—asserting that his old friends had changed their principles, and were now going such lengths as he could not consistently support;—but through good report and evil report he steadily adhered to the cause of civil and religious liberty. It happened in his instance that honesty led to prosperity, and he was applauded; but if he had failed, he would have been laughed at, and he would have seen successful renegades enjoying much more of general consideration than himself.

A dissolution of parliament taking place in the end of the year 1700, he found that he should have little chance in attempting to represent any large constituency, the popular cry being "The Church is in danger! Down with the Dissenters!" But having been recommended by his uncle to the Whig leaders, he was elected for the snug borough of Berealstone, which he represented in six parliaments, and which returned Whig lawyers for a great many years.

The Tories gained an overwhelming majority at this general election, and they threatened not only to impeach Lord Somers and the late Ministers, but to repeal the Toleration Act, and to revive all the most obnoxious laws against the Dissenters. The session was to begin in February, only a short time before the spring circuit. Locke, anxious that his nephew should do his duty in parliament, even at some considerable professional sacrifice, thus addressed him:—

"Jan. 27, 1701.

"Dear Cousin,

"I am as positive as I can be in anything that you should not think of going the next circuit. I do not in the meantime forget your calling; but what this one omission may be of loss to you, may be made up otherwise. I am sure there was never so critical a time when every honest member of parliament ought to watch his trust, and that you will see before the end of the next vacation. I therefore expect in your next a positive promise to stay in town. I tell you, you will not, you shall not repent it."

The young member seems to have sent a becoming answer; but his virtuous resolution was strengthened by another exhortation from the same quarter:—

"Jan. 31, 1701.

"Dear Cousin,

"Your staying in town the next vacation I look upon as resolved; and the reasons I find for it in your own letters, now that I have time to read them a little more deliberately, I think sufficient to determine you should, though I say nothing at all. Every time I think of it I am more and more confirmed in the opinion that it is absolutely necessary in all respects, whether I consider the public or your own private concerns, neither of which are indifferent to me. It is my private thought that the parliament will scarce sit even so much as to choose a Speaker before the end of the Term; but whenever he is chosen, it is of no small consequence which side carries it, if there be two nominated or at least in view, as it is ten to one there will be, especially in a parliament chosen with so much struggle. Having given all the help possibly you can in this, which is usually a leading point, showing the strength of the parties, my next advice to you is not to speak at all in the House for some time, whatever fair opportunity you may seem to have. But though you keep your mouth shut, I doubt not but you will have your eyes open to see the temper and observe the motions of the House, and diligently to remark the skill of management, and carefully watch the first and secret beginning of things, and their tendencies, and endeavor, if there be danger in them, to crush them in the egg. You will say, what can you do who are not to speak? It is true I would not have you speak to the House, but you may communicate your light or apprehensions to some honest speaker who may make use of it, for there have always been very able members who never speak, who yet, by their penetration and foresight, have this way done as much service as any within those walls: and hereby you will more recommend yourself when people shall observe so much modesty joined with your parts and judgment, than if you should seem forward though you spoke well."[1]

[1] The simplicity of the philosopher somewhat resembles that of the Emperor Alexander of Russia, who, being in England in 1814, said to a great Whig Lord, that "he had admired the OPPOSITION as a valuable part of the English Constitution, but he thought it would be better still if the members of Opposition were required to give their advice to Ministers in private instead of censuring them in parliament."

King's patriotic resolve was further fortified by the following letter:—

"Oates, 7th Feb.—01.

"Dear Cousin,
"I am glad to find by yours of January 30, that you are resolved to stay. Your own resolution, in case of *unforeseen accidents*, will always be in your own power. Or if you will make me the compliment that you will not go without my leave, you may be sure that, on any unforseen pressing occasion that may happen, you will not only have my leave, but my persuasion to go. But as things are, I think it your interest to stay."

The honorable and learned member for Berealstone accordingly gave up the spring circuit, which lawyers know must have been a considerable effort of patriotism, as he thereby not only sacrificed present profit, but hazarded his professional position. His stay in town was of little use in respect to the choice of a Speaker, for Harley, the Tory candidate, was elected in preference to Onslow the Whig, by a majority of 249 to 125.

What hints King communicated to the Whig leaders we know not, but he seems literally to have followed his uncle's advice, and never to have opened his mouth during the whole session, although there were such tempting subjects brought forward as the settlement of the Crown upon the House of Hanover, under the impracticable condition, maliciously introduced by the favorers of the exiled family, that no one holding any office under the Crown should sit in the House of Commons;—the impeachment of Somers and his late colleagues;—and the quarrel between the two Houses which led to an acquittal.

He still took great delight in theological reading, and he now published "The History of the Apostle's Creed, with Critical Observations on its several Articles." Coming out anonymously, it was ascribed to several eminent divines, and the world was astonished to learn that it was the production of a layman. So profound, accurate, and orthodox is the work, that it is still recommended by bishops to candidates for holy orders.

On the sudden revolution in public opinion which was produced by Louis XIV.'s recognition of the Pretender, and his threatened invasion, parliament being again dissolved, King was reinstated in the House of Commons by the Lord of Berealstone, and the Whigs now had a majority.

King still for some time remained silent in the House, but he was diligent in his attendance; and, there being no *Times* or *Morning Chronicle* in existence, he almost daily sent an account of the proceedings to Oates for the use of his kinsman, who still took a very lively interest in public affairs. The reports he furnished are not so full or interesting as might have been expected. I copy a specimen of them :—

"17th Feb. 1702.

"This day was expected to be the greatest day of this parliament, the business thereof being to consider of the rights and privileges of the House of Commons. Mr. Finch moved first, and he proposed the first question, which was assented to without any division, as were likewise two others, which were—

"1. That to assert that the House of Commons was not the representative of all the people of England, was subversive of the constitution of the House of Commons.

"2. The same as to asserting that the House of Commons had not power to imprison others besides their own members.

"3. The same as to libels on the House of Commons.

"A 4th question proposed was, that reflecting on the House of Commons, and praying a dissolution of the parliament, were tending to sedition, &c. That was opposed with courage and heat, so that the gentlemen who were for it moved to leave out the latter words about praying the dissolution of the parliament; upon which a motion was made to leave the chair, and therefore the Speaker took the chair and adjourned; by which means all the business of the committee is fallen to the ground, and is as if it never were—which is very great mortification to some people, though not to

"Your most affectionate
"Cousin and Serv[t],
"P. KING."[1]

On another occasion, describing the debate on the first

---

[1] This debate is never numbered or referred to in the "Parliamentary History."

day of the session, after giving a sketch of the Queen's speech, he says—

"Sir E. S———r was only for a general address of thanks, and not to thank particularly till the House had first considered the particular matters of the speech. But it was carried with a swing to thank her Majesty particularly for all those things mentioned in her speech, and to assure her that we will stand by, support, and maintain all her alliances already made or to be made."[1]

At last King made his maiden speech, which seems to have been successful; but we remain ignorant of the subject of it, and we should not have known that he had spoken but for the following letter from his cautious kinsman:—

"Feb. 29th, 1702.

"Dear Cousin,

"I am very glad the ice is broke, and that it has succeeded so well; but now you have showed the House that you can speak, I advise you to let them see you can hold your peace, and let nothing but some point of law, which you are perfectly clear in, or the utmost necessity, call you up again."

King, pleased with his *debut*, and considering how the fame of it might raise him into a nisi prius leader in the West, was about to join the circuit when he received the following admonition from his uncle:—

"March 3, 1702.

"Dear Cousin,

"I imagine by what you say of the circuit, that you have not duly considered the state in which we are now placed. Pray reflect upon it well, and then tell me whether you can think of being a week together absent from your trust in parliament, till you see the main point settled, and the kingdom in a posture of defense against the ruin that threatens it. The reason why I pressed you to stay in town was, to give the world a testimony how much you preferred the public to your private interest, and how true you were to any trust you undertook; this is no small character, nor of small advantage to a man coming into the world. Besides, I thought it no good husbandry for a man to get a few fees on circuit, and lose

[1] This is a fuller account of the debate than in the "Parliamentary History." See vol. vi. 151.

Westminster Hall. For I assure you Westminster Hall is at stake, and I wonder how any one of the House can sleep till he sees England in a better state of defense, and how he can talk of anything else till that is done."

At this time all seemed prosperous with the Whigs, and the appointment of a new ministry was every day expected, King's friends thinking that he had fair pretensions to the office of Solicitor General: but his hopes and those of his party seemed blasted forever by the death of William III., and the triumphant accession of the Tories to power under Queen Anne.

King continued in parliament, but almost abjured politics, and devoted himself to his profession—steadily advancing to the top of it.

In the following year he earnestly attempted to prevail on his kinsman to revisit the metropolis, thinking that a sight of his old friends would revive him, and received the following answer:—

"April 30th, 1703.

"In your last you seemed desirous of my coming to town; I have many reasons to desire to be there, but I doubt whether ever I shall see it again. Take not this for a splenetic thought; I thank God I have no melancholy on that account. But I can not but feel what I feel; my shortness of breath is so far from being relieved by the renewing season of the year as it used to be, that it sensibly increases upon me. I have several things to talk to you of, and some of present concernment to yourself, and I know not whether this may not be my last time of seeing you. I shall not die the sooner for having cast up my reckoning, and judging as impartially of my state as I can. I hope I shall not live one jot the less cheerfully the time that I am here, nor neglect any of the offices of life whilst I have it; for whether it be a month, or a year, or seven years longer, the longest any one out of kindness or compliment can propose to me is so near nothing when considered in respect of eternity, that if the sight of death can put an end to the comforts of life, it is always near enough, especially to one of my age, to have no satisfaction in living."

King's visits were now more frequent to his uncle, at whatever sacrifice; and he had the unspeakable satisfaction of prolonging the old man's days by his kindness, and rendering them more comfortable.

We must now take a glance at our hero playing the part of a lover. Having reached his thirty-fourth year, he either felt the tender passion, or he prudentially resolved to form a respectable matrimonial connection. The object of his choice was Anne, the daughter of Richard Seyes, Esquire, of Boverton in Glamorganshire, deceased. The young lady, beautiful and accomplished, possessed a very slender fortune, but she had great expectations from a maiden aunt who had brought her up. King, upon this occasion, consulted Locke as a father, and appears to have received from him some very prudent counsel, as we may conjecture from the following reply:—

"13th June, 1703.

"I thank you for your last letter, and the several kind hints in it. I believe the aunt will not come under any legal obligation for futurity, but she promiseth well. As to the young lady, she hath wit and sense, and will, I believe, be very easy in all those things you mention."

The courtship proceeded, but, from a difficulty about settlements, or some other cause not explained to us, it was not brought to a happy conclusion till the long vacation in the following year. Meanwhile, Locke, thinking that his last hour was at hand, wrote the following letter to his nephew:—

"June 1st, 1704.

"I remember it is the end of a term, a busy time with you, and you intend to be here speedily, which is better than writing at a distance. Pray be sure to order your matters so as to spend all the next week with me; as far as I can impartially guess, it will be the last week I am ever like to have with you; for, if I mistake not, I have very little time left in the world. This comfortable, and to me usually restorative, season of the year, has no effect upon me for the better: on the contrary, all appearances concur to warn me that the dissolution of this cottage is not far off. Refuse not, therefore, to help me to pass some of the last hours of my life as easily as may be, in the conversation of one who is not only the nearest, but the dearest to me of any man in the world. I have a great many things to talk with you, which I can talk to nobody else about. I therefore desire you again deny not this to my affection. I know nothing at such a time so desirable and so useful as the conversation of a friend one loves and relies on."

King, as may be supposed, instantly posted down to Oates, and did everything to soothe the sufferer which could be done by a pious son to a revered parent. His attentions proved successful, and, warm weather following, Locke had a wonderful revival, and was freer from pain than he had been for years past.

King's affair of the heart now took an auspicious turn, and it was agreed that after the summer circuit he should be united to the object of his affections. This news gave high delight to the philosopher, and his conduct on the occasion, places him in the most amiable point of view, forcing us to love him as much as to admire and to reverence him. Though conscious that when the severe season returned he could not long encounter his maladies, he took an unabated interest in the pursuits of his friends, and he was devotedly anxious to contribute to their happiness. He could not move from home, but he insisted on an immediate visit from the new married pair,—and on their wedding day thus wrote the author of the Essay on the human understanding, the Analysis of the Principles of Free Government, the Apostle of Toleration, the first intelligent Advocate of useful Education, the Founder of Free Trade in England :—

"Oates, 16th Sept.—04.

" Dear Cousin,

"I am just rose from dinner, where the bride and bridegroom's health was heartily drank, again and again, with wishes that this day may be the beginning of a very happy life to them both. We hope we have hit the time right ; if not, it is your fault who have misled us.

"I desire you to bring me down twenty guineas. The wooden standish, and the Turkish travels of the Exeter man, I know you will not forget. But there are other things of more importance on this occasion, which you ought not to omit, viz :—

" 4 dried neats' tongues.

" 12 Partriges that are fresh, and will bear the carriage, and will keep a day after they are here.

"4 Pheasants. The same I said of the partriges I say of the pheasants.

"4 Turkey poults, ready larded, if they be not out of season.

"4 Fresh Aburn Rabbits. if they are to be got.

"Plovers, or woodcocks, or snipes, or whatever else is good to be got at the poulterer's, except ordinary tame fowls.

"12 Chichester male lobsters, if they can be got alive—if not, six dead ones, that are sweet.

"2 large Crabs that are fresh.

"Crawfish and Prawns, if they are to be got.

"A double barrel of the best Colchester oysters.

"I have writ to John Gray to offer you his service. He was bred up in my old Lord Shaftesbury's kitchen, and was my Lady Dowager's cook. I got him to be messenger to the Council of Trade and Plantations, and have often employed him when I have had occasion in matters of this nature, when I have found him diligent and useful.

"I desire you also to lay out between 20 and 30 shillings in dried sweatmeats of several kinds, such as some woman skillful in those matters shall choose as fit and fashionable (excepting orange and lemon peel candied, of which we are provided). Let them be good of the kind, and do not be sparing in the cost, but rather exceed 30 shillings.

"These things you must take care to bring down with you, that I may, on this short warning, have something to entertain your friends, and may not be out of countenance while they are here. If there be anything that you can find your wife loves, be sure that provision be made of that, and plentifully, whether I have mentioned it or no.

"Pray let there be a pound of Pistachios, and some China oranges, if there be any come in."

In his affectionate zeal that the feast might pass off auspiciously, on the following day he again addressed the bridegroom :—

"Oates, 17th Sept.—04.

"Dear Cousin,

"Though I writ you yesterday, yet understanding by yours of the 10th, that the business is complete, at which I rejoice, I can not forbear to write you to-day to wish you and my cousin, your wife, joy, to whom, pray give my hearty service. I expected no more in your letter than you writ. It was enough for a man on his wedding-day;

and therefore I hope, though you say nothing, that you have prepared my present of a toilet furniture for my cousin, your wife, and will give it her from me before you come out of town; else I shall complain to her of you when I see her." [He then proceeds with a great many minute directions as to the provisions—the choosing of them—the packing of them—a statement that there would be eight at table, and a hope that John Gray would be able to make a bill of fare, concluding with these kind words,] " I shall be glad to bid you and my cousin, your wife, joy myself, and am

"Your most affectionate Cousin, and
" humble Servant,
" JOHN LOCKE."

John Gray performed his part to admiration, showing that he had served under a great master in the *scavoir vivre*. The philosopher himself could taste little beyond a crust of bread and a cup of water, but he was the most cheerful of the party, and felt true happiness in making others happy.

The wedding party had scarcely left him, when, the cold weather returning, his asthma and his other complaints were worse than they had ever been, and he knew that certainly his hour was come. But in the consciousness of a well-spent life, and far more in the firm faith of the great truths of the Gospel, his serenity was unclouded. He had before executed his will, leaving King the bulk of his property; and now he wrote to him the following letter, more fully to explain his wishes, and to bid him a last farewell:—

"Oates, 4th Oct. 1704.

" That you will faithfully execute all that you find in my will, I can not doubt, my dear cousin. Nor can I less depend upon your following my directions, and complying with my desires in things not fit to be put into so solemn and public a writing.

" You will find amongst my papers several subjects proposed to my thoughts, which are very little more than extempore views laid down in sudden and imperfect draughts, which though intended to be revised, and further looked into afterwards, yet, by the intervention of business, or preferable inquiries, happened to be thrust aside, and so lay neglected, and sometimes quite forgotten. Some of them, indeed did engage my thoughts at such a time of leisure, and in such a temper of mind, that I laid them not wholly by upon the first interruption, but took them in hand as occasion served, and went on in pursuance of my first design till I had satisfied myself in the inquiry I at first proposed. Of this kind is, 1. my discourse, 'Of seeing all things in God.' 2. My discourse 'Of Miracles.' 3. My 'Conduct of the Understanding.' 4. Papers inscribed 'Physica.' 5. My 'Commentaries upon the Epistle of St. Paul.'" [After directions respecting their publication, the management of his affairs and the payment of his legacies, he concludes, in a tone of great tenderness:]—"Remember it is my earnest request to you to take care of the youngest son of Sir Francis and Lady Masham, in all his concerns, as if he were your brother. He has never failed to pay me all the respect and to do me all the good offices he was capable of performing, with all manner of cheerfulness and deilght, so that I can not acknowledge it too much. I must therefore desire you, and leave it as a charge upon you, to help me to do it when I am gone. Take care to make him a good, an honest, and an upright man. I have left my directions with him, to follow your advice, and I know he will do it, for he never refused to do what I told him was fit. If he had been my own son he could not have been more careful to please and observe me.

"I wish you all manner of prosperity in this world, and the everlasting happiness of the world to come. That I loved you, I think you are convinced. God send us a happy meeting in the resurrection of the just! Adieu!

"JOHN LOCKE."

King on the receipt of this letter, left his bride in the West of England, and arrived at Oates in time to see how a Christian should die. Having been present when the last marks of respect were paid to the remains of his illustrious kinsman, he got possession, under his will, of his property and his MSS., and he most scrupulously fulfilled all his bequests and all his wishes, feeling himself, and transmitting to his posterity, the most profound veneration for the memory of the deceased.[1] Indeed, this relationship is, and

[1] On this occasion he wrote the following letter to his cousin, Mr. Peter Stratton, of Bristol, son of his aunt, Elizabeth Locke, the philosopher's other sister: "London, November 4, 1704.

"Cousin,

"This is principally to acquaint you that Mr. Locke died last Saturday.

I believe is felt to be a greater honor to them than if the Chancellor had been the son of a Duke, or a Knight of the Garter. The late Lord King, with true piety and talent, wrote an admirable Life of the Philosopher, and the name of " LOCKE " has become a patronymic in the family.

But we must now turn to the member for Berealstone, in the House of Commons. He attended diligently to his place during the short session which followed the accession of Queen Anne. There is no doubt that now and henceforth he took an active part in debate, but we know nothing of what he said or the particular occasions when he spoke. He has had worse luck in this respect than any other leader on either side, except Bolingbroke. Although he sat in parliament the whole of the present reign, and after the promotion of Lord Cowper to the Great Seal in 1705, was almost looked upon as the leader of the Whigs in the Lower House, his name is not once mentioned in the " Parliamentary History," and we trace his career in the House of Commons only by

By his will he has made me executor, and given several legacies to the value of above £4,500. Amongst other legacies he hath given you £50, and to your sister Hassell £5, both which I am willing and ready to pay. He hath not made any disposition of his lands by his will, but hath suffered them to descend according to the course of the law to his heirs, who are you and me ; so that one-half of his lands do now belong to me, and the other half to you. He frequently told me in his lifetime that he would let his lands go in this manner, and, believing that money would be more for your purpose than land, desired me to purchase of you your half. I have no occasion for it ; but, seeing he intimated such a thing to me, I will, if you please, purchase your half, and give the utmost and full value for it. My humble service to my cousin your good wife, to my aunt, to our friends at Sutton, and all our relations. " I am Sir,
" Your most affectionate Cousin and humble Servant,
" P. KING."

There is extant another orginal letter of Lord King, dated 23rd February, 1694, which I hope may satisfy those who say that he and the philosopher could not be "uncle and nephew" because they called each other "cousin," for his letter to William Stratton, the husband of Locke's sister, begins, " Honoured Uncle ;" and thus coucludes—" Do me the favor to present my service to all my friends with you, and in particular to my aunt. In anything wherein I can serve you I shall be always ready, and still endeavor to approve myself to be, " Your affectionate Nephew and Servant,
" PETER KING."

The above letters of 3rd Jan., 1698, 27th Jan., 1701, 31st Jan., 1702, 29th Feb., 1702, 50th April, 1703, 1st Jan., 1704, have been before in print. All the others I have selected from an immense mass of correspondence between him and Peter King, which s not so interesting as might have been expected, as it generally turns on matters of private business.

casual notices in contemporary writers. As the Administration became more and more Whiggish under Godolphin and Marlborough, his opposition to it was no doubt gradually softened, although he must have continued to fight many hard battles against the ultra-Tory bills which, for several years, were regularly carried in the Commons and thrown out in the Lords.

When the great case of "privilege" arose out of the Aylesbury election, he took the rational course, by contending that the action against the returning officer for maliciously refusing the vote of an elector was maintainable. In the "STATE TRIALS" there is preserved some account of his speech on this occasion:—*Mr. King.* " I am called upon by the strange assertion of the honorable gentleman who has just sat down, that the right of electing is only a service, and not a liberty or privilege. I desire that the act 20 Car. II. c. 9, may be read. [Members, *No, no.*] It is an act to enable the inhabitants of the county palatine of Durham to send members to parliament; and it recites, that they had not hitherto enjoyed that 'liberty and privilege.' I may surely call that a 'liberty and privilege' which is so called by the legislature; and if it be a 'liberty and privilege,' surely, for the wrongful violation of it, there ought to be a remedy. Gentlemen say, 'this is a new action, never heard of before.' True! this particular action is new; probably because the right to elect was never before so shamefully violated; but actions of the same nature, and grounded on the same principles, are as old as the common law of England. ' Et ubi eadem est ratio idem jus.' Was it ever heard, till the very late instance, that an action lay against an officer for denying a poll to one who stood candidate for the office of bridgemaster? But the injured party was found entitled to damages. No action was ever brought, till 16 Jac. 1., by a reversioner against tenant for life for refusing to let him enter to view waste; but the law always was, that the reversioner had the right. It stands upon the general maxim of law, 'if you do me a wrong, I must have a remedy.' It is said by a worthy gentleman, that in real actions there are no damages; but in real actions, if you do not recover damages, you recover the land itself. [Members, *The question! the question!*] I find gentlemen are very uneasy, I will trouble you no further. [Members, *Go on, go on.*] I agree the determining the right of election belongs to the House of Commons. This action does not relate to any disputed right of election, but is brought by a man who has the unquestioned privilege of voting against an officer for maliciously refusing his vote."[1] I presume that the interruption came from some Tory squires, who did not at all understand the subject, but were impatient to vote as they were ordered, and to get off to the "October Club," where they might drink "Church and Queen," with, perhaps, a bumper to JAMES III.,—the toast of "the King over the water" not yet being invented. The derided Peter, though so discourteously treated in this controversy, did not flinch, but continued resolutely to resist the tyrannical majority, who went on imprisoning plaintiffs and counsel, passing absurd resolutions against the Lords, and playing all manner of fantastic tricks, till they were sent adrift by a dissolution.

Although it did not suit party arrangements that King should be promoted to be a law officer of the Crown, he was now at the head of the bar for reputation and business, being not only the acknowledged leader of the Western Circuit, but retained in all the great causes which came before the common-law courts at Westminster. His first judicial appointment was as Recorder of Glastonbury, where it is said that his forefathers had been settled; but if this pleased his feelings, it brought him no emolument, and little *éclat*. He was introduced to the honors of the profession by the City of London, which has in several ages corrected the injustice of the government to eminent lawyers. On the death of Sir Salathiel Lovel he was elected Recorder of that great Corporation. Soon after, on the presentation of an address of congratulation from the City on Marlborough's bloody victory at Malplaquet, he was knighted by Queen Anne, although she looked upon him personally with no favor, by reason of his early connection with the Dissenters, and his present preference of the Low Church party.

At the meeting of the new parliament in 1708 there was a strong inclination to propose Sir Peter King as Speaker, but another section of the Whigs were resolved to have a country gentleman in the chair, and the whole

[1] 14 St. Tr. 770

party united in the election of Sir Richard Onslow, that they might keep out the Tory candidate.

When the trial of Sacheverell came on, Sir Peter, in respect of his ecclesiastical lore, was selected to support the second article of the foolish impeachment,—which charged the Doctor with having attacked the Toleration Act, by asserting " that he is a false brother with relation to God, religion, and the church, who defends toleration and liberty of conscience; that Queen Elizabeth was deluded by Archbishop Grindal, a false son of the Church, and a perfidious prelate, to the toleration of the Genevese discipline; and that it is the duty of true Christian pastors to thunder out anathemas against all who do not approve of the discipline as well as the doctrines of the Church of England." Sir Peter's speech at the bar of the House of Lords was very long and elaborate, but can not now be perused with much pleasure. He gives a history of the Reformation in England, with a list of the statutes to enforce conformity to the Church, and in ease of Protestant dissenters. He very ably defends Archbishop Grindal, and refutes the doctrine that the toleration of Protestant dissenters is antichristian; but he utterly fails in giving a satisfactory answer to the Doctor's plea, that "no words spoken of an archbishop 120 years since deceased will, in construction of law, amount to a high crime and misdemeanor," or in showing that the preaching of intolerance and bigotry from the pulpit was a fit subject of prosecution by the House of Commons. Says Sir Peter, in his peroration, " for the Doctor to come and say that 'though the Dissenters are tolerated by act of parliament, and though they are exempted by law from penalties, yet, be the law of the land what it may, let the ecclesiastical pastors do their duty, let them fulminate their excommunications, and thunder out their anathemas, and let the civil magistrate, the earthly powers, dare to reverse them if they can,' I submit this to your Lordships, whether this is not directly infringing the Queen's supremacy as well as weakening and censuring the toleration—which is what he is charged with in this article."[1] On a subsequent day he replied to the defense of the Doctor and his counsel on the second article, and turned, rather ingeniously, against them their argument that the Tolera-

[1] 15 St. Tr. 134-151.

tion Act could not alter the sin of schism. "Here is the force of the Doctor's argument: 'The Dissenters were schismatics before the Act of Toleration; as they were schismatics before, so they are schismatics still; it is the duty of all superior pastors to thunder out their anathemas against schismatics; when they thunder out these anathemas, they are ratified in heaven; whatever is ratified in heaven no power on earth can reverse; therefore, though the Dissenters be exempted from human penalties by the Toleration Act, and are thereby preserved in the free exercise of their religion and consciences, yet, notwithstanding that, let the superior pastors do their duty and thunder out their anathemas against them, and let any power on earth reverse those anathemas.' Have we not here an open defiance of the authority of parliament, and a direct incitement to a violation of the law of the land?"

Sir Peter was supposed to acquit himself very creditably, but was rather thought to be too forbearing in dealing with the High Church party, and did not please the Government by any means so much as Parker, who furiously assailed the Doctor and his adherents, covering them with odium and ridicule, and was therefore made Chief Justice of the Court of Queen's Bench, on the vacancy now occurring by the lamented death of Holt.[1]

Mr. Recorder King continued to practice at the bar, till the conclusion of this reign, with undiminished reputation; but there is only one reported trial in which I find any account of his pleading, which was in the famous prosecution of "Wicked Will Whiston," for heresy. This lover of eccentricity and paradox, when condemned before the Convocation and the Vice-Chancellor's Court at Cambridge, was without counsel; but when his case came, by appeal, before the DELEGATES, he was ably defended (without a fee) by our great theological lawyer, who showed that his notions of the Trinity were not Arian, but were founded on the Apostolical constitutions, and that, at any rate, the sentence against him was irregular, and ought to be reversed. Some bishops and doctors of the civil law, who were in the commission, were nevertheless strongly inclined to affirm the sentence, but no common-law judge would join them, and, King boldly threat-

[1] Ante, p. 361.

ening them with a *præmunire*, they concurred in the acquittal.¹ This prosecution, instituted by the High Church party, and meant as a set-off to Sacheverell's, was equally foolish and equally abortive. Bishop Burnet, who had tried to stifle it, said on the occasion, with excellent good sense, " I have ever thought that the true interest of the Christian religion was best consulted where nice disputing about mysteries was laid aside and forgotten."

About the same time .Dr. Fleetwood, a Whig bishop, but so warmly attached to the Church as to be a favorite of Queen Anne, having published a volume of Sermons, with a Preface, in which he lamented that " God, for our sins, permitted the spirit of discord to go forth and sorely to trouble the camp, the city, and the country, and to spoil for a time the beautiful and pleasing prospect which the nation had enjoyed,"—this was construed into an insult on the government,—and, to annoy a low churchman,

¹ 15 St. Tr. 703–716; Som. Hist. Anne, 426; Tindal, ix. 91; 15 St. Tr. Although King met with unbounded gratitude at the time, afterwards, because he would not adopt the fantastical notions which, as an advocate, he had attempted to palliate, Whiston attacked, maligned, and, I believe, grossly misrepresented him. " Upon my application to him," says Will, (probably in favor of a friend as wrong-headed as himself), " I found so prodigious a change in him, such strange coldness in matters that concerned religion, and such an earnest inclination to money and power, that I gave up my hopes quickly. Nay, indeed, I soon perceived that he disposed of his preferments almost wholly at the request of such great men as could best support him in his high station, without regard to Christianity; and I soon cast off all my former acquaintance with him. Now, if such a person as the Lord King, who began with so much sacred learning and zeal for Christianity, was so soon thoroughly perverted by the love of power and money at Court, what good Christians will not be horribly affrighted at the desperate hazard they must run if they venture into the temptations of a Court hereafter; *Exeat aulâ qui vult esse pius*."...." When I was one day with the Lord Chief Justice King, one brought up among the dissenters at Exeter, under a most religious, Christian, and learned education, we fell into a dispute about signing articles which we did not believe, for preferment; which he openly justified, and pleaded for it that ' we must not lose our usefulness for scruples.' Strange doctrine in the mouth of one bred among dissenters, whose whole descent from the legally established church was built on scruples! I replied, that ' I was sorry to hear his Lordship say so; and desired to know whether in their Courts they allowed of such prevarication or not?' He answered, ' they did not allow of it;' which produced this rejoinder from me, ' Suppose God Almighty should be as just in the next world as my Lord Chief Justice is in this, where are we then?' To which he made no answer. And to which the late Queen Caroline added, when I told her the story, ' Mr. Whiston, no answer was to be made to it.'" Archbishop Wake, Archbishop Potter, and Lord King, Whiston sets down as " three excellent men, utterly ruined by their preferment at Court."—*Whiston's Memoirs*, i. 35, 227, 314, 365.

a complaint was made in the House of Commons against the author. He was denounced as an enemy to religion and good government, and some very violent Tories, trying to outdo the folly of their antagonists, proposed that he should be impeached. Sir Peter King warmly took up his defense, and contended that the Bishop, whether right or wrong, had not exceeded the limits of fair discussion. The Commons waived the impeachment, but, by a majority of 119 to 54, "resolved this Preface to be malicious and factious, highly reflecting on the present administration of public affairs under her Majesty, and tending to create discord and sedition amongst her subjects;" and condemned it to be burnt by the hands of the common hangman.[1]

I can not find any other occasion on which Sir Peter King distinguished himself, except the debate on the 8th and 9th articles of the treaty of commerce concluded at Utrecht, providing "that no higher duties should be imposed on the importation of goods from France than were payable for the like goods brought from any other country in Europe." I am sorry to say that he joined General Stanhope and several other eminent Whigs in opposing this measure of free trade, on the ground that our rising manufactures of linen, silk, and paper would be ruined by French competition; and as it was defeated by the clamors they excited for "protection to native industry," the favorable opportunity for establishing a reciprocally advantageous commercial intercourse with France was forever lost. But I think my brother barrister may well be forgiven for his bad political economy in the very beginning of the eighteenth century, when we find an enlightened nobleman, in the middle of the nineteenth, still condemning this treaty, observing, with undoubting confidence in the soundness of the old *mercantile system*, " it has been calculated, on apparently good grounds, that, had the project passed, the annual balance against, or loss to, Great Britain would have been not less than £1,400,000;" and quoting, with applause, the saying of a bishop profoundly ignorant of such subjects, that the treaty would have been disgraceful "if even we had been

[1] Tindal's Cont. xix. 537. Bishop Fleetwood, in a letter to Bishop Burnet, giving an account of this affair, pays a compliment to the defense set up for him by Sir Peter King and other gentlemen of the long robe.

as often beat by the French as they had been beat by us."[1]

It has been alleged against Sir Peter King, that during the domination of the Tories in the latter part of Queen Anne's reign, he showed an inclination to go over to them, and that he used some harsh expressions against Walpole when that distinguished Whig was most infamously expelled the House of Commons and sent to the Tower for alleged corruption in his office of Secretary at War: whereas Sir Peter most steadily adhered to his party and his principles through good report and evil report, and what he said of Walpole was that "he *deserved as much to be hanged* as he deserved the punishment inflicted upon him, expulsion and imprisonment."[2] He was a most zealous friend to the succession of the House of Hanover, and took an active part in supporting the Regency Bill, and counteracting the machinations of the Jacobites. After Parker's elevation to the bench, he was by far the most eminent Whig lawyer in the House of Commons, and upon a change of government his promotion was considered certain—as he was so much esteemed by Lord Somers and Lord Cowper, who, in such an event, would regulate legal appointments. But the prospect still continued very gloomy till the death of the Queen, which suddenly reversed the respective positions of the rival factions.

At the head of the grand procession of the lord mayor, aldermen, and citizens of London, to meet King George when he first entered the limits of their jurisdiction in Southwark, walked Mr. Recorder Sir Peter King, who delivered a loyal and eloquent address (which must have appeared gibberish to the royal ear), hailing the happy arrival of a great Protestant Prince, who was to secure to us our religion and liberties, and, putting an end to all discord, was to make commerce, literature, and the arts forever flourish among us. As Madame von Schulenburg

[1] Lord Mahon, i. 49. On the first division on the subject, Ministers had a majority of 252 to 130; but the bill to carry these articles of the treaty into effect was thrown out by a majority of 194 to 185. Had it reached the House of Lords, I am afraid it would have had no chance there, where the Whig party was still so powerful. "Free trade" is a subject on which Whigs and Tories have changed principles; but the former have ever steadily favored free political institutions and liberty of conscience, and the latter high prerogative and civil disqualifications to protect the Church.
[2] Coxe's Life of Sir R. Walpole, i. 66; Tindal.

and the Baroness Keilmansegge did not make their appearance for a few weeks, and the other Hanoverians who afterwards declared that they had come "for all our *goods*"[1] were still kept in the background, not yet beginning the sale of offices or honors,—all at first went smoothly. Lord Cowper, having the Great Seal restored to him, was required to submit to his Majesty a *projet* for the settlement of Westminster Hall, the unlimited power being still exercised of removing Judges on a demise of the Crown. Part of the recommendation was that Lord Trevor, a good lawyer and a man of fair character, but a violent Tory, who had been one of Anne's batch of twelve Peers, should be replaced, as Lord Chief Justice of the Common Pleas, by Sir Peter King. His majesty, who hardly knew the difference between the office of Lord Chief Justice of the Common Pleas and Lord Mayor of London, of course graciously assented.[1]

CHAPTER CXXIV.

CONTINUATION OF THE LIFE OF LORD KING TILL HE WAS MADE LORD CHANCELLOR.

WHEN this change on the bench of the Court of Common Pleas had been publicly announced, and before it had formally taken place, the Chief Justice elect received the following magnanimous epistle from his falling predecessor:—

"Bromham, Oct. 12, 1714.

"Sir,

"I am informed it is his Majesty's pleasure to remove me from my office of Ch. Justice of the Co. Pleas, and to confer the same upon you—which I heartily wish you joy of, and am glad of, and am glad to see it placed in a person so worthy and much more capable to discharge the duty of it than myself. I am desired by an old servant who hath served me very faithfully when I was Attor. Gen[l]. and Ch. Justice, as Clerk of fines, to recommend him to you; and I desire the favor of you that you will be pleased to employ him as your Clerk in that employment, or as Cryer

---

[1] "And chattels, too," was the reply. [2] Ante, p. 222

if you are not engaged. I am confident you will find him a very good servant. His name is Bryan Whealon. In doing which you will very much oblige

"Your most faithful Friend and Servant,
"TREVOR."

When the appointment had taken place, thus was he congratulated by Majendie, a distinguished refugee Huguenot Minister, to whom he had shown great kindness:—

"d'Exeter, le 9. de Mai, 1715.

"Mylord,

"C'est avec un plaisir inexprimable que je mets ce noble titre au frontispice de cette lettre. et que je vous félicite de tout mon cœur, de ce qu'aprez vous avoir élevé à la dignité de Premier Juge dans un des premiers Barreaux de ce Roiaume, sa Majesté vous a approaché de son auguste persone et vous a admis au nombre de ses Conseillers, digne comme vous l'etes d'y occuper le premier rang, auquel je ne désespère pas de vous voir un jour arriver; digne, dis-je, nonseule' par votre vaste savoir, par votre pénétration, et par les qualities extraordinaires de votre esprit; mais encore par votre probité, par votre piété, et par la droiture de votre cœur.

"Ah! certes c'est à present que nous avons sujet d'espérer la réformation des mœurs, et l'avance' de l'intéret Protestant dans la Grande Bretagne, puisque nous avons dans le Conseil des personnes d'une piété si eminente, et qui ont si fort à cœur les intéréts de la gloire de Dieu, et du salut des ames. Bénit soit Dieu qui a élevé, come sur une haute montagne, un si éclatant flambeau, affin que sa belle lumière resplendit encore d'avantage, et fut salutaire à un plus grand nombre de persones. Mais je ne remarque pas que suivant les mouvemens de joie et d'admiration dont mon ame se sent ravie, je pourrois, Mylord, vous ennuyer par mes lignes peu correctes, choquer votre modestie et vous faire perdre des moments qui vous sont chers, et que vous donnez à des affaires tout autre' importantes."

Sir Peter King enjoyed the dignity of Lord Chief Justice of the Common Pleas for a period of eleven years, and he is universally allowed unqualified praise as a Common-Law Judge. To great learning in his profession and strict impartiality, he added considerable quickness of perception, immense industry and inexhaustible patience in listening to the drowsy sergeants who practiced before him.

His judgments, as handed down to us in the Reports, are marked by precision of definition, subtlety of distinction, breadth of principle, lucidness of arrangement, and felicity of illustration—his copious authorities being brought forward to fortify, not to overlay his reasoning.[1]

Criminal business being excluded from the Common Pleas, and the cases there, during his time, turning chiefly upon the law of real property, his decisions in his own court could not be made interesting or intelligible to the general reader. But he was occasionally called upon to act judicially in other tribunals,—to which we may follow him with some chance of useful instruction.

After the suppression of the rebellion of 1715, Lord Chief Justice King presided at the trial of the rebels, who being commoners, were brought before a jury. His report of the convictions to the Secretary of State is curious, and I give a few extracts from it, showing his humane desire to save those who, from mistaken loyalty, had forfeited their lives to the law :—

"*James Home*, alias *Hume*, was found guilty of levying war in the county of Lancaster. The evidence against him was plain and clear, that he came with the rebels from Scotland, and marched with them to Lancaster and Preston; and it was not much gainsayed by his counsel, but their principal defense for him was that his understanding was so low and weak as made him incapable of committing high treason, and several witnesses were produced for that purpose. The jury believed him to be a weak man, but not so weak as to excuse him from the commission of high treason. It did appear from his behavior at the trial, and from the evidence given that he is a very weak foolish man, of a very low understanding, and my humble opinion is that he is a proper object for his Majesty's grace and favor. He hath not yet received sentence. Whether his

---

[1] There was a labored eulogy upon him in the forty-ninth number of the *True Briton*, said to be from the pen of Duke Wharton. The writer, after pointing out the peril to which he was exposed, in being compared with his predecessor Trevor, and with Cowper, now Lord Chancellor, says, " Yet, under all these difficulties, which would have overwhelmed another, with the eyes of all the kingdom upon him, hath this truly great man acquitted himself in his high office to the universal satisfaction of both parties, contrary to the expectations of the one, and even beyond the hopes of the other. And if he had not been a prodigy of learning and wisdom, it would hardly have been possible for him to surmount so many disadvantages, and to appear in the same illustrious light as my Lord Trevor."

Majesty will be pleased to extend his favor by a *nolle prosequi* before sentence, or by a pardon after sentence, I humbly submit.

"*George Gibson* was tried on an indictment for levying war in the county of Northumberland. He was a tenant and servant of the late Lord Derwentwater—went with the Northumberland rebels to Kelso, and there joined the Scotch rebels—from thence came to Jedburgh—from thence came to his own house in Northumberland—from thence returned to the rebels in Scotland and came along with them to Preston, where he was taken with the rest. The jury without going from the bar found him guilty. He hath since sent me a petition to his Majesty, which is inclosed, alleging that he endeavored several times to escape, and a certificate of his good behavior, signed by several of his neighbors. It did not appear on his trial that he had used any acts of violence to his Majesty's subjects, but some instances were proved of his humanity to them. *John Windraham* was tried for high treason in levying war at Kelso, in the county of Tiviotdale. There were three witnesses produced against him, whereof one was rather a witness for him, and of the other two one proved him to be, together with several rebels, in a public coffee house at Kelso, and the other proved that he was quartered at the minister's house in Kelso—where the witness and two other rebels were also quartered; that he saw him dismount his horse at the minister's house—had sword, pistols, and jack-boots—dined with him twice or thrice there—that he was not under any restraint, and that he saw him several times afterwards among the rebel horse. *George Home*, of Wedderburn, was tried for levying war at Perth, in the county of Cumberland. The evidence against him was, that he was seen amongst the rebels, at a place called Armfeth Bridge, where the rebels staying to refresh themselves, most of the gentlemen alighted off their horses and gave them to their servants to lead whilst they stood all together in a close eating and drinking—amongst which number was the prisoner, who came from thence with the rebels, and a little beyond the bridge was seen in company with them on horseback." [The report having then detailed similar evidence against *George Home*, of Whitfield, goes on to say,] "The defense of these three prisoners was that they were brought into the rebels by force, and continued under force till the surrender of Preston. Upon the whole, the several juries, after consideration, found them all guilty; but inasmuch as the evidence was contradictory and doubtful, and one of the King's witnesses proved part of the prisoner's defense, I humbly submit whether these three persons may not be proper objects for his Majesty's mercy with respect to their lives."[1]

Among the convicts was a Jacobite parson, who had not only attended the rebels as their chaplain, but had very earnestly exhorted them to march into England, for the purpose of dethroning the usurper George. Deep horror was excited among the clergy by the prospect of a priest, apostolically ordained, suffering the ignominious and cruel sentence pronounced upon traitors—especially as the great bulk of rectors and curates fully participated his sentiments. A representation upon the subject was made to the bishops, who, although all professing to be well inclined to the Protestant succession, had among them hankerers after the exiled family, and were all sincerely animated, not only by the *esprit de corps*, but by genuine feelings of mercy. Accordingly Wake, the Archbishop of Canterbury, wrote the following letter to Lord Chief Justice King,—which would perhaps be a little censured for the levity of its tone, as not quite suitable to the solemnity of the occasion, if it did not proceed from the pen of the Primate of all England:—

"July 5, 1716.

"My Lord,

"I am desired by all my brethren, the bishops in town, who were to wait upon the King this morning, to recommend to your Lordship the case of an unfortunate brother of ours, Mr. Paul, who, they tell me, was arraigned and convicted before your Lordship.

"That he deserves to be hanged we all agree; and if all others be hanged who deserve it as well as he, we have nothing to say. But if others of the laity be spared, who are under the same circumstances, we hope this poor man shall not be made an example—merely for his office sake, and because he is a clergyman.

"We are told that a great deal depends upon the report which the Judges make of those whom they try. We hope

[1] MS. Report, dated 13th Jan. 1716.

your Lordship wi'l be as good so to report his case as favorably as you justly can, and whatever you shall please further to do for him, as he is an unworthy brother of the order, we shall all thankfully acknowledge to you. I am,

"My Lord, your Lordship's
"very affectionate friend and Servant,
"W. CANT."

In the year 1719, Lord Chief Justice King presided during a trial at the Old Bailey, which shows the extreme severity to which, from the multiplied plots to bring in the Pretender, the Government thought it necessary to proceed against the Jacobites. An act had passed, in the reign of Queen Anne, to make it high treason maliciously and advisedly to assert that the Pretender had a right to the throne; but it had been treated as a dead letter—till now that John Matthews, a printer, nineteen years of age, was indicted upon it for printing a pamphlet, entitled "Ex ore tuo te judico, vox populi, vox Dei," in which the writer somewhat jocularly contended that all parties should now acknowledge the Pretender, for the Tories believed, as a principle of religion, in the "divine right of Kings," and the Whig maxim of "Vox populi vox Dei" led to the same result, as the vast majority of the population of this country were now for King James. The poor printer contended that this could not be considered a *malicious* or *advised* asserting of the title of the Pretender, as he had only been acting in his trade, and the composition itself was merely thoughtless; but the Lord Chief Justice, according to the strict rigor of the law, laid down to the jury that " the fact implied *malice*, and that doing a thing *advisedly* is doing it with a consciousness of what is done;"—so there was a verdict of "guilty." The prisoner's counsel then moved in arrest of judgment that the indictment charged no crime, for being in Latin, it used the word "impressit" to predicate the *printing* of the book, whereas "imprimere," in the just meaning of the Latin tongue, has no such meaning, *printing* not being known among the Romans; and at all events the practice should have been followed which was proper where any doubt existed as to the meaning of a Latin word in law proceedings, and that the indictment should have run "IMPRESSIT, anglice *printed.*" But the

Chief Justice ruled that "imprimere" had acquired the meaning of " to print," as we may know from the " imprimatur " on books the printing of which was permitted. The frightful sentence was accordingly passed, and, I am shocked to say, was carried into full execution at Tyburn.[1] This appears to me the hardest case of treason which is to be found after the Revolution. The young man might properly have been imprisoned for some months for assisting in the publication of a libel; but it was a confounding of the real distinctions of crimes, to hang, embowel, behead, and quarter him as a traitor. From Sir Peter King's known humanity, I think we may safely infer that this execution took place against his recommendation.

Upon all occasions when we have sufficient means of examining his conduct, we uniformly find him exerting himself to mitigate the misfortunes and to soothe the sufferings of others. About this time, a complaint being made to him of some severities towards prisoners confined in the Fleet under Common Pleas process, and the warden having urged in answer the insecurity of the prison, whereby he incurred great responsibility from the danger of the prisoners escaping, the Chief Justice replied,— " Then you may raise your walls higher, but there shall be no prison within a prison where I bear rule."

Lord Chief Justice King went as Judge of Assize twice a year, and he broke through the old custom for a Judge to continue to " ride the same circuit," for he visited all the English circuits in their turn, or, as it has been since technically called in Westminster Hall, " he ran the gauntlet." When about to start on the Norfolk Circuit, in the summer of 1720, he received the following curious letter to excuse the non-attendance of the Vice-chancellor and Heads of Houses at Cambridge, on account of the controversy then raging between them and Bentley, the celebrated Master of Trinity, who, by ancient usage, had to lodge the Judges during the assizes in his college :—

" My Lord,

"I would have waited on your Lordship, but for the terrible apprehensions I am under, that my poor wife, who is lately brought to bed, will shortly breathe her last. Under this anxiety, I am forc'd by letters from Cambridge, to bear in mind the affairs of that University.

[1] 15 St. Tr. 1323-1404.

Thither your Lordship is quickly going, and believe me, my Lord, none upon earth are more ready to pay you due respect and honor than we are. But, my Lord, the Master of Trinity has taken a resolution, and put it in practice, to make the Vice-Ch^r and Heads wait in the open Court among the mob, or at least to be taken into a comon room among the footmen, when they come to pay their duty to you. Till he shall come to a better mind (which in this and all other respects I wish he may), I beg leave to depend on your Lordship's and Mr. Justice Blencoe's goodness, that you will favorably interpret this behavior of the University, and accept your usual present from the hands of the Bedell; if the Heads are not allow'd the constant customary convenience in waiting upon you. Pardon this trouble, my Lord, and the confusion I am in.

"I am, with the greatest respect,
"Your Lordship's most obedient, humble Servt,
"T. GOOCH.

"Great Russell Street, July 28, 1720."

A very noted case, though not of a political nature, came before Lord Chief Justice King two years after, at Bury St. Edmunds, in which, although substantial justice was done and the decision has been since recognized, I must confess it seems to me that the law was rather strained. Arundel Coke, Esq., a gentleman of fortune in the county of Suffolk, and John Woodburne, his servant, were capitally indicted on the "Coventry Act" for slitting the nose of Edward Crispe, Esq., Coke's brother-in-law, "with intent to maim and disfigure him." It appeared in evidence that Mrs. Coke was entitled to a large estate on the death of her brother, Mr. Crispe; that Mr. Coke, to get possession of this estate, resolved to murder Mr. Crispe; that with this view he inveigled Mr. Crispe

[1] *Lord Lovelace's MSS.*—Gooch, the Master of Caius, had been Vice-Chancellor in 1718, and had pronounced the famous sentence whereby Bentley was deprived of his degrees—till it was reversed by an appeal to the courts of law. The Judges being afterwards at Trinity Lodge, one of them took occasion to observe, "Dr. Bentley, you have not yet thanked us for what we have done for you." *Bentley:* "What am I to thank you for? Is it for only doing me justice after a long protracted law-suit? Had you, indeed, restored me at once to my rights, I might have expressed my obligations; but such have been your delays, that if I had not been an economist in my earlier years, I must have been ruined by the pursuit of justice."—*Life of Bentley*, by Monk, Bishop of Gloucester and Bristol, vol. ii. 211.

at midnight into a churchyard; that there Woodburne, by Mr. Coke's orders, assaulted Mr. Crispe with a bill-hook, and gave him several wounds, which were believed to be mortal; that he was left for dead in the churchyard; that he was nevertheless carried by some countrymen passing by to Mr. Coke's house, which was close by; that he recovered,—and that one of the wounds he received was a cut across the nose.

The prisoners being called upon for their defense, Coke boldly contended that this case did not come within the Coventry Act, 22 and 23 Car. II., which enacts that "if any person of malice aforethought, and by lying-in-wait, shall unlawfully slit the nose, &c., *with intent to maim or disfigure*, he shall be guilty of felony without benefit of clergy." Now the act, as was well known from its history, and as was apparent from its terms, was meant to apply to the outrage of maiming or disfiguring a man whom there was no intention to deprive of life, but who was afterwards to gratify the malice of an enemy by carrying about with him, and exhibiting in society, the mark of disgrace set upon his person. The attempt to put a fellow-creature to death might morally be a higher crime, but, not being the crime described in the statute, it remained as at common law, only an aggravated misdemeanor, to be punished by fine and imprisonment. The legislature might be hereafter called upon to make such an attempt a capital offense, but a court of justice could not properly extend to it a statute passed entirely *alio intuitu*. Now here there clearly was no wish that Mr. Crispe should live ridiculous with a mutilated visage; the intention was not to disfigure, but to murder him for his estate; the wound which merely cut the nose was intended, like others inflicted on different parts of his body, to be mortal, and both the accused persons when they left him in the churchyard believed that their real object had been fully accomplished.

However, Lord Chief Justice King ruled that if the prisoners maliciously inflicted a wound which amounted to a slitting of the nose, and which disfigured the prosecutor, the case was within the act, although the real object was to murder, not to disfigure; saying, "There are cases in which an unlawful or felonious intent to do one act may be carried over to another act done in prosecution thereof, and such other act will be felony, because done in prosecution of an unlawful or felonious intent. As if a man shoots at wild fowl wherein no one hath any property, and by such shooting happens unawares to kill a man; this homicide is not felony, but only a misadventure or chance-medley, because it was an accident in the doing of a lawful act: but if this man had shot at a tame fowl wherein another had property, but not with intention to steal it, and by such shooting had accidentally killed a man, he would then have been guilty of manslaughter, because done in prosecution of an unlawful act, viz. committing a trespass upon another's property; but if he had had an intention of stealing this tame fowl, then such accidental killing of a man would have been murder, because done in prosecution of a felonious intent, viz. an intent to steal. Here, although the ultimate intention was to murder, there might be an intermediate intention to disfigure, and one might take effect while the other did not. An intention to kill does not exclude an intention to disfigure. The instrument made use of in this attempt was a bill or hedging hook, which, in its own nature, is proper for 'cutting, maiming, and disfiguring.' The means made use of to effect the murder must be considered, and the jury will say whether every blow and cut, and the consequences thereof, were not intended—as well as the end for which it is alleged those blows and cuts were given." The prisoners were convicted and executed; but the case may be regarded as a pendant to that before Lord Chief Justice Sir James Mansfield, where a man who gave a horse a draught for the purpose of fraudulently winning a wager on a race, was hanged for killing the horse "out of malice to the owner," whose name he did not know.[1]

[1] In the spring of 1720, Lord Chief Justice King went the Northern Circuit with Mr. Justice Dormer; and there lies before me a very curious account of their joint expenses. In all its minute details it would be very interesting to circuiteering lawyers, but I can only venture to give the shortest abstract of it :—

	£	s.	d.
The expenses of the journey to York	9	16	7
——————at York	43	14	0
——————from York to Lancaster	6	6	1

[At Lancaster I copy at length as a specimen :]

	£	s.	d.
Corporation presented a quarter of beef, a mutton, a veal, and 2 dozen of wine	0	10	0

1718.]   LORD KING.   449

I shall only mention one other opinion of Sir Peter King while Chief Justice of the Common Pleas, which, though most honestly and conscientiously given, greatly pleased George I., and probably smoothed his way to the woolsack. This was on the dispute between the reigning Sovereign and his son, respecting the marriage and education of the royal grandchildren. "The question is," said he, "whether such marriage can be without the consent of the Crown? and I think it can not. As to marriage in fact in the royal family, nobody can instance any to be made these 500 years without the Crown's consent. Where the Crown has not been consulted, such a marriage has been considered a crime. The case of Lord Brandon, in Henry VIII.'s time, and the case of Lady Arabella Stuart, are strong precedents. If this had not been a crime, the Countess of Shrewsbury would not have been liable to any punishment. The House of Commons' address in

	£	s.	d.	£	s.	d.
Mr. Lawson, a present of apples	0	1	0			
The butcher's bill	0	8	10			
The house bill	18	7	7			
The vintner's bill	1	12	0			
The cook's bill	1	13	1			
The cook's wages	8	0	0			
The cook's horsekeeping and shoeing	0	7	10			
Gave to the servants	2	0	0			
Gave to the Sheriff's coachman	0	10	0			
Gave to the Sheriff's butler	0	2	6			
Gave to the poor	0	5	0			
Gave to the sexton	0	1	0			
	33	18	10			
				33	18	10
Journey back				13	9	0
Disbursed in all				107	4	6
Received for entries, &c. at York				31	13	4
———— for entries and recoveries at Lancaster				11	6	8
———— by 9 fines at York				3	0	0
———— by 34 fines at Lancaster				22	13	4
Received in all				68	13	4
Disbursed more than received				38	11	2
Each Judge's share				19	5	7

There is indorsed a receipt of this sum from "The R^t Honble the Lord Chief Justice King."

V.—29

1673, respecting the marriage of the King's nieces was ridiculous if he had no power over it. The instances of marriage apply equally to education. But it is objected, 'this invades the right of the father.' Not at all so: nor is this against the law of God in any sense; for duty to parents is still subject to the public good. Everybody knows that King William appointed the tutor of the Duke of Gloucester, son of Princess Anne, and that the House of Commons addressed the King to remove him. Why should the King remove him if he had no power over him? So that I am clear the King has this prerogative."[1]

Although Sir Peter King, while Chief Justice of the Common Pleas, escaped the imputation of being a political Judge, it is a curious fact that all this time he was, in a quiet way, one of the greatest boroughmongers in England. By reason of his high reputation in the West, his native country, many proprietors of boroughs there, from patriotic or from jobbing views, gave him the disposal of their seats in the House of Commons. I have perused an immense amount of electioneering correspondence, in which he bears the principal part, and which is very illustrative of the manners of the times, but which could only now be interesting to the families whose names occur in it. Among his correspondents was the greatest statesman of the eighteenth century, who kept the House of Hanover on the throne, and, by his pacific policy, added more to the real strength of his country than if he had gained battles and taken cities. Sir Robert Walpole's letters to Sir Peter King are curious, as they strikingly display the earnestness, energy, cleverness, and tact with which he brought all his negotiations, whether about a borough or a kingdom, to a successful issue. I will give one instance as a specimen. The borough of Berealstone —as close as Old Sarum—belonged to the Drakes; and Sir Francis Drake, the then head of the family, gave the managment of it to Sir Peter, who had put in, as one of its members, old Horace Walpole. It happened that before Sir Robert had established his ascendency, and while he was carrying on a struggle for power with Sunderland and Stanhope, Horace was to vacate his seat by the acceptance of a sinecure office, to which he was enti-

[1] 15 St. Tr. 1222.

tled under some reversionary grant; and a rumor had reached the Walpoles that Sir Peter had gone over to their rivals, and was about to return another member for Berealstone. Sir Robert at first contented himself with writing the following letter to Sir Peter, which he was in hopes might have been sufficient:—

"We have received such accounts of Mr. Blathwait's desperate state of health, that we have reason to apprehend my brother Horace's seat in parliament, to whom the reversion of Mr. Blathwait's place is granted, may be immediately vacant. As 'tis to you alone we owe the recommendation to Sir Francis Drake, you will not wonder that I make this early application to beg your friendship again, to have my brother re-elected. I have wrote to Sir Francis Drake, by this night's post, upon this subject, and I must entreat you to second my request, which, I am sensible, will be of the greatest weight and service to my brother; and, therefore, you may be assured we shall be both always ready to acknowledge so great an obligation in the best manner we are able."

But no satisfactory answer was received, and the rumor gained ground that a dependant of Lord Sunderland was to be returned. Thereupon Sir Robert penned the following irresistibly persuasive epistle, applying himself, with most inimitable dexterity, to all the motives which, upon such an occasion, could influence the mind of the man he was addressing:

"I hope you will forgive me if I write to you upon this occasion with some freedom and a little importunity. I am not at all insensible what applications will be made to you, and how acceptable it will be to some to give us this disappointment; but I flatter myself that I do not stand in that light with you, being not conscious that I have done anything that should make it a pleasure to you to put such a slight upon me. Experience teaches everybody how little of the regard that he meets with from the multitude is to be ascribed to himself, and how much is owing to his power only; but as I never could look upon you in that view, I can not persuade myself but friendship, old acquaintance, and a long knowledge of me in my public capacity, was my chief recommendation to you. It is not to be supposed but that Sir Francis Drake and yourself may have other friends that deserve as well or better

of you than we can pretend to, and that you may have
an equal inclination to serve; which, were this a common
case, and upon the election of a new parliament, I must
admit, would be a reasonable answer; but you will consider that a refusal now is an absolute exclusion of my
brother, and should you oblige anybody else, it must be
done at our expense; and I verily believe you will meet
no solicitations that will not be more out of a desire to
offer an indignity to me, than to oblige anybody else. I
will not tire your patience with more arguments. You
know the world too well not to be sensible how grievous,
to speak plainly, this disappointment must be to me at
this juncture, to have my enemies gain this triumph over
me. The satisfaction or advantage they can have by it,
unless in crossing my expectations, can be no ways equal
to the dissatisfaction and concern that, I very freely confess, it would give me. To others, your answer is plain
and ready—upon pre-engagements and present possession.
To me, I know but one—that you think me no longer
worth obliging. After I have expressed myself thus
plainly and earnestly to you, I can add nothing but to tell
you, that as I am sure this depends upon you alone, to
you alone I will ever own the obligation, which you may
plainly see I do really think as great as you can possibly
confer upon me; and if, after this, I should ever be wanting to show you a just sense of it, I should be worthy of
the last reproach. I must beg one thing more, that you
will give me a direct reply, which, if it is to be in favor of
my brother, will be an answer to all other solicitations. I
am, very much, your most faithful humble servant,

"R. WALPOLE."

It is possible that such a service, at such a pinch, was
remembered by Walpole, become sole ruler of the King
and kingdom, when, upon the impeachment of Lord
Macclesfield, the Great Seal was suddenly to be disposed
of. But I must do Sir Peter King the justice to say, that
in all the electioneering affairs in which he was engaged
he seems to have acted with honor and disinterestedness.
He makes no corrupt bargain for others, and he had no
ambitious views for himself. His great object was to support the Whig party and the Revolution settlement.

www.ingramcontent.com/pod-product-compliance
Lightning Source LLC
Chambersburg PA
CBHW032028150426
43194CB00006B/196